# The Economics and Law of Public Procurement

Public procurement makes up a significant part of national economies: 10–25% of gross domestic product (GDP), depending on the country. Appropriate laws and regulations are an essential tool to direct the action of procurers towards the public good and avoid corruption and misallocation of resources, while at the same time sustaining progress and social goals. The original approach of this book combines juridical, economic, and technical expertise to find common terrain and a common language in order to debate the specific issues that affect public administrations across the world that need advancing and modernizing. The book features contributions across four specific themes of interest to the procurer's day-to-day job in modern public purchasing organizations: preferences and political economy in public procurement, climate change, defence procurement, and human rights in public procurement. The aim is to let the new emerging trade-offs between competition and sustainability emerge, highlighting at the same time the possible synergies between the relevant policy objectives. The book takes into account sectoral specificities, reinforced by recent global events such as wars, natural disasters, and populism. The unique format features in each section an interdisciplinary debate between two experts across different disciplines who deliberate and engage one another so as to improve the mutual understanding across disciplines, followed by two additional contributions. This book will be of interest to scholars, researchers, and policymakers worldwide.

**Annalisa Castelli** is Associate Professor of Public Economics at the University of Cassino and Southern Lazio, Cassino, Italy.

**Gustavo Piga** is Professor of Economics at the University of Rome Tor Vergata, Rome, Italy.

**Tünde Tátrai** is Professor of Economics at Corvinus University of Budapest, Budapest, Hungary.

## Routledge Studies in Public Economics and Finance

**The Challenges of Public Procurement Reforms**
*Edited by Annalisa Castelli, Gustavo Piga, Stéphane Saussier and Tünde Tátrai*

**Public Financial Management in the European Union**
Public Finance and Global Crises
*Marta Postuła*

**Public Goods and the Fourth Industrial Revolution**
Inclusive Models of Finance, Distribution and Production
*Edited by Maria Płonka*

**The Privatisation of Knowledge**
A New Policy Agenda for Health, Energy, and Data Governance
*Massimo Florio*

**Rethinking Sustainable Development**
Economic Integration and Public Policy
*Seck Tan*

**The Economics and Law of Public Procurement**
New Global Scenarios
*Edited by Annalisa Castelli, Gustavo Piga and Tünde Tátrai*

For more information about this series, please visit: www.routledge.com/Routledge-Studies-in-Public-Economics-and-Finance/book-series/LICPUBECONFIN

# The Economics and Law of Public Procurement

## New Global Scenarios


**Edited by**
**Annalisa Castelli, Gustavo Piga and Tünde Tátrai**



Routledge
Taylor & Francis Group
LONDON AND NEW YORK

First published 2025
by Routledge
4 Park Square, Milton Park, Abingdon, Oxon OX14 4RN

and by Routledge
605 Third Avenue, New York, NY 10158

*Routledge is an imprint of the Taylor & Francis Group, an informa business*



*British Library Cataloguing-in-Publication Data*
A catalogue record for this book is available from the British Library

ISBN: 978-1-032-63169-1 (hbk)
ISBN: 978-1-032-63170-7 (pbk)
ISBN: 978-1-032-63172-1 (ebk)

DOI: 10.4324/9781032631721

Typeset in Times New Roman
by Newgen Publishing UK

**To Steen Treumer**

# Contents

# Figures

# Tables

# Contributors

**Valentina Bianchini** is Marie Sklowdoska-Curie Research Fellow, SAPIENS Network, University of Rome "Tor Vergata", Rome, Italy.

**Roberto Caranta** is Full Professor in the Department of Law at University of Turin, Turin, Italy.

**Annalisa Castelli** is Associate Professor of Public Economics at the University of Cassino and Southern Lazio, Cassino, Italy.

**Stefano Casu** is Legal Affairs and Procurement Officer at Sardegna Ricerche, Cagliari, Italy.

**Orsolya Diófási-Kovács** (PhD) is Associate Professor in the Department of Supply Chain Management at Corvinus University of Budapest, Budapest, Hungary.

**Michael Eßig** is Full Professor and Chair of Purchasing & Supply Management, and Director of the Procurement Work Area, Bundeswehr University Munich, Munich, Germany.

**Anna Freund** is Assistant Lecturer and a PhD student at Corvinus University of Budapest, Budapest, Hungary.

**Neli Garbuzanova** is Public Procurement Expert and Deputy Head of Transformation at National Health Service, England, Royston, United Kingdom.

**Giovanni Gaspa** is Policy Officer of Sardinia Region's EU Liaison Office in Brussels, Sardegna Ricerche, Cagliari, Italy.

**Andreas H. Glas** is Assistant Professor for Supply Management in Defence Sector, University of the Bundeswehr Munich, Munich, Germany.

**Jean Heilman Grier** is Trade Principal at Djaghe, LLC, Washington DC, United States.

**Annamaria La Chimia** is Professor and Director, PPRG, University of Nottingham, and Research Fellow at Stellenbosch University, Nottingham, United Kingdom.

**Enzo de Laurentiis** is World Bank's Chief Procurement Officer, Washington DC, United States.

**Sofia Lundberg** is Full Professor at Umeå School of Business, Economics and Statistics, Umeå University, Umeå, Sweden.

**Susanna Maxia** is Head of Office of Legal Affairs and Procurement, Sardegna Ricerche, Cagliari, Italy.

**Daniel Morris** is Senior Adviser at Danish Institute for Human Rights, Copenhagen, Denmark.

**Claire Methven O'Brien** is Reader in Law at Dundee Law School, School of Humanities, Social Sciences and Law, University of Dundee, Dundee, Scotland.

**Vincenzo Francesco Perra** is Legal Affairs and Procurement Officer at Sardegna Ricerche, Cagliari, Italy.

**Gustavo Piga** (PhD) is Full Professor of Economics in the Department of Economics and Finance, University of Rome Tor Vergata, Rome, Italy.

**Geo Quinot** is Professor in the Department of Public Law at Stellenbosch University, Stellenbosch, South Africa.

**Benjamin V. Rosa** is Assistant Professor, Business Economics and Public Policy, University of Michigan, Ann Arbor, MI, United States.

**Daniel E. Schoeni** is a U.S. Air Force judge advocate stationed at Space Systems Command at Los Angeles AFB, California.

**Keith F. Snider** is Emeritus Professor of Public Administration and Management at Naval Postgraduate School, Monterey, CA, United States.

**Tünde Tátrai** is Full Professor of Economics at Corvinus University of Budapest, Budapest, Hungary.

**Andrea Truppo** is an Italian MoD official, Italian Permanent Representation to the European Union, Brussels, Belgium.

**Martin Trybus** is Professor of European Law and Policy and Director of the Institute of European Law, University of Birmingham, Birmingham, United Kingdom.

**Kristina Vasileva** is a PhD candidate at Sofia University St. Kliment Ohridski and a State Expert at the Public Procurement Agency, Sofia, Bulgaria.

**Christopher R. Yukins** is Lynn David Research Professor in Government Procurement Law Program at the George Washington University Law School, Washington DC, United States.

# Introduction

## The economics and law of public procurement – New global scenarios

*Annalisa Castelli, Gustavo Piga, and Tünde Tátrai*

### I.1 The book

Governments have (varied levels of) market power when entering the public procurement arena for the acquisition of goods, services, and works. This power might be converted, through the levers and principles of competence and probity, in savings for the taxpayer, reduction in public debt and/or fiscal space for improved or enlarged public goods provision. Less acknowledged, but potentially even more strategic, is the use of such market power to contribute to public policy goals that go well beyond the transactional impact of economic efficiency. De Laurentiis (Chapter 13) in his piece, reminds us that it is also International Financial Institutions that play a role in helping countries to reach socio-economic and environmental objectives, promote economic growth, and improve public spending also thanks to their procurement activities. Obviously, as mentioned in this volume by Lundberg (Garbuzanova & Lundberg, Chapter 4), one should always aim at viewing public procurement geared for such additional goals in the context of all other existing policy instruments available to the policymaker. At the normative level, it is thus also important to weigh the advantages of procurement as a policy instrument in order to determine whether it is an appropriate tool for achieving policy objectives like effectiveness, efficiency, flexibility, equity, and transparency.

Whether all of this is done or not, a thorough analysis at the positive level of the consequences of such policy use of public procurement is extremely needed, if only because of its often-widespread use in many fields and across the world.

This volume, in recognition of the clearly rising role of such second (but not secondary) use of public procurement, concentrates on five fields of public policy where procurement by government, local or central, and state-owned establishments can have a relevant impact: in particular here the reader will find tackled public procurement issues in the field of human rights (Part I), in the climate-change context (Part II), in the political sphere of specific preferences for given social or economic groups (Part III), in the defence and security realm (Part IV), and within global and local perspectives (Part V). These five topics have been discussed during the Fifth Interdisciplinary Symposium held in September 2023 in Cagliari, Sardinia (Italy), with the by-now customary structure (see also the previous four Routledge volumes, co-initiated in 2011 by the late and brilliant juridical scholar and colleague Steen

DOI: 10.4324/9781032631721-1

Treumer, to whom this volume is dedicated): four topics debated by two invited scholars of different disciplines in a three-round alternation of opinions and replies, followed by two submitted papers written by additional scholars, also coming from different fields. The global and local view, equally needed in this debate, are included in the final part (Part V) of this volume, in which de Laurentiis (Chapter 13) reasons on the role of supranational institutions and Casu et al. (Chapter 14) describe the successful use of public funds that the Sardinia region did to support SMEs participation in national and international tenders.

That public procurement lends itself naturally to such interdisciplinary debate, a natural feature of our relevant topic, is confirmed by many authors in their specific works in this volume. Indeed, as La Chimia (La Chimia & Morris, Chapter 1) mentions, in public procurement 'significant synergies arise from collaborating with scholars from diverse backgrounds and disciplines; multidisciplinary collaboration is invaluable for its contributions to knowledge and addressing societal problems', while Garbuzanova (Garbuzanova & Lundberg, Chapter 4) states how issues in procurement 'should be addressed involving a wide range of stakeholders and, as a bare minimum, economists, climate change and procurement law experts'. This interdisciplinarity should characterize not only those who study public procurement, but should also affect how public procurement is organized. Significantly, Garbuzanova and Lundberg (Chapter 4) agree that the organization of the public sector and collaboration among civil servants from different areas of expertise is also important for effective implementation of procurement policies. Vasileva (Chapter 3) pointed out that the political agenda and the strong leadership in public sector organizations play a crucial role in supporting the application of sustainable principles in public procurement, including social considerations, which are strongly related to human rights and their protection. Towards this direction is the Sardinian use of innovative models in public procurement requiring interdisciplinary competences to become an effective tool to support local public administrations in improving the quality of public services (Casu et al., Chapter 14).

In what follows we highlight some, not all, of the major issues that arise as critical in this volume and that the reader will enjoy as we did during the symposium, deepening them while going over the dialogues and papers.

## I.2 In or out of the global political agenda?

Grier (Chapter 8) highlights that preferences in public procurement are creating tensions and divisions in the international trade system. While at the global level national concerns for transactional savings are usually accepted and even recommended, other local or national policy objectives for public procurement turn out to be contentious and often resisted at the global governance level. Even in the human rights arena there are fears, within the neoliberal paradigm, that distortions in competition policies could arise within the public procurement markets (see La Chimia & Morris, Chapter 1).

It is true, however, as mentioned by Quinot in his debate on preferences with Rosa (Quinot & Rosa, Chapter 7), that in the wake of the United Nation's millennium development goals, and now the United Nation's Agenda 2030 with its Sustainable Development Goals (SDGs), new public policy goals have gained significant force as an increasingly dominant part of the global policy agenda, and with it the relaxation of a stringent focus on transactional efficiencies which had dominated the debate in the late 1990s and early 21st century. SDG number 12.7 makes this clear by stating as target, to promote public procurement practices that are sustainable, a focus which must be in accordance with national policies and priorities. By so doing this 'mediates the policy tension experienced in procurement preferences between the global and local' (Quinot & Rosa, Chapter 7).

Garbuzanova (Garbuzanova & Lundberg, Chapter 4), looking at the climate-change issue where there is international consensus to act on it, suggest that strategies and policies for implementing such considerations should be globally led and coordinated but left for local implementation. Bianchini (Chapter 5) agrees with it when she suggests to improve supply chains resilience and sustainability, and that public buyers should also reduce rigidity in their supply chain configurations, prioritizing sourcing from local suppliers and those committed to sustainability. Garbuzanova and Lundberg (Chapter 4) note how this will require collaboration and cross-border coordination of all procurements within a country (minimum) or, which is preferable, within larger supranational entities and the magnitude of this joint planning and process organization shall not be underestimated. Truppo (Chapter 9), for example, clearly states that European countries have no choice but to converge towards an 'effective' common defence that, beyond political proclamations, establishes the conditions for a common market and the establishment of increasingly integrated armed forces, enabling a progressive transfer of sovereignty for the benefit of European Defence. Related to this is Grier's (Chapter 8) finding, that a high level of uncertainty effects a closer and symbiotic collaboration, while a low level of uncertainty calls for looser and maybe more competitive relationship between procurement and industry.

Generally speaking, as Morris (La Chimia & Morris, Chapter 1) mentions in this volume, looking across multiple jurisdictions two methodologies are used to implement these public policy goals through public procurement and can be broadly categorized as 'affirmative action' and 'due diligence'. Affirmative action consists of measures to ensure the social and economic empowerment of groups and it is often tailored to specific national contexts, while due diligence is based on identifying and addressing risks throughout the value chain to ensure that public procurement activities do no harm to people and the environment (in practice, these methodologies are often implemented separately or in an uncoordinated manner). In the field of human rights protection in public procurement La Chimia (La Chimia & Morris, Chapter 1) argues that the globalization of supply chains and the expansion of international markets have further underscored the necessity for fresh initiatives to strengthen the connection between procurement and human rights.

As Garbuzanova (Garbuzanova & Lundberg, Chapter 4) mentions, that the law perspectives contained in this volume often underline an overly conservative approach of international procurement regulation, which relies on excessive political correctness on topics on which often an international agreement to act at scale exists, like for the environment. For example, direct references to climate change are not included in the Government Procurement Agreement (GPA, 2012), as they are missing in the United Nations Commission on International Trade Law (UNCITRAL) Model Law on Public Procurement from 2011, which nonetheless mentions environmental policies and factors.

Inalienable rights like human rights may seem to fall into the category of policies with infinite value in democratic societies, to be pursued, that is, at all costs, while set-asides that prevent certain categories of firms to participate in tenders often generate a dilemma. Measures mandating the exclusion of companies that violate national labour laws or prohibiting participation in public tenders by companies based in (or conducting business with and/or offering products from) countries violating human rights would seem to be, in theory, destined to be accepted unanimously. However, as mentioned by La Chimia (La Chimia & Morris, Chapter 1), procurement and human rights measures often face national and international controversy. At the national level, measures taken by individual entities or councils might encounter political opposition at both local and national levels. At the international level, procurement and human rights measures are often regarded as conflicting with international agreements on market liberalization, such as the WTO GPA. According to O'Brien and Caranta (Chapter 2), solid obstacles to establishing direct mandatory due diligence requirements for public procurers, as well as indirect measures, such as reporting and assurance requirements, are not evident.

Sustainable public procurement (SPP) definitions are often considered vague and problematic for human rights because it has led to their 'subsumption under environmental sustainability' even though recent data demonstrate an increasing focus on the social and economic element of SPP (see Morris in La Chimia & Morris, Chapter 1). Garbuzanova (Garbuzanova & Lundberg, Chapter 4) underlines how what is experienced as climate-change consequences in the Northern Hemisphere could be different in impact and nature from the climate-change effects in the Southern Hemisphere.

Defence procurement generates in this volume a somewhat separated series of dilemma. For example, it is prone to be dominated exclusively by national agendas. Snider (Snider & Trybus, Chapter 10) underlines however how, for better or for worse, where defence acquisition is concerned, what happens in the United States has worldwide consequences. He concludes that the nations that rely on the United States to provide superior weaponry to meet their defence needs surely must hope, for the sake of their own national security, that the United States can achieve its acquisition reform goals.

## I.3 Cost challenges of public procurement geared towards new policy goals

These relatively new goals of procurement policy do not come without operational challenges. In the field of green public procurement (GPP), Lundberg (Garbuzanova & Lundberg, Chapter 4) argues that arguments in favour of choosing procurement as a policy instrument to tackle environmental concerns are more likely found in flexibility and equity rather than cost-based and objective-effectiveness. However, from the perspective of a contracting authority acting with a long-term view in mind, climate-change-sensitive products may actually be cheaper in economic and social terms, says Garbuzanova (Garbuzanova & Lundberg, Chapter 4).

Lower participation of firms due to preferences is often one of the reasons mentioned to underscore the greater cost of purchases: implementing climate-change considerations in public procurement, for example, may initially reduce the pool of bidders, in an attempt by firms to avoid regulation and any additional costs associated with adapting to climate-change requirements. As Lundberg (Garbuzanova & Lundberg, Chapter 4) writes, how GPP functions as a climate (or environmental) policy instrument has to include insights into how it affects potential suppliers' entry decision and the functioning of the market in question. Lundberg argues that we need to verify if the public sector is a large enough buyer to have the power to incentivize potential suppliers to invest in less polluting technologies, how will relative prices be affected, and how price sensitive are private consumers.

More complex is the evaluation of procurement policies which include the allocation of contracts to minorities or previously disadvantaged group, also utilized to proactively fulfil (promote and facilitate) the enjoyment of human rights within the enactment and implementation of measures specifically targeting certain human rights issues (see La Chimia in La Chimia & Morris, Chapter 1).

In their debate on procurement preferences, while Quinot (Quniot & Rosa, Chapter 7) underscores the difficulty into measuring the value of policy preferences when procurement focuses on reaching sustainable goals that are not economic per se, quoting the frequent intangibility of the notion of value, including its moral and normative dimensions, Rosa (Quinot & Rosa, Chapter 7) shows that although preferential policies with respect to certain social groups may appear more costly, there are situations where they may impact by lowering procurement costs either immediately or in the future, eliminating the often-quoted trade-off between economic efficiencies and the pursuit of different policy goals. This, Quinot (Quinot & Rosa, Chapter 7) suggests, might provide an alternative explanation for the tenacity of procurement preferences during much of the latter half of the previous century (we should add in most countries, but not in the European Union).

Specific trade-offs, and not just synergies, might often arise between different policy goals. Morris (La Chimia & Morris, Chapter 1) mentions as an example how, on the basis of what experts indicate, 'as much as 97% of solar panels could contain materials made by persecuted Uyghur workers who are trapped in forced labour schemes'.

Quinot and Rosa (Chapter 7) agree on the several operational challenges that may arise in the implementation of such preference schemes that may undermine development objectives, including gaming of the system, and suggest that we should focus on the issue of which one is the most appropriate design of a preference scheme that should be imagined under a given circumstance. As for transaction costs of preference schemes, there is evidence that benefits of preferential schemes may amply overcome any figure of process costs.

### I.4 Regulation vs. flexibility to ensure impact

Flexibility vs. regulation in the public procurement process is a strategic issue for procurers, often dependent on the growth professionalization of the related workforce and the strength of one country's institutions in terms of accountability and integrity.

In this volume, Snider and Trybus (Chapter 10) focus intensely on the appropriate level of regulation for a market where both the buying power of and the industrial preferences for specific suppliers by governments is typically high: the defence sector. This is an important issue particularly for large countries, where defence can reach, like in the United States, about 11% of all national spending, with the high-tech major systems that attract the lion's share of attention and external scrutiny (see Snider in Snider & Trybus, Chapter 10). Trybus (Snider & Trybus, Chapter 10) reminds us that since only a few countries have defence industries extensive enough to have domestic competition for major weapons systems, that makes the government somewhat responsible for the economic survival of any defence industrial capacity on their territory. This would frequently lead to direct awards to the domestic defence industries without competition and predictable consequences for price and quality. Countries with only limited domestic defence industries will still aim to protect whatever capabilities they have and often require the involvement of these domestic companies in the supply chains of foreign suppliers through offsets and similar arrangements which are also difficult to reconcile with a competitive procurement procedure. He states that defence procurement needs to be regulated; it is far too important to be left unregulated.

Snider (Snider & Trybus, Chapter 10) argues instead that the fact that the U.S. Department awards many high-value contracts, particularly those pertaining to major systems in the defence acquisition domain, outside the competitive regime in the absence of public outcry and opposition should suggest to question retaining a regulatory preference for competition in defence acquisition. He continues by noting that the continual accretion of regulations has led to high transaction costs in compliance and reporting requirements. In addition to increasing the workload for an already overburdened government workforce, these requirements lead, according to him, to increased contract prices from defence vendors. They also present, according to the author, barriers to entry into the defence market for potential new suppliers, which limits the military sector access to commercial innovation. Finally, they could even risk to lead to degradation of a nation's combat capabilities. Moreover, industrial symbiosis is a potential contribution to a substantially improved defence acquisition situation for procurement and defence industry (Glas & Eßig, Chapter 11).

Trybus (Snider & Trybus, Chapter 10), on the other hand, believes that limited regulation is possible, as long as it involves the exclusion of certain types of defence procurement from the scope of the regime that would be too complex or politically sensitive to be included. He suggests for the defence procurement to be ideally divided into three broad categories: (1) the procurement of non-military goods and services which should be conducted based on a competitive regime that is not adapted to the defence sector; (2) the procurement of specifically military goods and services that can be subjected to a competitive procurement regime that is in various ways adapted to the defence sector; and (3) the procurement of specifically military goods and services that for various reasons – rooted in national security, the complexity of large projects, or specific trans-national procurement practices – cannot be subjected to a competitive procurement regime and should therefore be excluded from such a regime on the basis of clearly defined exemptions. The question, he concludes, whether this approach can be called 'reduced' regulation depends, to an extent, on what share of the budget is attributed to the three categories, specifically the share that is completely excluded.

Snider (Snider & Trybus, Chapter 10) argues that in the defence procurement, professionalization is a worthy alternative to excessive regulation; procurement requires the workforce to be tuned towards innovation and flexibility, traits which are increasingly critical in today's procurement, possibly not only in the dynamic defence acquisition environment. This would imply strengthening administrative capacity in the form of a larger and more professional procurement workforce, with members who are trained to have business and public administration acumen, to be technologically savvy, and who are given sufficient administrative discretion to make sound decisions in the public interest. Trybus (Snider & Trybus, Chapter 10) disagrees with seeing better training as an alternative to regulation. While, on the one hand, nobody can deny the importance and utility of (better) training for procurement officers, training should, on the other hand, be continuously improved and updated in addition to good regulation, not as a substitute for it and include training on inevitably necessary regulation. Their debate has evidently significant implications also within the non-military sphere of public procurement.

The role of regulation or soft law affects other realms too. While La Chimia (La Chimia & Morris, Chapter 1) argues strongly that a hard law basis and hard (exclusion) measures are needed, Morris (La Chimia & Morris, Chapter 1) mentions that it alone does not guarantee that human rights respect is effectively incorporated into public procurement: laws in several countries introduce human rights objectives into public procurement but do not articulate how to practically implement these across the procurement cycle. At the contractual level, the normative power exercised through contracts remains persuasive rather than prescriptive in nature, argues La Chimia (La Chimia and Morris, Chapter 1), aligning with the approach of persuasion rather than prescription embraced by the United Nations Guiding Principles on Business and Human Rights and little progress can be registered in terms of using procurement to protect, facilitate, and promote human rights throughout the supply chain. When it comes to contractual issues, incorporating transparent mechanisms from the start for lawful modification of contracts at the contract-management stage is key, for example in the event of climate-change-related events, argues Garbuzanova (Garbuzanova & Lundberg, Chapter 4). Schoeni and Yukins (Chapter 12) point out that defence procurement and public procurement law operate within a legal and constitutional environment and this external environment is sometimes more important than the internal rules and regulations that govern a procurement system.

## I.5 Measuring impact and value of public procurement

One major issue in public procurement used for policy goals that are different from transactional efficiencies and monetary savings might be related to measuring the value of the former goals. Rosa's suggestion (Quinot & Rosa, Chapter 7) of turning to the contingent valuation literature to deal with the issue of valuing complexity is worth exploring. This would imply also assessing and quantifying procurers' stated preferences in relation to a range of sustainability criteria.

An issue that however often arises as a major problem in evaluating impact of specific procurement policies is the one regarding the lack of institutional structures dedicated to it. In the field of human rights, contract clauses must be associated with on-the-ground monitoring and verification mechanisms to be effective even within single companies and linked to substantial remedies for violating such conditions. A lack of data creates barriers in assessing the effectiveness of existing measures, including how they realize human rights of key stakeholders such as workers throughout value chains, impacted communities, and end users (see Morris in La Chimia & Morris, Chapter 1).

La Chimia (La Chimia & Morris, Chapter 1) adds that for the exclusion ground to apply, some form of definitive or quasi-definitive sentencing is needed and that this criterion is difficult to meet in some cases of human rights violations, especially when such violations occur abroad, because only a fraction of human rights violations is ascertained by a court and reach the status of res judicata. She suggests involving NGOs as an alternative in human rights for not only monitoring systems, instruments, and mechanisms which could be helpful in procurement but also prioritizing the capacity and professionalization of the procurement workforce, since they will implement the norms and policies linking procurement and human rights. Garbuzanova (Garbuzanova & Lundberg, Chapter 4) point out that technology and data-driven tools can help in planning for all climate-change consequences: the predictable and the unpredictable. Lundberg (Chapter 4) suggests we could assess the effectiveness of GPP in terms of dynamic efficiency, which pertains to its ability to stimulate the development of less polluting technologies. Also, GPP can be viewed as a signalling system that signifies a long-term commitment to influencing the market, encouraging investments in greener technology, and motivating consumer behaviour that reduces greenhouse gas emissions, allowing potential suppliers to adopt a long-term perspective on investment costs across multiple periods, potentially increasing the participation in the procurement process. On the environmental front, Garbuzanova and Lundberg (Chapter 4) agree, a life-cycle assessment approach (from raw material to disposal) is needed to address impacts outside immediate costs; this would cover not just costs but also wider climate-change consequences. As Diófási-Kovács and Freund (Chapter 6) note, the example of school food systems has great potential for transformation towards sustainability and for reducing the climate impact.

More generally, public procurement meant to satisfy or ensure the realization of specific goals requires the capacity to access information (more often than not also at the supply chain level of the buyer), making sure that those designing and implementing measures at the pre-award stage have the capacity and/or resources to identify and address risks in the post-award or contractual phase, a field in which they are not always knowledgeable and in which information is not readily accessible, ensuring that responsibility for introducing measures is clear and that the design and implementation of measures across multiple functions is made coherent, a task that can be difficult to achieve in practice. Garbuzanova (Garbuzanova & Lundberg, Chapter 4) mentions how consistent planning is needed and this also requires consensus on how to plan for the different consequences of contingencies. In the field of green procurement when one deals with climate change this implies addressing the unrepairable (adaptation and damage control); planning for measures to reverse the reversible; planning for preventing future negative impact and avoiding further irreparable damage; planning for the unforeseen and the unforeseeable. These are measures that should also be thought for the rest of the public procurement global and local strategies, building an organizational culture that allows such processes to become the norm rather than the exception.

# PART I

# Human rights in public procurement

# 1 Colloquium[1]

*Annamaria La Chimia and Daniel Morris*

## 1.1 Annamaria La Chimia – Introductory Remarks

The relationship between public procurement and human rights goes back as far as the 20th century. Procurement has long been linked to initiatives aimed at protecting and advancing human rights domestically (within the territory and jurisdiction of the state where the procurement entity is located) and internationally (concerning violations occurring abroad where suppliers are based or goods produced). However, as further elaborated below, this relationship is far from uncontroversial, and much more needs to be done to consolidate the link between procurement and human rights and harness the power of procurement to leverage human rights.

Procurement and human rights initiatives have involved measures aimed at ensuring respect and protection of human rights – often via *reactive* and *preventive* measures against human rights abuses (with a view to punish and prevent/deter abuses) – and via *proactive* efforts to fulfil (promote and facilitate) the enjoyment of human rights. Examples of measures falling within the first category include implementing measures mandating the exclusion of companies that violate certain national labour laws (see, e.g., Article 57 of the EU Directives 24/2014/EU). Similarly, this category – i.e. *reactive* and *preventive* measures against human rights abuses – encompasses measures prohibiting participation in public tenders by companies based in (or conducting business with) and/or offering products from countries violating human rights. Noteworthy initiatives in this category include those against the apartheid regime in South Africa or against the occupied territories of Palestine. For instance, in 2014, Leicester City Council approved a motion not to purchase goods from Israeli-Occupied Palestinian territories – a decision initially challenged by Jewish Rights Watch Ltd but upheld by the Court of Appeal (Jewish Rights Watch Ltd (T/A Jewish Human Rights Watch) Vs. Leicester City Council [2018]).[2]

Procurement has also been utilized to proactively fulfil (promote and facilitate) the enjoyment of human rights within the enactment and implementation of measures specifically targeting certain human rights issues, including the allocation of contracts to minorities or previously disadvantaged groups (notorious in this respect are the measures implemented by South Africa in the B-BBEE 2003 Act[3]).

DOI: 10.4324/9781032631721-3

However, procurement and human rights measures (reactive, preventive, and proactive) often face national and international controversy. At the national level, measures taken by individual entities or councils, as in the case of the Leicester City Council, might encounter political opposition at both local and national levels. As mentioned earlier, the measure implemented by the Leicester City Council faced a challenge in the national court from the Jewish Rights Watch. While the Appeal Court upheld the measure, the local opposition it encountered indicated its contentious nature, at least from a political perspective. The question of whether a local council or a single entity can act to respond to and prevent human rights violations committed abroad remains controversial to a considerable extent. The UK Parliament is scrutinizing a bill (HC Bill 325[4]), the UK Overseas Matter Bill 2022–2023 which if approved by the Parliament, will restrict the power of local councils to implement such measures. It is important to note that controversy at the national level over the linkages between procurement and human rights is not limited to the protection of human rights or violations committed abroad. For example, as Georgopolous notes, in the United Kingdom, the issue of whether private care home service providers are subject to the application of the ECHR through the Human Rights Act and can be regarded as 'performing functions of a public nature' (Georgopolous, 2014) required the intervention of the Parliament after a negative answer to this question in Y v Birmingham City Council ([2007] UKHL 27).

At the international level, procurement and human rights measures are often regarded as conflicting with international agreements on market liberalization, such as the WTO/Government Procurement Agreement (GPA). An example of such a conflict arose when the European Community (now European Union) challenged an Act passed by the Commonwealth of Massachusetts, which prohibited public authorities in Massachusetts from procuring goods or services from individuals or entities doing business with Burma (Act Regulating State Contracts 1996).[5] On 20 June 1997, The European Community lodged first a consultation request and later one to establish a panel with the WTO Dispute Settlement Body, claiming that Massachusetts' legislation violated their rights under the recently adopted 1994 WTO/GPA agreement.[6] The request was later suspended following a court ruling in the United States that prevented the implementation of the contested measure.[7]

To date, international economic law, the traditional branch of law associated with international public procurement, has not resolved this controversy or offered clear guidance on using procurement to advance human rights. The literature is still divided about the scope and extent to which the WTO/GPA allows the pursuance of HR objectives (Corvaglia & Li, 2018). Yet, much has changed in the past 20 years. The globalization of supply chains and the expansion of international markets have further underscored the necessity for fresh initiatives to strengthen the connection between procurement and human rights. As labour-intensive processes are increasingly outsourced to companies based in developing countries, which are often exploited by multilateral corporations imposing conditions and standards that workers in developed countries would never be expected to accept, the understanding that procurement can be a strategic tool for advancing broader human rights objectives has gained traction. Since the early 2000s, an important literature has developed tied to procurement and Corporate Social Responsibility (CSR) standards. During this period, initial steps were taken to prevent purchases from industries directly or indirectly involved in human rights violations throughout the supply chain. In this respect, for example, commendable were the efforts by Universities in the United States to 'end public purchases from sweatshops'[8]. Nonetheless, these proactive approaches initially remained relatively isolated, primarily implemented by individual procurement entities in response to specific instances of human rights violations.

Arguably, two major problems obstruct the implementation of these measures: on the one hand, the market's reluctance to fulfil the requests of pro-active public authorities, resulting in a lack of suitable suppliers; and secondly, the absence of a comprehensive normative framework that clarifies both the necessary and imperative nature of states' human rights purchasing responsibilities, limiting the effectiveness and impact of these initiatives (La Chimia, 2018). Both problems are complex and require strategic thinking by contracting authorities and different levels of intervention by the legislator. For example, the reluctance of businesses to adhere to human rights standards not only requires procurement entities to carefully consider what, where, and how to buy (if, for example, buying in collaboration with other authorities to increase the value of the purchases and attract more and different business entities) but also necessitates the intervention of the legislator to improve business conduct more generally, not just in relation to procurement. After all, procurement does not exist in a vacuum, and it is not a panacea for solving market problems. Instead, coordinated and structural actions are needed to change the market.

The second challenge, precisely the absence of a normative framework, saw some redress with the unanimous adoption of the United Nations Guiding Principles on Business and Human Rights (UNGPs) by the UN Council in 2011.[9] However, I argue that the UNGPs, while a step in the right direction, only partially fulfil the need for a comprehensive normative framework. The framework they offer is not adequate to drive the transformation needed to align procurement practices with human rights standards. My concern lies with the UNGPs' ambiguous and weak language regarding procurement, making them an insufficient instrument to effectively incentivize and overcome the reluctance of certain, more hesitant public authorities. As I delve into further detail below, the UNGPs fall short of being a robust catalyst for steering procurement practices towards full compliance with human rights standards.

Despite these limitations, it needs to be recognised, as many have argued in the literature (see below), that the UNGPs and the official commentary on those principles usher in a new and more articulated phase of the procurement and human rights debate, deserving praise for their contributions. This process of change has been further expedited by tragic events of the past decade, such as the collapse of the Rana Plaza factory in 2013. The dire and unsafe working conditions applied by companies that serve Western multilateral corporations were exposed to the world. Problematic for public procurers was the discovery that workers involved in the disaster were producing, among other garments, also U.S. defence uniforms (e.g., Stumberg et al. (2014) explicitly refers to both the UNGPs and the Rana Plaza tragic event).

Principles 6–8 of the UNGPs are dedicated to the state-business nexus, and recognize, to various degrees, states' responsibility for promoting respect for human rights by companies they do business with finance or have other forms of commercial and market transactions with. Thus, states must ensure that companies they support or finance (Principle 4), that they entrust with providing essential services (Principle 5), or that they do business with (Principle 6) respect and do not violate human rights. Principle 6, in particular, recognizes that states 'should promote respect for human rights by business enterprises with which they conduct commercial transactions'.[10] The official commentary on Principle 6 refers explicitly to public procurement as a key commercial transaction and a crucial expression of the state-business nexus. It draws a clear link between states' purchasing activities and states' obligations under international law to protect, respect, and fulfil human rights. This recognition consolidates the role of procurement in promoting human rights and brings it to the attention of business and human rights scholars who were previously less engaged with the potential influence of the public purse in advancing human rights. The international initiatives within the business and human rights domain injected new vigour into the debate on procurement and human rights (Jørgensen et al., 2003; Mc Crudden, 2006), generating a prolific literature advocating for the pursuit of human rights objectives through procurement (Stumberg et al., 2014, Martin-Ortega and O'Brien, 2019). The adoption of the UNGPs can be considered a turning point in establishing 'procurement and human rights' as a focal area for procurement lawyers.

Notably, the UNGPs provide the first international normative space *outside* the international trade framework to which procurement lawyers were typically accustomed to. Under this new framework, procurement is no longer viewed exclusively as a market integration tool but is explicitly identified as a leverage to promote human rights. This approach is further strengthened by the adoption of General Comment 24 (hereafter GC 24) by the United Nations Committee on Economic, Social and Cultural Rights, (UN Committee on ESCR (General Comment No. 24 (2017)). In its GC 24, the Committee articulates in a more comprehensive way how procurement can be used to promote human rights, including by pointing out that 'states' obligation to protect human rights includes taking administrative actions capable of ensuring effective protection of human rights' (GC 24 para 15).

In this author's view, the most significant merit of the new debate is to have raised awareness of the importance of procurement for protecting human rights beyond the limited framework in which it was previously constrained, extending beyond the actions of progressive yet isolated procurement entities. This new discourse now encompasses broader issues addressed by the business and human rights community, such as the focus on supply chains, while simultaneously helping to overcome some of the limitations typical of the business and human rights discourse. These limitations include concerns about the self-regulatory nature of the Business and Human Rights (BHR) approach and its reliance on voluntary codes of conduct by businesses (Eslava, 2015; and for the link between the peremptory nature of the public procurement, see Fox et al., 2002 and Mc Crudden, 2006). States, by regulating the procurement process through peremptory norms that discipline access to the public marketplace (and public contracts), wield enormous regulatory power capable of influencing changes in companies' behaviours. However, the normative power exercised through contracts remains persuasive rather than prescriptive in nature, aligning with the approach of persuasion rather than prescription embraced by the UNGPs.[11] The rules and standards imposed through public procurement only apply to companies that voluntarily enter into contracts with the state and are not universally applicable to all companies.

The limited effectiveness of the UNGPs is evident in the fact that, over ten years since chage the with their adoption, little progress can be registered in terms of using procurement to respect, protect, and fulfil human rights throughout the supply chain. While some states have undertaken individual initiatives – for example, in the area of 'modern' slavery (United Kingdom and Australia) and due diligence (Sweden) – these remain isolated approaches with a narrow focus and coverage, sometimes limited to soft law, non-binding initiatives (see OECD and OSCE). It is submitted that the initiatives so far undertaken simply pay lip service to the neoliberal principles endorsed by our damaged market economy and, to paraphrase Jessica Whyte's words in her brilliant work, these initiatives show that human rights are just used to moralize the market but not to substantially change it (Whyte, 2019). In other words, they are used to legitimize a competitive and individualist system based on profits and exploitation of workers in the global south.

This becomes evident when examining the actions undertaken at national level and the policy instruments issued, such as the National Action Plans (NAPs), to give effect to the UNGPs. It is argued here that these actions and policy instruments reflect the limited breadth of the current discourse on procurement and human rights, as well as the neoliberal vision of procurement endorsed by international economic law instruments that traditionally regulate procurement. The procurement and human rights discourse that emerged from the UNGPs does not offer an alternative conceptual framework, distinct from the existing framework of international trade agreements, rather it replicates it.

For example, the neoliberal frame of international economic law is evident in the NAPs endorsed by some states, where human rights objectives within the BHR discourse are pursued to offer a level playing field to companies in developed countries where such rights are upheld. Thus, the Italian 2018 NAP frames BHR as a competition issue that explicitly refers to the need to

> face the current global challenges with regard to *competition* and human rights in the context of the international market. Situations such as the distortion of market prices due to the import/export of goods and services from countries or enterprises not compliant with fundamental human rights …have serious economic implications on … competition. …addressing [these issues] is not only essential to improve their better protection [i.e. of HR] but it also proactively

> advances them by developing a sound business culture and seizing new opportunities for economic growth *within a system of fair competition*.
>
> (Italian NAP, 2018, emphasis added)

The competition link is further enhanced by the strong emphasis placed on the collaborative role between the Italian Competition Authority and the National Anti-Corruption Authority. However, this approach carries the risk of undermining human rights commitments to preserve competition objectives.

Further, this is evident in the fact that the procurement and human rights debate has been framed in terms of 'opportunity', 'benefits', rather than in terms of obligations, duties, and rights. As explained above, 'persuasion', not prescription, remains the approach of the UNGPs. This becomes especially evident when examining the actions suggested to promote human rights and the initiatives adopted since the endorsement of the UNGPs. It is submitted that such actions adopt an almost reverential approach to the market, ensuring that the proposed procurement measures remain 'respectful' of companies' capacity and willingness to contract with the state. There is a mindfulness to be seen as 'working with companies'. In practical terms, this approach has translated into toolkits and guidelines that are reticent to suggest the adoption of strong commitments to promote the respect of human rights through procurement. For example, this is evident in some of the toolkits developed by official institutions, such as the UK Modern Slavery Commissioner (Independent-Antislavery Commissioner and Local Government Association, 2015) and academics and practitioners (Davis-Ortega, 2016).

The limited breadth of these tools directly results from the narrow approach adopted within the procurement and human rights debate and the UNGPs' silence regarding the actions states should take through procurement to fulfil their human rights obligations. Indeed, while the UNGPs require states to take all 'appropriate steps to prevent, investigate, punish, and redress' any human rights abuse through 'effective policies, legislation, regulation, and adjudication' (UN Guiding Principle 1), no details are provided in the context of procurement regarding what these 'appropriate steps' entail. The commentary to Principle 6 simply states that commercial transactions provide 'unique *opportunities* [for states] to promote awareness of and respect for human rights by those enterprises, *including* through the *terms of contracts*, with due regard to States' relevant obligations under national and international law' (emphasis added). In the context of public procurement, this is a clear reference to the well-known use of contract conditions as a means to promote 'other' policy goals.[12]

As this author has argued elsewhere, although contract clauses are a good starting point to improve conditions regarding *single* contracts, they are not 'policy tools' and are ineffective at generating changes in the broader market (beyond single companies). Furthermore, contract clauses must be associated with on-the-ground monitoring and verification mechanisms to be effective even within single companies and linked to substantial remedies for violating such conditions. This is especially true if breaches of contract clauses result only in compensation arrangements related to non-disclosure agreements (as seen, for example, in Electronics Watch) and do not lead to the termination of contracts and debarment from future tender opportunities. Conversely, exclusions and termination of contracts are more effective ways of using procurement as a 'policy tool'. Yet, these are never suggested as measures; on the contrary, they are demystified. For example, the guide 'Modern Slavery: A Council Guide', issued by the UK independent anti-slavery Commissioner and the Local Government Association, states that 'Councils should consider when the best time is to look at human rights due diligence (HRDD). This may not always be during the competitive tendering process, when there may not be enough time to look into a supplier's supply chains' (Independent-Antislavery Commissioner and Local Government Association, 2015).[13]

As explained above, UNGP Principle 6 and its commentary do not explicitly refer to exclusions. However, this does not mean that contract clauses are the only means envisaged by the UNGPs. On the contrary, the language expressly used in the commentary, namely 'including', suggests that contract clauses are one of many measures that can be taken. This interpretation is confirmed by Comment 24 of the UN Committee on ESCR, which expressly refers to 'denying award of contracts' as possible actions to implement states' obligations (GC 24 Paragraph 50). Additionally, when interpreting what the wording 'appropriate steps' in Principle 6 entails, the Committee suggests (in Paragraph 16) that this includes the introduction of due diligence obligations to corporations and extending such due diligence obligations to the business entity's supply chain, subcontractors, suppliers, franchisees, or other business partners.

It could be argued that the fact that Principle 6 and its commentary do not explicitly refer to exclusions and debarment as possible actions (which, it is worth noting, are instead mentioned in Principle 7 linked to the development of procurement sectors) reveals a preference or, at least, an inclination for a 'weaker' or 'softer' approach to actions – typical of a performative approach to human rights that 'serves' but does not 'change' the market. Furthermore, such an approach fails to give impetus to states' endorsement of more ambitious measures. It is, therefore, not surprising that the normative value – and its imperativeness – of the procurement and human rights debate is still contested by some authors (Sanchez-Graells, 2019) and that the actions implemented by states over the past ten years reflect this weaker, softer, and unsatisfactory approach. Therefore, focusing on more decisive measures should be the first step for the future of procurement and human rights.

## 1.2 Daniel Morris – Introductory Remarks

States have international human rights law obligations to respect and protect human rights in their value chains and ensure remedy for human rights abuses which occur (Martin-Ortega & O'Brien, 2019). Public procurement has increasingly been used as a means of implementing human rights obligations in practice. States and international organizations are also embracing Sustainable Public Procurement (SPP). This element of the debate series begins by exploring how human rights fit within SPP.

There is no single definition of SPP. The United Nations Environment Programme (UNEP) notes that SPP is

> a process whereby public organizations meet their needs for goods, services, works and utilities in a way that achieves value for money on a whole life cycle basis in terms of generating benefits not only to the organization, but also to society and the economy, whilst significantly reducing, and if possible avoiding, negative impacts on the environment.
>
> (Multistakeholder Advisory Committee of the 10YFP SPP Programme, 2022)

The European Commission defines SPP as 'a process by which public authorities seek to achieve the appropriate balance between the three pillars of sustainable development – economic, social and environmental – when procuring goods, services or works at all stages of the project' (European Commission, 2021). A key feature of most SPP definitions is the joint focus on embedding economic, social, and environmental objectives in the procurement process (Stoffel et al., 2019; United Nations Global Marketplace, 2023; International Organization for Standardization, 2017).

Definitions in specific States explicitly link SPP to human rights. Sweden's central public procurement agency has stated that '[i]n a sustainable public procurement, you not only consider the benefits arising for your own organisation, but look at society as a whole. At the same time, you minimise environmental damage and safeguard certain social aspects such as equitable working conditions' (Upphandlingsmyndigheten, 2022). Environmental and labour rights are well recognized human rights. As such, links between human rights in SPP definitions exist, but are not universal. Treviño-Lozano and Ortega (2023, p. 15) have noted that 'SPP vagueness has been problematic for human rights because it has led to their subsumption under environmental sustainability, or in best case scenarios to their narrowed inclusion in the form of labour rights'.

The concept of SPP has its roots in measures to achieve sustainable development which arose in the 1980s and 1990s (Kumar, 2022). SPP was later included within the 2030 Agenda for Sustainable Development (2030 Agenda) and its associated Sustainable Development Goals (SDGs) and targets. SDG target 12.7 calls on all States to '[p]romote public procurement practices that are sustainable, in accordance with national policies and priorities' (United Nations General Assembly, 2015). A key feature of the 2030 Agenda is the introduction of a set of global indicators to measure progress. The associated indicator for SDG 12.7 relates to the '[n]umber of countries implementing sustainable public procurement policies and action plans'.

UNEP published a methodology to collect data on this indicator in 2020 which was updated in 2022. The updated methodology explicitly ties 'social, economic, and/or governance-related considerations' to ten focus areas, of which nine are grounded in human rights and human rights principles, including '1. [p]rotection against human rights abuses (for example, discrimination, unsafe working conditions child labour, forced labour, and human trafficking)',[14] '2. [p]rotection and promoting groups at risk (for example, minorities, indigenous peoples, persons with disabilities, migrant workers) through social inclusion, which may include employment', and '3. [p]romotion of compliance with ILO standards and decent work'[15] (Multistakeholder Advisory Committee of the 10YFP SPP Programme, 2022). The updated methodology also provides an Annex listing a wide range of international human rights and labour standards.

There is a question on whether such SPP indicators can be expected to drive the necessary inclusion of human rights in public procurement. The 'social, economic, and/or governance-related considerations' within the SDG 12.7 calculation methodology are often worded 'environmental *and/or* social [emphasis added]' (Multistakeholder Advisory Committee of the 10YFP SPP Programme, 2022). As such, a state can score well on implementing SPP without a focus on human rights.[16] Such 'pick and choose' frameworks do not clearly articulate that measures to realize human rights and address human rights abuses in state value chains should not be seen as optional extras.

However, SPP indicators can be designed to capture measures to realize human rights through public procurement. In 2019 the Sustainable Procurement working group of the UN High-Level Committee on Management Procurement Network (HLCM-PN, 2023) approved 12 indicators that allow for systematic monitoring, measuring, and reporting on sustainable procurement within the UN system under 4 pillars (environment, society, economy, and general). Indicators under the society pillar include 'human rights and labour issues', which is explicitly linked to international human rights standards, 'inclusion of persons with disabilities', and 'gender issues' (Sustainable Procurement (SP) working group of the HLCM Procurement Network, 2023). The Sustainable Procurement working group agreed a methodology to identify a sustainable tender 'as those that include at least three [sustainable procurement] criteria – one in each pillar of sustainable development: environmental, social and economic' (United Nations Global Marketplace, 2023).

While environmental objectives may have dominated SPP efforts, recent data demonstrates an increasing focus on the social and economic element of SPP. UNEP's Sustainable Public Procurement: 2022 Global Review highlights that 'certain socio-economic issues, such as the promotion of SMEs and the protection and promotion of groups at risk, were almost on par with the top environmental issues', which was not the case in the previous 2017 Global Review 'where in almost all instances environmental issues were prioritized over socio-economic concerns' (UNEP, 2022, p. xiv). The 2021 Annual Statistical Report on United Nations Procurement, which provides an overview of the majority of the procurement of the UN totalling $29.6 billion, highlights that '[t]he integration of the three recognized pillars of sustainability (environmental, social and economic) became more balanced in 2021. The inclusion of social considerations in procurement processes increased sharply, from 79 per cent in 2020 to 97 per cent in 2021' (UNOPS, 2022, p. 25).

Data is central to public procurement (Núñez, 2020), yet there is a general lack of data on implementation of SPP in practice, including in the EU (Caimi &

Sansonetti, 2023). A lack of data creates barriers in assessing the effectiveness of existing measures, including how they realize human rights of key stakeholders such as workers throughout value chains, impacted communities, and end users (Morris, 2020). The data which exists is not uniform or consistent (between and within states) (Caimi & Sansonetti, 2023), often does not disaggregate between human rights and environmental issues, originates from the 'global north' (Stoffel et al., 2019), and is self-reported with original documents to allow for verification not publicly available. The UNEP 2022 Global Review notes that 'the full extent of SP implementation and its impacts are still unclear, with only 24% of the national governments measuring SP outcomes' (UNEP, 2022, p. iii).

Some of the approaches to address human rights and the environment in public procurement were conceived before the adoption of SDGs and its focus on SPP, and/or are designed to meet fundamental environmental, human rights, and good governance commitments and obligations. While some approaches are designed to address 'human rights' broadly, there are a number of approaches pursuing more focused human rights objectives, such as gender-responsive procurement (Gollub et al., 2021), addressing human trafficking and forced labour in value chains (OSCE, 2020), and measures focused on certain rightsholder groups (Morris, 2020).[17]

Though the joint focus on economic, social, and environmental objectives is a key feature of SPP, these objectives are often pursued separately. States are encouraged and have developed 'green public procurement plans' or approaches to implement 'socially responsible public procurement', but often separately and without coherency. For example, a 2022 proposal for an EU Regulation establishing a framework for setting ecodesign requirements for sustainable products includes 'mandatory technical specifications, selection criteria, award criteria, contract performance clauses, or targets, as appropriate', but only for green public procurement (European Commission, 2022, Art. 58).

In addition, it is possible to identify different methodologies used to implement different objectives. Treviño-Lozano and Ortega (2023, p. 18) have noted that social and environmental objectives are treated differently in the EU. Socially responsible public procurement in the EU is broadly implemented through 'do good' measures and green public procurement as 'do no harm' through environmental protections. Looking across multiple jurisdictions, two methodologies used to implement SPP can be broadly categorized as 'affirmative action' and 'due diligence'. Affirmative action consists of measures to ensure the social and economic empowerment of groups with specific characteristics and are often tailored to specific national contexts. This includes measures to implement Black Economic Empowerment in South Africa (Shai et al., 2019), and a focus in Kenya on supporting enterprises owned by women, youth, and persons with disabilities and other disadvantaged groups through preferences and reservations (Office of the Attorney General et al., 2023). HRDD is laid out in the UNGPs and the OECD Guidelines for Multinational Enterprises and is based on identifying and addressing risks throughout the value chain to ensure that public procurement activities do no harm to people and the environment. In practice, these methodologies are often implemented separately or in an uncoordinated manner which is concerning given the interdependencies between the two methodologies: human rights are designed to empower rightsholders, and affirmative action, including economic empowerment measures, are often directed to specific rightsholder groups to address systemic inequality and discrimination.

While pursuing separate policy objectives through different methodologies can ensure that implementation measures are well-tailored to individual objectives it can lead to siloed approaches. Siloed approaches are problematic as the two methodologies outlined above often rely on the introduction of measures at similar stages of the procurement cycle (e.g., in requirements definitions and evaluation criteria) which can compete for relevance as public buyers are tasked with implementing multiple objectives, and buyers are required to respond to these. Furthermore, siloed approaches can result in key areas being overlooked, such as ensuring remedy for victims of human rights abuses and/or environmental harms in state value chains (Trusgnach & Martin-Ortega, 2022). Crucially, focusing solely on objectives and methodologies that can positively contribute can paradoxically overlook risks of adverse human rights impacts of business activities in a states' value chain and have negative impacts on communities and workers, which can undermine positive contributions (Morris et al., 2019). For example, a range of public bodies are looking to purchase solar panels, but 'experts indicate that as much as 97% of solar panels could contain materials made by persecuted Uyghur workers who are trapped in forced labour schemes' (UNISON et al., 2022). There are moves in the right direction with the International Responsible Business Conduct Agreement for the Renewable Energy Sector, 2023, providing in Article 2.21 'for RBC standards to be taken into account in renewable energy public procurement and tender processes involving the national government and/or local authorities, with a view to stimulating and rewarding responsible corporate practices that respect human rights and environmental standards'.

O'Brien, Martin-Ortega, and Conlon (2018) have proposed a definition of socially responsible procurement based on due diligence, and the OECD has urged its adherents to use 'public procurement as a strategic tool for RBC [responsible business conduct] and including RBC in procurement policies (regulatory and strategic frameworks), as well as promoting due diligence for RBC in public procurement' (OECD, 2022). However, the 2020 methodology to calculate how states are implementing SPP contained a scored indicator on 'Risk-assessment and impact prioritization', which was deleted from the updated 2022 methodology (Multistakeholder Advisory Committee of the 10YFP SPP Programme, 2020). The rationale for moving away from risk assessment and due diligence is unclear. This move is unfortunate as HRDD is key to addressing risks of human rights abuses and/or environmental harms occurring in state value chains. The EU taxonomy on sustainable finance has integrated human rights safeguards into objectives focused on advancing the green agenda and can provide some inspiration in this regard.[18]

For human rights to comfortably fit within SPP, there needs to be greater coherence between SPP objectives and methodologies, and human rights standards need to be integrated as a minimum safeguard across all SPP objectives, methodologies, and indicators.

## 1.3 Annamaria La Chimia – Response to Paper 2

Morris' paper proposes an interesting link between SPP, the SDGs, and human rights. The author makes it clear that a major issue in the current procurement and human rights approach is the lack of monitoring and measurement instruments associated with the SDGs and the measures taken to realize them. I certainly agree with the author's position concerning the need to advance knowledge on this aspect of the procurement and human rights debate.

I think this is important not only in terms of evaluating and monitoring the effectiveness of the actions taken but also in terms of damages, redress, and evaluation of past performance. This latter aspect, I believe, should be looked at carefully to contemplate the possibility of exclusion from future tenders, i.e., if a supplier does not comply with human rights norms and standards, they will not qualify to participate in the tender. As I explained in my first paper and other writing, I believe that procurement exclusions and contract terminations should be used in relation to human rights breaches, both in terms of reactive measures – post-violation – and as a form of dissuasion to avoid future violations. On this point, I have criticized other authors that endorse a mellower approach (La Chimia, 2018).

Yet, such an approach is challenging to implement because of the strict requirements imposed on contracting authorities by national and international law. Human rights violations should always be regarded as law violations and/or professional misconduct that would allow to exclude a supplier from a tender – whether as a mandatory/automatic or a discretionary exclusion. However, most systems have stringent criteria for establishing when a violation of law or professional misconduct qualifies as an exclusion ground. In line with the general principle of law that no one is guilty until definitively sentenced (see Article 27 of the Italian Constitution in this regard), most systems require, for the exclusion ground to apply, some form of definitive or quasi-definitive sentencing. This criterion is difficult to meet in some cases of human rights violations, especially when such violations occur abroad. This is because only a fraction of human rights violations is ascertained by a court and reach the status of res judicata. It is noteworthy, for example, that despite the many instances of child labour, few cases are officially reported or reach the status of res judicata in judicial proceedings.

A similar problem exists regarding the possibility of rescinding contracts. Countries adopt different stances on contract termination, especially when there are overarching reasons of public interest that would require the continuation of the contract. Furthermore, in many instances, proving that a violation has been committed is difficult, especially given the lack of adequate contract monitoring mechanisms, making the execution of the contract fertile ground for concealing violations. Hence, strong monitoring mechanisms are essential to facilitate procurement officials' decisions to terminate a contract and legitimize future exclusions when past performance can be used as an exclusionary ground.

In my view, it would be interesting to explore what human rights monitoring and verification mechanisms could be applied to the procurement cycle. In other words, it would be beneficial to investigate whether any mechanisms used to monitor compliance with human rights laws and standards could be applied to public procurement (and adopted by procurement lawyers). I believe that procurement professionals can learn much from human rights experts in this regard.

The work done by NGOs to monitor human rights abuses is essential in this respect. Reference to alternative human rights monitoring systems, instruments, and mechanisms would be helpful in procurement. Procurement is still entrenched in formal judicial proceedings and 'res judicata', which is impractical and ineffective in certain countries and cases of human rights abuses. Therefore, we need to ask how we can reconcile the reality on the ground with the strict procurement requirements. This question is important not only in relation to the exclusion of suppliers but also in relation to the termination of contracts or even the award of damages (the latter is another important aspect of procurement and human rights that still requires further attention).

Therefore, I believe there is a real need to collaborate with human rights practitioners, borrowing from their practices to use alternative methods of investigation, diversifying monitoring mechanisms in procurement, and improving dispute resolution mechanisms. This is especially important when official judicial systems are weak and unreliable.

The first part of Morris' paper addresses the link between SPP, HR, and the SDGs. I was surprised to see that Morris accepts the SDGs at face value, without any criticism, and reference to the wealth of critical literature that has questioned the SDGs. In this regard, for example, the literature is very vocal in criticizing the soft law nature of the SDGs, although the criticism of the SDGs goes further than this. In Morris' work, no questions are raised over the shortcomings of the neoliberal vision of HR projected by the SDG. Neither Morris questions whether the lack of any reporting obligation is sustainable and consistent with the international framework. Similarly, the work by UNEP is praised, but the author neglects to address the fact that the UNEP monitoring system relies on states' goodwill and willingness to report. Besides, because states do not have specific reporting obligations, they report only what they want. It is submitted that this is a weakness of the SDGs system that needs to be highlighted and addressed to give more credibility to the SDGs and its reporting mechanisms. The limits of the SDGs will be reflected in the methodology used to measure their impact, evaluate the action taken, and report.

Furthermore, Morris argues that 'definitions in specific countries explicitly link SPP to human rights' and highlights the example of Sweden's central public procurement agency, explaining that '[i]n sustainable public procurement, you not only consider the benefits arising for your own organization but also look at society as a whole. At the same time, you minimize environmental damage and safeguard certain social aspects such as equitable working conditions'. It is unclear how this definition reflects human rights standards. In my view, this definition remains too vague (consider, for example, the reference to 'certain social aspects') to be praised as a compliance model.

Additionally, when Morris mentions that the integration of the three pillars of sustainability became more balanced in 2021, 'with the inclusion of social considerations in procurement processes increased sharply, from 79 percent in 2020 to

97 percent in 2021', I believe it would be essential to understand if a distinction is made between human rights and environmental issues. If not, it could well be that the increase is to be attributed to environmental objectives.

Finally, the author might want to focus more on the implications of SPP for the procurement and HR discourse rather than the multidimensionality of the concept of SPP to avoid repeating existing work done by others on this topic (e.g., Stoffel et al., 2019.)

## 1.4 Daniel Morris – Response to Paper 1

The UNGPs are the foundational framework articulating how businesses can respect human rights by conducting HRDD. They are also the foundational framework articulating the link between human rights and public procurement, as La Chimia notes. HRDD, as articulated in the UNGPs, should underpin measures to incorporate human rights and sustainability into public procurement so that businesses are not faced with a range of different requirements from states. HRDD should be implemented through an effective 'smart mix' of mutually reinforcing hard and soft measures, tailored to the local context (Shift, 2019).

While the UNGPs are a soft law standard and do not create new international law obligations they reiterate human rights obligations contained in other hard law standards. The UNGPs built from the UN 'Protect, Respect and Remedy' Framework, which was developed by the UN Special Rapporteur, John Ruggie, with a mandate to, *inter alia*, 'identify and clarify standards of corporate responsibility and accountability with regard to human rights' (UN Commission on Human Rights, 2005, para. 1). La Chimia highlights that '[a]t the international level procurement and human rights measures are often regarded in conflict with international agreements on market liberalization'. However, the UNGPs are grounded in the existing international legal system and were not designed to address the structural challenges of neo-liberalism nor the fragmentation of international law (International Law Commission, 2006), although they provide that states should, 'when acting as members of multilateral institutions that deal with business-related issues', such as the WTO, '[s]eek to ensure that those institutions neither restrain the ability of their member States to meet their duty to protect nor hinder business enterprises from respecting human rights' (United Nations, 2011, Principle 10).

The UNGPs provide that states 'should consider a smart mix of measures – national and international, mandatory and voluntary – to foster business respect for human rights' (United Nations, 2011, Principle 3, Commentary). La Chimia argues that the UNGPs embrace an approach 'of persuasion rather than prescription'. However, states have flexibility under the UNGPs to adopt both hard and soft measures (i.e., prescription *and* persuasion) to ensure businesses respect human rights. Since the adoption of the UNGPs by the UN Human Rights Council in 2011, there has been a tendency to favour softer measures, which has led O'Brien (2019) to note there is more an 'invisible hand rather than SMART mix'. In recent years there has been a move towards mandatory measures, as can be seen with the adoption of mandatory HRDD laws, including those in Europe (European Coalition for Corporate Justice, 2022). This is a step towards recalibrating the balance between hard and soft measures to ensure a true smart mix.

In Germany, the 2016 NAP on business and human rights not only contained soft HRDD measures but also set a target that half of German businesses should implement core elements of HRDD. A 2020 survey showed that 83–87% of companies were not complying with the NAP requirements (EY, 2020, p. 4), which contributed towards the development of the German Supply Chain Due Diligence Law. This law came into force on 1 January 2023 and requires companies over a certain size to conduct HRDD. This data-driven approach shows how soft measures socialized HRDD in Germany and provided a basis for hard measures when soft measures were demonstrated to be ineffective in isolation. Evidence and lessons learned from Germany are informing HRDD developments in states designing softer measures and in states driving forward with mandatory HRDD legislation. Unfortunately, many mandatory HRDD legislative developments do not address leveraging public procurement to implement HRDD in practice.

La Chimia argues strongly that a hard law basis and hard (exclusion) measures are needed. While a hard law basis is important, it alone does not guarantee that HRDD is effectively incorporated into public procurement. Laws in several states introduce human rights objectives into public procurement but do not articulate how to practically implement these across the procurement cycle. Other states have laws which allow for the inclusion of human rights objectives rather than mandate them, which means many of these remain on paper or implemented piecemeal (Morris, 2020; O'Brien et al., 2016). When hard laws are not accompanied with and/or implemented through softer measures (including regulations, policies, standard tender documents, contractual clauses, guidance, and training for public buyers and/or suppliers), broad and optional human rights objectives can remain un-implemented. This is compounded by the risk-averse nature of procurement entities which wish to avoid litigation from unsuccessful suppliers. A European Parliament study on the social impact of public procurement (Caimi & Sansonetti, 2023, p. 68) notes that 'legislation is important but remains insufficient if not coupled with adequate policy frameworks, strategies and capacity-building programmes'.

A smart mix of measures can help raise the bar of what the market can deliver and be scored on in a procurement. A minimum standard to exclude suppliers convicted of serious human rights abuses winning tenders may be applied as a starting point. However, advanced HRDD criteria must be considered in light of other common procurement principles, including fair competition. In other words, advanced HRDD criteria should be tailored to the maturity of the market to ensure that there are suppliers which can meet mandatory criteria. In time, market maturity should be reassessed to ensure measures are effective, minimum standards should be raised, and more advanced HRDD criteria should be considered.

Certain soft measures can be implemented without a legal basis and without risk of litigation, such as voluntary training courses, questionnaires, and supplier dialogue. While such measures alone might not be sufficient to implement all elements of HRDD, they can be a good starting point where no hard law exists, and can help socialize human rights, change behaviors, and build capacity, which is important when trying to introduce inaugural or more advanced harder measures in the future.

La Chimia argues that 'the normative power exercised through contracts remains persuasive rather than prescriptive in nature'. While the normative power exercised through contracts only directly impacts the supplier which wins the tender and signs the contract (rather than other measures applicable to all tenderers), all measures implemented through public procurement only directly impact businesses which voluntarily choose to bid for/do business with the state, rather than the market as a whole. Therefore, all normative power exercised through public procurement can be considered 'persuasive rather than prescriptive in nature', including sanctions and exclusions. However, leveraging the contracting power of the state as a buyer to contractually require suppliers and potential suppliers to respect human rights can be a strong tool to drive change, especially as the state is often the largest buyer in a country, particularly in certain sectors. Furthermore, contractual protections are a key means to ensure suppliers respect human rights, for example, clauses to suspend suppliers, require corrective active action, and terminate contracts when HRDD is not conducted and/or human rights abuses occur and are not addressed. This aligns with the UNGPs which provide that '[i]f the business enterprise has leverage to prevent or mitigate the adverse impact, it should exercise it' (United Nations, 2011, Principle 19, Commentary).

La Chimia argues that 'little progress can be registered in terms of using procurement to protect, facilitate and promote human rights throughout the supply chain' and that there are only 'isolated approaches with a narrow focus and coverage, sometimes limited to soft law, non-binding initiatives'. While few states and public buyers have adopted a holistic approach to incorporating HRDD across the full public procurement cycle, there are a range of examples of how human rights can be incorporated at different stages through hard and/or soft measures. This includes measures related to planning, risk identification, assessment, sourcing, requirements definition, supplier qualification, evaluation and award criteria, contractual provisions, contract management and supplier dialogue, supplier monitoring, corrective action and disengagement, and sanctions (Morris, 2020; O'Brien et al., 2016). There are also measures which are not human rights measures *per se*, but are important to realize HRDD, such as contractual provisions around documentation, auditing, and sub-suppliers, for example, which allow a public buyer to effectively respond to allegations of human rights abuses. However, identifying good practice can be a challenge due to the different methodologies utilized to incorporate human rights into public procurement, including due diligence and affirmative action, and the multiple policy objectives (which may not be framed as human rights objectives) which can cause what good practice exists to be communicated in silos.

Asides from certain good practice examples, there is lack of publicly available data on how human rights are addressed in public procurement. Currently, it is not possible to say how many public procurement processes, tender documents, or contracts in a state include human rights protections, let alone say whether soft or hard measures, or measures at different stages of the procurement cycle, are more effective.

States should focus on developing and an implementing a data-driven approach to the incorporation of human rights within public procurement to help identify what an effective smart mix of soft and hard measures to prevent harm to rightsholders and remedy what harm occurs looks like in practice, provide a baseline to measure progress, and inform the development of hard laws. The development of more detailed indicators on human rights in public procurement would be a good starting point.

## 1.5 Annamaria La Chimia – Conclusions

Significant synergies arise from collaborating with scholars from diverse backgrounds and disciplines within law. Multidisciplinary collaboration is invaluable for its contributions to knowledge and its capacity to address societal problems. Within this collaborative spirit between human rights and procurement scholars, I foresee the future growth and development of the procurement and human rights debate.

Morris' approach and mine share similarities, perhaps more than one might initially perceive. We both emphasize the importance of advancing the debate. However, while Morris concentrates on what he considers essential to make 'procurement work for human rights', I emphasize the fact that, so far, the procurement and human rights approach has not yielded substantial results. My tone certainly carries a more critical edge. While Morris emphasizes the value of good practices and examples, albeit admitting that those are not enough, I often use the same examples to highlight their shortcomings. In my view, after 12 years of UNGPs, a handful of good practices are not enough.

In this final response, I want to focus on what is required to advance the procurement and human rights debate. As I explain below, I agree with some of the arguments made by Morris, but I would like the discourse on procurement and human rights to endorse stronger language and firmer commitments.

In his initial intervention, Morris stresses the need to introduce more evaluation mechanisms to monitor the implementation of policies to understand what countries do and how they achieve success. This theme is reiterated in his two-page response to my comments, where Morris further emphasizes the need for transparency, more information, and an evidence-based approach. Morris also points out that we currently lack comprehensive reporting, and I wholeheartedly agree with those points. I am in favour of increased transparency and reporting. I believe that open data and enhanced collaboration between contracting authorities – especially in accessing information about suppliers – could assist in this regard, along with the new opportunities offered by electronic and digital procurement systems. We have seen progress in specific areas, such as gender procurement.

I echo Morris' call for more information, an evidence-based approach, and greater transparency. Additionally, I advocate for identifying a clear pathway through innovation to achieve these objectives. I believe that open data and coordination of digital platforms will provide invaluable tools to harness the power of procurement effectively to protect and promote human rights. However, these instruments alone do not suffice and are insufficient. In my view, we need to reconsider the approach followed so far within the procurement and human rights debate, especially concerning the role that soft law instruments have within this debate.

Morris believes that soft law instruments have played a crucial role in paving the way for other measures. However, in my view, they have hindered the adoption of meaningful human rights measures through procurement, delaying the implementation of more substantial measures and giving companies an additional ten years to postpone the process of accountability and the prevention of human rights violations.

In his response, Morris uses Germany as an example and says that the soft-law approach has been successful in socializing HREDD. He explains that a 2020 survey showed that, and I quote: '83–87% of companies were not complying with the NAP requirements, which contributed to developing the German Supply Chain Due Diligence Law. This law came into force on January 1, 2023, and requires companies over a certain size to conduct HREDD'. Morris seems to see this as a success, whereas I view it as a failure of the German NAP. This was unable, by itself, to ensure companies' compliance with human rights standards to the extent that Germany had to resort to legally binding commitments.

Twelve years have passed since the adoption of the UNGPs, and countries have realized that a soft law approach does not suffice. Hence, there is a call for more robust measures at both the national and international levels. (In this respect, other countries are moving in the same direction as Germany; for instance, France and the new EU proposal are examples.) Yet, I think these new laws still fall short of fully accounting for procurement. While some of them do apply to procurement, they do so only above certain very high thresholds (see, for instance, the UK and Australian legislation on modern slavery). Furthermore, it is doubtful whether the specific measures targeted at procurement can truly be effective.

The fact that the procurement and human rights debate has, in many respects, replicated the soft law approach adopted by the BHR discourse is, in my view, a mistake. This legitimizes certain countries adopting a bland and hollow approach when implementing human rights standards within the procurement process. For example, consider the 'Modern Slavery a Council Guide' issued by the UK independent anti-slavery Commissioner and the Local Government Association. The Guide favours a soft and non-prescriptive approach under the justification that 'there might not be enough time to introduce due diligence during the procurement process'. As I have argued, this goes against a basic principle of good procurement practices: good planning. Furthermore, the guide also seems to discourage the adoption of 'inconvenient' or 'conflictual' measures. As I have argued before,

> to treat the implementation of human rights standards simply as an issue of preference or appropriateness is highly problematic from a legal point of view. It suggests that it is acceptable not to provide an effective remedy when an abuse

> and/or violation takes place. In other words, it is acceptable to consider how 'appropriate' or otherwise inconvenient such a remedy would be for the company or the state.
>
> (La Chimia, 2018)

This is especially important if we want to use procurement as leverage for companies to protect human rights more broadly, not just when supplying goods and services to the state.

This approach has mainly been justified by the difficulties that procurement officials would face in implementing these requirements and the fear that companies might end up concealing abuses rather than collaborating. While these problems certainly exist, they could have been addressed in other ways, such as by increasing monitoring and better planning. In certain cases, the approach adopted seems to assimilate and treat human rights objectives as mere 'secondary or horizontal' policies rather than human rights obligations. As a result, not only have companies failed to change their behaviours, and procurement has not been utilized to advance human rights, but procurement entities have been left alone to address the human rights aspects of their procurement processes. Furthermore, this approach has exposed procurement officials – both those who wanted to pursue human rights and those who were more risk-averse – to criticism (and possibly litigation).

I believe we are missing fundamental strategies at the macro and transnational levels to address the human rights obligations linked to the procurement process. We cannot delegate actions to individual officials; states must take uniform measures. For example, states should identify sectors with high risks for the supply chain and specify actions to address those risks. We need to connect the different phases of the procurement process, such as execution and termination, linked with qualification and selection, possibly via past performance. Coordination between entities and countries is essential, and we should take advantage of the interoperability of new digital platforms.

It will not be easy, but it is necessary; otherwise, we risk hollowing out human rights standards, pretending that the procurement and human rights discourse is somehow estranged from human rights abuses. This is not just a question of hard law and punitive actions per se but of synergy between actions, coherence, and legality within the process.

Morris argues in his response that 'the UNGPs are grounded in the existing international legal system and were not designed to address the structural challenges of neo-liberalism nor the fragmentation of international law', well, I would argue, maybe this is why 12 years on, we are looking for new, more effective ways to push the procurement and human rights debate forward.

Finally, Morris reminds us that the 'UNGPs provide that states should, 'when acting as members of multilateral institutions that deal with business-related issues', such as the WTO, '[s]eek to ensure that those institutions neither restrain the ability of their member States to meet their duty to protect nor hinder business enterprises from respecting human rights' (Morris, first paper). This is an essential reminder that should guide the procurement and human rights debate and bear a direct influence in international procurement, including, but not limited to, the WTO/GPA working groups (and any negotiations made to ender the GPA, especially by developing countries) and the actions of other international institutions, such as international development banks that work in and for the most vulnerable countries and people. We need synergy among actors and agents within the procurement and human rights community at both national and international levels. This entails involving all institutions – such as the OECD, the World Bank, and the EU – that wield power and influence in the realm of procurement. Consider, for instance, the work done by these institutions on procurement reforms as they set strategies and agendas. However, we also require a more assertive role for parliaments, signalling unequivocally that there will be no ifs and buts when it comes to procurement and human rights. This is not solely the responsibility of individual procurement entities; a clear and strong political message is necessary. Lastly, we must prioritize the capacity and professionalization of the procurement workforce because they will implement the norms and policies linking procurement and human rights.

## 1.6 Daniel Morris – Conclusions

Certain challenges in effectively working on human rights and public procurement have been highlighted in the previous elements of this debate and by other authors, including siloed approaches, multiple and overlapping policy objectives, the lack of hard laws and legal certainty, the lack of support for public buyers and suppliers, the lack of indicators and monitoring, and the lack of access to remedy for victims (O'Brien et al., 2016; Trusgnach & Martin-Ortega, 2022). However, other challenges exist and are relevant when developing hard measures to implement HRDD in public procurement, including through the exclusion of suppliers for human rights abuses.

It is noteworthy that the use of exclusions in response to human rights abuses is growing. The United States is increasingly utilizing the Tariff Act of 1930 to prohibit the imports of goods made with forced labour (Casey et al., 2023; U.S. Customs and Border Protection, 2023). The U.S. Customs and Border Protection can self-initiate investigations or investigate based on information received and detain imported goods when there is reasonable evidence that they have been produced with forced labour. Suppliers have three months to demonstrate that goods are not produced with forced labour. The reversal of the burden of proof when there are reasonable grounds for suspicion is welcome as it places the onus on suppliers to address human rights risks rather than creating administrative burdens for buyers. The EU has proposed a Regulation on Prohibiting Products made with Forced Labour although the latest version does not reverse the burden of proof in the same manner.[19] Policy and regulatory developments on exclusions means that public buyers will have to work with them more moving forwards. These developments may help address some of the challenges in using exclusions which La Chimia highlights, including challenges arising from '*res judicata* (i.e., needing a final sentence to exclude suppliers from a tender)'.

A clear challenge for public buyers effectively working on human rights and public procurement is access to information. For example, the first stage of HRDD involves identifying risks of potential human rights impacts across the value chain. However, value chain maps beyond higher tiers are often unavailable to public buyers. Even where maps are available, value chains can be vast and complex, crossing multiple sectors and jurisdictions where human rights risks vary. Many softer human rights measures focus on generating information for use in future procurements and at the post-award stage. Introducing measures at the post-award stage means that focus can be placed on addressing risks associated with one supplier's value chain(s) requiring access to less information and fewer resources. As La Chimia notes, reliable information is needed to underpin the use of exclusions. A second challenge is that in many jurisdictions priority is given to the post-award stage and contract implementation. Those designing and implementing measures at the pre-award stage often have little capacity or resources to identify and address risks in a field in which they are not knowledgeable and in which information is not readily accessible. Capacity, resources, and knowledge are necessary, for example, to design requirements and both score and verify how tenders meet these. This is especially true when it comes to exclusions, which may be challenged by potential suppliers.

A third challenge for public buyers arises from varied understandings of the breadth of public procurement. Certain procuring entities see public procurement as the simple act of buying; supplier engagement, supplier training, supply chain management, and/or contract management can be seen as beyond the purview of public procurement. This is despite the fact that measures to ensure suppliers respect human rights can be incorporated at these stages, if they are built in and/or valued at the buying stage. A fourth challenge is identifying responsibility for implementing measures to realize human rights through public procurement ensuring coherence as the 'full' public procurement cycle can cross multiple functions. For example, in some jurisdictions a 'requisitioner' may initiate a process, supported by a 'procurement officer', in turn supported by 'legal', and once a contract is in place, responsibility for delivery may rest with a 'contract management team'. Responsibility for introducing human rights measures can be unclear and ensuring coherence in the design and implementation of measures across multiple functions can be difficult to achieve in practice.

In conclusion, effectively introducing measures to implement HRDD into public procurement requires a system-wide approach to recalibrate the distribution of resources within entities conducting public procurement and/or seek greater synergies between procurement entities to enhance efficiency and policy coherence.

## Notes

1 The Annamaria La Chimia, La Chimia A, is thankful to the BA-Leverhulme for funding part of the work underpinning this research (grant number: SG152483).

2 The measure read: 'insofar as legal considerations allow [...] until such a time as [Israel] complies with international law and withdraws from Palestinian Occupied territories'. Leicester City Council, Agenda and minutes, 13 November 2014. The Decision of Leicester City council was upheld by the Court of Appeal; see Jewish Rights Watch Ltd (T/A Jewish Human Rights Watch) Vs Leicester City Council [2018] EWCA Civ 1551 Case No: C1/2016/2887.

3 See South Africa's Broad-Based Black Economic Empowerment Act 53 of 2003 (B-BBEE Act).

4 Economic Activity of Public Bodies (Overseas Matters) Bill. Available at https://bills.parliament.uk/bills/3475/publications.

5 The Act was enacted on 25 June 1996 entitled Act Regulating State Contracts with Companies Doing Business with Burma (Myanmar).

6 The EC claimed that Articles VIII(B), X and XIII of the, at the time infant, 1994 WTO/Government Procurement Agreement. The EC also claimed that the measure nullified 'benefits accruing to it under the GPA, as well as impeding the attainment of the objectives of the GPA, including that of maintaining balance of rights and obligations'. On 8 August 1998 the EC made a formal request for the establishment of a panel, and on 21 October 1998, a panel was established. Yet on 10 February 1999, at the request of the complainants the panel was suspended.

7 The Panel was established on 21 October 1998, composed on 6 January 1999 and lapsed on 11 February 2000. Available at www.wto.org/english/tratop_e/dispu_e/cases_e/ds88_e.htm.

8 Sweat Free Purchasing Consortium and the work done by student unions and universities across America, more information at http://buysweatfree.org/

9 The UNGP are based on the 'Protect, Respect and Remedy' Framework elaborated by the Secretary-General's Special Representative on Business and Human Rights (SRSG) and presented to the Human Rights Council in 2008. This framework is mirrored in the three-pillar structure of the UNGPs, namely Pillar I: Protect (State), Pillar II: Respect (companies), and Pillar III: Remedy. The obligations linked to procurement are placed under the first pillar of State's obligation to protect. See www.undcs.org/a/hrc/8/5.

10 Principles 4–7 impose human rights due diligence obligations on the state, its agencies, and the companies they do business with. See www.ohchr.org/EN/Issues/Business/Pages/StateEconomicActor.aspx

11 Approach endorsed by Ruggie, the former Special Representative of the Secretary-General on Human Rights and Transnational Corporations and Other Business Enterprises (SRSG) drafter of the UNGPs.

12 The terms of contracts are often included in the bidding documents and therefore suppliers are aware of the responsibilities involved when 'doing business with the state' – and can decide whether to participate or not to a tender based on whether they can meet the contract terms.

13 The council guidance also says that 'whilst councils may wish to end a contract if issues are discovered this can be counterproductive, as it could move the problem, and could create an atmosphere of fear and concealment in the industry'. See www.antislaverycommissioner.co.uk/media/1201/modern-slavery-a-council-guide.pdf.

14 The text continues and includes an explicit reference to the UN Guiding Principles on Business and Human Rights.

15 One focus area does not contain a clear link to human rights: '5. Promotion of SMEs'.

16 It should be noted that measures focused on the environment, such as addressing poor air quality, can have impacts on human rights. Furthermore, there is a growing recognition of a right to a healthy environment.

17 See, for example, the approaches in Uruguay (rehabilitation of prisoners), Brazil (vulnerable food producers), Sweden (those who have been outside the labour market for a long period of time), Colombia (persons with disabilities), and the United States (veterans), detailed in Morris, D. (2020), *Driving Change Through Public Procurement*, Danish Institute for Human Rights, Denmark. Available at www.humanrights.dk/publications/driving-change-through-public-procurement [Accessed 13 November 2023].

18 The EU taxonomy on sustainable finance draws heavily from environmental standards without fully integrating human rights safeguards. However, it demonstrates how to ensure some consideration of human rights when pursuing environmental objectives (see European Commission, 2023).

19 Other relevant EU Regulations include the Conflict Minerals Regulation and Regulation on Deforestation-free products.

## References

Caimi, V. and Sansonetti, S. (2023), *The Social Impact of Public Procurement – Can the EU Do More?*, European Parliament, Directorate-General for Internal Policies of the Union, Luxembourg. Available at https://data.europa.eu/doi/10.2861/05187 [Accessed 13 November 2023].

Casey, C.A., Cimino-Isaacs, C.D., and Weber, M.A. (2023), *Section 307 and Imports Produced by Forced Labor*, Congressional Research Service. Available at https://crsreports.congress.gov/product/pdf/IF/IF11360#:~:text=Section%20307%20of%20the%20Tariff%20Act%20of%201930,Customs%20and%20Border%20Protection%20%28CBP%29%20enforces%20the%20prohibition [Accessed 13 November 2023].

Corvaglia, M.A. and Li, K. (2018), 'Extraterritoriality and public procurement regulation in the context of global supply chains' governance', *Europe and the World: A Law Review*, 2(1). https://doi.org/10.14324/111.444.ewlj.2018.06

Davies-Ortega's Guide(2016), *Protecting Human Rights Through the Supply Chain: A Guide for Procurement Practitioners*, CIPS. Available at www.apuc-scot.ac.uk/docs/A%20Guide%20Protecting%20Human%20Rights%20in%20the%20Supply%20Chain.pdf [Accessed 28 November 2023].

Eslava, L. (2015), 'Corporate Social Responsibility & development: A knot of disempowerment', *Sortuz: Oñati Journal of Emergent Socio-Legal Studies*, 2(2), pp. 43–71.

European Coalition for Corporate Justice (2022), *Comparative Table: Corporate Due Diligence Laws and Legislative Proposals in Europe*. Available at https://corporatejustice.org/wp-content/uploads/2022/03/Corporate-due-diligence-laws-and-legislative-proposals-in-Europe-March-2022.pdf [Accessed 13 November 2023].

European Commission (2021), *Green and Sustainable Public Procurement.* Available at https://ec.europa.eu/environment/gpp/versus_en.htm#:~:text=Sustainable%20Public%20Procurement%20(SPP)%20is,all%20stages%20of%20the%20project [Accessed 2 May 2023].

European Commission (2022), 'Proposal and annexes for a regulation establishing a framework for setting ecodesign requirements for sustainable products and repealing directive 2009/125/EC'. Available at https://environment.ec.europa.eu/publications/proposal-ecodesign-sustainable-products-regulation_en [Accessed 2 May 2023].

European Commission (2023), *EU Taxonomy Navigator*. Available at https://ec.europa.eu/sustainable-finance-taxonomy/ [Accessed 13 November 2023].

EY (2020), *Final Report, Monitoring of the Status of Implementation of the Human Rights Due Diligence Obligations of Enterprises Set Out in the National Action Plan for Business and Human Rights 2016–2020*. Available at https://globalnaps.org/wp-content/uploads/2021/05/Germany-nap-monitoring-process.pdf [Accessed 13 November 2023].

Fox, T., Ward, H., and Howard, B. (2002), *Public Sector role in Strengthening Corporate Social Responsibility: A Baseline Study*, World Bank Publication. Washington DC.

Georgopoulos, A. (2014), 'The EU accession to the ECHR: An attempt to explore possible implications in the area of public procurement', in: Kosta, V., Skoutaris, N., and Tzevelekos, V. (eds.), The EU Accession to the ECHR 48. Hart Publishing, Oxford.

Gollub, A., Lusamba, C.M., and ElShazly, J. (2021), *Rethinking Gender-Responsive Procurement: Enabling an Ecosystem for Women's Economic Empowerment*. ILO and UN Women, New York and Geneva. Available at www.unwomen.org/sites/default/files/Headquarters/Attachments/Sections/Library/Publications/2021/Rethinking-gender-responsive-procurement-en.pdf [Accessed 13 November 2023].

HLCM Procurement Network (2023), *Sustainable Procurement Indicators*. Available at www.ungm.org/Shared/KnowledgeCenter/Pages/SustainableProcurementIndicatorProject [Accessed 2 May 2023].

Independent-Antislavery Commissioner and Local Government Association (2015), *Modern Slavery: A Council Guide*. Available at www.antislaverycommissioner.co.uk/media/1201/modern-slavery-a-council-guide.pdf.

International Law Commission (2006), *Fragmentation of International Law: Difficulties Arising from the Diversification and Expansion of International Law*. United Nations, Geneva, pp. 400–423. Available at https://doi.org/10.18356/ad144936-en [Accessed 13 November 2023].

International Organization for Standardization (2017), ISO 20400 International Standard, Sustainable Procurement Guidance, ISO 20400:2017(E).

International Responsible Business Conduct Agreement for the Renewable Energy Sector (2023), *Integrating Sustainability and Human Rights in the Energy Transition*. Available at www.imvoconvenanten.nl/-/media/imvo/files/hernieuwbare-energie/convenant_hernieuwbare_energie_engels.pdf [Accessed 13 November 2023].

Italian Government, National Action Plan on Business and Human Rights 2016-2021, available at: https://respect.international/wp-content/uploads/2018/01/Italian-National-Action-Plan-on-Business-and-Human-Rights-.pdf

Jørgensen, H.B., Pruzan-Jørgensen, P.M., Jungk, M., and Cramer, A. (2003), *Strengthening Implementation of Corporate Social Responsibility in Global Supply Chains*. World Bank, IFC.

Kumar, S. (2022), *Understanding Sustainable Public Procurement, Springer eBooks*. Available at https://doi.org/10.1007/978-3-031-08258-0 [Accessed 13 November 2023].

La Chimia, A. (2018), 'Development aid procurement and the UNGPs', in: Elegbe, W. and Quinot, G. (eds.), *Public Procurement Regulation for the 21st Century Africa*, Juta & Co., pp. 31–78, ISBN 9781485128694 (Chapter 3).

La Chimia, A. (2023), 'UN Guiding Principle 6', in Barnali, C. (ed.), *Commentary to the UN Guiding Principles on Business and Human Rights*. Edward Elgar. Cheltenham, UK; Northampton, USA.

Martin-Ortega, O. and O'Brien, C.M. (2019), 'Public procurement and human rights: Interrogating the role of the state as buyer', in: Martin-Ortega, O. and O'Brien, C.M. (ed.), *Public Procurement and Human Rights Opportunities, Risks and Dilemmas for the State as Buyer*. Edward Elgar, Cheltenham.

McCrudden, C. (2006), 'Corporate Social Responsibility and Public Procurement', in: Mc Barnet, D., Voicilescu, A., and Campbell, T. (eds.), *The New Corporate Accountability: Corporate Social Responsibility and the Law*. Cambridge University Press, Cambridge.

Morris, D. (2020), *Driving Change Through Public Procurement*, Danish Institute for Human Rights, Denmark. Available at www.humanrights.dk/publications/driving-change-through-public-procurement [Accessed 13 November 2023].

Morris, D., Wrzoncki, E., and Lysgaard, S.A. (2019), *Responsible Business Conduct as A Cornerstone of the 2030 Agenda – A Look at the Implications, a Discussion Paper*, Danish Institute for Human Rights, Denmark. Available at www.humanrights.dk/publications/responsible-business-conduct-cornerstone-2030-agenda-look-implications [Accessed 13 November 2023].

Multistakeholder Advisory Committee of the 10YFP SPP Programme (2020), *SDG Indicator 12.7.1., SPP Index Calculation Methodology, Version 5.0 Post IAEG*, United Nations Environment Programme. Available at https://sdghelpdesk.unescap.org/sites/default/files/2020-05/sdg_12.7.1_final_post_ieag_.pdf [Accessed 13 November 2023], paragraph 8.7, D(c).

Multistakeholder Advisory Committee of the 10YFP SPP Programme (2022), *SDG Indicator 12.7.1., SPP Index Calculation Methodology, Version 6*. United Nations Environment Programme. Available at https://wedocs.unep.org/bitstream/handle/20.500.11822/37332/SPPICMG.pdf?sequence=3&isAllowed=y [Accessed 13 November 2023].

Núñez Ferrer, J. (2020), *The EU's Public Procurement Framework, How Is the EU's Public Procurement Framework Contributing to the Achievement of the Objectives of the Paris Agreement and the Circular Economy Strategy?*, European Parliament, Luxembourg. Available at www.europarl.europa.eu/RegData/etudes/BRIE/2020/648770/IPOL_BRI(2020)648770_EN.pdf [Accessed 13 November 2023].

O'Brien, C.M. (2019), *EU Business and Human Rights Policy: Still More 'Invisible Hand' Than 'SMART Mix'*, Finnish Government Finland. Available at www.researchgate.net/publication/340789360_EU_business_and_human_rights_policy_still_more_'invisible_hand'_than_'SMART_mix [Accessed 13 November 2023].

O'Brien, C.M., Martin-Ortega, O., and Conlon, E. (2018), *Guidance on Socially Responsible Public Procurement: Response to Consultation of the European Commission by the International Lab on Procurement and Human Rights*. Available at www.bhre.org/current-news/2018/7/20/guidance-on-socially-responsible-public-procurement-response-to-consultation-of-the-european-commission-by-the-international-learning-lab-on-procurement-and-human-rights [Accessed 1 May 2023].

O'Brien, C.M., Meulen, N.V, and Mehra, A. (2016), *Public Procurement and Human Rights: A Survey of Twenty Jurisdictions*, International Learning Lab on Public Procurement and Human Rights. Available at https://globalnaps.org/wp-content/uploads/2018/08/public-procurement-and-human-rights-a-survey-of-twenty-jurisdictions.pdf [Accessed 13 November 2023].

OECD (2022), *OECD Recommendation on the Role of Government in Promoting Responsible Business Conduct*. Available at https://legalinstruments.oecd.org/en/instruments/OECD-LEGAL-0486 [Accessed 13 November 2023].

Office of the Attorney General and Department of Justice, Kenya National Commission on Human Rights, and the Danish Institute for Human Rights (2023), *A Review of the Legal Framework Governing Human Rights and Public Procurement in Kenya*. Available at www.humanrights.dk/publications/review-legal-framework-governing-human-rights-public-procurement-kenya [Accessed 13 November 2023]

OSCE Office of the Special Representative and Co-ordinator for Combating Trafficking in Human Beings (2020), *Compendium of Relevant Reference Materials and Resources on Ethical Sourcing and Prevention of Trafficking in Human Beings for Labour Exploitation in Supply Chains, Second Updated Edition*, OSCE, Vienna. Available at www.osce.org/files/f/documents/8/c/450769.pdf [Accessed 13 November 2023].

Sanchez-Graells, A. (2019), 'Public procurement and "core" human rights: A sketch of the EU Legal Framework', in: Martin-Ortega, O and O'Brien, C.M. (eds.), *Public Procurement and Human Rights: Risks, Dilemmas and Opportunities for the State as a Buyer*. Edward Elgar, Cheltenham and Camberley.

Shai, L., Molefinyana, C., and Quinot, G. (2019), 'Public procurement in the context of Broad-Based Black Economic Empowerment (BBBEE) in South Africa—Lessons learned for sustainable public procurement', *Sustainability*, 11(24), p. 7164.

Shift (2019), *Fulfilling the State Duty to Protect: A Statement on the Role of Mandatory Measures in a 'Smart Mix'*. Available at https://shiftproject.org/fulfilling-the-state-duty-to-protect-a-statement-on-the-role-of-mandatory-measures-in-a-smart-mix/ [Accessed 13 November 2023].

Stoffel, T, Cravero, C, La Chimia, A, and Quinot, G. (2019), 'Multidimensionality of sustainable public procurement (SPP) – Exploring concepts and effects in Sub-Saharan Africa and Europe', *Sustainability*, 11(22), p. 6352.

Stumberg, R.K., Ramasastry, A., and Roggensack, M. (2014), *Turning a Blind Eye? Respecting Human Rights in Government Purchasing*, International Corporate Accountability Roundtable, Washington.

Sustainable Procurement (SP) Working Group of the HLCM Procurement Network (2023), *Sustainable Procurement Indicators*. Available at www.ungm.org/Shared/KnowledgeCenter/Pages/SustainableProcurementIndicatorProject [Accessed 2 May 2023].

Treviño-Lozano, L. and Martin-Ortega, O. (2023), 'Sustainable public procurement of infrastructure and human rights: Linkages and gaps', in: Treviño-Lozano, L. and Martin-Ortega, O. (eds.), *Sustainable Public Procurement of Infrastructure and Human Rights*. Edward Elgar, Cheltenham, pp. 2–27.

Trusgnach, M. and Martin-Ortega, O. (2022), *Remedy for Human Rights Violations in Global Supply Chains: Essential Elements*, University of Greenwich. Available at https://electronicswatch.org/remedy-for-human-rights-violations-in-global-supply-chains-essential-elements-july-2022_2618868.pdf [Accessed 13 November 2023]. University of Greenwich, UK.

U.S. Customs and Border Protection (2023), *Uyghur Forced Labor Prevention Act*. Available at www.cbp.gov/trade/forced-labor/UFLPA [Accessed 13 November 2023].

UNEP (2022), *Sustainable Public Procurement: 2022 Global Review (Parts I and II)*, UNEP, France. Available at www.oneplanetnetwork.org/knowledge-centre/resources/sustainable-public-procurement-2022-global-review-parts-i-and-ii [Accessed 13 November 2023].

United Nations Committee on Economic, Social and Cultural Rights, General Comment No. 24 (2017), *State Obligations under the International Covenant on Economic, Social and Cultural Rights in the Context Of Business Activities (E/C.12/GC/24)*. Available at http://tbinternet.ohchr.org/_layouts/treatybodyexternal/Download.aspx?symbolno=E/C.12/GC/24&Lang=en.

United Nations Global Marketplace (2023), *The Sustainable Procurement (SP) Indicators*. Available at www.ungm.org/Shared/KnowledgeCenter/Pages/SustProcIndicators [Accessed 2 May 2023].

United Nations (2011), *Guiding Principles on Business and Human Rights: Implementing the United Nations 'Protect, Respect and Remedy' Framework*. United Nations, Geneva and New York.

United Nations Commission on Human Rights (2005), *Human Rights and Transnational Corporations and Other Business Enterprises*. Available at https://view.officeapps.live.com/op/view.aspx?src=https%3A%2F%2Fap.ohchr.org%2Fdocuments%2FE%2FCHR%2Fresolutions%2FE-CN_4-RES-2005-69.doc&wdOrigin=BROWSELINK [Accessed 13 November 2023].

United Nations General Assembly (2015), *Transforming Our World: The 2030 Agenda for Sustainable Development*. United Nations, New York.

UNOPS (2022), *2021 Annual Statistical Report on United Nations Procurement*, UNOPS, Denmark. Available at www.ungm.org/Shared/KnowledgeCenter/Pages/asr_report [Accessed 13 November 2023], p. 25.

UNISON, The Helena Kennedy Centre for International Justice at Sheffield Hallam University, and Stop Uyghur Genocide (2022), *Clean/Dirty Energy – Sourcing Solar Energy without Uyghur Forced Labour*. Available at www.unison.org.uk/content/uploads/2022/08/Clean-dirty-energy-1.pdf [Accessed 13 November 2023].

Upphandlingsmyndigheten (2022), *Sustainable public procurement*. Available at www.upphandlingsmyndigheten.se/en/sustainable-public-procurement/#socially_sustainable_public_procurement [Accessed 13 November 2023].

Whyte, J. (2019), *The Morals of the Market: Human Rights and the Rise of Neoliberalism*, Verso, London.

# 2 Should EU public procurement law integrate sustainability due diligence requirements?

## EU institutions' procurement as a case study

*Claire Methven O'Brien and Roberto Caranta*

### 2.1 Introduction

Globally, expectations on businesses to manage human rights and other sustainability risks are becoming increasingly 'more detailed, demanding and widespread' (Methven O'Brien & Martin-Ortega, 2019c). Since 2011, taking point of departure in the UN Guiding Principles on Human Rights (UN Human Rights Council, 2011) and related 'responsible business conduct' standards (OECD, 2011, 2018, 2023), the European Union (EU) and other policy actors have contributed to this trend by adopting a range of instruments encouraging businesses to implement sustainability 'due diligence' to give effect to their 'corporate responsibility to respect' human rights (EC, 2011b; Council of Europe, 2016; Methven O'Brien, 2021; Methven O'Brien & Botta, 2023; Methven O'Brien & Caranta, 2024). Due diligence processes, so understood, entail that businesses should identify, assess, prevent, cease, or mitigate and remediate harms to human rights and the environment resulting from their own activities or to which they are directly linked via business partners. The scope of corporate human rights due diligence, correspondingly, extends to procurement activities.

In particular, the EU has enacted new laws establishing mandatory sustainability due diligence requirements for specific industry sectors and value chains.[1] Besides, negotiations are underway on legislation to establish 'horizontal' (that is, cross-sectoral) corporate sustainability due diligence duties.[2] This follows in the wake of national 'horizontal' corporate due diligence laws already enacted in France, Germany, and Norway (République Française, 2017; Deutscher Bundestag, 2021; Norwegian Storting, 2021) and official due diligence guidelines launched by other major economies (Japan Ministry of Economy Trade and Industry, 2022). Corporate due diligence is now widely identified as pivotal to securing realization of the UN 2030 Agenda and Sustainable Development Goals (SDGs), as well as the global green energy transition and commitments contained in the Paris Climate Agreement (Methven O'Brien & Ologhadien, 2024).

Given this, as well as the economic significance of public procurement within the global economy, and the potential for public buyers to influence suppliers towards more sustainable forms of production, there is a clear rationale to consider

DOI: 10.4324/9781032631721-4

whether new due diligence requirements should extend to government as well as to private procurement activity (Martin-Ortega & Methven O'Brien, 2019; Methven O'Brien & Martin-Ortega, 2019c). If they should, it then falls to be asked, more specifically, how this might be achieved, taking into account the existing form, focus, content, and policy concerns of public procurement laws. The use of public buying to advance 'strategic' concerns has increasingly been acknowledged as legitimate and necessary in recent years (OECD, 2015; Burgi, 2022). While this logic surely extends to environmental and social sustainability, nevertheless, competition, fairness, and due process objectives are still perceived by some as limiting regulatory space for the extension of due diligence duties into the realm of government buying (Sanchez-Graells, 2019b). Whereas procurement law has moved gradually towards greater flexibility in accommodating sustainability-based buyer preferences, based on existing jurisprudence, and given the persisting strictures imposed by existing statutory rules and case law, it seems such objections may not yet be rejected out of hand (Methven O'Brien & Caranta, 2024).

This chapter approaches the question of whether sustainability due diligence requirements should apply to government through the lens of EU procurement legislation. More specifically, given the EU legislator's prominence in advancing mandatory due diligence norms for companies, it considers whether rules on EU entities' *own procurement* could incorporate due diligence requirements, and opportunities and challenges that might be associated with doing so. This is a novel investigation. While earlier work has considered the interface between human rights due diligence and public procurement law (Methven O'Brien & Martin-Ortega, 2020); the increasing infiltration of mandatory sustainability requirements in EU procurement rules (Janssen & Caranta, 2023); and, recently, interactions between the foreseen European Union Corporate Sustainability Due Diligence Directive (EUCSDDD) and EU Procurement Directives (Treviño-Lozano & Uysal, 2023), the case of EU institutions, including the European Commission (EC), European Parliament (EP), and EU agencies, has not yet been addressed by scholarship. Considering this topic besides has wider importance beyond EU institutions, given that the applicable legal rules apply *mutatis mutandis* to procurements under EU law at the level of the member states. Given the 'Brussels effect', in policy terms, the inquiry may have broader significant still.

Section 2 analyses general EU procurement rules, their application to EU institutions' own account procurement and their incorporation of sustainability concerns. Section 3 addresses international and EU norms on human rights and environmental due diligence, their assimilation into EU sustainable business regulations and their interaction, to date, with public procurement regulations. Section 4 investigates the role of due diligence in the sustainable procurement frameworks and practices of the EC, EP, and EU independent agencies, while Section 5 considers how this role could be extended. Section 6 concludes, arguing that the policy case for assimilating sustainability due diligence measures in the public buying context makes this an urgent priority not just for the EU but also for other regulators.

## 2.2 EU institutions' procurement: legal framework, strategic and sustainable procurement

### *2.2.1 EU institutions' procurement: legal framework*

EU law establishes common procedural legal rules on the award of public procurements and concessions applicable at national level.[3] These rules were enacted with a view to achieving the Internal Market[4]: as clarified by the Court of Justice, 'the principal objective of the Community rules in the field of public procurement is to ensure the free movement of services and the opening-up to undistorted competition in all the Member States'.[5]

The EU Public Procurement Directive seeks to achieve this goal by three principal means—prohibiting discrimination, implementing transparency, and removing barriers to access in competition for public contracts (Arrowsmith, 2012). Under EU law, the procurement procedure is articulated around four steps: (i) selection: choosing a contractor complying with fundamental ethical standards and suitable to perform the contract; (ii) technical specifications, describing the characteristics of the goods or services to be purchased; (iii) award – here criteria aim to achieve the best value for money; and (iv) contract performance clauses, including the general and specific contract clauses applicable to a given contract.

The legal rules on the award of contracts by European institutions on their own account are specified in the EU Financial Regulation[6]; in turn, this provides that such rules and principles should be based on the rules set out in the EU Public Procurement and Concessions Directives[7]; detailed procurement rules are enacted in Annex I to the Financial Regulation. These provisions are duly reflected in tenders issued by EU institutions and the respective internal policies procedures and contract terms advanced by the EC, EP, and various EU agencies (Methven O'Brien & Caranta, 2024).

Procurement by EU institutions and bodies must in addition comply with general principles specific to the Financial Regulation. Under its Article 6 *Respect for budgetary principles*, 'The budget shall be established and implemented in accordance with the principles of unity, budgetary accuracy, annuality, equilibrium, unit of account, universality, specification, sound financial management and transparency as set out in this Regulation'. Of additional relevance are the principles of sound financial management and performance, and the principle of transparency. Article 33(1) of the Financial Regulation specifies these principles as covering (a) the 'principle of economy which requires that the resources used by the Union institution concerned in the pursuit of its activities shall be made available in due time, in appropriate quantity and quality, and at the best price'; (b) the 'principle of efficiency which concerns the best relationship between the resources employed, the activities undertaken and the achievement of objectives'; and (c) 'the principle of effectiveness which concerns the extent to which the objectives pursued are achieved through the activities undertaken'.

Because of the articulation between the Financial Regulation and the EU Public Procurement Directive and EU Concession Directives, the case law and scholarship developed regarding both the Financial Regulation and the EU Directives already mentioned are also relevant with reference to EU institutions' own procurement, with limited differences between the two bodies of rules. These include rules regarding the integration into procurement of sustainability concerns, as considered in the next section.

### *2.2.2 EU procurement law: strategic and sustainable procurement*

The primary objective of procurement may be understood as 'delivering goods and services necessary to accomplish government mission in a timely, economical and efficient manner' (OECD, 2015, p. 6). Both inside and beyond the EU, the goal of procurement laws – of achieving best value for money – was for many years understood as maximum quantity or quality for least price. Yet with recent reforms, exclusive focus on the lowest price has been gradually superseded in many jurisdictions. Rather, for a growing number of regulators, procurement law increasingly aims to weigh secondary, non-price or 'horizontal' (Arrowsmith & Kunzlik, 2009) factors against the primary procurement objective (OECD, 2015, p. 6). Such horizontal goals include 'sustainable green growth, the development of small and medium-sized enterprises, innovation, standards for responsible business conduct or broader industrial policy objectives' (OECD, 2015, p. 6).

Hence, the notion of strategic procurement (SP) emerged in EU procurement policy in 2011. In its Green Paper on the modernization of public procurement, the EC applied this term to denote the 'use of public procurement in response to new challenges', including in the social, labour, and environmental domains (EC, 2011a, p. 10). Strategic procurement thus combines the objective of enhancing procurement efficiency with that of using procurement to support 'common societal goals such as protection of the environment..., combating climate change, promoting innovation, employment and social inclusion' (EC, 2011, p. 2). Similarly, according to the EU Public Procurement Directive, 'Public procurement plays a key role…as one of the market-based instruments to be used to achieve smart, sustainable and inclusive growth while ensuring the most efficient use of public funds' (EU Public Procurement Directive, Recital 3).

Accordingly, in implementing the EU Public Procurement Directive, member states must 'take appropriate measures to ensure that in the performance of public contracts economic operators comply with applicable obligations in the fields of environmental, social and labour law' (Article 18(2) of Directive 2014/24). Further, the Court of Justice has held 'that such a requirement constitutes, in the general scheme of that directive, a cardinal value with which the member states must ensure compliance' (Case C-395/18, *TIM*, para. 38). As is well known, SPP in the EU has been nurtured by the case law of the Court of Justice since C-31/87 *Beentjes* to arrive at C-395/18, *TIM*, and T-578/19 *Sophia Group*. Notably, in *Sophia Group*, the General Court upheld award criteria chosen by the EP concerning equal treatment, combatting sexual harassment, the inclusion of persons with disabilities and fair working conditions as well as certification schemes attesting to quality systems.

In parallel, the cheapest price has given way to 'Value for money' in interpreting public procurement's primary objective, with the former increasingly understood as the 'most advantageous combination of cost, quality and sustainability to meet defined requirements' (OECD, 2019) or 'most economically advantageous tender' (MEAT).[8] Value for money and MEAT are also, in the EU, to be assessed on a full life cycle basis (Article 68 of Directive 2014/24 and Article 167 of the Financial Regulation). Responding to such evolving norms, and to help domestic contracting authorities and entities willing to engage in SPP, for its part the EC has issued sustainable procurement guidance and tools reflecting this same trajectory (EC, 2016; EC, 2021a; EC, 2023). Many initiatives under the Circular Economy Action Plan, the European Green Deal (EC, 2019a) and the European Pillar of Social Rights likewise assume or imply a need for SPP. These include, for example:

- Requesting contracting authorities to buy high environmentally performant products.[9]
- Requesting contracting authorities to play an exemplary role in SPP.[10]
- Requiring that member states take appropriate measures to ensure that, in the awarding and performance of public procurement or concession contracts, economic operators and their subcontractors comply with the applicable obligations regarding wages, the right to organize and collective bargaining on wage-setting.[11]

Even if such measures may not explicitly refer to SPP, nevertheless they comprise part of the 'applicable obligations' recalled in Article 18(2) of the EU Public Procurement Directive. Further, such proposals are significant in shifting EU public procurement rules from regulating only the award procedure ('how to buy') to regulating which products and services contracting authorities shall prefer ('what to buy') and from which supplier they should not buy ('whom not to buy from') (Janssen & Caranta, 2023). As explained above, such norms should further apply, *mutatis mutandis*, to EU institutions' own account procurement: EU institutions are expected to adhere at least to standards imposed on contracting authorities and entities in the member states.

## 2.3 Human rights and sustainability due diligence

### *2.3.1 Due diligence: international and EU standards*

According to the UN Guiding Principles on Business and Human Rights ('UNGPs'), international human rights treaties, besides the duties they establish amongst states, entail a 'corporate responsibility to respect human rights', that requires businesses to avoid infringing human rights through their own actions or those of their business partners (UNHRC, 2011). Businesses should accordingly seek to prevent, mitigate and/or remediate negative impacts on human rights that they have 'caused or contributed to', as well as those 'directly linked' to their operations, products, or services through business relationships, whether contractual or non-contractual

(UNHRC, 2011, UN Guiding Principle 13). In terms of scope, the corporate responsibility to respect human rights refers to all 'internationally-recognised' human rights, not just those that are binding in the domestic law of any one jurisdiction (UNHRC, 2011, UN Guiding Principle 11).

'Human rights due diligence' as described by the UNGPs is a process through which corporations fulfil their 'responsibility to respect' human rights. Its first step is adopting a corporate policy to respect human rights (UNHRC, 2011, UN Guiding Principle 15). Next, due diligence requires four further steps comprising a continuous improvement cycle (UNHRC, 2011, UN Guiding Principles 17–20): (1) Assessing actual and potential, direct and indirect impacts of the business' activities on human rights; (2) Integrating appropriate measures to address impacts into company policies and practices; (3) Tracking the effectiveness of measures taken in preventing or mitigating adverse human rights impacts; and (4) Communicating publicly about the due diligence process and its results. Given the right of victims of business-related human rights abuses to access effective remedies, companies should also take steps to remediate adverse impacts of their activities on rights-holders (UNHRC, 2011, UN Guiding Principle 22; see further Methven O'Brien & Holly, 2021).

Since 2011, the UNGPs' due diligence concept has been widely assimilated amongst international institutions. The Council of Europe, in its business and human rights guidance called for member states to 'apply such measures as may be necessary' to encourage or require business enterprises to apply human rights due diligence 'throughout their operations' (COE, 2016, Appendix, para. 20). The OECD integrated due diligence into its Guidelines for Multinational Enterprises (OECD, 2011, 2023), followed by its Due Diligence Guidance for Responsible Business Conduct (OECD, 2018), and sector-specific due diligence guidance documents (OECD, 2017, 2023b, 2023c). Significantly, such OECD standards extended the subject-matter scope of the due diligence exercise beyond human rights to environmental and other sustainability and governance issues. The International Finance Corporation Performance Standards, and human rights guidance under the Equator Principles as well as a range of other individual and sector business policies and tools have been UNGPs-aligned (see further Methven O'Brien & Botta, 2023).[12]

In the EU, the EC espoused support for the UNGPs and corporate due diligence already in 2011 with its Communication on Corporate Social Responsibility (EC, 2011b). This called for enterprises 'to identify, prevent and mitigate their possible adverse impacts' on human rights as well as environmental and social concerns. 'Large enterprises', it stated, 'and enterprises at particular risk of having such impacts, are encouraged to carry out risk-based due diligence, including through their supply chains' (EC, 2011b). Representing a significant transition from voluntary to mandatory in the conceptualization of corporate responsibility in EU policy (Methven O'Brien & Dhanarajan, 2016), this has been followed by a range of EU legislative initiatives giving effect, indirectly and directly, to corporate due diligence duties (Methven O'Brien, 2021).

In terms of *indirect* measures, due diligence has gradually assumed a central role in EU corporate governance and investment regulation. The 2014 EU

Non-Financial Reporting Directive foresaw public disclosures of company impacts on human rights; their policies (including due diligence processes); outcomes, principal risks, and risk management arrangements; and key performance indicators (KPIs).[13] Non-binding EC Guidelines on reporting of non-financial and climate-related information subsequently introduced the concept of 'double materiality', according to which companies should report on material risks to company value as well as risks to people and the environment (EC, 2019c).

Later, from this foundation, the EU Corporate Sustainability Reporting Directive was enacted.[14] Effective from 2026, under this instrument relevant companies will be required to generate annual sustainability reports according to European Sustainability Reporting Standards: now mandatory, these standards refer to due diligence, while companies are also obliged to obtain external assurance of their annual sustainability reports.[15] More specifically, the EU Corporate Sustainability Reporting Directive amended Article 2(17) of Directive 2013/34/EU to the effect that 'sustainability matters' means environmental, social and human rights, and governance factors, including sustainability factors defined in point (24) of Article 2 of Regulation (EU) 2019/2088. Under the new Article 19a(2), sustainability reporting includes a description of 'the due diligence process implemented by the undertaking with regard to sustainability matters' (pp. f, i).

The intention of such measures, evidently, is to encourage large companies and small and medium-sized enterprises (SMEs) to implement a due diligence process, indirectly, by requiring that they formally report on it. Alongside, however, the EU legislator has enacted various *direct* due diligence duties for enterprises. First amongst these was the EU Conflict Minerals Regulation.[16] Due diligence requirements also feature in the Batteries Regulation[17]; updated Deforestation Regulation[18]; and the proposed EU Forced Labour Regulation[19] (Methven O'Brien & Weatherburn, 2023).

Such measures, in restricting their focus to specific human rights risks, value chains or commodities, still however fall short of the UNGPs' position that due diligence, because it is flexible and scalable according to enterprises' size and characteristics, is applicable to all businesses and all human rights. Accordingly, some European states have enacted 'horizontal' laws establishing due diligence duties for larger companies on a cross-sectoral basis. These include France's Loi de Vigilance (République Française, 2017) and the German 'Act on Corporate Due Diligence to Prevent Human Rights Violations in Supply Chains' (Deutscher Bundestag, 2021). Norway has also passed due diligence legislation (Norwegian Storting, 2021). Though varying significantly in their exact terms, these laws all establish statutory due diligence duties and penalties for default; France's Loi de Vigilance further attaches civil liability to harms to human rights and the environment linked to corporate due diligence failures (Methven O'Brien & Botta, 2023). In the UN, a draft business and human rights treaty laying down duties for states to enact domestic corporate human rights and sustainability due diligence laws is under discussion (Methven O'Brien, 2022).[20]

In this context, a draft EU corporate sustainability due diligence directive (EUCSDDD) has been advanced by the EC (EC, 2022b; Methven O'Brien &

Martin-Ortega, 2022). Under the EC's proposal, large limited liability companies, including EU and third-country companies operating in the EU market and smaller companies in designated 'high-risk' sectors (EC, 2022b, Art. 2) would be required to identify, prevent, mitigate, and account for their adverse human rights impacts, and also their environmental impacts, in their own operations but also their subsidiaries, contractors, and subcontractors, to the extent of their 'established business relationships'. Echoing France's due diligence law, under the draft EU Directive, harms resulting from failures of due diligence might attract both administrative sanctions or exposure to civil liability in proceedings brought by damaged parties (EC, 2022; Methven O'Brien & Martin-Ortega, 2022). The draft EUCSDDD obtained qualified support in the EP[21] and concluded trilogue negotiations in 2023 (EP, 2023).

### *2.3.2 Public procurement and due diligence: an evolving relationship*

The UNGPs' (UNHRC, 2011) fundamental rationale derives from the duty of states, arising under human rights treaties, to take positive action to protect human rights and ensure their practical effectiveness in relations between individuals in society, as well as between individuals and government. The 'corporate responsibility to respect human rights', reflected in due diligence laws, proceeds from, and is secondary to, this role of states as the 'primary duty bearer' under human rights law (Methven O'Brien & Martin-Ortega, 2019a).

It may be thought paradoxical, given this, that the UNGPs, and consequent laws and policies seeking to give effect to them nationally and regionally, have sought to establish due diligence duties for corporations, but not for the state or state entities (Methven O'Brien & Martin-Ortega, 2019c). The UNGPs highlight, under Pillar I, the duty of governments to 'promote respect for human rights by business enterprises with which they conduct commercial transactions' (UNHRC, 2011, UN Guiding Principle 6) and 'to exercise adequate oversight in order to meet their international human rights obligations when they contract with, or legislate for, business enterprises to provide services' (UNHRC, 2011, UN Guiding Principle 5). Yet a specific injunction on state buyers to undertake due diligence as such, or to require their suppliers to do so, was not included in the 2011 UNGPs text. Moreover, public procurement was not addressed by the OECD in its 2011 Guidelines for Multinational Enterprises or its later Responsible Business Conduct guidance (OECD, 2011, 2018). Neither is public procurement within the identified scope of the French national due diligence law (French Republic, 2017).

Likewise, the proposed EU corporate sustainability due diligence Directive proposal does not extend in personal scope to public buyers (EC, 2022b, para. 63). In addition, the 2014 EU procurement reform, while post-dating clear EU commitments to uphold the UNGPs and policies advocating due diligence for corporations, did not integrate the due diligence concept. Although it did include notable measures intended to advance room for strategic procurement (Dragos & Neamtu, 2014), and scope to exclude suppliers in breach of certain minimum social standards, the EU Public Procurement Directive voided the possibility for contracting authorities to refer to 'criteria and conditions relating to general corporate policy, which cannot be considered as a factor characterising the specific process of production or provision of the purchased works, supplies or services' (Recital 97). This may be understood as effectively removing room for public buyers to assess whether suppliers undertake human rights and environmental due diligence and how well. If so, this would appear strongly to undermine the objectives of the EU legislator and EU policies to promote the uptake of due diligence across the market as described above.

Within the EU, permitting references to suppliers' due diligence in public procurement laws and processes has been suggested by some scholars to entail significant risks to fundamental requirements and values of procurement law. It has been argued, for instance, that this might undermine fair competition, because the implementation of corporate due diligence is not adequately verifiable, whether pre- or post-award, and thereby runs the risk of creating new possibilities for discriminatory purchasing if not for outright corruption. The use of certifications, as proxies for due diligence, in terms of technical specifications, has been challenged for the same reason. References to due diligence might, it has been suggested, be impermissible by virtue of the requirement under the 2014 Directives for a link to the subject matter. By the same token, due diligence might also be thought to pose difficulty in evaluations of MEAT (Sanchez-Graells, 2019b, cf. Marx, 2019).

Such concerns may not be totally without foundation, and if valid, they would, as analysed above, be relevant for EU institutions' procurements as for procurement undertaken by EU member states. Yet at the same time it requires to be recognized that the divergence of public and private buyers' due diligence duties derives partly from the 'lexical priority afforded to market integration over human rights concerns within the EU legal order' (Methven O'Brien, 2021). Notwithstanding the constitutional status afforded human and fundamental rights since the Lisbon Treaty, historically this orientation has had a 'chilling effect' on the application of 'social' considerations in EU procurements by public authorities, while it even recently has continued to condition EC interventions in the procurement arena.[22] Besides the legislative omissions mentioned above, for instance, the latest EC 'Buying Social' guidance falls short of EU due diligence commitments in its definitions and principles (EC, 2021a; see further Methven O'Brien, Martin-Ortega, & Conlon, 2018).

Slowly, nonetheless, EU policy is aligning EU public procurement regulation towards support of agreed Union-wide legal and policy objectives addressing sustainability, or at least its green (rather than social) dimensions. For example, the 2019 European Green Deal gives SPP a prominent role (EC, 2019a). The 2020 Circular Economy Action Plan goes a step further, from promoting an exemplary role to insisting upon mandatory SPP:

> [t]o tap into this potential, the Commission will propose minimum mandatory green public procurement (GPP) criteria and targets in sectoral legislation and phase in compulsory reporting to monitor the uptake of Green Public

Procurement (GPP) without creating an unjustified administrative burden for the public buyers.

(EC, 2020a, para. 2.2; Tátrai & Diófási-Kovács, 2021)

As the Circular Economy Action Plan avows, this shift towards mandatory SPP criteria is born of a realization that instruments such as the EU GPP criteria mentioned above 'have reduced impact due to the limitations of voluntary approaches' (EC, 2020a, para. 2.1). A recent judgment by the General Court has affirmed the legality of awarding points for certification schemes attesting to quality systems, including ISO 9001 or equivalent (T-578/19 *Sophia Group*).

Hence, space appears to be growing for discussion on whether, and how, EU law might establish requirements that public bodies undertaking EU procurements refer to due diligence. At minimum, it would seem relevant that economic operators required by other EU legislation (e.g. the EUCSDDD, conflict minerals, timber or forced labour regulations) to perform due diligence should not be awarded contracts if determined by regulators as non-compliant (Methven O'Brien & Weatherburn, 2023; Methven O'Brien & Caranta, 2024).

Equally, it seems plausible to consider whether EU entities might be subject to free-standing due diligence requirements on a mandatory basis. In the alternative, or in addition (and akin to the indirect measures addressed by the EU to companies discussed above) EU entities might be subjected to new statutory duties formally to report on their supply chain due diligence processes; to obtain external assurances of such reports; and to publish them. This might also provide a basis for the exercise of oversight via audit by the European Court of Auditors, and thereby for accountability to democratic principals in the EP (Methven O'Brien & Caranta, 2024).

Some normative developments beyond the EU seem to lend tentative support for such a progression, by indicating a gradual crystallization of due diligence duties in the public procurement domain. In its 2016 Recommendation, for instance, the Council of Europe provides that states should 'apply additional measures to require business enterprises to respect human rights, including, where appropriate, by carrying out human rights due diligence...' when member states 'own or control business enterprises; grant substantial support and deliver services through agencies, such as export credit agencies and official investment insurance or guarantee agencies, to business enterprises' or 'conduct commercial transactions with business enterprises, including through the conclusion of public procurement contracts' (Council of Europe, 2016, Appendix, para. 22, hereinafter COE Recommendation). Further, the COE Recommendation counsels that 'Member States should evaluate the measures taken and respond to any deficiencies' and 'provide for adequate consequences if such respect for human rights is not honoured'. Although the OECD's 2015 public procurement Recommendation does not refer explicitly to due diligence (OECD, 2015), subsequent OECD guidance material has sought to bridge and bring into coherence the OECD's sustainable procurement, responsible business conduct and due diligence agendas (OECD, 2020). Germany's more recent supply chain due diligence law provides for due diligence-based exclusions from public procurement (Deutscher Bundestag, 2021, Section 22).

Besides, the UN Security Council and General Assembly have called on the 'UN system organizations to step up their efforts to strengthen protections against human trafficking in all UN procurement',[23] leading to adoption of a 'common approach to combat human trafficking and forced labour in UN supply chains' and amendments to the General Conditions of Contract and UN Supplier Code of Conduct.[24] The Organization for Security and Cooperation in Europe (OSCE) has highlighted the role of public procurement in tackling modern slavery and concluded guidance on implementation of anti-trafficking measures in OSCE's own procurement across its executive structures and aligning the OSCE's mandates with its own processes (OSCE, 2021). Finally, public buyers in some EU and OECD member states have already for some years engaged in innovative practices that promote their own due diligence practices and/or the engagement in such practices by their suppliers and tenderers (DIHR, 2020; EC, 2021a; OECD, 2020), notwithstanding a lack of mandatory requirements at national or EU levels.

## 2.4 EU institutions' procurement and due diligence policy and practice: case studies

Such innovations are clearly aligned and intended to further the human rights duties and policy objectives described above. Given this, and the EU's specific human rights and due diligence commitments, it appears appropriate to explore whether EU institutions themselves are implementing due diligence standards that the EU legislator has sought to direct towards private buyers, and which moreover are being advanced via public procurement 'best practices' on due diligence at the level of member states. With this goal, research was undertaken by the authors of this chapter on behalf of the EP in 2023, to investigate the current state of due diligence practice by the EC, EP, and three selected EU independent agencies (EU Fundamental Rights Agency (FRA), the European Border and Coast Guard Agency (FRONTEX), and the EU Agency for the Space Programme (EUSPA)). This section highlights key findings, based on stakeholder interviews and documentary analysis (Methven O'Brien & Caranta, 2024).

### *2.4.1 European Parliament*

Procurement rules for the EP are convergent with the EU Financial Regulation, the 2014 EU Public Procurement Directive, and EU Concession Directives: in other words, the EP is generally bound by the same procurement rules as member state authorities when conducting procurements governed by EU law. EP procurement activity is largely decentralized across its Directorate Generals. Nevertheless, it is constrained, guided and supported, besides transversal EU legal rules, by EP internal policies, tools, templates, and systems, that appear to be closely observed in practice. Sustainability considerations are to an extent integrated within this framework, with practical SPP support provided to EP buyers by entities including the EP Eco-Management and Audit Scheme (EMAS) Unit,[25] a Steering Group on Environmental Management and Steering Committee for Environmental Management, and EP Procurement Forum which help define Green Public Procurement targets (GPP), and an EP Annual Environmental Statement.[26] A Central Financial Unit plays a key role, developing standard tender procurement documents, general guidance, and subject-specific procurement guidance documents.

On this basis, some EP procurements apply measures to address suppliers' compliance with minimum environmental and social requirements; abnormally low tenders; technical specifications, selection criteria, and award criteria, linked to GPP or, albeit infrequently, SPP objectives. Some EP policy and guidance materials reflect the specific meaning of due diligence as per recent EU and international policies on responsible business conduct, and EU legislation. However, 'due diligence' is still predominantly understood, in the context of EP procurement, as synonymous with ensuring sound and efficient buying practices. Dedicated supply chain or procurement due diligence policies and practices are not yet observable in EP purchasing activity, either at corporate level or within individual DGs.

Although some steps have been taken, such as publication of an EP Guide for Socially Responsible Public Procurement at the European Parliament (SRPP Guide), EP policies and practices relating GPP are more mature and extensive than those concerning SPP, and social risks, including risks to human rights, do not appear to have been subjected to specific identification, assessment or management exercises with reference to EP spend breakdown or supply chains. SPP KPIs and reporting are also lacking. In terms of securing suppliers' compliance with minimum environmental and social obligations during contract performance, the EP generally assumes that national authorities fulfil this role where production or service delivery occurs within EU member states. Proactive monitoring during contract performance is hence not widely undertaken; this is also true of supplier exclusions or contract terminations based on either green or social criteria. Overall, while EP sustainable procurement goals appear institutionally well supported, they do not yet comprise a functional substitute for supply chain due diligence as envisaged by international and EU standards, in particular, lacking full coverage of social as well as green issues, and comprehensive approaches for the management of material sustainability risks.

### *2.4.2 European Commission*

Rules on EC procurement also reflect the EU Financial Regulation and the 2014 EU Public Procurement Directive and EU Concession Directives. As for the EP, while procurement activity is largely decentralized, it is also subject to EC internal policies, tools, templates, and systems that seem closely honoured in practice. Within this framework, EC procurements apply some approaches relevant to sustainability, for instance, via generally applicable measures to address suppliers' compliance with minimum environmental and social requirements; scrutiny, where relevant, of abnormally low tenders; and, in some cases, technical specifications, selection criteria and award criteria, linked to GPP objectives. Analogously to the EP, even if some EC materials reflect the specific meaning of due diligence as per recent EU and international policies on responsible business conduct, and EU legislation, generally 'due diligence' is understood as ensuring sound and efficient buying practices, including taking stock of lesson learned. As for the EP, sustainability due diligence is lacking in EC procurement activity, and the EC does not, at corporate level or in individual DGs, perform supply chain due diligence itself or require this of suppliers. Mechanisms to facilitate complaints and remediation concerning harms linked to EU institutions' procurement are not in place, while data on the scale and character of EC procurement, as well as its environmental and social footprint are also lacking.

On the other hand, EMAS certification has been a driver for GPP by the EC, which is more extensive and mature than SRPP in EC procurements, and EU GPP criteria are referred to in this context. In terms of securing suppliers' compliance with minimum environmental and social obligations during contract performance, like the EP, the EC generally assumes that national authorities fulfil this role; declarations of honour are mostly relied on as guarantees of suppliers' past compliance with environmental and social obligations at award stage.

### *2.4.3 EU agencies*

The EU's decentralized agencies undertake procurements encompassing general and specialist goods and services, of significant monetary value and impact, with diverse sustainability risk profiles, according to each agency's respective policy mission, mandate, and functions. EU agency procurements are governed by the same legal framework as the EP, EC, and member state authorities and according to our research, EU agencies implement this similarly to the EP and EC, including in the sustainability area, for instance, adopting some measures to address suppliers' compliance with minimum environmental and social requirements, and scrutiny of abnormally low tenders. Where possible and cost-effective, EU agencies may also account environmental and social aspects of procurements via technical specifications, selection criteria, and award criteria. 'Due diligence' is interpreted by EU agencies as applying sound and efficient buying practices, and not with the specific meaning given to it in recent EU and international policies on responsible business conduct. Hence, dedicated due diligence policies, corporate-level processes of sustainability risk identification, assessment, management, monitoring, and reporting, as counselled by UN, EU, and OECD standards, are absent.

In terms of prospects for integrating due diligence into procurement, EU agencies remain under strong pressure to achieve their respective missions while containing costs, which could limit or de-prioritize efforts to develop or implement due diligence policies and practices voluntarily. On the other hand, EU agencies' established procurement systems and institutional and professional capacity provide a strong foundation for the integration of sustainability due diligence, if mandated. Transversal EU institutional guidance on due diligence as well as other aspects of sustainable procurement seem likely to be well received by EU agencies. The EU Agencies Network could be an appropriate vehicle for cross-EU agency coordination and peer learning on due diligence and SPP. The use by EU agencies of framework contracts negotiated by the EC or other entities could likewise help to consolidate the use of due diligence and SPP and its impact.

## 2.5 Sustainability in EU institutions' procurement: a case for new due diligence requirements?

Overall, despite clear injunctions directed by the EU legislator to EU businesses to perform sustainability due diligence and to integrate due diligence measures into their supply chain approaches and management, EU institutions themselves have yet to adopt significant efforts in this area. While EU bodies appear generally to adhere to the EU Financial Regulation and 2014 EU Procurement Directive, these rules do not require public buyers to engage in human rights or environmental due diligence; neither do they require public buyers' consideration of prospective or contracted suppliers' due diligence during the procurement process. Indeed, aspects of the current EU procurement regime, such as the requirement for a 'link to the subject matter', rather tend to constrain public buyers from considering suppliers' due diligence, a 'chilling effect' evident across EU institutions.

Due diligence as analysed in Section 3 is counselled by UN, EU, and OECD standards as a key tool to operationalize 'responsible business conduct' and hence to advance progress towards green transition and sustainable development. If, despite this, due diligence is lacking across EU institutions' procurement, it appears important to ask whether new due diligence norms should be established for EU institutions, and if so, through which legal, policy, or practical approaches. This section reflects on these questions, outlining pertinent technical as well as policy issues and evaluating options that might be deployed to this end, with reference inter alia to the foreseen EUCSDDD as well as other instruments.

### *2.5.1 Supply chain due diligence for EU institutions*

Institutional due diligence processes (UNHRC, 2011; OECD, 2023, 2018) are advocated as an effective mechanism for managing operational, litigation, and reputational risks, including as they arise from supply chain relationships. Echoing this view, the OECD's 2015 Public Procurement Recommendation urges adherents to develop an appropriate strategy for integrating secondary objectives into public procurement systems; to establish appropriate planning, baseline analysis, risk assessment, and target outcomes as the basis for the development of action plans or guidelines for implementation; to employ appropriate impact assessment methodology to measure the effectiveness of procurement in achieving secondary policy objectives; to measure the results according to appropriate milestones to provide policymakers with necessary information regarding the benefits and costs of such use, addressing both the level of individual procurements, and against policy objective target outcomes; and to periodically assess the aggregate effect of pursuing secondary policy objectives on the public procurement system to address potential objective overload (OECD, 2015, p. 12).

A first and key observation, then, is that the existing legal rules governing EU institutions' procurement, as EU procurements generally, following the analysis advanced above, do not pose any obstacle to the adoption of such processes. Key elements of procurement due diligence for EU institutions, in line with the cited international standards, should include risk identification and assessment; measures to cease, prevent, or mitigate identified supply chain risks; tracking and implementation of results; internal and external communication of results, on an iterative basis; as well as steps to provide for or cooperate in remediation (Methven O'Brien & Caranta, 2024). Given human resource and financial capacity constraints and other limiting factors, there would be clear value in this context in cross-EU institutional pooling of resources, burden-sharing, and a coordinated approach. Pilot exercises, best practices from member states' procurement bodies and guidance can readily inform EU institutions in taking first steps in this respect (Göthberg, 2019; DIHR, 2020). Organized cross-body due diligence processes might also provide a more transparent and consistent basis for EU contract monitoring commitments and targets in relation to material risks of environmental or social harms associated with EU procurements.

### *2.5.2 Extending sustainable procurement practice within the existing legal framework*

Second, measures already available under the existing legal framework for EU institutions' procurement can be pursued more tenaciously to secure compliance by suppliers with minimum legal obligations, both statutory and contractual. For example, companies convicted of certain offences may be excluded from EU tender procedures. Under the EU Financial Regulation (Article 136), exclusionary grounds include grave professional misconduct and serious breach of contract. In principle, this is broad enough to capture most breaches of environmental and social obligations and to justify suppliers' exclusion from EU institutions' own account tenders on that basis. Likewise, more could be made of existing provisions permitting EU buyers to monitor compliance during contract performance of suppliers with applicable obligations in the fields of environmental, social, and labour law; and on SPP contract clauses, while still meeting current 'link to the subject matter' and transparency requirements (Methven O'Brien & Caranta, 2024).

### *2.5.3 Articulating EU institutions' procurement law and EU sustainability and due diligence standards*

If significant advances towards sustainable EU institutions' procurement can be made within the existing normative framework, nonetheless, that framework could undoubtedly be made more favourable to this goal. A number of measures appear worth considering in this regard. These include: integrating due diligence and binding sustainable procurement goals into the EU Financial Regulation; ensuring the Financial Regulation is continuously updated to articulate with EU sustainable procurement requirements; extending the basis for mandatory exclusions; integrating sustainable procurement into general EU budgetary control mechanisms; measures to link EU institutions' own procurement with the anticipated EUCSDDD; and finally, revision of the 2014 EU Public Procurement Directive in particular to reconsider the requirement of the link to the subject matter to allow public buyers to take suppliers' due diligence and sustainability performance into account in their procurements (Methven O'Brien & Caranta, 2024).

#### *2.5.4 Strengthening sustainable procurement and due diligence efforts and capacity across EU institutions*

Finally, regardless of whether the integration of sustainability due diligence proceeds under existing or new legal rules, it will require concerted action amongst EU institutions to generate and process relevant data, enhance technological and data infrastructure relating to their contracts, and secure cross-institutional coordination and pool resources to realize consistent enforcement. Whereas some initiatives to foster mutual support and dissemination on SPP across EU bodies are already underway, greater effort is needed to secure policy coherence, while more synergy in SPP measures would likely enhance both their cost-effectiveness and impacts. Development of guidance, trainings, and exchange of good practices together form one discrete area of requirements (Methven O'Brien & Caranta, 2024).

The prospect of adding further, sustainability-focused requirements to EC tenders could both limit competition for EU contracts and extend internal capacity requirements, as well as contract costs. Market analysis and market consultation would therefore be prerequisite in assessing which SPP criteria relevant economic operators can comply with. While such concerns, alongside pressure on budgets, might constrain efforts to develop or implement due diligence policies and practices voluntarily, strong institutional and professional capacity would support effective implementation of sustainability due diligence, if mandated. Framework contracts managed by the EC could offer a relevant focal point for piloting due diligence approaches across EU institutions. Establishing accessible whistleblowing and remediation mechanisms should also be considered in this context.

### 2.6 Conclusion: risk and resilience in EU and EU institutions' supply chains – the role of due diligence

Globally and at European level, society faces multiple threats to stability and sustainability. EU institutions as a result are engaged in intensive activity to address environmental and social concerns, including via new supply chain standards. Anchoring sustainability due diligence inside corporations that are established or operate in the EU via mandatory due diligence requirements has fast become a central plank of such measures. Public procurement due diligence has, to date, been an area of oversight for such rules. In closing, this section reiterates why this gap should be more deliberately and urgently addressed by legislators and policymakers, not just as regards EU institutions' own procurements, but public buying in general.

First, this promises a direct contribution to sustainable development. A 'crucial pillar of strategic governance and services delivery for governments' (OECD, 2015; EC, 2011a), globally public procurement amounts to over $13 trillion annually (World Bank, 2021). EU institutions' procurement, while hard to quantify precisely, accounts for likely hundreds of billions of euro in each budget cycle, and across the EU, public procurement accounts for 13.3% of gross domestic product (EC, 2019b). On this scale, sustainable public procurement has potential to contribute *directly* to securing sustainable consumption, in line with the UN 2030 Agenda and SDGs[27] and global and EU climate objectives (EC, 2020b). It can help to address not only the triple planetary crisis, but also salient socio-economic issues such as human and labour rights, diversity, inclusion, and gender equality (UNEP, 2022).

Second, through due diligence governments can both lead and support responsible business conduct by market actors. *Indirectly*, by better integrating sustainability considerations, including via due diligence, public procurement may influence suppliers and the market at large to adopt new measures or enhance existing measures to advance environmental and social objectives. Demonstrable sustainable public procurement practices by EU institutions themselves, such as due diligence, should help communicate a commitment to policy coherence by the EU legislator and associated institutions. Sustainable procurement by EU bodies is also an opportunity to demonstrate sustainability leadership, practical relevance, and the 'value-added', in terms of efficiency and other gains, of EU sustainability standards to market actors and member state authorities. As stated in the Communication on the European Green Deal, 'Public authorities, including the EU institutions, should lead by example and ensure that their procurement is green' (EC, 2019b, p. 8). In addition,

> mandatory GPP promotes the availability of information on the market, further standardisation, and more legally certain and efficient procurement processes for the authorities. Furthermore, a mandatory GPP approach is likely to increase market demand and innovation and lower the costs of environmentally-friendly products and services.
>
> (Mélon, 2020)

Third, due diligence in public procurement advances policy coherence in the sustainability domain. Practical implementation of corporate due diligence, allied with strengthened non-financial corporate reporting requirements[28] and a broader framework of new sustainable investment regulation[29] has assumed a central role in securing the green transition as well as sustainable development and global decent work commitments. More firmly aligning the procurement expenditure of EU public institutions, via due diligence, to legal and policy commitments in the areas mentioned, would contribute to advancing fulfilment of policy objectives, and thereby also to effective and efficient use of resources.

Fourth, due diligence in public procurement is prerequisite for the fulfilment of established legal duties. Under Article 2, Treaty on the Functioning of the European Union (TFEU),

> The Union is founded on the values of respect for human dignity, freedom, democracy, equality, the rule of law and respect for human rights, including the rights of persons belonging to minorities. These values are common to the Member States in a society in which pluralism, non-discrimination, tolerance, justice, solidarity and equality between women and men prevail.

Article 7, TFEU, requires the Union to 'ensure consistency between its policies and activities, taking all of its objectives into account and in accordance with the principle of conferral of powers'. To this end, the Union must aim to eliminate inequalities, and to promote equality, between men and women (TFEU, Article 8), to promote a high level of employment and fight against social exclusion (TFEU, Article 9), to combat discrimination based on sex, racial, or ethnic origin, religion or belief, disability, age, or sexual orientation (TFEU, Article 10). Finally, 'Environmental protection requirements must be integrated into the definition and implementation of the Union's policies and activities, in particular with a view to promoting sustainable development' (TFEU, Article 11). Human rights and all the other relevant aspects considered in due diligence are thus at the core of the EU constitution.

Positive obligations arising under international treaties provide a basis for reasonable due diligence by public actors (Methven O'Brien & Martin-Ortega, 2019), whereas due diligence also appears as an appropriate tool and mechanism for identifying and seeking to reconcile multiple overlaid legal duties and policy objectives facing public buyers (DIHR, 2020; Martin-Ortega & Methven O'Brien, 2019). Indeed, Article 207(1), TFEU, requires that development of the common commercial policy must be 'conducted in the context of the principles and objectives of the Union's external action', namely respect for and promotion of human rights. From the point of view of human rights, the feasibility of aligning public procurement to a greater extent with state and EU human rights duties have been highlighted (Martin-Ortega & Methven O'Brien, 2017, 2019).

As already indicated, while not yet modifying the 2014 EU Public Procurement Directive, the EU legislative framework is changing, via new mandatory sustainability and due diligence requirements (Janssen & Caranta, 2023). The broader legislative framework must hence be carefully interpreted anew, in light of current challenges and the range of values enshrined in the EU Treaties as related above. Public procurement must play its role in addressing societal changes, and contractors' compliance with common goals must be ensured. Equally, governments and private sector actors are increasingly subject to legal challenges linked to failure to implement human rights and climate change obligations and action directed towards EU institutions linked to public buying decisions cannot in future be ruled out (Kulovesi et al., 2024).

Fifth, sustainability due diligence in public procurement is a mechanism for securing economic value and efficiency. In principle, scientific literature is supportive of the shift towards SPP, and GPP, identified as holding 'great potential to decarbonise the economy, also relative to other decarbonization policies that are currently being implemented or discussed' (Chiappinelli & Zipperer, 2017; Schotanus & Nicolas, 2023). It has been stressed that, in place of the 'tyranny of the lowest price' (Schooner & Speidel, 2020), procurement should be considered an investment (Feliu, 2020) with greater focus on the real costs (including societal and environmental costs) rather than the mere price tag of what is bought (Caranta, 2023). EU institutions have been recently criticized for weak GPP efforts (Badell & Rosell, 2021).

Perhaps, there is little economic evidence about the actual effectiveness and efficiency (or lack thereof) of SPP. Yet case studies seem to disprove general theoretical economic assumptions strongly tilted against regulatory action. Carreras and Vannoni's analysis, for example, seems to question the efficacy of initiatives for promoting inclusion and supplier diversity (e.g. SMEs and women- or minority-owned businesses) through set asides and similar tools, by comparison with those dedicated to *hardcore* social objectives (e.g. respect for human and labour rights; Carreras & Vannoni, 2023).

On the other hand, competition-based arguments against SPP have been robustly countered. Sanchez-Graells' suggestion, for instance, that Article 18(1) of the EU Public Procurement Directive imposes on contracting authorities both a procedural and a substantive burden to demonstrate that sustainability requirements do not restrict competition more than necessary to achieve cross-cutting goals (Sanchez-Graells, 2019a) met with criticism and it is unclear why 'competition' should take precedence over 'sustainability' (Kunzlik, 2013). State support, via public contract awards, for companies that are violating basic human rights, labour rights, social protections, and environmental standards is anyway market-distorting (Methven O'Brien & Martin-Ortega, 2019b, 2020). More recent contributions tend to assess the extent to which individual EU law provisions on different stages of the procurement cycle allow for SPP (Sabockis, 2022).

The potential to advance the positive values and outcomes identified above should weigh heavily, for legislators and regulators, in favour of incorporating due diligence into public procurement law, policy, and practice. On the other hand, there remain certain obstacles to this goal. Chief amongst them is the issue of institutional capacity and resources. Concerns are regularly expressed by public procurers regarding capacity and resource constraints, in face of multiple, overlaid, and potentially conflicting secondary objectives (EU Committee of the Regions, 2012; Sack & Sarter, 2022). Demonstrating value-added and the practical feasibility of applying due diligence in public procurement, and providing meaningful benchmarks in this area, is admittedly crucial.

However, according to UNEP about 80% of procurement professionals already consider SPP to be either more or much more important since 2017 (UNEP, 2022, figure 2.6, p. 14). Moreover, 'All stakeholders, both public and private, indicated that the achievement of the SDGs was a key consideration in their SP policies.

While SDG 12 on responsible consumption and production and SDG 13 on climate action were most frequently cited, recent policies considered responsible business conduct (SDG 8 on decent work and economic growth) and innovation and competitiveness (SDG 9 on industry, innovation and infrastructure)' as well (UNEP, 2022, pp. iv, f). Accordingly, Recommendation 4.2 of the 2022 UNEP SPP Global Review invited procurement authorities to 'emphasize training, capacity-building and incentives'. Indeed, 'training, capacity-building and incentives are effective ways to embed SP practices more fully into an organization's purchasing patterns by helping create a shared understanding around SP and highlighting its importance throughout the organization' (UNEP, 2022, p. 73). Similarly, the OECD's 2015 Recommendation on Public Procurement stresses the need (i) not just to balance different considerations, but also to have staff ready to work on sustainable public procurement including concerning monitoring; (ii) to develop a sustainable public procurement strategy (a suggestion in line with UNEP's Sustainable Public Procurement Implementation Guidelines; UNEP, 2021); and (iii) to assess the results of SPP to evaluate their cost and benefits (OECD, 2015, p. 9). This last point binds with Recommendation X (OECD, 2015, p. 11) which more generally invites public authorities to enhance 'evaluation of the effectiveness of the public procurement system from individual procurements to the system as a whole, at all levels of government where feasible and appropriate'. Besides training, capacity building, and incentives, it is also necessary to lower the administrative burden on procurement officials. Compliance with human rights, social and labour rules, and environmental obligations must avoid duplication of efforts. Collation of data on contractors' non-compliance is therefore imperative, alongside integration of due diligence into existing resources and facilities, such as the GPP training kit for contracting authorities in the member states (EC, 2023).

Against this background, the 'soft-pedalling' to date amongst policymakers as regards the assimilation of due diligence into public procurement law, policy, and practice is noteworthy. As detailed in this chapter, this ought to yield sustainability dividends. On the other hand, its oversight may attract a range of reputational, political, operational, and legal risks. Further, according to the analysis presented here, solid obstacles to establishing direct mandatory due diligence requirements for public procurers, as well as indirect measures, such as reporting and assurance requirements, are not evident. Dialogue involving all actors should hence now be intensified on whether closer links between due diligence and public procurement in EU law and policy can any longer be avoided.

## Notes

1 These include Regulation (EU) 2017/821 laying down supply chain due diligence obligations for Union importers of tin, tantalum and tungsten, their ores, and gold originating from conflict-affected and high-risk areas, OJ L 130/1, 19 May 2017; Regulation (EU) 2023/1542 concerning batteries and waste batteries, amending Directive 2008/98/EC and Regulation (EU) 2019/1020 and repealing Directive 2006/66/EC (Art. 85) OJ L 191, 28 July 2023; Regulation (EU) 2023/1115 of the European Parliament and of the

Council of 31 May 2023 on the making available on the Union market and the export from the Union of certain commodities and products associated with deforestation and forest degradation and repealing Regulation (EU) No 995/2010 (Art. 25) OJ L 150, 9 June 2023).

2 If enacted, the EU Corporate Sustainability Due Diligence Directive (hereinafter CSDDD) would extend responsibilities, civil liability and exposure to administrative penalties to larger economic actors in respect of human rights and environmental impacts: EC Proposal for a Directive on Corporate Sustainability Due Diligence (EU) 2019/1937, COM/2022/71 final, 23 February 2022, hereinafter 'CSDDD'). See now Directive (EU) 2024/1760 of the European Parliament and of the Council of 13 June 2024 on corporate sustainability due diligence and amending Directive (EU) 2019/1937 and Regulation (EU) 2023/2859.

3 Henceforward 'public procurement', to be understood as including concessions unless otherwise specified. These are found in Directive 2014/24/EU of the European Parliament and of the Council of 26 February 2014 on public procurement (hereinafter 'Public Procurement Directive'); Directive 2014/23/EU on the award of concession contracts (hereinafter 'Concession Directive') and Directive 2014/25/EU of the European Parliament and of the Council of 26 February 2014 on utilities procurement (hereinafter 'Utilities Directive').

4 Consolidated version of the Treaty on the Functioning of the European Union (hereinafter TFEU), Part Three: Union Policies and Internal Actions, Title VII: Common Rules on Competition, Taxation and Approximation of Law, Chapter 3: Approximation of laws, Article 114 (ex Article 95 TEC) OJ C 115, 9.5.2008, pp. 94–95 provides: 1. … The European Parliament and the Council shall, acting in accordance with the ordinary legislative procedure and after consulting the Economic and Social Committee, adopt the measures for the approximation of the provisions laid down by law, regulation or administrative action in Member States which have as their object the establishment and functioning of the internal market, while e.g. under Article 114(6) national measures in relevant areas should not constitute 'means of arbitrary discrimination or a disguised restriction on trade between Member States' that presents 'an obstacle to the functioning of the internal market'.

5 Case C-454/06 *pressetext Nachrichtenagentur* [2008] ECR I-4401, paragraph 31; see also Case 26/03 *Stadt Halle and RPL Lochau* [2005] ECR I-1, paragraph 44.

6 Regulation (EU, Euratom) 2018/1046 of the European Parliament and of the Council of 18 July 2018 on the financial rules applicable to the general budget of the Union, amending Regulations (EU) No 1296/2013, (EU) No 1301/2013, (EU) No 1303/2013, (EU) No 1304/2013, (EU) No 1309/2013, (EU) No 1316/2013, (EU) No 223/2014, (EU) No 283/2014, and Decision No 541/2014/EU and repealing Regulation (EU, Euratom) No 966/2012 (hereinafter 'the Financial Regulation').

7 EU Financial Regulation, Recital 96.

8 Article 67 of the EU Public Procurement Directive and Article 167 of the EU Financial Regulation.

9 For example, Regulation (EU) 2023/1542 concerning batteries and waste batteries, amending Directive 2008/98/EC and Regulation (EU) 2019/1020 and repealing Directive 2006/66/EC (Art. 85) OJ L 191, 28 July 2023.

10 Proposal for a Directive amending Directive (EU) 2018/2001 of the European Parliament and of the Council, Regulation (EU) 2018/1999 of the European Parliament and of the Council and Directive 98/70/EC of the European Parliament and of the Council as regards the promotion of energy from renewable sources, and repealing Council Directive (EU) 2015/652 (COM/2021/557 final), Article 15a(3).

11 Directive 2022/2041/EU on adequate minimum wages in the European Union, Article 9.

12 The International Finance Corporation (hereinafter IFC) Performance Standards on Environmental and Social Sustainability provide IFC clients with 'guidance on how to identify risks and impacts…to help avoid, mitigate, and manage risks and impacts as a way of doing business in a sustainable way' and apply to IFC-funded project activities: IFC (2012), Performance Standards on Environmental and Social Sustainability, available at www.ifc.org/content/dam/ifc/doc/2010/2012-ifc-performance-standards-en.pdf. The Equator Principles provide guidance on sustainability considerations as applicable to project finance provided by banks and other financial institutions; since 2020 they recognise the corporate responsibility to respect human rights provide supplementary guidance on human rights assessments: Equator Principles, *Guidance Note on Implementation of Human Rights Assessments under the Equator Principles*, available at: https://equator-principles.com/app/uploads/Human_Rights_Assessment_Sept2020.pdf.

13 Directive 2014/95/EU of the European Parliament and of the Council of 22 October 2014 amending Directive 2013/34/EU as regards disclosure of non-financial and diversity information by certain large undertakings and groups, hereinafter EU Non-Financial Reporting Directive.

14 Directive (EU) 2022/2464 of the European Parliament and of the Council of 14 December 2022 amending Regulation (EU) No 537/2014, Directive 2004/109/EC, Directive 2006/43/EC and Directive 2013/34/EU, as regards corporate sustainability reporting.

15 Commission Delegated Regulation (EU) 2023/2772 of 31 July 2023 supplementing Directive 2013/34/EU of the European Parliament and of the Council as regards sustainability reporting standards C/2023/5303 OJ L, 2023/2772, 22.12.2023.

16 Regulation (Regulation (EU) 2017/821 of the European Parliament and of the Council of 17 May 2017 laying down supply chain due diligence obligations for Union importers of tin, tantalum and tungsten, their ores, and gold originating from conflict-affected and high-risk areas.

17 Regulation (EU) 2023/1542 of the European Parliament and of the Council of 12 July 2023 concerning batteries and waste batteries, amending Directive 2008/98/EC and Regulation (EU) 2019/1020 and repealing Directive 2006/66/EC).

18 Regulation (EU) 2023/1115 of the European Parliament and of the Council of 31 May 2023 on the making available on the Union market and the export from the Union of certain commodities and products associated with deforestation and forest degradation and repealing Regulation (EU) No 995/2010.

19 Regulation of the European Parliament of The Council on prohibiting products made with forced labour on the Union market, COM(2022)453 final (EC 2022).

20 UN Human Rights Council, Open-ended intergovernmental working group on transnational corporations and other business enterprises with respect to human rights, Updated draft legally binding instrument (2023), available at: www.ohchr.org/en/hr-bodies/hrc/wg-trans-corp/igwg-on-tnc.

21 www.europarl.europa.eu/doceo/document/TA-9-2023-0209_EN.html. Unusually, however, at time of writing it remains doubtful whether the law will pass during the current European Parliamentary term.

22 Article 1a inserted into the Treaty on European Union (hereinafter TEU) by the TFEU, provides: 'The Union is founded on the values of respect for human dignity, freedom, democracy, equality, the rule of law and respect for human rights, including the rights of persons belonging to minorities. These values are common to the Member States in a society in which pluralism, non-discrimination, tolerance, justice, solidarity and equality between women and men prevail.'

23 UN Security Council Resolution S/RES/2388; UN General Assembly Resolution 76/7.
24 Available via UN System Chief Executives Board for Coordination, Combatting Human Trafficking and Forced Labour in UN Supply Chains, https://unsceb.org/combatting-human-trafficking-and-forced-labour-un-supply-chains.
25 EMAS is the EU Environmental Management System: Regulation (EC) No 1221/2009 on the voluntary participation by organisations in a Community eco-management and audit scheme (EMAS), repealing Regulation (EC) No 761/2001 and Commission Decisions 2001/681/EC and 2006/193/EC.
26 E.g. EP, 2023 Annual Environmental Statement covering 2022, available at: www.europarl.europa.eu/about-parliament/files/organisation-and-rules/ecological-footprint/en-ep-environmental-statement.pdf.
27 Target 12.7 of the UN Sustainable Development Goals is to 'Promote public procurement practices that are sustainable, in accordance with national policies and priorities': UN General Assembly, Resolution 70/1, Transforming our world: the 2030 Agenda for Sustainable Development (UN Doc. A/RES/70/1, 20 October 2015).
28 Regulation (EU) 2019/2088 on sustainability-related disclosures in the financial services sector, OJ 317/1, 9 December 2019).
29 Regulation (EU) 2020/852 on the establishment of a framework to facilitate sustainable investment, and amending Regulation (EU) 2019/2088, Regulation (EU) 2019/2088 on sustainability-related disclosures in the financial services sector.

## References


Arrowsmith, S. (2012), 'The Purpose of the EU Procurement Directives: Ends, Means and the Implications for National Regulatory Space for Commercial and Horizontal Procurement Policies', *Cambridge Yearbook of European Legal Studies*, 1.

Arrowsmith, S. and Kunzlik, P. (eds.) (2009), *Social and Environmental Policies in EC Procurement Law: New Directives and New Directions*, Cambridge University Press, Cambridge.

Badell, D. and Rosell, J. (2021), 'Are EU Institutions Still Green Actors? An Empirical Study of Green Public Procurement', *Journal of Common Market Studies*, 59, p. 1555.

Burgi, M. (2022), 'More or Less Internal Market, Competition or Strategic Procurement: The ECJ's Case– Law over Time', in: Risvig Hamer, C. et al. (eds.), *Into the Northern Light – in memory of Steen Treumer*, ExTuto, Copenhagen.

Caranta, R. (2023), 'Public procurement for the SDGs – Rethinking the basics', in: Mélon, L. (ed.), *Sustainability in Public Procurement, Corporate Law and Higher Education*, Routledge, London.

Carreras, E. and Vannoni, D. (2023), 'Mandatory Requirements in Sustainable Public Procurement: The Economic Perspective', in: Janssen, W. and Caranta, R. (eds.), *Mandatory Sustainability Requirements in EU Public Procurement Law*, Hart, Oxford.

Chiappinelli, O. and Zipperer, V. (2017), 'Using Public Procurement as a Decarbonisation Policy: A Look at Germany', *DIW Economic Bulletin*, 49, p. 523.

Council of Europe (2016), *Recommendation CM/Rec (2016) 3 of the Committee of Ministers to Member States on Human Rights and Business*.

Danish Institute for Human Rights (DIHR) (2020), *Driving Change Through Public Procurement: A Toolkit on Human Rights for Procurement Policy Makers and Practitioners*, DIHR, Copenhagen.

Deutscher Bundestag (2021), *Gesetz über die unternehmerischen Sorgfaltspflichten in Lieferketten (German Supply Chain Due Diligence Act), 2021.*

Dragos, D.C. and Neamtu, B. (2014), 'Sustainable Public Procurement in the EU: Experiences and Prospects', in: Lichère F., Caranta R., and Treumer S. (eds.), *Modernising Public Procurement: The New Directive*, DJOEF, Copenhagen.

EC (2011a): European Commission (2011a), *Green Paper on the Modernisation of EU Public Procurement Policy. Towards a More Efficient European Procurement Market* (COM/2011/0015 final).

EC (2011b): European Commission (2011b), *A renewed EU strategy 2011–14 for Corporate Social Responsibility* COM(2011) 681 final.

EC (2016): European Commission (2016), *Buying Green! A Handbook on Green Public Procurement.*

EC (2019a): European Commission (2019a), *Communication on the European Green Deal* (COM(2019) 640 final).

EC (2019b): European Commission (2019b), *Public Procurement Indicators 2017.* Available at https://ec.europa.eu/docsroom/documents/38003.

EC (2020a): European Commission (2020a), *A new Circular Economy Action Plan For a Cleaner and More Competitive Europe* (COM/2020/98 final).

EC (2020b): European Commission (2020b), Communication from the Commission to the European Parliament, the Council, the European Economic and Social Committee and the Committee of the Regions, *Stepping up Europe's 2030 Climate Ambition Investing in a Climate-Neutral Future for the Benefit of Our People* (COM/2020/562 final).

EC (2021a): European Commission (2021a), *Buying Social – a Guide to Taking Account of Social Considerations in Public Procurement* (2nd edition).

EC (2021b): European Commission (2021b), *Report from the Commission to the European Parliament, the Council and the Court of Auditors on Annual Management and Performance Report for the EU Budget – Financial Year 2020* (COM (2021) 301 final).

EC (2021c): European Commission (2021c), *Report on the Implementation and Best Practices of National Procurement Policies in the Internal Market* COM(2021) 245 final.

EC (2022a): European Commission (2022a), *Commission Work Programme 2023 A Union Standing Firm and United* (COM(2022) 548 final).

EC (2022b): European Commission (2022b) *Proposal for a Directive on Corporate Sustainability Due Diligence and amending Directive (EU) 2019/1937, COM/2022/71 Final, 23 February 2022*, Council of the European Union, 2022.

EC (2023): Green Public Procurement Toolkit, accessible via https://green-business.ec.europa.eu/green-public-procurement/gpp-training-toolkit_en

EU Committee of the Regions (2012): *Report on the REGPEX Early Warning System File on the Revision of EU Legislation on Public Procurement 27 March 2012.*

EP (2023): European Parliament (2023), *Corporate Sustainability Due Diligence at a Glance*, 25 May 2023. Available at www.europarl.europa.eu/thinktank/en/document/EPRS_ATA(2023)747901.

Feliu, G.J.M. (2020) 'La visión estratégica en la contratación pública en la LCSP: hacia una contratación socialmente responsable y de calidad', *Revista Economía Industrial*, 415, p. 8.

Göthberg, P. (2019), 'Public procurement and human rights in the healthcare sector: the Swedish County Councils' collaborative model', in: Martin-Ortega, O. and Methven O'Brien, C. (eds.), *Public Procurement and Human Rights: Opportunities, Risks and Dilemmas for the State as Buyer*, Edward Elgar Publishing, Cheltenham.

Janssen, W. and Caranta, R. (eds.) (2023), *Mandatory Sustainability Requirements in EU Public Procurement Law*, Hart, Oxford.

Japan Ministry of Economy Trade and Industry, Guidelines on Respecting Human Rights in Responsible Supply Chains (2022), www.meti.go.jp/english/press/2022/pdf/0913_001a.pdf.

Kulovesi, K., Sebastian, O., Harro, H. and Savaresi, A. (2024), 'The European Climate Law: Strengthening EU Procedural Climate Governance?', *Journal of Environmental Law*, 20, p. 1.

Kunzlik, P. (2013), 'Neoliberalism and the European Public Procurement Regime', *Cambridge Yearbook of European Legal Studies*, 15, p. 283.

Martin-Ortega, O. and Methven O'Brien, C. (2017), 'Advancing Respect for Labour Rights Globally through Public Procurement', *Politics and Governance*, 5(4), pp. 69–79.

Martin-Ortega, O., and Methven O'Brien C. (eds.) (2019), *Public Procurement and Human Rights: Opportunities, Risks and Dilemmas for the State as Buyer*, Edward Elgar, Cheltenham.

Marx, A. (2019), 'Public Procurement and Human Rights: Current Role and Potential of Voluntary Sustainability Standards', in: Martin-Ortega, O., and Methven O'Brien C. (eds.), *Public Procurement and Human Rights: Opportunities, Risks and Dilemmas for the State as Buyer*, Edward Elgar, Cheltenham.

Mélon, L. (2020), 'More Than a Nudge? Arguments and Tools for Mandating Green Public Procurement in the EU', *Sustainability* 12, p. 1003.

Methven O'Brien, C. (2022), 'A Defining Moment for the UN Business and Human Rights Treaty Process', *Verfassungsblog: On Matters Constitutional*, https://nbn-resolving.org/urn:nbn:de:0301-20221026-110229-0-1.

Methven O'Brien, C. (2021), 'Business and Human Rights in Europe 2011–2021: A Decade in Review', in: Czech, P. et al. (eds.), *European Yearbook of Human Rights*, Intersentia, Brussels.

Methven O'Brien, C. and Caranta, R. (2024), *Due Diligence in EU Institutions' Own-Account Procurement: Rules and Practices*, Report for the European Parliament Committee on Budgetary Control, www.europarl.europa.eu/thinktank/en/document/IPOL_STU(2024)758335.

Methven O'Brien C. and Dhanarajan, S. (2016) 'The corporate responsibility to respect human rights: A status review', *Accounting, Auditing and Accountability Journal*, 29(4), p. 542.

Methven O'Brien, C. and Martin-Ortega, O. (2019a), 'Public procurement and human rights: interrogating the role of the state as buyer', in: Martin-Ortega, O. and Methven O'Brien, C. (eds.), *Public Procurement and Human Rights: Opportunities, Risks and Dilemmas for the State as Buyer*, Edward Elgar, Cheltenham, p. 2.

Methven O'Brien, C. and Martin-Ortega, O. (2019b), 'Public Procurement and the Erosion of the EU Social Model: Outline of a Polanyian Perspective and the Emerging Regulatory Role of Human Rights?', in Hinojosa Martinez, L.M. and Martin Rodriguez, P. J. (eds.), *International Markets Regulation and the Erosion of the European Political and Social Model*, Thomson Reuters, Madrid, p. 239.

Methven O'Brien, C., and Martin-Ortega, O. (2019c), 'Public Procurement and Human Rights: Discretion, Divergence, Paradox' in Bogojevic, S., Groussot, X. and Hettne, J. (eds.), *Discretion in EU Procurement Law*, Hart, Oxford.

Methven O'Brien, C. and Martin-Ortega, O. (2020), 'Human Rights and Public Procurement of Goods and Services', in: Deva, S. and Birchall, D. (eds.), Research Handbook on Human Rights and Business, Edward Elgar, Cheltenham, p. 245.

Methven O'Brien, C. and Martin-Ortega, O. (2022), Commission *Proposal* on *Corporate Sustainability Due Diligence*: *Analysis* from a *Human Rights Perspective*. European Union. Available at www.europarl.europa.eu/thinktank/en/document/EXPO_IDA(2022)702560.

Methven O'Brien C., Martin-Ortega, M. and Conlon, E. (2018), *Guidance on Socially Responsible Public Procurement: Response to consultation of the European Commission by the International Learning Lab on Procurement and Human Rights*, University of Greenwich, BHRE Research Series, Policy Paper No.5, July 2018.

Methven O'Brien C. and Holly, G. (2021), '*Human Rights Due Diligence Laws: Key Considerations. Briefing on Civil Liability for Due Diligence Failures*', DIHR, October 2021.

Methven O'Brien, C. and Botta, G. (2023), 'The Corporate Responsibility to Respect Human Rights: An updated status review', in: da Silva Almeida, J. L. (ed.), *Responsabilidade Social Corporativa e Governança Socioambiental: Greenwashing e Direitos Humanos*, Lumen Iuris, Rio de Janeiro, p. 1. Available in English at https://papers.ssrn.com/sol3/papers.cfm?abstract_id=4179257.

Methven O'Brien, C. and Weatherburn, A. (2023), *Commission Proposal for a Regulation on Prohibiting Products Made with Forced Labour on the Union Market: The Issue of Remedies*. European Parliament. Available at www.europarl.europa.eu/thinktank/en/document/EXPO_BRI(2023)702583.

Methven O'Brien C. and Ologhadien, N. (2024), 'Climate Change Mitigation, Investment and Human Rights: The Emerging Legal and Policy Framework?', in: Martinez Romera, B., Nordlander, L. and Monti, A. (eds.), *Human Rights and Investment Law for Climate Change: Trends and Prospects*, Edward Elgar, forthcoming. Available at https://discovery.dundee.ac.uk/en/publications/human-rights-in-the-context-of-climate-change-emerging-investment).

Norwegian Storting (2021), *Act relating to Enterprises' Transparency and Work on Fundamental Human Rights and Decent Working Conditions (Transparency Act)* LOV-2021-06-18-99, 2021.

OECD (2011): Organization of Economic Co-operation and Development (2011), *OECD Guidelines for Multinational Enterprises 2011 Edition*, OECD, Paris.

OECD (2015): Organization of Economic Co-operation and Development (2015), *Recommendation of the Council on Public Procurement* OECD/LEGAL/0411, OECD, Paris.

OECD (2017): Organization of Economic Co-operation and Development (2017), *Due Diligence Guidance for Responsible Supply Chains in the Garment & Footwear Sector*, OECD, Paris.

OECD (2018): Organization of Economic Co-operation and Development (2018), *OECD Due Diligence Guidance for Responsible Business Conduct*, OECD, Paris.

OECD (2019): Organization of Economic Co-operation and Development (2019), *Reforming Public Procurement: Progress in Implementing the 2015 OECD Recommendation*, OECD, Paris.

OECD (2020): Organization of Economic Co-operation and Development (2020), *Integrating Responsible Business Conduct in Public Procurement*, OECD, Paris .

OECD (2022): Organization of Economic Co-operation and Development (2022), *Pilot on Integrating OECD Due Diligence into Public Procurement in the Garment Sector*, OECD, Paris.

OECD (2023a): Organization of Economic Co-operation and Development (2023a), *OECD Guidelines for Multinational Enterprises, Due Diligence*, OECD, Paris, https://mneguidelines.oecd.org/duediligence/.

OECD (2023b): Organization of Economic Co-operation and Development (2023b), *Business Handbook on Due Diligence in the Cocoa Sector*, OECD, Paris.

OECD (2023c): Organization of Economic Co-operation and Development (2023c), *OECD-FAO Business Handbook on Deforestation and Due Diligence in Agricultural Supply Chains*, OECD, Paris.

OSCE (2021): Organisation for Security and Cooperation in Europe (2021), *Combating Trafficking in Human Beings and Labour Exploitation in Supply Chains Guidance for OSCE Procurement*. Available at www.osce.org/cthb/502383.

République Française (2017), *Loi no. 2017-399 du 27 Mars 2017 relative au devoir de vigilance des sociétés mères et des entreprises donneuses d'ordre, 2017*.

Sabockis, D. (2022), *Competition and Green Public Procurement in EU Law*, Jure Forlag, Stockholm.

Sack, D. and Sarter, E.K. (2022), 'To comply or to be committed? Public procurement and labour rights in global supply chains' *Global Social Policy*, 22(3), pp. 521–539.

Sanchez-Graells, A. (2019a), 'Some Reflections on the 'Artificial Narrowing of Competition' as a Check on Executive Discretion in Public Procurement', in: Bogojevic, S., Groussot, X. and Hettne, J. (eds.), *Discretion in EU Procurement Law*, Hart, Oxford, p. 79.

Sanchez-Graells, A. (2019b), 'Public procurement and 'core' human rights: a sketch of the European Union legal framework', in: Martin-Ortega, O. and Methven O'Brien, C., *Public Procurement and Human Rights: Opportunities, Risks and Dilemmas for the State as Buyer*, Edward Elgar, Cheltenham.

Schooner, S.L. and Speidel, M. (2020), '"Warming Up" to Sustainable Procurement', *Contract Management*, 60(10), p. 32.

Schotanus, F. and Nicholas, R. (2023), 'Coercive, Memetic and Normative Influences on the Uptake of Sustainable Public Procurement: An Institutional Perspective', in: Janssen, W. and Caranta, R. (eds.), *Mandatory Sustainability Requirements in* EU Public Procurement Law, Hart, Oxford.

Tátrai, T. and Diófási-Kovács, O. (2021), *European Green Deal – the way to Circular Public Procurement* 22 ERA Forum 523.

Treviño-Lozano, L. and Uysal, E. (2023), 'Bridging the gap between corporate sustainability due diligence and EU public procurement', *Maastricht Journal of European and Comparative Law*, 1.

UNHRC (2011): UN Human Rights Council (2011), *Guiding Principles on Business and Human Rights: Implementing the United Nations 'Protect, Respect and Remedy' Framework* ('UNGPs'), A/HRC/17/31.

UN System Chief Executives Board for Coordination (nd), Combatting human trafficking and forced labour in UN supply chains. https://unsceb.org/combatting-human-trafficking-and-forced-labour-un-supply-chains.

UNEP (2021): United Nations Environment Programme (2021), *Sustainable Public Procurement How to 'Wake the Sleeping Giant'*. Available at https://wedocs.unep.org/bitstream/handle/20.500.11822/37045/SPPWSG.pdf.

United Nations Environment Programme (2022): UNEP (2022) Sustainable *Public Procurement: 2022 Global Review*. Available at www.oneplanetnetwork.org/sites/default/files/2023-01/377_I_UNEP_Global_Report_2022_EN.pdf.

World Bank (2021), 'A Global Procurement Partnership for Sustainable Development – An International Stocktaking of Developments in Public Procurement', https://documents1.worldbank.org/curated/en/173331642410951798/pdf/Synthesis-Report.pdf.

# 3 Socially responsible public procurement

## How to transform will into reality

*Kristina Vasileva*

### 3.1 Introduction

Public procurement acquired new dimensions in recent decades, going beyond the elementary satisfaction of certain needs. Public procurement is connected to public policies through its horizontal nature. It could be also perceived as an important demand-side policy instrument that maximizes policy results in different areas. A key argument supporting the view that public procurement is an important policy instrument is that it accounts for about 14% of the European Union (EU) GDP (European Commission, 2017). On a different note, the protection and promotion of human rights is a milestone of all European policies and actions. The EU makes sure that fundamental rights are taken into account when developing EU law and actions, and it promotes human rights in its external relations. The protection of fundamental rights is a horizontal issue that affects all fields of EU activity. This means they must be taken into consideration by all government bodies in their work, regardless of their level or the topics they cover. Right here is the point of contact between human rights and public procurement. Socially responsible public procurement (SRPP), as a form of strategic procurement, can be seen as complementing the traditional mechanisms of protection of human rights. SRPP can furthermore reinforce and extend EU-level policy, including its interaction with international policies. The issue of social considerations in public procurement is not a new one and it is already on the EU strategic agenda, because public procurement is recognized as a strategic tool to support sustainable, social policy objectives and innovation. The relevance of that issue has increased also due to the unprecedented events of recent years and the subsequent economic and social crisis. Public procurement consideration is a matter of relevance and is reinforced by the complexity of tasks to be solved on the agenda of governments and modern public administrations. Some European member states (MSs) have taken appropriate measures and are achieving results in SRPP, while others are not coping so well. There are already lessons learned which indicate that new approaches and practices of social and strategic procurement in general should be adopted so that the wish turns into reality. It is necessary to apply strategic approaches and practices systematically in order to achieve optimal results through public procurement as a policy instrument. This can be facilitated by broad political and practical support.

DOI: 10.4324/9781032631721-5

This report examines human rights issues in the context of the EU political, strategic, and regulatory framework in the field of public procurement, and it also makes analysis of some aspects that are applied in the practice. Based on this, conclusions are drawn and recommendations provided to improve the practice and results of a social approach to public procurement.

## 3.2 Socially responsible public procurement

### *3.2.1 Strategic public procurement*

One of the main characteristics of the public procurement concept is that procurement is awarded in areas intended to satisfy public needs. Public procurement can be defined as 'acquisition by one or several contracting authorities through public procurement contracts for works, supplies or services from contractors chosen by them, intended for the needs of public buyers, and in the case of utilities – for the implementation of sectoral activities' (Pavlova, 2017, p. 12). At the same time, the rationale, purpose, and starting point of public procurement should always be related to the solution of public issues and meeting human needs or global challenges such as environmental or health problems. The concept of sustainable development from the point of view of public procurement brings procurement into a strategic dimension beyond the elementary satisfaction of certain needs (Pavlova & Vasileva, 2023). strategic public procurement (SPP) involves the award of environmental ('green'), socially responsible and innovative public procurement.

Although the notions of sustainable and strategic public procurement are often used interchangeably, a broader concept stands behind the notion of SPP, including innovative public procurement. Sustainable public procurement is defined as a process whereby public authorities purchase goods, services, and works in a value-for-money way based on the lifecycle costing of products and services, thus generating benefits not only for the organization, but also for the society and the economy, while minimizing environmental damages. On the other hand, 'green' public procurement can be considered as a process by which public authorities seek to obtain products, services, and works of a reduced environmental impact. SRPP takes into account one or more social considerations to achieve social goals, and innovative procurement involves purchasing the process of innovation or the results of innovation. In any case, SPP objectives go beyond the point of simply meeting a specific need identified by public authorities.

### *3.2.2 Strategic public procurement as a policy instrument*

As it was already mentioned, public procurement represent a significant share of the EU GDP, around €2 trillion per year. It amounts to over $13 trillion annually at global level (United Nations, 2022). Public procurement is not only a main pillar of strategic management and service delivery, but also a key economic activity. If used strategically, it can improve the competitiveness of market economies, as well as help deliver important policy outcomes in response to today's societal and economic challenges, especially when it comes to creating sustainable growth and jobs. Public procurement that takes into account social, economic, and environmental aspects plays a strategic role in transforming the markets of more sustainable products and services. This justifies the consideration of public procurement as a policy instrument that can be used to support the efforts to address not only the 'triple planetary crisis',[1] but also important socio-economic issues such as human and labour rights, diversity, inclusion, and gender equality.

Public procurement is connected to public policies through its horizontal nature. It is an overall instrument of all sectorial policies due to the fact that all MSs' policies are implemented through expenditure of public funds in compliance with the common legislation.

On the other hand, the study of public policy refers to what the state does in its activity with respect to community cohesion and upholding the order in the society. The public policy approach is a continuation of theories about the modern state which through its legitimate institutions brings rationality to society. A classic understanding of public policy is that it is whatever governments choose to do or not to do (Dye, 2008). The truth is that a single definition does not exist – there is a whole concept behind the notion. The concept of public policies refers to the measures any government stands behind, which trigger a change in the behaviour of individuals and ultimately in community development (Tomova, 2022). One of the basic assumptions of public policy science is that public policy can be defined as a temporary organization for achievement of goals. In the same vein, public policy could be considered as government-supported actions that are taken to change the social environment in a direction desired by the community (Tomova, 2022).

The measures by which legitimate authorities and their institutions achieve the goals formulated at political level are in fact the public policy instruments (Tomova, 2003). The instruments are part of the actual implementation of public policy (Borrás & Edquist, 2013) and may serve different purposes and lead to different results and effects. This implies that the choice of policy instruments is an important point in policy formulation, as it has a direct effect on the implementation outcomes. In other words – and this could be taken as a conventional and general definition – the public policy instruments are a set of techniques used by government bodies to exercise their powers in an attempt to ensure support and effect (or prevent) social change. They represent management techniques that in one way or another involve the use of state power or deliberate limitation thereof. It comes as no surprise that the instruments can be, and have been, categorized in a variety of ways in scientific literature. Thus, for example, by their nature they can be mandatory or voluntary, and by their aims – social or economic, etc. Public procurement can be considered as an economic instrument of public policy implementation. Some authors even view public procurement as part of a new generation of innovation policy instruments. On another note, according to its inherent market impact, public procurement is also a demand-side market mechanism. Supply and demand are major catalysts in the 'Smith's invisible hand'[2] notion. It is well known that demand should be supported not only by willingness and a need of goods, but also by sufficient resources for their provision. Hence, a key argument supporting the view of public procurement as an important policy instrument is the significant amount of public expenditures through the public procurement system. Considering its high funding potential, public procurement can be regarded as an important demand-side policy instrument (Borrás & Edquist, 2013; Rolfstam, 2009; Edler & Georghiou, 2007) that affects both the speed and the direction of development.

Conceptually, at least two types of participants interact in the public procurement process – a contracting authority and a candidate/participant(s). In the case of SPP, this interaction aims to solve a specific 'problem'; what is more, it is meant to satisfy an identified need of public interest. The solution itself is achieved by using the available knowledge among the participants, which implies mobilization of the existing knowledge and potential of the market. Considered as an act, SPP is a special case of consumer-supplier interaction (von Hippel, 1988). Within this interaction, interactive learning per se takes place (Lundvall, 1992) as a social process governed by institutions. In this way, public authorities participate in market supply formation through the public procurement system.

All mentioned above leads to the logical conclusion that SPP can be used as an instrument of pursuit of various political goals, including the protection and support of EU values such as human dignity, freedom, democracy, equality, rule of law, and of course human rights.

### *3.2.3 Social dimensions of public procurement*

SRPP is about achieving positive social outcomes in public procurement contracts. Procurement affects a large number of people: users of public services, those involved in production and delivery, and the staff of the buying organization. Apart from those directly affected, SRPP also has the potential to influence the wider market on both its demand and supply sides. As mentioned above, SRPP is defined as public procurement that considers one or more social considerations to achieve social goals.

SRPP covers a wide range of social considerations, such as promoting fair employment opportunities and social inclusion, accessibility and design for all, delivering high-quality social, health, education, and cultural services, etc.

Through SRPP, public procurement fulfils its function of a policy instrument – a strategic way to spend public funds in an efficient and sustainable way. SRPP takes into consideration the societal impact of goods, services, and works purchased by the public sector. In addition to the most economically advantageous offer, when applying SRPP, the contracting authorities also pursue social goals, i.e. public procurement achieves social benefits as well, and prevents or mitigates adverse social consequences during procurement implementation. This also includes compliance with the obligations and principles established by the Treaty on the Functioning of the EU (TFEU, 2016) and the Charter of Fundamental Rights of the European Union (2012), as well as the United Nations (UN) Convention on the Rights of Persons with Disabilities (2006), such as dignity, solidarity, equality before the law, and non-discrimination. Human rights that are protected by the Charter of Fundamental Rights of the EU cover the right of non-discrimination on the basis of gender, racial or ethnic origin, religion or belief, disability, age or sexual orientation, the right of personal data protection, and the right of access to justice. The use of SRPP can also contribute to the implementation of international commitments such as the UN Sustainable Development Goals[3] (SDG, 2015). Social goals can be attained by setting requirements and conditions at all stages of the procurement process through exclusion grounds, selection and award criteria, technical specifications, contract implementation requirements, etc., provided that they are not discriminatory and are relevant to the subject matter. In addition to the TFEU and the mentioned international human rights acts and agreements, public procurement in the EU, SRPP included, must be awarded in compliance with the 2014 Public Procurement Directives (Directive 2014/24/EU and Directive 2014/25/EU) and Directive 2009/81/EC if applicable, as well as international agreements to which the EU is a party, for example the World Trade Organization Agreement on Government Procurement (GPA, 2012) and others alike in the field.

### *3.2.4 Public procurement and human rights*

Humans and their prosperity are at the core of societies' development, social progress, and scientific and technological achievements. The exercise of human rights gives rise to responsibilities and obligations, not only towards other individuals, but also towards the society in general and to the future generations. Human rights are therefore one of the pillars of sustainable development and any effort to uphold them is worth considering.

Human rights are rights that are inherent to all human beings. They are universal legal guarantees protecting individuals and groups against actions that interfere with fundamental freedoms and human dignity.

Human rights are:

- Applicable to all human beings;
- Equally valuable, meaning that there is no hierarchy of human rights;
- Universal, meaning that they should be enjoyed by everyone equally, irrespective of race, gender, ethnic origin, religion, age, or other protected status.

Human rights consist of various rights and freedoms, which are thematically separated into two main groups: civil and political rights; and economic, social, and cultural rights. Civil and political rights protect people mainly against the state power and its unjustified interference in their lives. Cultural rights are related to education and enjoyment of the benefits of cultural freedom and scientific progress. Economic and social rights ensure that every person is provided with conditions to enable them to satisfy their basic economic and social needs; those rights are closely related to public welfare. Therefore, states should take the necessary steps to enable citizens to fully exercise their economic and social rights.

Public procurement is essential in facilitating the states to discharge their duties to protect, respect, and fulfil human rights. In fact, public procurement can also build upon this function. As 'mega-consumers', governments potentially have the purchasing power to set standards that can shift markets towards more humane norms of practice and competition, and to exercise leverage over suppliers responsible for any transgressions (Methven O'Brien et al., 2016). In other words, public procurement can stimulate the emergence of socially conscious markets, as well as support integration and inclusion.

As a rule, the public procurement cycle consists of planning, an award process, and contract management. The range of goods, services, and works procured by public authorities is quite diverse – from large-scale infrastructure and urban development projects, acquisition of complex items such as weapons systems or procurement of essential public services in the health and social care sectors, to the purchase of common goods such as stationery, furniture, and groceries. The wide scope of public procurement subjects implies an unavoidably high risk of human rights violations, including along the supply chains in the public procurement implementation process.

The nature of those potential risks and their link with public procurement is an essential question. Different examples of public procurement practices associated with abuse of human rights could be presented. It was found out that licensed apparel for U.S. military stores, purchased through public procurement, was produced in a factory in Bangladesh where one-third of the workforce were children (Methven O'Brien et al., 2016). Violations of the ban on child labour also occur in the electronics sector due to the extractive industries that supply raw materials, for example, as many as 1.5 million children worked in gold mines, as of 2016. Forced labour is another example of violation of human rights: it was revealed that the rubber content of plastic gloves procured by the public healthcare sector in Denmark had been sourced from plantations relying on forced labour. Human rights abuse by means of forced labour has also been exposed in supply chains in the IT sector, where systematic exploitation of Chinese students occurs in production. Furthermore, human rights abuse in relation to working conditions can be pointed out too, for example illegal wages and working hours. In Chinese factories that supply goods to many governments' contractors in the United States and Europe, working conditions are sometimes very harsh. For example, overtime is dramatically above the allowed threshold – 286 hours per month against a legal limit of 36 hours. What is more, this work is often unpaid. Unsafe working conditions are one of the most common violations. Licensed insignia for U.S. military service were found in the garbage of a factory that killed 112 workers in Bangladesh. In Peru, workers who extract minerals for the electronics industry are exposed to mercury without personal protective equipment. A large share of common surgical instruments, such as scissors and forceps, used by healthcare providers in Sweden and the United Kingdom, are manufactured in Sialkot, Pakistan, where hazardous working conditions were also revealed. The right of freedom of association can be affected by the public procurement system too. For example, the Danish government was found to procure military uniforms from a factory in Bangladesh within an Export Processing Zone where trade unions were prohibited.

Of course, the aforementioned list of examples where the set of rights may be violated in the public procurement process is by no means exhaustive. Similar examples are: discrimination and unequal treatment, violation of freedom and security rights, etc. These practices show how public procurement markets have a negative impact on human rights due to low requirements for participation in the procedures, weak contract implementation control or insufficient supply chains verification, to mention just a few.

As shown, contracting authorities may happen to violate human rights during the procurement process, albeit indirectly and not by conscious actions. Therefore, public procurement should be first approached as a mandatory instrument of fulfilling the obligations related to human rights, and second as a policy instrument to turn those obligations into pursuit of sustainable development goals.

### *3.2.5 SRPP in the context of EU public procurement legislation*

After World War II, international concern for human rights rose at a global level. As a result, human rights were introduced in international and regional treaties and declarations. There are several 'core' human rights treaties that set out states' obligations with regard to human rights, namely:

- Universal Declaration of Human Rights – 'The Universal Declaration of Human Rights (UDHR, 1948) is a milestone document in the history of human rights. Drafted by representatives with different legal and cultural backgrounds from all regions of the world, the Declaration was proclaimed by the United Nations General Assembly in Paris on 10 December 1948 (General Assembly resolution 217 A) as a common standard of achievements for all peoples and all nations. It sets out, for the first time, fundamental human rights to be universally protected and it has been translated into over 500 languages. The UDHR is widely recognized as having inspired, and paved the way for, the adoption of more than seventy human rights treaties, applied today on a permanent basis at global and regional levels (all containing references to it in their preambles)' (UDHR, 1948).
- International Covenant on Civil and Political Rights: A Global Treaty for Human Rights – the International Covenant on Civil and Political Rights (ICCPR, 1966) was opened for signature on 19 December 1966, and entered into force on 23 March 1976. The ICCPR elaborates upon most of the civil and political rights set forth in the UDHR, including the right to non-discrimination. It also mentions several rights that are not listed in the UDHR, for example the right of all peoples to self-determination and the right of ethnic, religious, and linguistic minorities to enjoy their own culture, religion, and language (Burns, 2023).
- International Covenant on Economic, Social and Cultural Rights (ICESCR, 1966) – it came into force in 1976 and is one of the main legally binding instruments of worldwide application. It was drafted in order to expand on the rights outlined in the UDHR, and to give them legal force.

The UDHR, ICESCR, ICCPR, and their respective Optional Protocols altogether form the International Bill of Rights[4] – a cornerstone of international human rights law. Other core human rights treaties further elaborate on the rights of specific groups, including women, children, people with disabilities, and migrant workers, and expand the prohibition of racial discrimination, torture, etc. In addition, the core labour standards of the International Labour Organization (ILO) also aim at human rights protection: non-discrimination in the workplace, freedom from child labour, freedom of association and collective bargaining, and freedom from forced labour. These are complemented by many other important ILO standards in areas such as health and safety at work, wages, and social protection. Public procurement refers to the process by which public bodies, such as government departments/ministries, local or municipal authorities, and state-owned enterprises purchase works, goods, or services from businesses. This means that public procurement actually touches upon all aspects of human rights that can be affected during the process.

At EU level, the Convention for the Protection of Human Rights and Fundamental Freedoms, better known as the European Convention on Human Rights (European Court of Human Rights), was opened for signature in Rome on 4 November 1950 and entered into force on 3 September 1953. It was the first instrument to give effect to some of the rights set out in the Universal Declaration of Human Rights and make them binding in the EU. The respect for it is enshrined in the Treaty of Amsterdam (1997). Moreover, the Treaty contains provisions on specifically empowering the Community to combat discrimination based on gender, racial or ethnic origin, religion or belief, disability, age, or sexual orientation (Article 6a). Declaration 22 on persons with disabilities to the Treaty of Amsterdam states that when preparing measures for the gradual creation of the internal market, the Community institutions must take into account the needs of persons with disabilities. With the Treaty of Lisbon (2007), Europe committed to achieving 'a highly competitive social market economy that aims at full employment and social progress' and to 'combat social exclusion and discrimination [and] […] promote social justice and protection, equality between women and men, solidarity between generations and protection of the rights of the child' (Art. 3, para. 3 from the Treaty of Lisbon).

All principles and obligations stated in the Treaties are reflected in the secondary EU legislation. Public procurement is no exception. The obligations of the states in the field of human rights are applicable to all public bodies and organizations when purchasing goods, services, and works through the public procurement system.

### *3.2.6 The spirit of EU law*

The principles of the Treaties should be respected in the development and application of secondary EU legislation. Based on everything mentioned above, it follows that respect for human rights is one of the basic obligations of states, and therefore its aspects are reflected in a number of provisions of the current European legislation and also in the field of public procurement. Approaches and opportunities to include special social considerations in the public procurement process are laid down in the legislation of 2014 – Directive 2014/24/EU and Directive 2014/25/EU (hereinafter: Public Procurement Directives). Apart from the specific provisions of the legislative acts, the foundation and the starting point for the implementation of the legislation are the principles underlying it – or in other words, the spirit of the law.

Procurement principles are traditionally considered to include equal treatment, non-discrimination, transparency, and proportionality. The Public Procurement Directives include two new principles. Firstly, the new legislation states that procurement shall not be designed with the intention to exclude it from their scope or to narrow competition artificially. Secondly, MSs should take appropriate measures to ensure compliance with the environmental, social, and labour law established by EU legislation, national law, collective agreements, or international provisions. These two new principles can be interpreted as the principle of open competition and the sustainability principle (Andhov, 2023). It should be pointed out that there are varied opinions in the academic and professional circles as to whether the two new 'additions' can be truly accounted for as public procurement principles.

On the one hand, compliance with the mandatory social and labour legislation at the stages of public procurement award and contract implementation is not a matter of choice, but an obligation under the provisions of the Public Procurement Directives. Article 18, para. 2 of Directive 2014/24/EU, which is a new addition to the procurement principles (resp. Art. 36, para. 2 of Directive 2014/25/EU) states the following: 'Member States shall take appropriate measures to ensure that in the performance of public contracts economic operators comply with applicable obligations in the fields of environmental, social and labour law established by Union law, national law, collective agreements or by the international environmental, social and labour law provisions listed in Annex X'. The inclusion of Article 18(2) in the Directive 2014/24/EU is viewed as a milestone in achieving sustainable public procurement market. However, the provision raises some questions and there are diverse opinions on whether this is truly a principle. First comes the question of the binding nature of the provision. Inasmuch as the text creates a somewhat generic duty, since it is addressed to MSs rather than the contracting authorities, the legal consequences of this provision are unclear. This could be considered as a prerequisite for potentially limited enforceability (Andhov, 2023.). The EU Court of Justice in turn provides some clarity on the application of the provision (Curia, C-395/18 Tim SpA), confirming that the new legislation of 2014 sought to establish the provision of Article 18(2) as a principle. Article 18(2) lists sources of the applicable obligations; these include national and EU law, and international laws that were referred to before the mentioned Annex X. The core ILO Conventions, for example the ones on abolition of forced labour discrimination, employment, and occupation or equal remuneration, etc. are included. The clarification that appropriate measures should be applied to ensure compliance and performance of public contracts is given in recital 40 of Directive 2014/24/EU. The recital indicates that the relevant control should be performed at all stages of the public procurement award process.

If the understanding of the provision of Article 18 of the Directive 2014/24/EU as an introduction of a principle is adopted, i.e. not restrictively as an obligation to comply with the minimum requirements defined in special legislation, this will overturn the general understanding of sustainable considerations in the decision-making process in public procurement. There is no one-size-fits-all approach to incorporating human rights requirements into public procurement.

Human rights and their protection can be seen not only as a policy, but also as a political goal, and therefore as a starting point. This makes them interrelated with the principles of any legislation. This is why the adoption of the principle of sustainability as a principle of public procurement is crucial. Should this happen, it seems reasonable to assume that sustainability aspects should be discussed in principle in the context of public procurement and that such conditions and requirements should be set whenever possible. The requirements laid down in certain procedures may go beyond the minimum level set out in the relevant legislation and thus allow MSs or individual contracting authorities to introduce enhanced human rights protection of their own design. For example, recent amendments (effective from 1 January 2021) to the Public Procurement Act (PPA Czech) in the Czech Republic aimed to promote innovative procurement in the country. A new paragraph (in section 6) was introduced adding a new principle in public procurement – 'strategic procurement' – which includes social, environmental, and innovative aspects. It means that contracting authorities have to consider the strategic aspects of every procedure. Moreover, they are obliged to draw a report explaining their approach. In addition, legal definitions of 'socially responsible public procurement', 'environmentally responsible public procurement', and 'innovation' are introduced. The amendments to the Public Procurement Law in the Czech Republic were adopted by an accelerated procedure, and so far there is no evidence that the adopted approach achieved its goal; however, a significant positive effect is expected.

### *3.2.7 Respect for human rights in the public procurement process: is it a matter of choice?*

As already noted, the provision of Article 18, para. 2 of the Directive (Art. 18(2) Dir. 2014/24/EU) is mandatory. With respect to scientific debates, it should be pointed out that some researchers and experts in EU law are of the opinion that the wording of the said provision fails to make clear to whom the binding nature refers: contracting authorities or MSs (Andhov, 2023).

It should be also taken into account that Article 57(1) of Directive 2014/24/EU contains mandatory grounds for exclusion. They cover situations whenever an economic operator has been convicted of criminal offences related to involvement in a criminal organization, corruption, human trafficking, or breach of tax-related obligations. Further to this, discretionary grounds for exclusion pursuant to Article 57(4) EU include the possibility for public authorities to exclude suppliers whenever the contracting authority can demonstrate by any appropriate means a violation of applicable obligations referred to in Article 18(2).

Article 69 of Directive 2014/24/EU is also compliant with social considerations and human rights protection. It requires contracting authorities to reject tenders that are abnormally low due to poor human rights standards, in case the supplier is unable to account for the low price in a satisfactory manner. It is perfectly reasonable to assume that an excessively low price may imply bad and dangerous working conditions, forced or child labour, including the phenomenon of modern slavery, etc., and therefore the presence of such circumstances should be carefully checked by contracting authorities.

Furthermore, the EU public procurement legislation includes provisions directly aimed at providing opportunities for organizations in the social economy sector and social enterprises. The social economy business models aim at reinvesting most of the profits back into the organization and/or a social cause, and having a participatory/democratic form of governance. Social economy encompasses a variety of businesses, organizations, and different legal entities. They share the objective of consistently putting people in the first place, producing a positive impact on local communities and pursuing a social cause. Social economy organizations may include non-profit associations, cooperatives, mutual societies, associations and foundations, and social enterprises.[5] Their primary goal is to have a social impact rather than maximize incomes for owners or shareholders (European Commission, 2021). For example, Articles 20 and 77 of Directive 2014/24/EU and Articles 38 and 94 of Directive 2014/25/EU contain provisions aimed at promoting social inclusion by reserving contracts for social enterprises. The legislation provides the possibility for MSs to reserve the right to participate in public procurement procedures (the so-called reserved procurement) for protected sheltered workshops and economic operators whose main aim is the social and professional integration of disadvantaged persons or persons with disabilities. It is also possible for such a contract to be implemented in the context of structured and stable sheltered employment programmes. To benefit from the reservation, at least 30% of the employees of such workshops, economic operators, or sheltered employment programmes must be persons with disabilities or disadvantaged persons. It is also allowed to reserve certain lots of a contract. Additionally, Article 77 of Directive 2014/24/EU gives the possibility to MSs to reserve procurements for certain services. 'Reservation' may be seen as an effective tool to add social value through public procurement.

It should be pointed out that the above-mentioned provisions are dispositive and do not create an obligation for the contracting authorities according to the 2014 Public Procurement Directives. The reason that reservation is enshrined in the secondary EU legislation as an option, rather than obligation, is probably due to the specific national legislation of MSs in the field of human rights, labour legislation, etc. Consequently, fine-tuning is a matter of national regulation. For example, reservation in Bulgaria is mandatory for the public procurement of certain services, according to the provisions of the Public Procurement Act (Art. 12). The Council of Ministers, at the proposal of the Minister of Labour and Social Policy and by means of written decisions, determines a list of the goods and services according to the Common Procurement Vocabulary,[6] which are intended for award to specialized undertakings or cooperatives of disabled people, or to economic entities whose basic purpose is the social and professional integration of disabled people or people in disadvantaged situations and/or programmes for generation of protected jobs under which contracting authorities have the right to keep procurements. When drawing up the list or adopting the programmes, contracting authorities should take into consideration any current national policies, implemented strategies and programmes, as well as the capacities and the nomenclature of goods and services provided by the undertakings, persons with disabilities or economic operators having the main purpose of social and professional integration of disabled people or people in disadvantaged situations; if needed, the list and the programmes are updated. Central purchasing bodies are excluded from the obligation to reserve procurements which fall within the scope of the quoted list. This example shows the possibility for MSs to establish social obligations for contracting authorities under different conditions through the national legislation.

The provisions of Article 46 of Directive 2014/24/EU and Article 65 of Directive 2014/25/EU, although not directly addressed, may also be considered in the context of the SRPP. These provisions are related to the obligation of contracting authorities to divide contracts into lots whenever possible. This obligation is meant not only to ensure wider access to the public procurement market, including by Small and Medium-Sized Enterprises (SMEs), and to increase competition, but also to provide opportunities for access by organizations from the social economy sector. Whenever contracting authorities are non-compliant with this requirement, they are obliged to indicate the main reasons for their decision. However, the other public procurement principles and the obligation of contracting authorities to protect the public interest in the first place should not be neglected. In this regard, if the division of the contract into lots poses risks to its implementation, the right decision is the one that benefits a larger part of the society.

Although the 2014 Public Procurement Directives are the main EU legislation in this area, one more legislative act deserves attention, given that the main topic is SRPP. A big step towards promoting the practice of SRPP is Directive (EU) 2019/882, also known as the Accessibility Directive. It covers products and services that have been identified as the most important for persons with disabilities while being most likely to have diverging accessibility requirements across the EU countries. It sets out common standards and obligations to harmonize accessibility requirements for these products and services. In the scope of the Accessibility Directive fall products and services such as computers and operating systems, payment terminals and ATMs, smartphones, e-books, etc. Mandatory accessibility requirements for these products and services are applicable from 28 June 2025.

### *3.2.8 Practical aspects of SRPP*

In 2020, the Danish Institute for Human Rights published a toolkit on human rights for policymakers and public buyers. A part of the toolkit is guidance on public procurement – driving change through public procurement (Danish Institute for Human Rights, 2020). The guidance and the tools to support the SRPP application include a description of step-by-step processes so as to achieve optimal results when implementing this type of procurement, minimizing the risks of failure due to lack of capacity, as well as organizational planning.

From a practical point of view, the public procurement cycle involves several stages, and at each stage specific actions may be undertaken with the purpose to integrate human rights considerations. At the planning stage it is crucial to acquire knowledge about human rights, since it is the foundation of the entire process. An essential part of this stage is utilizing public data to identify any reports on human rights issues that may be associated with specific geographic regions, countries, sectors, or businesses relevant to the tender. Additionally, it is vital to initiate dialogue with various stakeholders, such as supplier associations, workers, civil society actors, and communities potentially impacted by human rights abuses. This dialogue would help gain a deeper understanding of the human rights context on the specific market and identify areas where immediate progress could be made, as well as areas requiring longer-term change.

During the preparation stage, several considerations are at play. An essential step is the introduction of exclusion grounds for suppliers found responsible for committing serious abuse of human rights by courts or other official bodies. This stage also involves identifying social labels or certificates relevant to the procured goods, services, or works. The selection criteria should be simple, transparent, easily achievable by suppliers and assessable by public buyers, requiring from the suppliers to, for example, have a policy in place addressing human rights. The award criteria should consider human rights protection by using quality assessment indicators as part of the evaluation methodology. Contract implementation requirements are also crucial at this stage, including a demand for suppliers to disclose reports on labour issues, discrimination, harassment, and other relevant concerns. Suppliers may also present a risk-management strategy related to human rights and cascade these contractual requirements down to their sub-contractors.

At the contract management and implementation stage it is of paramount importance to establish dialogue with suppliers about goals, risks, expectations, and their plans to comply with the contractual requirements related to human rights. The development of monitoring and control systems for contract implementation concerning human rights is also a key aspect. An appropriate approach is to ask suppliers to report annually on their compliance with human rights requirements under the contract, and these reports should be discussed with suppliers to help them develop action points addressing identified risks and opportunities. Finally, it is also important to adapt existing termination and escalation clauses to include cases of severe abuse of human rights as grounds for remedial action and termination, ensuring a comprehensive approach to human rights integration in the entire public procurement cycle.

It is necessary to discuss some features at the stages of preparation and conduct of the procedure, and the obstacles that may appear during this process. Undoubtedly, the first and most important step towards SRPP is to recognize social goals as a policy line at the highest political level, and public procurement as an instrument to maximize the results of these policies. At the organizational level, too, everything begins with the desire and will to achieve results in this field. SRPP requires leadership and commitment across management structures, from the political level to key decision-makers and budget holders (European Commission,

2021). On organizational level, some public buyers already have procurement policies or strategies in place about green or sustainable procurement. These could be an appropriate fundament for identification of SRPP opportunities. By analysis of priorities and mapping of current procurement policies and activities, for example, the social objectives of the highest relevance can be identified.

#### *3.2.8.1 Planning and forecasting stages*

SRPP is not an end in itself. No public procurement of this type starts on the idea that social procurement should be made. This process begins with needs identification. Once those needs have been identified, it is time to decide how they could be met. At this point the social element may be introduced for the first time. Can we satisfy the needs by incorporating social considerations? Stakeholders and experts in the field of human and labour rights can best answer this question, and their involvement in the decision-making process is appropriate at this early stage. Unlike green public procurement, which gained popularity in recent years and has practical tools at its disposal already developed within the EU and at national level in many MSs to help contracting authorities, knowledge and skills seem limited regarding the implementation of SRPP. For example, there are various guides and toolkits available to contracting authorities, which define product groups particularly suitable for the inclusion of green requirements and proposals for such specific requirements, while guides and toolkits for SRPP are not yet sufficiently widespread.

In the realm of public procurement, several good practices have emerged across Europe, highlighting the integration of sustainable and socially responsible approaches. One such initiative is the Procura+ Network,[7] a collaboration of European public authorities and regions dedicated to sustainable and innovative procurement. This network serves as a platform for members to connect, share insights, and take collective action in the field of sustainable procurement.

Another good example is SRPP strategy development. In Germany, the Competence Centre for Sustainable Procurement at the Federal Ministry of the Interior, developed jointly with the Federal Association for Information Technology, Telecommunications and New Media (Bitkom) a common strategy, published in May 2019, aimed at the procurement of sustainable information and communications technology (ICT) products and services (European Commission, 2021, p. 26). The primary objective of this joint initiative is to ensure that public buyers and suppliers collaborate effectively to uphold social standards and fair working conditions within the global ICT production supply chain, encompassing various ILO Conventions. The process included stakeholder consultations with feedback from over 20 representatives of civil societies, churches, and other public buyers.

Meanwhile in Finland, Hansel, a central purchasing body, focused on embedding social responsibility in the procurement of computers and laptops (European Commission, 2020). This focus stemmed from the recognition that these products are frequently manufactured in countries with insufficient enforcement of human and labour rights. To address this issue, Hansel produced a Code of Conduct (Code of Conduct for Suppliers, 2018) that aimed to promote and ensure decent working conditions across the entire supply chain of computers and other ICT products.

These practices exemplify how public procurement can be leveraged to foster sustainable and socially responsible outcomes, demonstrating a commitment to ethical standards and the betterment of working conditions globally.

At the planning stage, a decision should be made regarding the type of procedure, the value and type of the contract (contract or framework agreement), the use of lots, variants of offers, etc. In practice, there are generally two opposing views on the choice of type of procedure. The first is that the procedures introduced by the 2014 Public Procurement Directives are not flexible enough and do not meet the modern needs of contracting authorities. On the other hand, there is a view that public procurement procedures are too formalized, which complicates, delays, and limits the procurement process and the application of sustainability principles. In this point of view, the 'hard' original contract conditions, which must be observed until the final procurement phase, and the prohibition of amending the contracts outside the cases specified in the legislation, leave contracting authorities with their hands tied. However, there is the opposite opinion that each of the formally stated procedures can be conducted in an innovative way that provides the necessary flexibility. An example of the application of an innovative, and at the same time legally compliant, approach with regard to a completely routine procedure is Dublin City Council's procurement of safety ring buoys (European Assistance for Innovation Procurement, 2019). The selected type of procedure is an open procedure in combination with a two-phase evaluation approach (including a testing phase) for the award of a framework agreement. In addition, the 2014 Public Procurement Directives allow the choice of procedures with a negotiation stage or development stages under certain conditions.

Another practical issue to be addressed here is the practice of appeals and audit bodies in the context of social procurement. Social requirements should be in compliance with the legislation. When deciding on such requirements, contracting authorities should take caution and avoid possible discriminatory nature of the requirements or restriction of competition. Public procurement should be awarded lawfully in the first place. It is a valid point that the fear of sanctions and the delay or procedure termination could act as a disincentive for contracting authorities to apply SRPP. The yet untrodden path of SRPP requires from the contracting authorities to show not only skills and creativity, but also courage to initiate and carry out such a project.

Next comes the discussion, even at this early stage, on how the contract type and duration could affect the social value of public procurement. Long-term contracts can lead to less competition, as well as higher costs, for the contracting authority, but on the other hand they can act as an incentive for suppliers to offer solutions with higher social returns, due to the potential to win multiple contracts and therefore recoup any additional expense involved in implementing these solutions. There is also the natural clash between the usual considerations related to competition, equality, economic efficiency, etc., and those of achieving social benefits.

Dividing the contract into lots can, on the one hand, guarantee wider opportunities for participation by smaller operators, organizations from the social economy sector, or social enterprises. On the other hand, the use of lots may in some cases jeopardize the quality of implementation due to the need to coordinate different contractors under the respective lots. Therefore, the volume and nature of specific public procurement, and its complexity as a whole, should be taken into account and a balanced decision should be made.

#### *3.2.8.2 Preparation stage*

The preparation stage of the public procurement cycle is perhaps the one at which social considerations can be approached most broadly. This is the stage of procedure programming. Requirements are formulated of what we want to purchase and who we will purchase it from, under certain conditions. In order to set requirements that achieve the pursued social goals as much as possible, good knowledge of the relevant market and supply chains is necessary. The usual supply chains' opacity can affect the procedure negatively. This is where stakeholder expertise comes in, which can be helpful in formulating the requirements. Knowledge of labels and certifications related to social objectives can also be used at this stage. It should be borne in mind, however, that despite the formulation of appropriate requirements in pursuit of social goals, those requirements should still be consistent with the capacity of market participants to fulfil them and, respectively, the expected quality and quantity of bids. Just as the right diagnosis in medicine constitutes 90% of the treatment, the choice should be the right one to meet the relevant needs: appropriate requirements for products, services, and works, for those who will supply/perform them, and an evaluation approach to tenders which implies efficiency and high procurement results (with added value, contributing to sustainable development).

Accessibility, fair trade, social inclusion, and employment opportunities for disadvantaged groups may be promoted through various good practices in public procurement, for example use of technical specifications, selection criteria, award criteria, and contract conditions.

Technical specifications, for example, should reflect the needs of all people, including those with physical disabilities. Here the importance of requirements of fair trade, sustainable farming and responsible sourcing can also be highlighted.

In terms of selection criteria, bidders could be required to demonstrate their ability to manage their staff with disadvantaged groups, to apply quality management systems, including those for disabled access, or to apply good practices or standards of staff management.

The award criteria could include allocation of a certain percentage of available points for tenders based on the number and quality of employment opportunities for disadvantaged workers, with specific plans for their recruitment, training, and retention.

A good example of draft contractual terms focused on accessibility and social inclusion are those related to ICT equipment. Contractors could be required to provide accessible equipment for persons with disabilities, including training sessions and dedicated helpdesk support. Or under advertising contracts, for example, contractors should reach out to the target groups mentioned in the specifications and implement special measures to involve elderly users, persons suffering from social isolation, and persons without internet access. Draft contracts should foresee regular reviews of the measures, while contractors are expected to implement any necessary remedial measures.

#### *3.2.8.3 Pre-award stage*

The pre-award stage (or the stage of conducting procurement) runs from the moment of publication until the contract award, and it seems to involve the least concrete SRPP supporting actions. At this stage, procurement rules are observed, and this includes implementation of the already determined evaluation methodology. The focus at this stage is primarily on the application of the general procurement principles and legality. Despite this, evaluation committees have some instruments to support SRPP. Assessment of abnormally low tenders and the use of the possibility to verify declared circumstances and request additional information about the bid are an appropriate way to achieve the necessary assurance that social requirements will be met during contract implementation. In an effort to address the issue of abnormally low tenders in public procurement, the Walloon Public Procurement Commission in Belgium initiated a commendable practice under its Action Plan on Responsible Procurement (Plan d'actions achats publics responsables 2017–2019, 2017). To tackle this challenge, the Commission established a working group consisting of a diverse range of experts and stakeholders. Their primary focus was to investigate the causes and implications of abnormally low tenders in procurement processes. A key outcome of this initiative is the mandatory rejection of bids where abnormally low pricing is identified as a result of non-compliance with applicable social and labour laws or collective agreements. By taking such measures, the Commission not only promotes ethical standards in procurement but also safeguards the rights and well-being of workers and the integrity of the procurement process.

#### *3.2.8.4 Contract implementation stage (contract management)*

The contract implementation stage can be seen as the most important procurement stage in terms of achieving the set objectives and expected outcomes. As Figure 3.1 shows, most of the actions that could be directed to SRPP support are part of the preparatory stage. But it is equally important to control the contract implementation stage and above all the parties' compliance with the obligations.

The report Sustainable Public Procurement: Global Review 2022 (United Nations, 2022, p. 22) of the United Nations Environment Program makes an attempt to identify the most effective stages of the procurement cycle introducing sustainable procurement considerations. The report includes the results of a conducted survey. Based on the answers of 263 respondents, it was found out

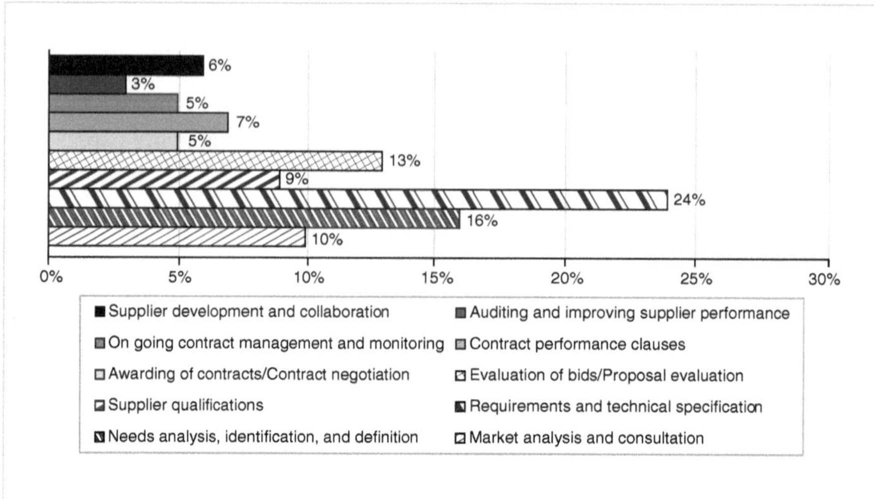


*Figure 3.1* The most effective stages of the procurement cycle to introduce sustainable procurement considerations.

*Source:* Own compilation based on UN (2022, p. 22.).

that the preparatory stage comes first (requirements in the technical specification), followed by the planning stage (needs analysis) and the award stage (bid evaluation) (Figure 3.1).

Although the cited results reveal attitudes and practices related to sustainable procurement in general, a reference to SRPP as a type of sustainable procurement is made. The results show a clear focus on the preparation stage. This sounds reasonable because, as already said, the excellent programming of public procurement is a prerequisite for its high-quality result. On the other hand, even professionally prepared and conducted procurement may not produce the expected result, if contract implementation is not carefully monitored. Figure 3.1 shows that ongoing contract control and ex-post audit are not among the public procurement cycle phases that the respondents find most effective in the context of sustainable procurement. However, could we claim for sure that the introduction of a social clause in the public procurement contract would guarantee its adherence during implementation? Would that be sufficient for contractors to declare that tax-, labour-, and environment-related legislation will be respected in the course of contract implementation? In this sense, the possibilities of the contract implementation stage of the public procurement cycle and the assessment of implementation are worth further discussion.

Commission Notice Buying Social – a guide to taking account of social considerations in public procurement (2nd edition) also indicates that 'It is during the performance of a contract that SRPP commitments are truly put to the test' (European

Commission, 2021, p. 81). Without appropriate contract conditions/clauses – and the means to monitor and enforce them – SRPP will be ineffective. Undoubtedly, the contracting parties are responsible for the implementation of the contract and they should develop and implement an appropriate monitoring and evaluation system. Designating responsible persons for the implementation and reporting of this system on the part of both the contracting authority and the contractor is good practice. It is essential that these persons have the necessary time, information, and motivation to carry out effective control of the compliance with social clauses. The key word here is motivation. What would motivate these persons, which would be their incentives to approach the implementation of the contract beyond the usual formality, to engage personally and impartially? The answer is complex and gives grounds to think in the direction of not what the motivation would be, but who should be motivated. This question is also key in identifying the stakeholders in general, when any project is implemented. Every single public procurement can be considered as an independent project. Stakeholders who have direct interest in the fulfilment of social commitments could be various unions, organizations for protection of the rights of people with disabilities, accessibility experts, non-governmental organizations, citizens, or end users.

A possible way to overcome the weakness in SRPP contract implementation is to involve the stakeholders, including end users, not only in the process of procurement planning and preparation, but also at the stage of contract implementation.

## 3.3 Closing the gap between the will and the results: possible approaches

### *3.3.1 All-level leadership*

Leadership is one of the keys for success in SRPP. This means political commitment in the first place and also top-down leadership coming from the organization's management structures. In principle, it should be fairly easy for all public authorities to take political decisions in this vein. Moreover, the issue of social responsibility in public procurement has already been placed on the EU agenda and an agreement has been reached in this regard, including in the context of European human rights policy and the European social model as a whole. The focus should be on organizational leadership. Continued leadership and a strategic vision are needed to ensure sustained implementation of strategic procurement practices. Practitioners need strong, supportive and ongoing leadership that sets a vision of how objectives would be achieved and how procurement strategies and practices would support this vision.

### *3.3.2 Cooperation and stakeholder involvement*

Contract clauses are only one part of the solution. In order to achieve success, dialogue and partnership with the suppliers is essential. This should start before the tender is launched and continue throughout the implementation of the contract. This means that an appropriate instrument is needed to be used at all stages of the procurement process. Actually, a similar tool is already available to contracting authorities. The so-called Integrity Pact[8] aims to ensure a transparent and fair procurement process at all stages (Transparency International, 2021). If adapted appropriately, it could be used to improve the results of the implementation of SRPP.

Integrity Pacts are primarily seen as a tool to effectively tackle corruption by ensuring greater transparency and accountability (Transparency International, 2022). This is no doubt true, but it does not exhaust the functions and capabilities of this tool. In fact, its application can also strive to achieve other goals, for example, of social nature. Typically, an Integrity Pact is defined as a mechanism for cooperation between a public authority and one or more civil society organizations to ensure that authorities and tenderers act within legal constraints, take action in relation to corruption hazards, and promote public trust in the procurement process. In broader terms, Integrity Pacts can be seen as collective action to achieve a specific goal or goals. In this sense, the use of such a mechanism to ensure more efficient SRPP awarding seems appropriate and would help solve the main question – how to practically enhance the effect of SRPP. Integrity Pacts tend to boost civil society's and citizens' engagement and trust in public institutions, and promote awareness and better understanding of public procurement.

There are generally three parties in the process of using Integrity Pacts: in addition to the contracting authority and representatives of civil society organizations, and the economic operator/s, candidates/participants, and contractors may be also involved. Bidder participation is optional but recommended. Contracting authorities and bidders may formally agree to refrain from corrupt practice and conduct a transparent procurement process for each single contract. In all cases, the parties commit through public agreement to refrain from corrupt behaviour and to improve transparency and accountability throughout the public procurement process. Some of the advantages of Integrity Pacts are (Transparency International, 2022):

- Making public procurement more transparent and accountable;
- Increasing public policy transparency and accountability;
- Increasing citizens' trust in the process and in the administration;
- Involving civil society in the monitoring of public procurement;
- Providing end users with the opportunity to participate in the public procurement process and to evaluate contract implementation.

This form of agreement (Integrity Pact) provides for an independent mechanism led by a civil society organization to monitor compliance with the agreement. The mechanism implies the possibility of involving independent observers and representatives of the civil society in the process of awarding specific public contracts, including in the activities of control and reporting of contract execution. The instrument is an expression of the recognition of the role and effect of the civil society on the monitoring of public contracts. If the instrument (and hopefully other instruments of similar nature) turns into regular practice, the results of public procurement will be perhaps better. Creating more opportunities for citizen-led monitoring should be also prioritized in SRPP.

Apart from being a form of potential response against corruption, Integrity Pacts can be qualified by other functional aspects too. One such aspect is the ability to involve stakeholders, including end users, and the civil society as a whole, in the overall decision-making and implementation process related to public procurement. This makes it particularly relevant in the context of SRPP, where the ultimate beneficiaries of the outcomes – be it infrastructure, generated jobs, or better and decent working conditions – may guide the process, participate in monitoring, and actually assess the outcomes. It should be noted at this point that SRPP is usually defined as such if it contains any of the social conditions and requirements already listed above. Its results are respectively measured through formulated indicators, primarily related to the (non-)fulfillment of these conditions or requirements. For example, during contract implementation, no cases of non-fulfilment of the obligations of labour law enforcement bodies were registered; or two facilities were built for people with disabilities; or 10 working places were opened for people from marginalized groups; and so on. This is evaluation based on constituent indicators. These are obvious (observable) indicators. But this approach seems to be insufficient in order to obtain a sufficient and real picture of the results of the administration's activity and the level of administrative capacity in particular. So-called reflective evaluation indicators could be more appropriate for this purpose. For example, such a methodology has already been used in Bulgaria to measure administrative capacity (Bulgarian Institute of Public Administration, 2023). The reflective indicators represent the opinions of the socio-economic partners of the administration. In other words, this is evaluation based on reflective indicators. By applying both approaches simultaneously in a single study and by comparing the results, it is possible to assess the real condition of the object. Used in the context of SRPP, this approach – especially in times when this type of procurement is still in its infancy in a number of countries in Europe – would allow for better in-depth measurement of the impact, the results, and, accordingly, its improvement in the future.

Integrity Pacts can be used in SRPP to enable the application of the mentioned combined approach to the assessment of specific procurement. In this way, the contracting authority's finding that no violations of labour law have been registered (according to the relevant competent authority) can be compared with the assessment of an independent observer from an on-site inspection; or a reported constructed installation for people with disabilities can be assessed by its actual users in terms of accessibility, convenience, and safety.

Other benefits of using such agreements could be discussed. First of all, there is no need of legal changes. The form of cooperation under the instrument is voluntary and hence its regulation is not necessary. The partners under this project (each specific public procurement may be considered an independent project) hold negotiations and voluntarily agree on the terms of the agreement. This possibility of ad hoc use makes it, above all, highly flexible. The parties have the opportunity to take into account the specifics of the order, for example specific market. Next, the use of such an agreement is short-term (quick-acting). It does not impose an administrative burden, does not complicate or delay contract award, but instead follows the process in parallel.

### *3.3.3 Professionalization of public procurement*

Culture changes and the increased focus on the use of strategic procurement need a wider scope of agile practices, market knowledge, and innovative means. Changes require experts with the right skills. The reasoning of some authors and their research (Bandiera et al., 2008) may lead to the reasonable assumption that the lack of professional skills in public procurement can be seen as a substantial problem. The European Commission also finds that the low level of professionalization of public buyers is a systemic problem in many MSs; therefore, it recommends development of long-term strategies for professionalization at the national level (European Commission, 2017). As said above, the implementation of SRPP requires specific knowledge and skills in a wide range of areas, apart from the specific area of public procurement of course. Undoubtedly, the next important key step to promote the practice of SRPP is to build appropriate capacity through the professionalization of public procurement.

### *3.3.4 Development and popularization of tools for SRPP implementation*

As already mentioned, the instruments for application of SRPP are still limited at EU level. Practical tools are needed to help procurement experts. Building up communities to exchange experiences, discuss problems, and strengthen the cooperation in general among experts in this field at the European level could be helpful. The newly created Public Buyers Community Platform,[9] which complements the European Commission's strategy to improve public procurement in the EU by bringing together public authorities and other stakeholders, can be used for this purpose. Such collaborative forums can help identify the needs of practical tools and adapt them to an internationally applied model. They will then help promote these tools and learn from their practical application. Ideas and experiences can be more easily and widely shared in a peer-to-peer environment.

### *3.3.5 Improving data wholeness and transparency*

It is difficult to make a snapshot of SRPP at the European level. Public procurement notices (old standard forms) published in Tenders Electronic Daily (TED) failed to provide structured information on the use of social elements. Contracting authorities have been completing new and updated standard forms (eForms) since 25 October 2023, when Commission Implementing Regulation (EU) 2019/1780 enters into force. New standard forms allow them to provide information on the use of social considerations and accessibility criteria in their public procurement. The updated standard forms include fields that indicate the fact that a procurement procedure seeks to achieve a social goal. The introduction of the new forms is expected to help improve the knowledge and analysis capabilities of SPP in the EU in general. However, any decision concerning the mandatory provision of this data in the announcements should be taken at national level. In Bulgaria, for example, it is stipulated that this data must be indicated in the new forms. On the other hand, contracting authorities are obliged to provide information in TED only for procedures above the EU thresholds. In this way, the information on national public procurement below the EU thresholds remains outside the scope of the data. Therefore, in order to improve the overall picture, consideration should be given to possible establishment of a reporting order for MSs on SRPP, with the results being disseminated.

Next, as already discussed, it is necessary to discuss the possibility of registering the cases in which violations of human rights have been established in SRPP, and any negative experience in the implementation of such projects. To be effectively complete, SRPP also implies post-contract management, i.e. assessment and lessons learned. Data about economic operators who have violated the rules, any registered problems of the supply chains and other information would help contracting authorities be aware of the possible risks in procurement procedures having different subjects and objects, as well as on specific markets. At the same time, information about the number and type of SRPP, as well as detected violations and obstacles, can be maintained in a centralized place, if a European SRPP register is built, for example. Such registry seems appropriate for SPP in general. Currently, various platforms and initiatives exist to support 'green', 'social', or 'innovative' procurement, but the access to information stored in them is fragmentary. The establishment of a single access point for all information about this type of procurement would definitely improve the awareness of interested parties (as well as contracting authorities and economic operators) on the issues of strategic procurement and the opportunities in this area.

## 3.4 Conclusion

From a legal point of view, the consequences of some provisions in the 2014 Public Procurement Directives are unclear. However, this is a separate issue that could be the subject of individual research. The conclusion in this chapter is that compliance with the mandatory social and labour rules is not a matter of choice and it derives from public procurement legislation.

Leadership and strategic vision ensure more resilient implementation of strategic approaches. The political agenda and the strong leadership in public sector organizations play a crucial role in supporting the application of sustainable principles in public procurement, including social ones. Social considerations, on the other hand, are strongly related to human rights and their protection. Public procurement may have strategic contribution to the implementation of EU, regional, and national policies in different areas. This means that the principle of sustainability should be recognized as a principle of public procurement in general. The added value of SPP requires the presence of leading institutions that are capable of translating a given policy into a strategy with concrete, actionable steps, and which create opportunities for different stakeholders, including economic operators, end users, etc. for collaboration, networking, and peer learning. Building up a network of stakeholders in the field of strategic procurement, promoting partnerships for collaboration and opportunities for sharing awareness practices and lessons learned are also needed.

To sum up, it seems that SRPP as a process requires the consideration of sustainable principles at all its stages, but in practice they are applied mainly at the stages of planning, forecasting, and preparation. To be effectively complete, SRPP also implies post-award management – assessment and lessons learned. The evaluation of contract implementation shows real achievements and results. This is precisely the stage at which more efforts are needed.

## Notes

1 'The triple planetary crisis' refers to the three main interlinked issues that humanity currently faces: climate change, pollution and biodiversity loss.

2 'Invisible hand' is metaphor, introduced by the 18th-century Scottish philosopher and economist Adam Smith, that characterizes the mechanisms through which beneficial social and economic outcomes may arise from the accumulated self-interested actions of individuals in free markets.

3 UN Sustainable Development Goals (SDGs) include 17 goals, which are at a heart of the 2030 Agenda for Sustainable Development, adopted by all United Nations Member States in 2015, which provides a shared blueprint for peace and prosperity for people and the planet, now and into the future. SDGs are an urgent call for action by all countries - developed and developing - in a global partnership. They recognize that ending poverty and other deprivations must go hand-in-hand with strategies that improve health and education, reduce inequality, and spur economic growth – all while tackling climate change and working to preserve our oceans and forests.

4 'The International Bill of Rights' is a term used to refer to a group of international human rights treaties and declarations that together form the cornerstone of international human rights law. It includes the Universal Declaration of Human Rights (UDHR), the International Covenant on Economic, Social and Cultural Rights (ICESCR), and the International Covenant on Civil and Political Rights (ICCPR), along with their respective Optional Protocols.

5 Social enterprises are organizations that, regardless of their legal form, combine entrepreneurial activity with a social purpose.

6 The Common Procurement Vocabulary establishes a single classification system for public procurement aimed at standardising the references used by contracting authorities and entities to describe procurement contracts.

7 Procura+ is a network of European public authorities and regions that connect, exchange and act on sustainable and innovation procurement. Available at https://procuraplus.org/home/.

8 'Integrity Pact' is a tool developed by Transparency International for tackling corruption in public procurement.

9 'The Public Buyers Community Platform (2023)' is a European Commission initiative dedicated to facilitating joint action in public purchasing across the EU. It is a space for European public procurers and the European Commission to meet and work together to actively advance public purchasing.

## References

Accessibility Directive: Directive (EU) 2019/882 of the European Parliament and of the Council of 17 April 2019 on the accessibility requirements for products and services.

Andhov, M. (2023), *Procurement Principles, Sustainable Public Procurement Law Course, Sapience Network*. Available at https://sapiensnetwork.eu/trainings/spp-law-course/.

Bandiera, O., Prat, A., and Valletti, T. (2008), *Active and Passive Waste in Government Spending: Evidence from a Policy Experiment*, Economics, Political Science CEIS: Centre for Economic & International Studies Working Paper Series. Available at https://art.torvergata.it/bitstream/2108/37070/1/AER.pdf.

Borrás, S. and Edquist, C. (2013), *The Choice of Innovation Policy Instruments*, Centre for Innovation, Research and Competence in the Learning Economy (CIRCLE, Lund University). Available at https://charlesedquist.files.wordpress.com/2013/02/201304_borrasedquist-21.pdf.

Bulgarian Institute of Public Administration (2023), Metodika za prouchvane na administrativnija kapacitet na dyrzhavnata administracija, na bazata na otrazjavashti pokazateli i ocenka na kapaciteta na administracijata za 2022. Available at www.ipa.government.bg/sites/default/files/m-admin_kapacitet_doklad_final_0.pdf.

Burns, N. (2023), Historical Development of the Human Rights, Britanica. Available at www.britannica.com/topic/human-rights.

Charter of Fundamental Rights of the European Union (2012), OJ C 326, 26.10.2012, pp. 391–407. Available at https://eur-lex.europa.eu/legal-content/EN/TXT/?uri=CELEX%3A12012P%2FTXT.

Code of Conduct for Suppliers (2018), Hansel. Available at www.hansel.fi/media/filer_public/4f/8d/4f8d84e4-bafc-4460-9db3-ee0fcbf483ff/code_of_conduct_132018_eng.pdf.

Commission Implementing Regulation (EU) 2019/1780 of 23 September 2019 establishing standard forms for the publication of notices in the field of public procurement and repealing Implementing Regulation (EU) 2015/1986 (eForms) (Text with EEA relevance). Available at https://eur-lex.europa.eu/eli/reg_impl/2019/1780/oj.

Convention on the Rights of Persons with Disabilities (2006), adopted on 12 December 2006 by Sixty-first session of the General Assembly by resolution A/RES/61/106. Available at www.ohchr.org/en/instruments-mechanisms/instruments/convention-rights-persons-disabilities.

Danish Institute for Human Rights (2020), *Driving Change through Public Procurement*,| The Danish Institute for Human Rights. Available at www.humanrights.dk/publications/driving-change-through-public-procurement.

Directive 2014/24/EU, Directive 2014/24/EU of the European Parliament and of the Council of 26 February 2014 on public procurement and repealing directive 2004/18/EC. Available at https://eur-lex.europa.eu/legal-content/en/TXT/?uri=CELEX:32014L0024.

Directive 2014/25/EU, Directive 2014/25/EU of the European Parliament and of the Council of 26 February 2014 on procurement by entities operating in the water, energy, transport and postal services sectors and repealing directive 2004/17/. Available at https://eur-lex.europa.eu/legal-content/en/TXT/?uri=CELEX%3A32014L0025.

Directive 2019/882, Directive 2019/882 of the European Parliament and of the Council of 17 April 2019 on the accessibility requirements for products and services. Available at https://eur-lex.europa.eu/legal-content/EN/TXT/?uri=CELEX%3A32019L0882.

Dye, T. R. (2008), *Understanding Public Policy*, 12th ed. Pearson/Prentice Hall, Upper Saddle River, N.J., pp. 1–3.

Edler, J. and Georghiou L. (2007), 'Public procurement and innovation—Resurrecting the demand side', *Research Policy,* 36(7), pp. 949–963.

European Assistance for Innovation Procurement (2019), *Dublin City Council – Smart Dublin*. Available at https://eafip.eu/assistance/procurers-receiving-assistance/smart-dublin/.

European Commission (2017), *Communication from the Commission to the European Parliament, the Council, the European Economic and Social Committee and the Committee of the Regions Making Public Procurement Work in and for Europe* , COM/2017/0572 final. Available at https://eur-lex.europa.eu/legal-content/EN/TXT/?uri=COM%3A2017%3A572%3AFIN.

European Commission (2020), *Making Socially Responsible Public Procurement Work, 71 Good Practice Cases*. Available at https://op.europa.eu/en/publication-detail/-/publication/69fc6007-a970-11ea-bb7a-01aa75ed71a1.

European Commission (2021), *Buying Social – A Guide to Taking Account of Social Considerations in Public Procurement*, 2nd ed., p. 81. Available at https://ec.europa.eu/docsroom/documents/45767.

European Convention on Human Rights (2013), *European Court of Human Rights*. Available at www.echr.coe.int/Documents/Convention_ENG.pdf.

European Court of Justice (2020), C-395/18 of 30 January 2020 – Tim SpA. Available at https://curia.europa.eu/juris/liste.jsf?num=C-395/18.

GPA (2012), *Agreement on Government Procurement*, as amended on 30 March 2012. Available at www.wto.org/english/tratop_e/gproc_e/gpa_1994_e.htm&gt.

Greco, A. (2023), *Introduction to the Integrity Pacts Presentation*. European Institute of Public Administration, European Commission. Available at Inforegio – Training on Cohesion Policy for EU Member State Experts (europa.eu).

ICCPR (1966), International Covenant on Civil and Political Rights, adopted on December 1966 General Assembly resolution 2200A (XXI). Available at www.ohchr.org/sites/default/files/ccpr.pdf.

ICESCR (1966), International Covenant on Economic, Social and Cultural Rights, adopted on December 1966 General Assembly resolution 2200A (XXI). Available at www.ohchr.org/sites/default/files/cescr.pdf.

ILO Conventions, International Labour Organization Conventions. Available at www.ilo.org/moscow/areas-of-work/gender-equality/WCMS_249143/lang--en/index.htm.

Methven O'Brien, C., Meulen, N. V., Mehra, A., Martin-Ortega, O., Stumberg, R., & Andrecka, M. (2016), *Public Procurement and Human Rights: A Survey of Twenty Jurisdictions*. International Learning Lab on Public Procurement and Human Rights. UK. Available at www.humanrights.dk/sites/humanrights.dk/files/media/migrated/public-procurement-and-human-rights-a-survey-of-twenty-jurisdictions-final.pdf.

Lundvall, B-A. (1992), *National Systems of Innovation. Towards a Theory of Innovation and Interactive Learning*. Pinter Publishers, London.

Pavlova, M. (2017), 'Obshtestveni porychki – upravlenie i kontrol', Izdatelski kompleks UNSS, p. 12.

Pavlova, M. and Vasileva, K. (2023), 'Public procurement as a demand-side policy instrument', *Industry 4.0*, 8(1), pp. 28–31. Available at www.academia.edu/99217258/Public_Procurement_as_a_Demand_Side_Policy_Instrument.

PPA Bulgaria (2016), Public Procurement Act of Republic of Bulgaria (Prom. SG. 13/16 Feb 2016). Available at www2.aop.bg/wp-content/uploads/2022/08/PublicProcurementAct_20220805.pdf.

PPA Czech (2016), Public Procurement Act (Act No. 134/2016), Czech Republic Available at www.uohs.cz/en/legislation/public-procurement.html.

Plan d'actions achats publics responsables 2017-2019 (2017), Wallonie, Service Public de Wallonie. Available at www.oneplanetnetwork.org/sites/default/files/201070503_plan_apr_complet.pdf.

Public Buyers Community Platform, European Commission (2023). Available at https://public-buyers-community.ec.europa.eu/.

Rolfstam, M. (2009) 'Public procurement as an innovation policy tool: The role of institutions', *Science and Public Policy*, 36(5), pp. 349 – 360.

SDG (2015), Sustainable Development Goals, United Nations. Available at www.un.org/sustainabledevelopment/.

TFEU (2016), *Consolidated Versions of the Treaty on European Union and the Treaty on the Functioning of the European Union, Consolidated Version of the Treaty on European Union Consolidated Version of the Treaty on the Functioning of the European Union Protocols Annexes to the Treaty on the Functioning of the European Union Declarations annexed to the Final Act of the Intergovernmental Conference which adopted the Treaty of Lisbon, signed on 13 December 2007, OJ C 202, 7.6.2016*, pp. 1–388.

Tomova. T. (2003), 'Publichnite politiki Podhodi i metodologija na izsledvaneto i analiza', Habilitacionen trud, Specializiran nauchen syvet po sociologija, politologija i naukoznanie, p. 77.

Tomova, T. (2022), 'Procesyt na politikite: upravlenie, osnovano na stesnenijata', UI 'Sv. Kliment Ohridski', pp. 39–59.

Transparency International (2021), Safeguarding EU-Funded Investments with Integrity Pacts – A Decision-Maker's Guide to Collaborative Public Contracting Monitoring. Available at https://ec.europa.eu/regional_policy/policy/how/improving-investment/integrity-pacts_en.

Transparency International (2022), *Integrity Pacts in the EU: Suitability, Set Up and Implementation*. Available at https://ec.europa.eu/regional_policy/sources/policy/how/improving-investment/integrity-pacts/practical_guide_en.pdf.

Treaty of Amsterdam amending the Treaty on European Union (1997), Official Journal C 340, 10/11/1997 pp. 0001 – 0144. Available at https://eur-lex.europa.eu/legal-content/BG/TXT/?uri=celex%3A11997D%2FTXT.

Treaty of Lisbon amending the Treaty on European Union and the Treaty establishing the European Community (2007), signed at Lisbon, 13 December 2007, OJ C 306, 17.12.2007, pp. 1–271.Available at https://eur-lex.europa.eu/legal-content/EN/TXT/?uri=CELEX:12007L/TXT.

United Nations, Universal Declaration of Human Rights. Available at www.un.org/sites/un2.un.org/files/2021/03/udhr.pdf.

Universal Declaration of Human Rights (1948), *United Nations*. Available at www.un.org/en/about-us/universal-declaration-of-human-rights.

United Nations (2022), *Sustainable Public Procurement: Global Review*. Available at www.oneplanetnetwork.org/knowledge-centre/resources/sustainable-public-procurement-2022-global-review-parts-i-and-ii.

von Hippel, E. (1988), *The Sources of Innovation*. Oxford University Press, Oxford.

# PART II

# Climate change in public procurement

# 4 Colloquium

*Neli Garbuzanova and Sofia Lundberg*

## 4.1 Neli Garbuzanova – Introductory remarks

The international scientific consensus (NASA, 2019) is that the Earth's climate has significantly warmed since the late 1800s and is still warming, predominantly due to greenhouse gas emissions produced from human activity such as burning of fossil fuels like coal and oil (Lynas, Houlton, & Perry, 2021). The impact of climate change on the planet, wildlife and humans is devastating. To name a few from a long list of actual and predicted consequences: temperatures and sea levels rise, leading to extreme weather (such as rainfalls, heatwaves and droughts) affecting the social, economic and health conditions of everyone (European Commission, 2024).

Climate change is ubiquitous, highly visible and in some cases irreversible. Our actions must correspond to the nature of the challenge at hand and must be universal, transparent and coordinated – managing the preventable, the reversible and the unrepairable in a holistic manner. Public procurement can help humanity in addressing climate change and its destructive consequences only if climate change considerations play a central role throughout all stages of the procurement cycle.

The aim of the legal position presented in this debate is to make the case for shifting the perception of climate change factors in public procurement from 'trivialized, nice to have and scattered' to 'established, planned for and prioritized'. Even more boldly, to imagine and enable a theoretical, legal and practical procurement framework where climate change is seen as a stand-alone priority consideration in every procurement strategy and procurement exercise. This demands a change of mindset and the adoption of a dynamic whole-cycle procurement model (Garbuzanova, 2019) focusing on planning and needs identification before running a tendering process. To accelerate the change of practices in public procurement, we need a more strategic approach to procurement and the use of technology in planning for climate change events. As climate change consequences traverse human-drawn borders, collaboration and cross-border procurement become an important vehicle for joint planning and process organization. Importantly, international procurement regulation plays a key role in recognizing and implementing climate change factors in procurement legislation affecting the practical implementation of public procurement projects. The conclusion proposes potential avenues for bringing this discourse forward.

DOI: 10.4324/9781032631721-7

### *4.1.1 Change in mindset and adoption of a dynamic whole-cycle procurement approach*

Climate change affects everyone and should be a priority consideration for all future planning exercises. It requires visible, constant, consistent and coordinated efforts in all sectors, including public procurement. With recent news that the planet's warming is set to break the 1.5°C limit for the first time (McGrath, 2023), it becomes even more difficult to disentangle acting to address climate change from acting in the public interest when spending taxpayers' money. For the United Kingdom, for example, there is an expectation for increased rainfalls (ibid.), and this should be considered in the planning of public procurement projects.

Social circumstances are rapidly changing, and so should our mindset, laws and approaches to public procurement. The debate is no longer about to what extent procurement laws allow for 'green', 'environmental' and 'sustainability' considerations. It is about facilitating more opportunities to address climate change specifically throughout all stages of the procurement cycle. This calls for further debate on a working legislative definition of 'climate change' and associated climate change measures and on the risks around misusing any flexibility provided in the law when implementing such requirements. These points should be addressed by involving a wide range of stakeholders and, as a bare minimum, economists, climate change experts and procurement law experts.

A dynamic phenomenon like climate change requires a dynamic and agile approach to the whole procurement cycle. A typical whole-cycle procurement includes stages such as needs identification, strategy development, process, contract management and review. The model becomes dynamic when it facilitates the proactive build-up of channels, at the outset, enabling the flow of information and feedback at each stage and allowing the procurement practitioners to confidently adjust the approach upon change of circumstances. For example, incorporating transparent mechanisms from the start for lawful modification of contracts at the contract management stage in the event of climate change-related events.

### *4.1.2 Strategic planning, collaboration and use of technology*

Climate change considerations should feature in all stages of a dynamic whole-cycle procurement model. Holistic planning for the necessary activities throughout the model should happen at strategic – international, national, regional – and individual project levels.

Goal 13 of the United Nations (UN) Sustainable Development Goals (SDGs) asks for urgent actions from countries and societies to combat climate change and its impacts and includes specific targets for implementation (United Nations, 2022). As acknowledged by the UN Secretary-General, action on climate change is the 21st century's greatest opportunity to drive forward all SDGs (United Nations, 2023). The European Union (EU) also introduces some specific targets for its member countries, such as cutting greenhouse gas emissions by at least 55% by 2030 (European Council, 2023). The climate change profiles of countries and regions (Climate Adapt, 2023) including produced greenhouse emissions (United

Nations Environmental Programme, 2021) or adaptation status of countries are examples of helpful available tools for a transparent and coordinated planning approach to climate change.

These are all already very specific targets and tools that could help in planning and determining the climate change 'needs' of a region or a country and which could be implemented in national and regional procurement strategies and legislation and throughout the procurement cycle. Consistent planning also requires consensus on how we plan for the different consequences of climate change: addressing the unrepairable (adaptation and damage control); planning for measures to reverse the reversible; planning for preventing future negative impact and avoiding further irreparable damage; planning for the unforeseen and the unforeseeable. What used to be considered as 'unforeseeable' is now transforming to 'increasingly possible', such as the increased occurrence of extreme events like wildfires and floods. That is why there is a strong argument that for procurement planning purposes these events could be seen as foreseeable (Farmer et al., 2020), and should therefore be accounted for. Concrete climate change plans and prioritization strategies for the short, medium and long term will make it easier to incorporate climate change targets in individual procurement projects. On a holistic level, consideration of the varying (and changing) needs of countries and populations in different parts of the globe is essential. What is experienced as climate change consequences in the Northern Hemisphere could be different in impact and nature from the climate change effects in the Southern Hemisphere. In illustration, the expectation for increases in drought occurrences is likely to impact crops and ecosystems in the Northern Hemisphere under the warmest future scenario (Balting et al., 2021).

Due to the ubiquitous effect of climate change, collaboration and cross-border procurement are becoming increasingly important. A contracting authority in northern Italy, for example, can no longer plan and make procurement decisions in isolation from the decision-makers in southern Austria or eastern France. This applies to procurements in all public sectors, for example, infrastructure, health and agriculture. Collaborations between national Ministries (e.g., Environmental Minister and Finance Minister) and organizations and procurement functions should be the norm, not the exception. Climate change experts should be part of all stages of the dynamic whole procurement cycle, and at least in the planning, procurement design and evaluation.

Technology and data-driven tools can help in planning for all climate change consequences – the predictable and the unpredictable. For example, forecasting best and worst-case scenarios or statistical models and Artificial Intelligence (AI) to model scenarios predicting heatwaves or floods and the timespan for such changes (Edwards, 2023). For illustration, a recent study (Pickering et al., 2022) claims to be able to discover and forecast the probability of extreme events via active learning in neural operators (Brown University News, 2022). Thus, a robust climate needs identification in each project, facilitated by technology and based on solid evidence, will inform the design of the process and the content of the procurement documents. Technology can also help to quickly coordinate resources and equipment in the case of procurement due to climate change emergencies and can enhance communication between countries and the use of collaborative procurement in the event of crises.

In summary, with appropriate 'needs identification' at the strategic level and implementation of a coordinated, collaborative and technology-assisted approach to planning, procurement authorities can better determine the holistic needs at the individual procurement project level and incorporate climate change factors. For example, procuring electric vehicle charging points or buildings that withstand floods or heatwaves or deciding on the appropriate level of inventory (also kept in a climate change neutral manner) to address unpredictable crises as a result of climate change.

### *4.1.3 Climate change and the role of international procurement regulation*

Leading by example, the international and European Union (EU) procurement regulations play a key role in facilitating the inclusion of explicit climate change factors in procurement. The international regulations, however, currently refer to climate change in a handful of cases, presumably incorporating such consideration through the terminology of 'environmental', 'green' or 'sustainable' (Garbuzanova & Blyahova, 2023a).

The United Nations Commission on International Trade Law (UNCITRAL) Model Law on Public Procurement from 2011 (UNCITRAL Model Law, 2011, art. 2, option II, (o). does not mention climate change specifically but allows for environmental policies and factors, for example, environmental qualifications of suppliers (ibid., art. 9) and evaluation criteria related to the environmental characteristics of the subject matter (ibid., art. 10 and art. 11).

The Guide to Enactment (UNCITRAL Guide to Enactment, 2012) and the Guidance on Procurement Regulations (UNCITRAL Guidance, 2013) provide further explanation on environmental considerations and refer to 'sustainable procurement', 'sustainability', 'innovation' and 'green' (UNCITRAL Guide to Enactment, 2012, pp. 4–7). Notably, the Guide to Enactment (ibid., p. 87, para 9) references the level of carbon emissions as evaluation criteria if linked to the subject matter of the procurement. There is no link to the subject matter, for example, in relation to the manner in which the procuring entity may dispose of by-products of a manufacturing process or offset carbon emissions from the production of the goods or services at issue (ibid., p 86, para 7).

The Model Legislative Provisions on Public-Private Partnerships (UNCITRAL Model Provisions, 2019) also do not refer to climate change explicitly, although the Preamble makes a bold attempt to cross-reference to long-term sustainability, the SDGs and climate-related resolutions (United Nations, 2015). The Model Legislative Provisions further articulate how environmental considerations can be included at different stages of the procurement, for example, in pre-procurement during feasibility studies (UNCITRAL Model Provisions, 5, para 3(a)), pre-selection (ibid., 10(a)) and as evaluation criteria (ibid., 19, para 1(b)). There is no requirement for a link to the subject matter of the contract.

The associated Legislative Guide (UNCITRAL Legislative Guide, 2019) is somehow more ambitious. It refers to the international regime of environmental protection (ibid., p. 262, para 49) and to climate change-relevant international acts as well as to 'climate finance' as a way of mitigating global warming (ibid.). The Legislative Guide reviews environmental considerations in PPP projects in more detail, including the role of special bodies and advocacy groups in preventing environmental damage or issuing environmental licences (ibid, p. 261, para 48). This is a welcomed inclusion and should be further expanded to explicitly mention climate change impact.

Similarly, there is no direct reference to climate change in the Government Procurement Agreement (WTO, 2012). Instead, there are a few references to environmental aspects in adopting technical specifications (ibid., art. X, para 6) or as part of the evaluation criteria (ibid., para 9). Terminology such as 'green', 'research and development' or 'innovation' is also lacking. The GPA, however, recognizes the need for further work on sustainable procurement (ibid., art. XXII, para 8) in line with the principle of 'best value for money' (WTO, 2012, p. 444). Thus, climate change and the need for public procurement regulation based on climate change policy instruments was also discussed as part of a dedicated work programme (GPA Key Take-Aways, 2017).

The Treaty on the Functioning of the European Union (European Union, 2012) refers to integrating environmental protection requirements in policies and activities (TFEU, 2012, art. 11) and to promoting measures to preserve the environment and, in particular, combating climate change (ibid., art. 192). Compared to the previous EU procurement Directives, the Directives from 2014 (Directive 2014/23/EU; Directive 2014/24/EU; Directive 2014/25/EU) expand the scope for including social and environmental considerations throughout the whole-cycle procurement, although the number of provisions directly referring to 'climate' in the context of climate change is less ambitious and is only two. For example, when defining technical specifications in terms of environmental and climate performance levels (ibid., Annex VII; ibid., Annex VII; ibid., Chapter II, art. 36) and in life-cycle costing when defining costs imputed to environmental externalities.,[1] Such costs may include the cost of emissions of greenhouse gases and of other pollutant emissions and other climate change mitigation costs (Directive 2014/24/EU, art. 68; Directive 2014/25/EU, art. 83). The inclusion of provisions for preliminary consultations (which could potentially include climate change experts) and cross-border procurements is welcomed in the context of climate change. Soft instruments, such as the Buying Green! Handbook (European Commission, Buying Green!, 2016) and EU Green Public Procurement Criteria (European Commission, Environment, 2023) are a good attempt to explain how environmental considerations can be implemented in procurement but require more explicit reference to climate change-related considerations.

The law review above illustrates an overly conservative approach to international procurement regulation that relies on excessive political correctness on a topic on which an international agreement to act at scale exists. Climate change usually appears as part of a wider category of environmental considerations instead of giving it a central role in public procurement legislation and practice. Guidelines, Guides and soft law documents are the main drivers for including climate change considerations in public procurement. This does not set the right tone and lacks ambition.

#### *4.1.4 Key points and recommendations*

If countries and societies are truly committed to collaboratively tackle the climate change challenges, we should not shy away from calling for bolder measures and explicit introduction of climate change targets and measures as key considerations in every public procurement. As a starting point, this should be a mandatory requirement at the planning and strategy formation stage at the country and project level. It is therefore proposed to:

- Agree a more strategic approach to climate change in procurement with a focus on planning, needs identification and risk management.
- Be bolder in using 'climate change' targets and precise measures and mandatory conditions in legislation.
- Discuss and agree on a working legislative definition of climate change and the measures to tackle it.
- Identify opportunities for inclusions of climate change factors alongside a dynamic whole-cycle procurement model.
- Agree steps to facilitate cross-functional and organizational collaboration and involvement of climate change experts in all stages of procurement and, as minimum, at the planning stage.

### 4.2 Sofia Lundberg – Introductory remarks

The main focus of this discussion is on green public procurement (GPP) as an instrument of environmental or climate policy. That is, a situation where contracting authorities use a competitive tendering process to allocate public contracts while also using green criteria in the supplier selection process aiming for secondary – societal – objectives related to environment or climate (European Commission, 2008).

The question of GPP as a policy instrument is not entirely straightforward. There are a couple of distinctions that need to be made. To begin with, it is important to differentiate between impact and effectiveness. Its potential to achieve this depends on whether public procurement with green requirements is considered an instrument within environmental or climate policy. Furthermore, it must be seen in the context of policy instruments at the local, regional, or global level. In the following, these aspects will be the starting point and addressed. It should be noted, however, that governance through public procurement should adopt a systemic perspective to identify any goal conflicts that, if present, require prioritization. In the analysis that follows below, the focus is solely on environmental and climate aspects.

Further, regardless of whether public procurement is viewed as an environmental or climate policy instrument, its design and potential for impact must be seen in the context of existing policy instruments. In the case of climate policy, this becomes especially complex because we have climate policy at the European level (EU ETS and ESR), while such policies are also implemented at the national level (such as a carbon tax). A difference between environmental and climate policy through public procurement is that the former can be targeted towards local issues, while the latter must be seen as part of a larger context contributing to reduced emissions at the national level at least. Local initiatives through, for example, public procurement may be motivated if existing policies are deemed insufficient.

### *4.2.1 Motivation and evaluation of policy instruments for environmental or climate change*

From an economic standpoint, a policy instrument is warranted when there are non-priced positive or negative effects, that is, externalities, associated with consumption or production. An example of a negative externality would be the harmful impact of a production facility on the environment or climate, while a positive externality could be the creation of new knowledge that benefits others in addition to the innovator. Policy instruments set a price on these externalities, and if the price is equal to the cost of the negative effect or the value of the positive effect, the externality is considered internalized, that is, fully compensated for. In designing policy instruments, it is crucial to consider both the value for money aspect, given the scarcity of resources, as well as other potential justifications for implementing the instrument. Overall, policy instruments can be an effective means of addressing market failures or promoting positive externalities.

According to the literature, environmental policy and their direct or indirect effects can be evaluated or motivated by four criteria: effectiveness, efficiency, flexibility and equity (Hanley et al., 2007). Effectiveness pertains to the impact of the instrument – will it lead to the achievement of environmental or climate objectives? Efficiency, on the other hand, concerns how the impact can be achieved at the lowest possible cost to society with the externality internalized. Cost-effectiveness requires globally coordinated policies. Effectiveness without achieving cost-effectiveness can be achieved at the European or national level. A flexible instrument is one that can adapt to a changing world, including changes in technology and markets. Policy instruments, such as criteria in public procurement, can also be motivated by concerns related to the distribution or redistribution of responsibility, or equity. Another literature strand, Bennear and Stavins (2007), suggests that policy instruments should be evaluated based on process transparency, from the implementation of the instrument to impact measurement. An indirect effect can be achieved by providing producers with incentives to adopt new technology and thereby contribute to the spread of new, less climate-damaging innovations.

In evaluating or designing environmental policies, it is crucial to consider these criteria in order to promote the most effective and efficient use of resources while also accounting for equity and flexibility. It is worth noting that an instrument may fulfil more than one criterion or none at all. Consequently, an instrument can, for example, contribute to an objective without fulfilling it, come to a higher societal cost than the lowest possible, but lead to redistribution of resources and target a local environmental problem. In this case, the motives for the implementation of the instrument are found in equity and flexibility.

### *4.2.2 Public procurement as an instrument of policy*

Previous studies suggest that public procurement as an instrument of environmental policy may not be cost-effective (Lundberg & Marklund, 2013), is unlikely to be objectively effective (Lundberg, et al., 2016) and may not be as transparent as desired from a societal perspective (Lundberg, et al., 2016). However, arguments in favour of using public procurement as a policy instrument for a better environment can be found in its flexibility and potential to promote equity (Lindström & Lundberg, 2022).

It is important to weigh the advantages and disadvantages of public procurement as a policy instrument in order to determine whether it is an appropriate tool for achieving environmental policy objectives. While it may have limitations in terms of cost-effectiveness and transparency, its flexibility and potential to promote equity should also be considered. Furthermore, the public sector is organized at various governmental levels, such as national, regional (e.g., counties) or local (e.g., municipalities), which means that the implementation of GPP is decentralized. This justifies an analysis of the fifth criterion mentioned above, political process transparency – that is, whether and how political environmental and climate ambitions with regards to public procurement translate into calls for tenders.

An important distinction is between the effect GPP may have on the contracting authority's own operations and its' potential to tackle negative external effects from production and consumption. When designing a procurement auction and selecting suppliers, it is essential for the contracting authority to consider the life-cycle costs (LCC) of its business, such as minimizing energy costs over time (European Commission, 2016). However, to address external effects, in this case negative environmental and climate effects that extend beyond the authority's own operations, a life-cycle assessment (LCA) approach is necessary.

Both LCC and LCA can be integrated into the public procurement process via mandatory criteria or into the scoring rule as a price – value – on the external effects. In brief, if this also translates to (i.e., is included) the price paid to the suppliers, the negative effect is internalized. This approach considers a product's total impact on the environment or climate, from raw material extraction to disposal.

The administration of public procurement is primarily carried out by civil servants, and Bouwer et al. (2006) found that the main obstacle to implementing green criteria relates to resource issues, political factors (e.g., lack of organizational resources and promotional policies), as well as cognitive factors (e.g., lack of training and competence). The organization of the public sector and collaboration among civil servants from different areas of expertise are also important for effective implementation (Testa, et al., 2012; De Giacomo, et al., 2019).

Public procurement as an instrument of environmental policy is in its construction to be classified as a command and control instrument. Further, as the public sector is to lead the way for private consumers to follow, the idea is that good practices from the public sector are an information signal. The classification originates from the nature of the procurement auction since it can include green mandatory or optional criteria related to the production process, the product, or the supplier. Note that it is not, as sometimes argued, a market-based instrument as defined in economic theory (Hanley, et al., 2007). Market-based instruments are incentive-based and rely on the assumption that market actors are cost-minimizing at all points in time and what they have in common is that they work by changing relative prices and, in doing so, create incentives to cut costs by reducing pollution without regulating how this is done.

### *4.2.3 Market conditions for GPP to have impact*

Assuming that private and public buyers co-exist on the market and that there are brown and green alternatives of a product that in all other characteristics are equal, it follows from previous research, that the conditions listed here must be fulfilled for GPP to contribute to reduced environmental or climate impact: The contracting authorities have significant purchasing powers, producers are price sensitive, and consumers are price insensitive (Marron, 1997; Lundberg, et al., 2015).

With significant purchasing powers and binding green requirements, GPP will increase the price of green products and make conventional ones relatively cheaper. If the price-sensitive conditions are not met, GPP may have counterproductive effects. Price-insensitive producers will continue to produce conventional products, while price-sensitive consumers will switch from green to conventional products – opposite of the intentions of GPP.

The potential of GPP to have an impact is conditioned on it being integrated throughout the supplier selection process and the contract clauses. In addition, for GPP to be binding and have an impact (effect), the green criteria must go beyond existing standards for at least one of the bidders, that is, at least one potential supplier must have transitioned from brown to green production, all things equal. To maximize impact, GPP must encourage as many potential suppliers as possible to adapt to the environmental standards it implements, not just the winning supplier.

One of the reasons for this is that GPP is a self-regulating policy targeting secondary objectives. As such, potential bidders can avoid regulation and costs associated with adapting to environmental or climate requirements by not participating in the procurement auction. Instead, they can choose to deliver to market segments with lower green requirements.

### *4.2.4 Horizontal and vertical coordination*

A public sector that is organized at different levels – nationally, regionally, or locally – and the decentralized implementation of GPP raise questions about whether it can contribute to solving environmental or climate problems at the most decentralized level (Nijaki & Worrel, 2012). The implementation of GPP should primarily focus on local environmental problems or national climate problems. Focusing on environmental problems, the implementation of GPP with flexibility in mind will require green mandatory and evaluation criteria to be tailored to the local problem.

Another important aspect is the need for horizontal coordination of procurement auctions and control of their effects so that they contribute to solving the local or national problem. While flexibility may not always be cost-effective, it may motivate the use of GPP if it targets unique environmental problems in a specific local area that cannot be addressed by taxes or other instruments implemented at the EU or national level.

Another flexibility feature of GPP is the ability to redistribute resources and equalize welfare if green requirements target upstream production nodes in other geographical areas beyond national and EU borders and regulatory jurisdictions. This requires vertical coordination and control, which is the bridge to equity, that is, supply chain management (Preuss, 2009; Boström & Karlsson, 2013).

With equity in mind, GPP may also include socially responsible procurement objectives (McCrudden, 2004). Monitoring of the supply chain is crucial to avoid moral hazard and adverse selection issues and successfully use GPP (tailored to addressing equity concerns). Overall, GPP strongly relates to sustainable public procurement and social concerns. GPP tailored to addressing equity concerns should be implemented with care and with attention to the local environmental problem. Horizontal and vertical coordination are crucial for ensuring that GPP contributes to solving local or regional problems while also being cost-effective.

### *4.2.5 Summary and conclusions*

In contrast to the political argumentation in favour of GPP, previous research proves it is not cost- or objective-effective. GPP can, at best, have a positive impact on the environment (Marron, 1997; Lundberg & Marklund, 2013) or on the climate (Konjunkturinstitutet, 2020). Arguments in favour of GPP as a policy instrument are more likely found in flexibility and equity rather than cost- and objective-effectiveness.

The flexibility argument builds on the importance of the correct design of the procurement process and the horizontal coordination of procurement auctions and control of its effects so that all procurements together contribute to local or regional environmental problems or, in the context of climate, to global or national problems. Another flexibility feature of GPP makes it possible to redistribute resources and equalize welfare if the green requirements target upstream production nodes in other geographical areas, beyond national borders and regulatory jurisdictions. This will, however, require vertical coordination and control of the supply chain.

A difference between environmental and climate policy through public procurement is that the former can be targeted towards local issues, while the latter must be seen as part of a larger context contributing to reduced emissions at the national level at least. From a policy perspective, the recommendation is to adopt supplier selection criteria accordingly, include them in the contract, invest in follow-up routines, including green performance and apply incentive schemes to avoid moral hazard. Note that the use of green criteria can – regardless of political ambitions – be motivated from the perspective of the authority considering its own operational life-cycle costs, LCC.

## 4.3 Neli Garbuzanova – Response to Paper 2

### *4.3.1 Cross-country collaboration and coordination*

The economic and legal positions in this debate concur on many points. For example, climate change requires cross-country collaboration and policy setting and should be considered in the context of existing wider climate change policies at EU, UN and international level. As there is international consensus to act on climate change, strategies and policies for implementing such considerations should be globally led and coordinated but left for local implementation. This will contribute not only to cost effectiveness but will also have positive effects that are not monetary, such as consistency and alignment of approaches between countries.

As climate change is a ubiquitous phenomenon, so should be the policies that address it. The effects of climate change can be grave and, in some cases, irreversible, impacting all future generations, which demands from national and international policymakers to coordinate efforts. Thus, existing climate change policies cannot tackle climate change in isolation from other policies, such as public procurement. Making room for climate change in public procurement policies and regulation would not open the gate for other non-core procurement policies since climate change is a special case in that it affects everything and everyone and is now universally accepted by experts and society. For climate change, local, uncoordinated actions will not achieve sustainable results and value for money. I agree with Prof. Lundberg on the need for mandatory (or minimum) climate change standards and flexibility (e.g., in selection and evaluation criteria) to tailor requirements to local problems.

Another key point made by Prof. Lundberg, which I agree with, is that the organization of the public sector and collaboration among civil servants from different areas of expertise are important for effective implementation of climate change considerations in public procurement. This means proactive actions and investment in climate change resources, training and experts as well as the involvement of climate change experts in projects throughout the entire procurement cycle and in this debate going forward.

### *4.3.2 Climate change terminology and 'primary' vs. 'secondary' consideration*

Climate change is usually 'bundled' with the wider category of environmental considerations or policies. Prof. Lundberg refers to environmental and climate change considerations together but also accepts that there is a difference between environmental and climate policy. The former can be targeted towards local issues, while the latter must be seen as part of a larger context contributing to reduced emissions.

There is merit in 'unbundling' the two categories and focusing future economic and legal analysis on climate change only. This will provide more accurate conclusions and will have a powerful effect in influencing the political discourse on the matter. For example, a political debate framed around public procurement as an instrument of environmental and climate change policy altogether may slow down the process of implementing specific climate change considerations in public procurement. The discussion should shift towards public procurement policy and regulation 'catching up' with countries, citizens and companies' efforts to collectively address and manage the effects of climate change. If this mindset is adopted, climate change objectives can no longer be seen as 'secondary'. Thus, the label 'secondary' should be avoided as it does not convey the right message, and for these reasons, public procurement practitioners are also moving away from using this terminology.

### *4.3.3 Alignment with core procurement objectives and principles*

Implementing climate change considerations is also in line with the core objectives and principles of public procurement. If we accept that the core purpose of public procurement is to *'satisfy a public need by doing 'the most good with what we have' in a principled and transparent way'* (Garbuzanova, 2019, p. 89) we can easily link to climate change objectives by adding '*having a long-term view on our actions*' to this working definition. The principles that guide the modern procurement regulatory framework and practical delivery – accountability, transparency and integrity – are also easily reconcilable with the implementation of climate change considerations. Such factors can be considered alongside all stages of the procurement cycle (e.g., needs identification, award criteria) and not just the selection or competitive tendering stage. In fact, the planning and needs identification stages are critical when it comes to planning for the short-, medium- and long-term needs of a country. For example, addressing predicted temperature increases leading to heat waves or flooding. Because of the impact of climate change in every aspect of public sector delivery and its long-term consequences, not taking the opportunity to implement climate change factors in public procurement would go against the public interest in spending public money responsibly and the core objectives and principles of public procurement.

### *4.3.4 'Green public procurement' and the bidders' pool*

The Buying Green! Handbook (European Commission, Buying Green!, 2016) provides helpful insights into implementing environmental and climate change considerations as part of the EU public procurement directives. It refers to a definition of 'green public procurement' (GPP) as a 'process whereby public authorities seek to procure goods, services and works with a reduced environmental impact throughout their life cycle when compared to goods, services and works with the same primary function that would otherwise be procured' (ibid., p. 4). However, the description of 'reduced environmental impact' compared to goods and services that would otherwise be procured is vague, does not specifically refer to climate change and is insufficient in relation to climate change-related aspects (which are often specific and indisputable).

Prof. Lundberg points out that 'green criteria' must go beyond existing standards for at least one of the bidders. It is not clear if this pool relates to potential bidders in an existing or a fictitious market or to actual bidders participating in a specific procurement exercise. This is important as climate change considerations should be part of the preparatory and needs assessment stage, which precedes the actual tendering process when bidders participating in the process become known. This would also mean that climate change considerations are left to be determined by the bidders' pool for a particular project taking a reactive position to climate change implementation by contracting authorities. Climate change is as important as other fields, such as labour and tax, for which there is little flexibility for bidders to determine the key factors that should be included in a procurement exercise. For these reasons, climate change factors should not be 'voluntary' and left for bidders (market) to lead on but should feature as clear minimum requirements implemented at various stages of the whole procurement cycle. State aid for adopting new technology, a point made by Prof. Lundberg, may provide some temporary benefits but is not likely to address the gravity of the impact of climate change in the long term.

Implementing climate change considerations in public procurement may initially reduce the pool of bidders in an attempt to avoid regulation and any additional costs associated with adapting to climate change requirements. However, if we take a longer term perspective on climate change, we should be ready to accept this trade-off in the short term as it will bring benefits in the long run. This may be different for the 'wider' environmental factors category, and a targeted approach can be adopted for these.

The efforts of all contracting authorities should also be coordinated, covering all sectors and levels – regional, national and international. A firm stance on climate change and any associated requirements held by all contracting authorities will discourage bidders to 'shop around' and deliver to a market segment with lower climate change requirements. Thus, if we look from the perspectives of taxpayers, consumers and contracting authorities (rather than just suppliers), including climate change factors will be seen as a positive step. This will improve the reputation of contracting authorities who will be actively helping to achieve net zero and other specific targets, which the citizens of the (near) future will be closely scrutinizing and demanding when their money is being spent for public products and services.

#### *4.3.5 Life-cycle approach and impact of climate change considerations*

Prof. Lundberg and I agree that a life-cycle assessment approach (from raw material to disposal) is needed to address impacts outside immediate costs. This would cover not just costs but also wider climate change consequences.

It is claimed that for climate change considerations to have an impact, the following conditions must be satisfied: significant purchasing powers, producers are price-sensitive and consumers are price-insensitive (Marron, 1997; Lundberg, et al., 2016). In the context of climate change, these conditions require re-assessment with a reference to some of the specific characteristics of climate change, such as immediate and long-term effects, state of urgency and irreversibility. For example, price sensitivity for producers and price insensitivity for consumers should be considered with these characteristics in mind. Prof. Lundberg suggests that significant purchasing power and binding climate change requirements will increase the price of green products and make conventional ones relatively cheaper.

However, from the perspective of a contracting authority acting with a long-term view in mind, climate change products may actually be cheaper – in economic and social terms. This is especially true if a product or service life-cycle assessment approach is adopted. Furthermore, suppliers will not have the incentive to continue to produce cheap products if all public buyers future-proof (taking into account climate change impact) the products and services they buy. As public procurement does not exist in isolation, there would be additional regulatory mechanisms from other public sectors (energy, environment) that would not allow suppliers to produce, sell or buy products or services that fail below agreed climate change levels and standards. Thus, price sensitive customers should not be able to easily switch to providers who are below certain minimum climate change-related standards.

### *4.3.6 Conditions for the introduction of a policy instrument*

Prof. Lundberg explains that from an economic perspective, policy instruments are introduced where there are non-priced positive or negative effects, or externalities, associated with consumption or production. In the case of climate change, there could also be positive or negative 'priced' effects, especially with the view of the various consequences of climate change that require addressing and if we think holistically and in the long term. We could incorporate these effects in the assessment of what constitutes 'value for money' by including a reference to climate change from the outset. This is justifiable as climate change is a special case that can not only lead to scarcity of resources but also to grave societal damage and ultimately extinction.

Climate change policy is likely to cover all four criteria cited by Prof. Lundberg for motivating a policy instrument – effectiveness, efficiency, flexibility and equity. The effectiveness criteria are satisfied in the case of climate change, as the impact of including climate change considerations in public procurement can be very large. For example, many governments across the globe have committed to binding international obligations to act on climate change and yield very high purchasing power. Public procurement is more than 12% of countries' Gross Domestic Product (GDP) (OECDiLibrary, 2023). Furthermore, climate change can significantly affect the GDP as we measure it (Jones, 2022) and the concept of GDP has considerably evolved to take into account sustainability (Pilling, 2014), including climate change. The UK Office for National Statistics, for example, has started publishing climate change insights alongside GDP with options for measuring emissions as part of their plan to go 'Beyond GDP' measures of inclusive income (McKeown, 2022).

Prof. Lundberg also refers to flexibility to redistribute resources and equalize welfare linking to socially responsible objectives. This and all of the above criteria should be carefully assessed in the light of climate change considerations specifically instead of the wider terminology of environmental considerations. The point on how political environmental and climate ambitions (or policy instruments) with regard to public procurement translate into calls for tenders (political process transparency) is especially important. It should focus on climate change aspects for which there is already international consensus, like reduction of $CO_2$ emissions and other climate actions pursued as part of the UN SDGs and climate change agenda.

Prof. Lundberg suggests a control-and-command policy instrument as opposed to market-based (where market actors are minimizing costs at all times) or voluntary agreement to act. This choice, however, may differ if we consider climate change as a standalone factor outside the wider category of environmental policy instruments. For climate change, the public sector is expected to lead the way (not as a sole leader but as part of wider efforts, strategies and policies), and this is likely to be demanded by taxpayers. It could be reasonable to consider a mixed policy instruments approach, starting with command-and-control for agreed minimum requirements (e.g., climate change passport for companies) and market-based or voluntary agreements for climate change-related aspects beyond that (e.g., for companies or contracting authorities who decide to go beyond minimum requirements).

### *4.3.7 Summary of debate points*

For climate change, we may need to adopt a mix of horizontal and vertical actions at the international, country and local levels. Such actions should be globally coordinated and regionally delivered. Wider environmental problems do not have the urgency, global impact and long-term effect present in climate change. Analysis on climate change considerations specifically (as defined in an agreed working definition) focusing on the short-, medium- and long-term effects and trade-offs should assess if using climate change considerations in public procurement will be cost-effective (in the sense of life-cycle assessment) or objectives-effective. There are many opportunities to implement climate change factors at different stages of a whole cycle procurement process without distorting the useful effects of healthy and climate change compliant competition and with a long-term perspective in mind.

Finally, one point is not up for debate – the Earth's climate has significantly warmed and is still warming, predominantly due to greenhouse gas emissions produced from human activity, and we need to act to avoid a global catastrophe.

## 4.4 Sofia Lundberg – Response to Paper 1

Is climate change a key consideration in public procurement? A more correct question is, perhaps, if climate should be a key consideration in public procurement. As pointed out in previous research, the political argumentation in favour of GPP leans on cost- or objective-effectivness, while the arguments in favour of GPP are better found in equity and flexibility. It follows from the design of the procurement process and its qualities as a policy instrument – command and control feature – that GPP, at best can have a positive impact on the environment (Marron, 1997; Lundberg & Marklund, 2013) or on, as discussed here, the climate (Konjunkturinstitutet, 2020). As pointed out in Lundberg and Marklund (2018), a guiding principle when designing effective environmental or climate policies is that policy instruments should be designed to operate as close to the source of the problem(s) as possible, that is, they should target the source as directly as possible. This eases impact and cost results. Both are ingredients in optimal policy design.

### *4.4.1 Public procurement and climate change, is it fit for purpose?*

A difference between environmental and climate policy through public procurement is that the former can be targeted towards local issues, while the latter must be seen as part of a larger context contributing to reduced emissions at the national level at least. As pointed out by Neli Garbuzanova, climate change via public procurement will require collaboration and cross-border coordination of all procurements within a country (minimum) or, which is preferable, within the European Union (EU). The magnitude of this joint planning and process organization shall not be underestimated.

Further, a distinctive feature of GPP compared to more traditional climate policy instruments such as emissions taxes or the EU Emissions Trading System (EU ETS) is the element of discretion. For climate impact, the requirements on potential suppliers have to go beyond existing standards and create incentives for suppliers to invest in less polluting technology, or lead to a replacement of brown (polluting) suppliers with green (less polluting) suppliers – alternatively, a combination of these two effects. Participation in public procurement is optional and also contingent on potential suppliers' expected pay-off from entering into GPP schemes. This feature will impact the climate effect or cause it to be absent. As long as there is a cost for adjusting to the climate-related requirements, potential suppliers will weigh this cost against the expected profit from the contract. It has to be non-negative for adaption to greener technology to occur and entry to the procurement auction to happen.

In brief, this is one of the major reasons why GPP as a climate policy instrument is potentially weaker than taxes, tradable permits, subsidies and standards (see, e.g., Heyes, 2009). It follows that understanding of how GPP functions as a climate (or environmental) policy instrument has to include insights into how it affects potential suppliers' entry decisions and the functioning of the market in question. Is the public sector a large enough buyer to have the power to incentivize potential suppliers to invest in less polluting technology? How will relative prices be affected and how price-sensitive are private consumers (co-existing on the same market)? Is there a counteractive effect? (Lundberg, et al., 2016).

### *4.4.2 Policy design*

From a climate change point of view, it is crucial that the requirements on suppliers stipulated in the call for tenders take place with reference to defined objectives and, as stated above, go beyond the current standard of the technology of the polluting suppliers. Another important feature for change to happen is that potential suppliers, who contribute to the climate change problems, find it beneficial to submit a bid and decide to adjust their product accordingly. Further, as mentioned by Neli Garbuzanova, visible, constant, consistent and coordinated efforts – translated to requirements and contract clauses – in all parts of the public sector (preferable in all sectors) – are called for. It follows from the arguments presented in Lundberg and Marklund (2018) that the contracting authority should be transparent in terms of the link between the climate change factors and the targeted objective(s), to facilitate evaluation of the impact and the cost of the policy – a difficult task when it comes to climate change since it traverses geographical borders.

The same authors illustrate how the so called Tinbergen rule (Tinbergen, 1952) translates to GPP schemes. The rule states that the number of policy instruments should equal the number of goals, that is, if the goal is climate change communicated as, for example, an emission level – there should only be one instrument targeting this problem. Consequently, public procurement should only include climate change factors if existing policies are insufficient. If so, the climate change factors should be designed to complement the existing policy. These features need to be added to the list of next steps suggested by Neli Garbuzanova, and they also need to be included in handbooks such as the Buying Green Handbook published by the EU Commission.

### *4.4.3 Diffusion of innovation, changes in technology*

According to an analysis of climate policy and public procurement performed by the National Institute of Economic Research (Konjunkturinstitutet, 2020), climate change factors in public procurement may have zero impact. The Swedish government's climate policy action plan is quite comprehensive, and in it, references are made to public procurement as a way to reach national climate goals. The plan and existing policy instruments, such as taxes, give relatively strong incentives for private and public actors to reduce their carbon emissions. On the European level, the EU Commission has adopted a series of legislative proposals to achieve climate neutrality and the intermediate target of an at least 55% net reduction in greenhouse gas emissions by 2030. One proposal is limiting the caps on the EU ETS allowances. With existing policy instruments in mind, emissions from one area risk to be redistributed to another area. For real impact on the climate, the public procurement design has to focus on sectors where the general climate policy is weak.

A more plausible impact is the indirect impact on the climate through the spread of new low-emission technology.

As mentioned above, public procurement and supplier selection based on climate change factors can contribute to the spread of low-emission technology. That is, if market conditions apply and countries commit to collaboratively join forces on climate change via public procurement. In practice, however, public procurement is a control instrument, which makes it difficult to design accurately. A market-based, or economic, policy instrument is incentive-based and works through market price signals without explicitly prescribing the use of a certain technology – a feature that makes them cost-effective with the potential to contribute to emission targets.

This contrasts with public procurement, where supplier selection criteria often stipulate delivery processes, technical specifications and use of materials. Technical specifications and quantitatively regulated emission levels are typical features of command and control instruments, features that make them cost-ineffective but with potential to impact – an impact that in GPP schemes will be indirect and uncertain.

### *4.4.4 Do we have the courage to be responsible?*

True commitment to collaboratively tackle the climate change challenges via public procurement will also depend on the competence and priorities within each and every contracting authority in the EU. Existing research referred to in Lindström et al. (2022) tells about financial restrictions and perception of green products being relatively more expensive, lack of organizational resources, lack of training and competence as barriers to implementing GPP.

The analysis presented here implies that bolder measures and explicit introduction of climate change targets and measures as key considerations in every public procurement *will not be enough* to tackle the climate change challenges – the urgent need to tackle the climate change requires bold measures that are of a different and more politically difficult nature, for example, higher carbon taxes, redistribution of taxes, or further limitations of the cap on the number of emission allowances in the EU – difficult measures as they are *direct in impact and tangible in societal and private costs* – not necessarily a successful way to attract voters. As things stand today, the price on emissions is too low, all things equal.

## 4.5 Neli Garbuzanova – Conclusions

Climate change must feature as a key consideration in public procurement. With July 2023 set to be the world's warmest month on record mainly due to fossil fuel use (BBC News, 2023), policymakers, regulators and authorities responsible for spending public money have no excuse for inaction.

I agree with Prof. Lundberg that public procurement alone will not tackle the climate change challenges, and bolder measures of political nature are also needed. However, solving complex problems requires a holistic approach, and in the case of climate change, this includes coordinated actions via all possible avenues, including public procurement. One policy instrument tackling the problem may not be sufficient in the case of climate change. However, there may be one main policy instrument and multiple auxiliary ones to achieve impact. It is also questionable if existing policies are sufficient and if they actively contribute to tackling climate change. Research cited by Prof. Lundberg suggests that climate change factors in public procurement may have zero impact and focus should be in sectors with weak climate change policy. The evidence from this research is not conclusive ('may'), but it should be critically reviewed and considered. Public procurement features in all sectors, including sectors with weaker climate change policies.

As a big spender of public money, the public sector can have a positive impact if climate change considerations are appropriately implemented in public procurement. The public buyer is powerful enough to demand and set standards, including key climate change requirements. Once these standards are set, suppliers and public authorities can explore mutually beneficial solutions. Implementing climate change factors does not need to happen abruptly and could be phased in with clear milestones in mind. I agree that climate change policy instruments should operate as close to the problem as possible. Ideally, climate change in public procurement should be nationally and globally coordinated and regionally implemented. Cross-border collaboration and joint planning will require significant efforts and resources in order to tackle a complex and challenging problem.

As for the market, many suppliers are already investing in green and climate change-responsive products. To a great extent, this is because of increased demand and a shift in perception about green products due to greater awareness of the effects of climate change. For example, in the electric vehicle market, technology is developing rapidly, and the products become more affordable and include options for monthly payments. Any replacement of polluting suppliers/products with non-polluting suppliers/products will be implemented in a staged manner, considering the impact on markets too.

Participation in public procurement is optional but, in many cases, very attractive too. If a supplier wants to do business with the public sector, key climate change commitments should be met or there should be comprehensive plans for meeting these in the longer term. There are payment and costing mechanisms that can be explored to allow for gradual adjustment to climate change requirements by suppliers. For example, initially costs can be shared or risk can be allocated in a more favourable manner for suppliers. Tax exemptions and other incentives, such as longer contracts or guaranteed minimum payment, can be attractive for suppliers willing to adjust to climate change requirements. A fair comparison of polluting and green suppliers' costs would include the long-term cost of polluting suppliers' cheaper products against the current and long-term costs of the green suppliers' products throughout the entire product life cycle. In the future, and similarly to product safety costs, climate change costs should not be questioned by the market.

Entry to market decisions of suppliers and effect on markets is important but should not be the only consideration. For some markets, a climate change requirement may actually expand the market rather than have a negative effect on competition. A good point that prompts further research is the effect on relative prices and price sensitivity of private consumers – in the short and in the long term.

Prof. Lundberg rightly points out that there should be transparency in terms of the link between the climate change factors and the targeted objectives, a challenging task given climate change goes beyond political and geographical boundaries. However, technology, data and computer models and simulations of actions and impacts on climate change are becoming more sophisticated and mature. Therefore, in the near future, we can expect to see models helping to support decision making on the most impactful policies and public procurement tools.

Public procurement is not a static discipline, and procurement policies, regulations and processes have developed over time to become more flexible and to allow for environmental considerations. Technical specifications have evolved and are often outcome-based and developed in collaboration with the market. Being explicit about climate change measures and requirements will send a strong message and will help the market and public authorities to jointly find the right solution, which may even be a cheaper one. Working with public procurement practitioners will allow us to identify these flexibilities alongside the procurement cycle and design appropriate processes. A key party that should be part of this debate is the climate change experts. In addition, country-specific studies on climate change and public procurement in the context of individual countries climate change profiles, policies and regulatory frameworks can further stimulate the debate (Garbuzanova & Blyahova, 2023b).

We should all agree that we need to urgently act on climate change and that this is the right (ethical) thing to do – for us, for future generations and for the planet. Action is needed in all aspects of life and sectors of society, including procurement. Once we are in agreement on the ethical justification, the legal and economic arguments will naturally flow to support our case.

## 4.6 Sofia Lundberg – Conclusions

It follows from the most recent IPPC synthesis report (IPCC AR6 SYR) that "… global greenhouse gas emissions have continued to increase, with unequal historical and ongoing contributions arising from unsustainable energy use, land use and land-use change, lifestyles and patterns of consumption and production across regions, between and within countries and among individuals (high confidence)". The IPPC states that regulatory and economic instruments can support emission reduction – given that there is political commitment, well-aligned multilevel governance, institutional frameworks, laws, policies and strategies and financial support. Adaption will cost, and current gaps are explained by financial restraints in general and in developing countries in particular.

In line with the IPPC reporting, Neli Garbuzanova points out the importance of collective efforts from different stakeholders within and across nations. One key issue here is *how* the collective efforts can be achieved. Public procurement is a highly decentralized process in most countries. Moreover, GPP serves as a policy instrument that exemplifies self-regulation, with its primary aim being the procurement of goods, services, or works to satisfy a public need. While societal objectives are important, they should be viewed as secondary within this framework, regardless of the noble intentions behind them. Instead, greater emphasis should be placed on crafting an efficient policy rather than solely prioritizing the delivery of the right message. The most impactful message is one that is backed by a policy with a demonstrated, measurable and positive effect on reducing greenhouse gas emissions. I therefore disagree with the advice to avoid the label 'secondary' in the GPP context. Transparency and accountability necessitate the practice of accurately labelling things based on their true nature.

Garbuzanova argues that from the perspective of a contracting authority acting with a long-term view in mind, climate change products may actually be cheaper – in economic and social terms. In both the short and long term, the concept of economic terms encompasses not only financial considerations but also societal costs and benefits, including external effects that are not accounted for in market prices. It is important to note that policy instruments are necessary precisely because negative external effects resulting from consumption and production are not adequately priced by the market. A challenge arises in the fact that contracting authorities, in most instances, tend to adopt a one-year perspective focused primarily on operational costs and revenues, rather than considering the wider implications for welfare effects and societal costs and benefits. This disparity raises an important issue, as it fails to capture the impact and long-term perspective.

The effectiveness of policy instruments, such as GPP, can be assessed in terms of dynamic efficiency, which pertains to their ability to stimulate the development of less polluting technologies. If GPP were dynamically efficient, it could outweigh the disadvantage of being cost-ineffective in a static sense (Lundberg & Marklund, 2013). However, GPP functions as a command-and-control policy instrument that relies on direct controls. Previous research indicates that direct controls provide fewer incentives for promoting technological development compared to economic instruments like emission taxes.

Nevertheless, GPP can be viewed as a signalling system that signifies a long-term commitment to influencing the market, encouraging investments in greener technology and motivating consumer behaviour that reduces greenhouse gas emissions. It is important to acknowledge the potential risk of relative price effects leading to counterproductive outcomes. However, GPP, as a signalling system, allows potential suppliers to adopt a long-term perspective on investment costs across multiple periods, potentially increasing their participation in the procurement process.

To enhance the impact of GPP, a preferable approach could involve designing the procurement auction to prioritize functionality rather than relying on the current practice of mandating specific technologies. This shift away from technology-specific requirements is crucial as it hampers innovation (Porter & van der Linde, 1995). It follows that a key question for future research is: Can technology-neutral calls for tenders effectively facilitate the broader adoption and diffusion of new and greener technologies?

## Note

1 Directive 2014/24/EU (Art. 2 (20)) and Directive 2014/25/EU (Art. 2 (16)) define life cycle as: *'all consecutive and/or interlinked stages, including research and development to be carried out, production, trading and its conditions, transport, use and maintenance, throughout the existence of the product or the works or the provision of the service, from raw material acquisition or generation of resources to disposal, clearance and end of service or utilisation'.*

## References


Balting, D.F., AghaKouchak, A., Lohmann, G., and Ionita, M. (2021), 'Northern hemisphere drought risk in a warming climate'. *npj Climate and Atmospheric Science*, 4(1), pp.1–13. Available at https://doi.org/10.1038/s41612-021-00218-2 [Accessed 28 November 2023].

BBC News (2023), *Climate Change: July Set to Be World's Warmest Month on Record.* 27 July. Available at www.bbc.co.uk/news/science-environment-66322608 [Accessed 28 November 2023].

Bennear, L. S. and Stavins, R. N. (2007), 'Second-best theory and the use of multiple policy instruments'. *Environmental and Resource Economics*, 37(1), pp. 111–129.

Boström, M. and Karlsson, M. (2013), 'Responsible procurement, complex product chains and the integration of vertical and horizontal governance'. *Environmental Policy and Governance*, 23(6), pp. 381–394.

Bouwer, M. et al. (2006), *Green Public Procurement in Europe 2006 – Conclusions and Recommendation.* Virage Milieu & Management, AJ Haarlem.

Brown University News (2022), *Study Shows How Machine Learning Could Predict Rare Disastrous Events, Like Earthquakes or Pandemics.* Available at www.brown.edu/news/2022-12-19/extreme-events [Accessed 28 November 2023].

Climate Adapt (2023), *Country Profiles – English.* Available at https://climate-adapt.eea.europa.eu/en/countries-regions/countries [Accessed 28 November 2023].

De Giacomo, M. R., Testa, F., Iraldo, F., and Formentini, M. (2019), 'Does green public procurement lead to life cycle costing (LCC) adoption?', *Journal of Purchasing and Supply Management*, 25(3), pp. 1–10.

Directive 2014/23/EU of the European Parliament and of the Council of 26 February 2014 on the award of concession contracts [2014] OJ L 94.

Directive 2014/24/EU of the European Parliament and of the Council of 26 February 2014 on public procurement and repealing Directive 2004/18/EC [2014] OJ L 94.

Directive 2014/25/EU of the European Parliament and of the Council of 26 February 2014 on procurement by entities operating in the water, energy, transport and postal services sectors and repealing Directive 2004/17/EC [2014] OJ L 94.

Edwards, C. (2023). *A Dire Forecast: Scientists Used Ai to Find Planet Could Cross Critical Warming Threshold Sooner Than Expected, CNN.* Available at https://edition.cnn.com/2023/01/30/world/global-warming-critical-threshold-climate-intl/index.html?utm_source=substack&utm_medium=email [Accessed 28 November 2023].

European Commission (2008), *Communication from the Commission to the European Parliament, the Council, the European Economic and Social Committee and the Committee of the Regions* – Action plan for a better environment, s.l. European Commission, COM(2008) 0400. Available at https://eur-lex.europa.eu/legal-content/EN/TXT/?uri=celex%3A52008DC0400 [Accessed 23 October 2024]

European Commission (2024), Consequences of Climate Change. Available at https://climate.ec.europa.eu/climate-change/consequences-climate-change_en [Accessed 22 September 2024.

European Commission, Directorate-General for Environment (2016), *Buying Green! A Handbook on Green Public Procurement*, 3rd ed. Publications Office. Available at https://data.europa.eu/doi/10.2779/837689 [Accessed 28 November 2023].

European Commission, Environment (2023), *EU Green Public Procurement Criteria*. Available at https://ec.europa.eu/environment/gpp/eu_gpp_criteria_en.htm [Accessed 28 November 2023].

European Council (2023), *Climate Change: What the EU is Doing*. Available at www.consilium.europa.eu/en/policies/climate-change/#:~:text=Under%20the%20European%20climate%20law [Accessed 28 November 2023].

European Union (2012), 'Consolidated version of the Treaty on the Functioning of the European Union (TFEU)', *OJ L. 326/47-326/390*. Available at https://eur-lex.europa.eu/legal-content/EN/TXT/?uri=celex%3A12012E%2FTXT [Accessed 28 November 2023].

Farmer, A., Foote, M., and Morawetz, J. (2020), COVID-19 offers force majeure lessons for climate planning. Available at www.kirkland.com/publications/article/2020/07/covid19-force-majeure-lessons-climate-planning [Accessed 28 November 2023].

Garbuzanova, N. (2019), 'A dynamic whole-cycle approach to public procurement: A practitioner's perspective on best practice methodologies', *African Public Procurement Law Journal*, 6(2). Available at https://applj.journals.ac.za/pub/article/view/34. DOI: https://doi.org/10.14803/6-2-34 [Accessed 28 November 2023].

Garbuzanova, N. and Blyahova, Y. (2023a), 'Climate change considerations in public procurement and concessions in Bulgaria (part I), *European Procurement & Public Private Partnership Law Review*, 18(1), pp.50–64. Available at https://doi.org/10.21552/epppl/2023/1/8 [Accessed 19 November 2023].

Garbuzanova, N. and Blyahova, Y. (2023b), 'Climate change considerations in public procurement and concessions in Bulgaria (Part II). *European Procurement & Public Private Partnership Law Review*, 18(3), pp. 164–176. Available at https://doi.org/10.21552/epppl/2023/3/4.

GPA (2017), *Key Take-Aways from the Committee's Symposium on Sustainable Procurement, Annex E*. Available at https://docs.wto.org/dol2fe/Pages/FE_Search/FE_S_S009-DP.aspx?language=E&CatalogueIdList=240250,240219,236605,233339,233038,225097,128999,128861,120376,113691&CurrentCatalogueIdIndex=2&FullTextHash=&HasEnglishRecord=True&HasFrenchRecord=True&HasSpanishRecord=True [Accessed 28 November 2023].

Hanley, N., Shogren, J. F., and White, B. (2007), 'Environmental economics', In *Theory and Practice*. Palgrave Macmillan, New York.

Heyes, A. (2009), 'Is environmental regulation bad for competition? A survey', *Journal of Regulatory Economics*, 36(1), pp. 1–28.

Jones, M. (2022), *Climate Change Putting 4% of Global GDP at Risk, New Study Estimates, Reuters*,28 April. Available at www.reuters.com/world/climate-change-putting-4-global-gdp-risk-new-study-estimates-2022-04-27/ [Accessed 28 November 2023].

Konjunkturinstitutet (2020), *MIljö ekonomi och politik 2020 upphandling med klimathänsyn*. Konjunkturinstitutet, Stockholm.

Lindström, H. and Lundberg, S. (2022), *Att upphandla med miljöhänsyn – när, hur och varför?*. Konkurrensverket, Stockholm.

Lindström, H., Lundberg, S., and Marklund, P-O (2022), 'Green public procurement: An empirical analysis of the uptake of a organic food policy', *Journal of Purchasing and Supply Management*, 28(3), pp. 1–18.

Lundberg, S. and Marklund, P-O (2013), 'Green public procurement as an environmental policy instrument: Cost effectiveness', *Environmental Economics*, 4(4), pp. 75–83.

Lundberg, S. and Marklund, P-O (2018), 'Green public procurement and multiple environmental objectives', *Journal of Industrial and Business Economics*, 45(1), pp. 37–53.

Lundberg, S., Marklund, P-O, and Strömbäck, E. (2016), 'Is environmental policy by public procurement effective?', *Public Finance Review*, 44(4), pp. 478–499.

Lynas, M., Houlton, B.Z., and Perry, S. (2021), 'Greater than 99% consensus on human caused climate change in the peer-reviewed scientific literature', *Environmental Research Letters*, 16(11), p.114005. Available at https://doi.org/10.1088/1748-9326/ac2966 [Accessed 28 November 2023].

Marron, D.B. (1997), 'Buying green: Government procurement as an instrument of environmental policy', *Public Finance Review*, 25(3), pp. 285–305.

McCrudden, C. (2004), 'Using public procurement to achieve social outcomes', *Natural Resource Forum*, 28(4), pp. 257–267.

McGrath, M. (2023), 'Global Warming Set to Break Key 1.5C Limit for First Time', *BBC News,* 17 May. Available at www.bbc.co.uk/news/science-environment-65602293 [Accessed 28 November 2023].

McKeown, L. (2022), 'Looking beyond GDP and providing insights on climate change'. *Office for National Statistics*. Available at https://blog.ons.gov.uk/2022/05/12/looking-beyond-gdp-and-providing-insights-on-climate-change/ [Accessed 28 November 2023].

NASA (2019), 'Scientific consensus: Earth's climate is warming', *Climate Change: Vital Signs of the Planet*. Available at https://climate.nasa.gov/scientific-consensus/ [Accessed 28 November 2023].

Nijaki, L. K. and Worrel, G. (2012), 'Procurement for sustainable local economic development', *International Journal of Public Sector Management*, 25(2), pp. 133–153.

OECDiLibrary (2023), *Size of Public Procurement*. Available at www.oecd-ilibrary.org/sites/18dc0c2d-en/index.html?itemId=/content/component/18dc0c2d-en [Accessed 28 November 2023].

Pickering, E., Guth, S., Karniadakis, G. E., and Sapsis, T.P. (2022), 'Discovering and forecasting extreme events via active learning in neural operators'. *Nature Computational Science*, 2(12), pp.823–833. Available at https://doi.org/10.1038/s43588-022-00376-0 [Accessed 28 November 2023].

Pilling, D. (2014), 'Has GDP outgrown its use?', *Financial Times*. Available at www.ft.com/content/dd2ec158-023d-11e4-ab5b-00144feab7de.

Porter, M. E. and van der Linde, C. (1995), 'Toward a new conception of the environment: Competitiveness relationship', *Journal of Economic Perspectives*, 9(4), pp. 97–118.

Preuss, L. (2009), 'Addressing sustainable development through public procurement: the case of local government', *Supply Chain Management: An International Journal*, 14(3), pp. 213–223.

Testa, F., Iraldo, F., Frey, M., and Daddi, T. (2012), 'What factors influence the uptake of GPP (Green Public Procurement) practices? New evidence from an Italian survey', *Ecological Economics*, 82(2), pp. 88–96.

Tinbergen, J. (1952), *On the Theory of Economic Policy*. Holland Publishing Company, Amsterdam: North.

UNCITRAL Guidance on Procurement Regulations (2013), *United Nations Commission on International Trade Law*. Available at https://uncitral.un.org/sites/uncitral.un.org/files/media-documents/uncitral/en/guidance-on-procurement-regulations-e.pdf [Accessed 28 November 2023].

UNCITRAL Guide to Enactment of the UNCITRAL Model Law on Public Procurement (2012), *United Nations Commission on International Trade Law*. Available at https://uncitral.un.org/sites/uncitral.un.org/files/media-documents/uncitral/en/guide-enactment-model-law-public-procurement-e.pdf [Accessed 28 November 2023].

UNCITRAL Legislative Guide on Public-Private Partnerships (2019), *United Nations Commission on International Trade Law*. Available at https://uncitral.un.org/sites/uncitral.un.org/files/media-documents/uncitral/en/19-10872_uncitral_ppp_e_ebook_2021.pdf [Accessed 28 November 2023].

UNCITRAL Model Law on Public Procurement (2011), *United Nations Commission on International Trade Law*. Available at https://uncitral.un.org/en/texts/procurement/modellaw/public_procurement [Accessed 28 November 2023].

UNCITRAL Model Legislative Provisions on Public-Private Partnerships (2019), *United Nations Commission on International Trade Law*. Available at https://uncitral.un.org/sites/uncitral.un.org/files/media-documents/uncitral/en/19-11011_mlpppp_e.pdf [Accessed 28 November 2023].

United Nations (2015), *Resolution 69/313 Addis Ababa Action Agenda of the Third International Conference on Financing for Development (Addis Ababa Action Agenda), A/RES/69/313*. Available at www.un.org/en/development/desa/population/migration/generalassembly/docs/globalcompact/A_RES_69_313.pdf [Accessed 28 November 2023].

United Nations (2022), 'Goal 13: Take urgent action to combat climate change and its impacts', Sustainable Development Goals. Available at www.un.org/sustainabledevelopment/climate-change/ [Accessed 28 November 2023].

United Nations (2023), *Secretary-General's briefing to the General Assembly on Priorities for 2023*. Available at www.un.org/sg/en/content/sg/speeches/2023-02-06/secretary-generals-briefing-the-general-assembly-priorities-for-2023 [Accessed 28 November 2023].

United Nations Environmental Programme (2021), *State of the Climate*. Available at www.unep.org/explore-topics/climate-action/what-we-do/climate-action-note/state-of-climate.html?gclid=CjwKCAjwjYKjBhB5EiwAiFdSflz5kp1W_BUhWl2iKX7iIn50vqo6zCmNXQGbKu42aE2tpm1qeoNsOBoCGZoQAvD_BwE [Accessed 28 November 2023].

World Trade Organization (WTO) (2012), *Agreement on Government Procurement 2012 and Related WTO Legal Texts (GPA 2012)*. Available at www.wto.org/english/docs_e/legal_e/rev-gpr-94_01_e.pdf [Accessed 28 November 2023].

# 5 Using public procurement to build supply chains resilience to climate change[1]

*Valentina Bianchini*

## 5.1 Introduction

The recent COVID-19 pandemic highlighted the vulnerability and interconnectedness of global supply chains (GSCs) (Gereffi, 2020), which are increasingly subject to external shocks, including those produced by climate change, wherein effects compound year by year (Kara et al., 2021), or better to say, 'centigrade by centigrade'.

Climate change-related disruptions have far-reaching consequences on GSCs, affecting multiple industries, countries and stakeholders, necessitating a re-evaluation of GSCs strategies and risk management approaches (Sarkis et al., 2020).

Paradoxically, while GSCs are affected by climate change, they also significantly contribute to it. Recent studies estimate that emissions from GSCs related to climate change surpass operational emissions by a factor of 11.4 (CDP, 2023). These emissions result from activities associated with sourcing, production, transportation and disposal across the entire supply chain. Thus, investigating what is and what can be done to make GSCs more resilient while reducing their impact on climate change is very compelling.

While the private sector has been increasingly recognizing the impact of climate change on supply chains and has started integrating climate change considerations into their global sourcing strategies, the specific role played by public procurement in enhancing GSC resilience to climate change-related disruptions remains an understudied area.

So far, the business management literature has investigated how firms are addressing climate change in their GSCs as a problem of information asymmetry (Jira & Toffel, 2013; Dahlmann & Roehrich, 2019) requiring focal firms to enact suppliers' engagement strategies for information gathering, processing and transferring, or as a risk and performance management component (Kara et al., 2021).

While, in the public procurement literature, contributions emerged on how to measure public organizations' carbon footprints (Correia et al., 2013) and more widely on how to use public procurement as a leverage for "greening the market" in the form of 'Green Public Procurement' (GPP) (Cheng et al., 2018).

Yet, little is known about: Which procurement strategies do public authorities use to address climate change-related risks within their (global) supply chains?

DOI: 10.4324/9781032631721-8

This chapter addresses this question by taking stock of the literature on public procurement and GSCs resilience in the context of climate change and by presenting the case of three public administrations in the United States participating in the Carbon Disclosure Project (CDP) Public Authorities Programme.[2] To guide the analysis, the lens of transaction cost economics (TCE) Theory is employed (Williamson, 1985) and applied to public procurement (Rokkan & Haugland, 2022).

The TCE Theory sees public buyers as decision-makers that are rule-bounded and seeking to optimize the procurement process according to the transaction attributes (Williamson, 1996; Flynn & Davis, 2014). The increased uncertainty associated with climate change effects requires specific governance structures, which, according to TCE, evolve to minimize transaction costs stemming from uncertainty, asset specificity and frequency of transactions (Williamson, 1996). Within the context of GSCs and climate change, TCE can thus offer valuable insights into understanding governance strategies adopted by public buyers to face increasing complexity due to high environmental uncertainty, as well as high asset specificity and behavioural uncertainty.

This chapter provides several contributions to the literature on sustainable public procurement and the global scenarios ahead. First, it offers one of the first analyses of public buyers' strategies in addressing climate change issues in their supply chains. Secondly, it contributes to theorization efforts in the field of public procurement (Flynn & Davis, 2014; Koala & Steinfeld, 2018) by adopting TCE Theory for exploring the adaptation of public procurement governance to new risks. Thirdly, it provides a fresh perspective on the newly released data from the CDP Public Authorities Programme, previously investigated by others only from the Suppliers Engagement Programme (Jira & Toffel, 2013; Dahlmann & Roehrich, 2019).

The chapter's structure is organized as follows. First, a literature review of the nexus between globalization and resilience in supply chains is provided, together with a review of the potential role that procurement can play. Secondly, the TCE Theory is reviewed, providing the rationale for investigating the role of public procurement through its lenses. The theoretical framework developed is then applied to the case of three Public Authorities (PAs) in the United States, focusing on public procurement governance and transaction attributes, and performance assessed as the ability to adapt to higher complexity. Finally, the conclusions about the use of public procurement to enhance supply chains resilience to climate change are provided, together with some managerial and policy implications and study limitations.

## 5.2 Globalization and supply chains resilience

Globalization and supply chain resilience are two closely intertwined aspects of modern business operations. Globalization refers to the interconnectedness and integration of markets, economies and societies on a global scale (Petrella, 2005). Whereas resilience is the ability to anticipate, prepare for, respond to and recover from disruptions (Sheffi & Rice, 2005). These disruptions can range from natural disasters and geopolitical tensions to economic downturns and pandemics. Thus, a resilient supply chain is one that can quickly adapt and recover from shocks, minimizing negative impacts and maintaining business continuity.

In the last 40 years, the global economy has become more interconnected thanks to increased international trade. Between the fall of the Berlin Wall and the global financial crisis of 2007–2008, we lived in a period of hyper-globalization driven by advances in information and communication technologies and the progressive liberalization of trade flows between countries (Subramanian & Kessler, 2013). These factors stimulated the implementation of international production segmentation strategies and the expansion of supply chains across borders, creating increasingly complex and interdependent networks.

However, globalization has changed and is continuing to change. At present, globalization appears to be decelerating due to a variety of factors, such as (I) the reduction of labor cost advantages in countries that have been more actively involved in offshoring processes (e.g., like China); (II) the technological changes caused by the advent of Industry 4.0; (III) the growing protectionist trends in some advanced countries like the United States in response to the loss of their industrial base and new geopolitical tensions (Mariotti, 2022). These changes, combined with further disruptions resulting from the COVID-19 pandemic and conflicts, are continuing to slow down globalization and increasing regionalism (Panwar et al., 2022).

Changes in the globalization phenomenon have strong repercussions on the resilience of supply chain networks (Davis et al., 2021). On one hand, globalization offers numerous advantages to supply chains, such as access to diverse markets, cost-effective labor, specialized expertise and a broader range of suppliers. On the other hand, it also exposes supply chains to higher risks due to increased complexity, dependencies, longer lead times and potential disruptions across different geographical and political landscapes.

To enhance supply chain resilience in a globalized context, firms adopt several strategies. At strategic level, firms are diversifying their supplier base and spreading their sourcing across different regions to lower their risk exposure. This strategy helps in reducing dependency on a single location and minimizes the risk of complete disruption, for instance, due to climate-related events in a particular area. Diversification also allows for better risk management and ensures a steady supply even in the face of climate disruptions.

Reconfiguration and supply chain re-design are other adopted strategies. During the COVID-19 pandemic, firms needed to reconsider how they configured their supply chains, assessing whether re-shoring part of their productive capacity back home (back-shoring) or closer (near-shoring), also supported by new industrial policies that provided incentives to critical productive sectors (e.g. the pharmaceutical industry) (Coveri & Zanfei, 2023). Secondly, firms needed to rethink about their business models, assessing whether to reintroduce redundancy in critical supply chain components to provide backup options in case of disruptions. Overall, supply chains are increasingly designed to be agile and adaptable, allowing for quick adjustments in operations, sourcing and logistics to respond to changing conditions and unexpected events.

To anticipate disruptions, firms are also conducting a thorough mapping of their supply chains to identify vulnerabilities, including potential climate change-related risks. This involves assessing the geographical locations of suppliers and evaluating the exposure to climate hazards like extreme weather events, flooding, or sea-level rise (De Marchi & Gereffi, 2023). By understanding these risks, firms can devise strategies to mitigate disruptions and enhance supply chain resilience. To do so, firms work closely with their suppliers to assess and understand the environmental impact of their operations and encourage them to adopt sustainable practices.

Finally, firms increasingly invest in Information and Communication Technology (ICT) integration, data analytics and early warning systems to facilitate real-time monitoring and data sharing across the supply chain, enabling rapid responses to disruptions (Wang, 2023). For instance, by analyzing historical climate data and utilizing predictive analytics, they can proactively prepare for potential disruptions, adjust sourcing strategies and make informed decisions to mitigate supply chain risks.

## 5.3 Procurement as a leverage for resilience and sustainability in the public and private sectors

To increase both resilience and sustainability of GSCs, rethinking the sourcing and procurement strategies of both public and private sector organizations is key. Despite being motivated by different reasons, adopting sustainable procurement strategies allows both types of organization to reduce the environmental impact of their supply chains and reduce their reputational risks and financial losses.

For private sector organizations sustainable procurement can be a source of competitive advantage and business opportunities, allowing firms to attract new customers and investments by showing their reduced environmental impact and measuring their contributions towards sustainability. While pursuing both resilience and sustainability goals, firms are increasingly required to adopt a whole supply chain approach to their GHG emissions, accounting also for those generated upstream by their suppliers and sub-suppliers, and downstream, those generated by the end-users or customers (De Marchi & Gereffi, 2023). These together are called "Scope 3 emissions" – to differentiate them from the emissions directly produced by firms during their activities (Scope 1) or produced to energetically sustain their activities (Scope 2) – and represent the largest share of firms GHG emissions.

To reduce their contributions to climate change, public and private sector organizations can integrate sustainability criteria into their procurement processes and prioritize suppliers who follow sustainable practices, including reduced GHG emissions, sustainable sourcing of raw materials, ethical labour practices and circular economy principles.

Furthermore, they can incorporate climate resilience clauses into contracts and agreements with suppliers. These clauses define responsibilities and actions to be taken in case of climate-related disruptions. They may include contingencies, alternative supply sources, or provisions for adaptive strategies to ensure continuity in the supply chain during climate change-related events.

The procurement role has increasingly expanded also in the public sector, becoming a more strategic function of the organization (den Butter & Linse, 2008). The strategic role of public procurement arises primarily from its economic weight in terms of market size. In 2019, public procurement accounted for 12.6% of OECD Countries Gross Domestic Product (OECD, 2021). Therefore, what public administrations buy can significantly influence what the market offers. Secondly, efficiency and value for money considerations remain a priority in public spending. To minimize waste, it is therefore very important for governments to spend wisely.

In recognition of the strategic role public procurement, public purchases goals have been widened from focusing on cost, quality and time to encompass other objectives, such as reducing the negative environmental and social impact of economic activities. This new focus allows public procurement to contribute to wider policy goals and to fulfilling public organizations mandates. Public buyers are increasingly called to implement green public procurement (GPP) policies and regulations (Cheng et al., 2018).

GPP involves the selection and sourcing of products and services with lower environmental impact throughout their lifecycle (Rainville, 2017). This can include choosing products made from recycled materials, energy-efficient technologies, or goods with reduced carbon footprints.

By favouring environmentally responsible options, public buyers can stimulate market demand for sustainable products and services. Moreover, they can better face the risks posed by climate change on their supply chains.

Public authorities can develop guidelines and adopt standards such as Ecolabels to ensure that suppliers meet specific environmental sustainability goals (Sönnichsen & Clement, 2020), including reducing greenhouse gas emissions, minimizing waste, using renewable energy and adhering to sustainable sourcing practices. By setting these requirements, public buyers encourage suppliers to adopt environmentally friendly practices and contribute to climate change mitigation. Public authorities may also provide incentives or preferences to suppliers who follow sustainable practices in tenders award criteria, further encouraging the adoption of environmentally responsible behaviour (Bergman & Lundberg, 2013).

Moreover, public authorities can monitor and evaluate suppliers' compliance with sustainability and climate-related criteria (Sönnichsen & Clement, 2020). This includes tracking emissions, waste reduction and adherence to sustainable sourcing practices. Public buyers may also require reporting on environmental performance, encouraging suppliers to meet established sustainability targets, thereby reducing climate change contributions at the supply chain level.

To understand market readiness and foster sustainable innovative solutions, public authorities can also engage in transparent dialogues with suppliers to understand and address climate change risks within the supply chain. However, this can be done to a lesser extent compared to the private sector, as public buyers need to show compliance with principles of transparency, fair competition and anti-corruption.

Despite these impediments in supplier engagements, building partnerships also with third parties (e.g., NGOs, auditing firms, etc.) is crucial for public buyers to increase internal knowledge and the ability to enforce environmental standards, as well as conducting supplier monitoring and verification.

Finally, just like private sector firms, public buyers can conduct comprehensive risk assessments to identify vulnerabilities within the supply chain that may be exacerbated by climate change (Erridge & Mcllroy, 2002). These assessments are key for understanding how climate-related events such as extreme weather, resource scarcity, or disruptions in transportation can impact their extended supply chains.

Consequently, climate change risk mitigation strategies and contingency plans can be developed to ensure continuity of supply even when dealing with extended and complex supply chains.

## 5.4 Transaction cost economics, public procurement and climate change

In this chapter, the TCE lenses are adopted to analyze how public authorities address climate change-related disruptions in GSCs. The study's underlying assumption is that by considering the transaction attributes, public authorities can tailor their procurement strategies (governance) to mitigate climate change risks, ultimately contributing to a more sustainable and resilient supply chain network.

Coined by Coase during the 1930s in his renowned work "The Nature of the Firm" (Coase, 1937) and subsequently advanced by Williamson (Williamson, 1985), the TCE theory is founded on the discriminating alignment proposition, where transactions with diverse attributes align with governance structures to achieve cost-efficient outcomes (Williamson, 1985). Transaction costs encompass all expenses involved in acquiring goods and services, whether through the transfer of ownership rights in a market transaction or the transfer of responsibilities via an informal agreement (den Butter & Linse, 2008). These costs emerge to mitigate information asymmetries and opportunistic behaviours between the parties involved.

The rational or natural selection of governance mode depends on the fundamental transaction attributes, namely asset specificity, frequency and uncertainty (Williamson, 1998). Asset specificity refers to the unique physical and human assets underpinning the transaction and forming the basis of the exchange relationship. Relationship-specific investments in TCE denote investments that hold value exclusively within a specific transaction. The greater the asset specificity in a transaction, the more essential appropriate governance mechanisms become. Transaction frequency also dictates the necessary governance; a one-time purchase with no expectations of continuity requires a different governance mechanism than recurring purchases. For example, in the context of public procurement, public buyers may establish long-term contracts and collaborative endeavours with suppliers to ensure continuity and safeguard the relationship-specific asset.

Uncertainty refers to the sources of disruptions necessitating adaptation (Williamson, 1998), which can be linked to the external environment and to the behaviour of the actors involved. Climate change amplifies environmental uncertainty and unpredictability in suppliers' behaviours in response to environmental challenges, resulting in new transaction risks. These risks are heightened in extended supply chains, where interdependencies among suppliers' behaviours are robust.

The TCE theory underscores that heightened uncertainty mandates more intricate governance structures. The increased complexity demands adaptive strategies and transactional flexibility, implying that the governance mechanisms of public buyers should be adaptable to a changing environment. Consequently, public buyers, facing heightened uncertainty due to climate change, are expected to tailor the procurement strategy considering these pivotal attributes.

However, public buyers operate in a highly regulated environment, and when procuring, they need to respect the principles of equal treatment of suppliers and transparency (Knight et al., 2012), which may restrict their buyer–supplier relationship governance choices. When analyzing the differences between the public and the private sector in implementing green procurement, New et al. (2002) found them to be related mainly to the consequences of the application of regulations to the procurement process, which ties public procurers to bureaucratic procedures and gives them less flexibility in prioritizing sustainability over other criteria. Moreover, while firms can more easily adopt collaborative engagements with suppliers, public authorities need to justify that while they do so they do not breach any transparency principle- or process-related requirements, which makes them more likely to adopt transactional or market-based governance (Lian & Laing, 2004).

Because the regulatory boundaries public authorities are subject to take precedence to efficiency considerations in public procurement, Rokkan and Haughland (2022) theorized a specific TCE extension to public procurement, proposing that: (I) Public buyers generally lean towards utilizing market mechanisms to manage relationships with suppliers, and when they adopt non-market approaches, they usually take a unilateral approach rather than a bilateral one; (II) Enhancing the competence and decision-making autonomy of public buyers, especially when combined, will encourage the use of non-market strategies; (III) The traditional governance mode of public procurement is best suited for less intricate transactions, especially those involving the protection of specific assets, rather than to govern transactions characterized by high environmental and behavioural uncertainty.

However, enhanced competence and decision-making autonomy are expected to boost public procurement performance, especially in complex transactions. In the following section, the approach taken by three public authorities in the United States to govern climate change risks is explored against these theoretical propositions.

## 5.5 Case study: U.S. Public Authorities' responses to climate change risks in their supply chains

Public procurement officers in the United States allocate around $2 trillion per year for the acquisition of goods and services (Volcker, 2016), of which approximately

$1.3 trillion are spent at the state and local government levels, involving approximately 89,000 PAs (Baldus & Hatton, 2020). Because of the size of their expenditures, exploring U.S. PAs response to climate change risks is relevant both in terms of potential reductions in GHG emissions and in terms of potential for "green" market orientation.

The Carbon Disclosure Project (hereinafter CDP), an international non-profit environmental organization, launched in 2022 a new program for PA environmental impact disclosure to be piloted in North America, and then extended to Europe. The model for disclosure is intended to provide information to stakeholders about PA risk exposure and contribution to climate change. During its first year of operation, only three pioneering PAs have submitted and made publicly available information about their environmental impact: two local Public Utilities companies from California, the Los Angeles Department of Water and Power and the Sacramento Municipal Utility District and the International Airport of Philadelphia.

The Los Angeles Department of Water and Power (LADWP) is the largest municipal utility in the United States, responsible for delivering water and electricity to the city's residents and businesses, governed by a Commission and financed through service revenues and bonds, with its operations divided into Power, Water and Joint business systems.

The Sacramento Municipal Utility District (SMUD) is the nation's sixth-largest community-owned electric utility, is governed by a Board and recognized for its innovative energy efficiency, renewable power technologies and sustainable environmental solutions, including pioneering solar facilities, tree planting programs, green energy initiatives and a commitment to achieving absolute zero carbon emissions by 2030.

Owned by the City of Philadelphia, the Philadelphia Airport System (PAS) comprises two airports—Philadelphia International Airport (PHL) and Northeast Philadelphia Airport (PNE)—both financially self-sustaining entities managed by the City's Division of Aviation, with PHL being a major hub airport serving over 19.6 million passengers in 2021, while PNE primarily serves as a reliever airport for PHL.

In the next section, the data they provided in the CDP questionnaire are analyzed, according to the theoretical framework, namely in terms of buyer–supplier governance strategies, changes in procurement transaction costs and the role of competence and decision-making autonomy to address climate change risks.

### *5.5.1 Buyer–supplier relationship governance to address climate change risks*

The three U.S. PAs investigated have developed (LDWP and SMUD), or are developing (PAS), tailored Climate Change plans to guide their organization in devising strategies to achieve their GHG emissions reduction targets and embed climate change risks into the organization risk management framework. These plans vary in terms of ambitions, methodology and stakeholders' engagement, reflecting different maturity levels of sustainability integration into the organizations' strategies and operations.

*Table 5.1* Comparative table showing the goals and the buyer–supplier governance strategies adopted by the three public authorities to address climate change risks

| | *LDWP* | *SMUD* | *PAS* |
|---|---|---|---|
| GHG EMISSIONS TARGETS | Carbon neutrality by 2030 | Carbon neutrality by 2045 (as prescribed by California law) | Carbon neutrality by 2050 |
| SUSTAINABLE PROCUREMENT | Climate-related criteria in contracts | Climate-related criteria in contracts | Not mentioned |
| SUPPLIERS ENGAGEMENT | GHG tracking via Third-party verifications | Engaged in Climate Plan consultations; direct suppliers' evaluation; info used to inform risk management; suppliers' development | Engaged only to gather info about their energy and waste generated emissions |

*Source:* Own compilation.

The LADWP's climate plan (LA 100) outlines strategies, developed with research centres, to achieve 100% renewable energy supply for Los Angeles by 2045, while SMUD's climate plan (SMUD 2030 Zero Carbon Plan) is even more ambitious, aiming for carbon neutrality by 2030 due to climate change threats, utilizing qualitative and quantitative climate-related scenario analysis after stakeholder consultations. On the other hand, the PAS has two distinct plans to integrate sustainability into their strategy and address climate change risks, both striving for carbon neutrality by 2050, although they haven't employed climate-related scenario analysis in their strategy development.

The SMUD is the only authority that involved its suppliers in the consultations for formulating its climate change plan (Table 5.1) and that used supply chain risks to inform its overarching strategy, whereas LDWP involved them more selectively to inform its operations risk management strategy and PAS has not involved them at all at strategic level.

The LDWP adopts a risk-based approach to its buyer–supplier relationship, aiming to enhance tracking of GHG emissions within its supply chain by 2023 through risk and vulnerability identification, engaging suppliers via third-party programs like the CDP Supply Chain program and EcoVadis for sustainability ratings.

Aligned with a relational governance approach, LDWP incorporates climate-related criteria within supplier contracts; however, direct monitoring of Scope 3 emissions from its procurement processes is not conducted. Suppliers capable of calculating these emissions are expected to comply using their specific methodologies, reflecting a governance model grounded in trust among parties and reinforced by third-party monitoring tools like CDP and EcoVadis. At present, 17% of the

LDWP GHG Scope 3 emissions are calculated by using data derived from suppliers or value chain partners.

Contrarily to the LPWD and the SMUD, the PAS sustainability integration into their operations is at a very early stage, with supply chain risks and engagement not proactively sought. The PAS is in the process of updating its risk management strategy to embed climate-related risks, and at present, supply chain considerations are absent. Suppliers are engaged marginally on special projects, such as in ground support equipment electrification, and only their energy and waste generated emissions are calculated. This limited attention to supply chain sustainability is reflected also in the organization's sustainability targets, which tackle only Scope 1 and 2 emissions.

The SMUD stands as a pioneer in embracing sustainability strategies, surpassing both federal (EPA Clean Air Act) and state (SB-100, SB-32, SB-350) carbon emissions reduction mandates. Californian laws set already ambitious goals for public authorities, aiming for 60% renewable energy by 2030 and 100% by 2045. It's mandatory for SMUD to integrate climate-related risks into its organizational strategy, with a strong focus on mitigating supply chain risks within its climate plan and procurement governance.

The procurement policy at SMUD adheres to a comprehensive set of principles and strategies, including competition, inclusiveness, economic development, environmental procurement, responsible bidding, best value procurement, strategic alliances and supply chain risks. To enforce these principles, SMUD has instituted an environmentally sustainable purchasing program that ensures supplier compliance with climate change requirements through suppliers' evaluations. In 2022, SMUD asked all its suppliers about green procurement and climate change practices and used the information gathered by this assessment and by risk management to change its supply chain configuration. For instance, SMUD decided to shift to local manufacturers for purchasing cable and wires, priorly procured from suppliers in the southeast United States, reducing its transportation emissions by 234 MT of CO2 equivalent. Moreover, SMUD has started embedding sustainability requirements in the request for proposal to "encourage suppliers to propose cost-effective environmentally sustainable alternatives", with the aim of orienting the market by clarifying the organizations' expectations.

While this centralized governance approach provides SMUD with heightened control over climate change risks, it does entail increased transaction costs. Beyond supplier evaluation costs, the SMUD also provides suppliers with business development opportunities with programs specifically targeted to local small businesses. These proactive and centralizing efforts to mitigate climate change risks are motivated by increasing concern about their effects on the organization's operations but also by the opportunity to achieve competitive advantage, both enshrined in the Climate Emergency Declaration adopted in 2020 by the SMUD Board (SMUD, 2021).

In conclusion, we can affirm that the different procurement governance approaches adopted by the three PAs appear to be coherent with the maturity level of their knowledge about climate change-related risks impacting their organization.

Higher knowledge is linked to a more proactive attitude in considering supply chain-related uncertainties also in the procurement governance strategies. Moreover, higher knowledge about climate-related impacts on the organization also allowed the SMUD and the LWPD to design climate change-related programs that help position them in new customer segments, supporting not only the organization's resilience to shocks but also creating competitive advantages.

### *5.5.2 Changes in transaction costs due to climate change uncertainties*

The increased uncertainty brought by climate change-related events has been captured by the three PAs through climate-related risk management processes, whereby climate change risks were defined and assessed also in terms of increased operational costs.

Both the LWDP and the SMUD have set up climate change risk assessments occurring more than once a year, whereas the PAS frequency of risk assessment has not yet been defined (Table 5.2). Again, here the risk-spanning horizon and the sophistication level employed in the risk identification techniques reflect different maturity levels of sustainability embedded in the organization's risk management frameworks. For instance, the SMUD assesses risks across its upstream, downstream and direct operations.

Moreover, beyond calculating the impact and probability of the climate change-related risks, it has added the parameter of "velocity" defined as "the speed at which the risk will occur", accounting for the increased frequency of shocks. According to their risk assessment, the climate change-related risk that would seriously impact the organization operations is that of wildfires, which is expected to affect critical suppliers and increase indirect operating costs, motivating a more hands-on procurement governance strategy.

*Table 5.2* Comparative table showing the risk management focus adopted by the three U.S. public authorities and the anticipated cost increases to address climate change disruptions

| | *LDWP* | *SMUD* | *PAS* |
|---|---|---|---|
| SCOPE | Upstream, Organization, Downstream | Upstream, Organization, Downstream | To be defined |
| FREQUENCY | more than once a year | more than once a year | To be defined |
| COST INCREASES | Increasing procurement costs to ensure electric grid reliability and to procure more fuel due to temperatures rises; estimated financial impact 4–10 million dollars increase | Increase in indirect operating costs because of wildfires affecting critical suppliers | To be defined |

*Source:* Own compilation.

The LDWP risk assessment focuses more on the downstream dimension of the supply chain, giving more importance to climate change-induced changes in consumption behaviours, such as increases in electricity demands because of higher future temperatures. These changes are projected anyway to result in increasing procurement costs to ensure electric grid reliability and to procure more fuel due to temperature rises, with an estimated financial impact ranging from about 4 to 10 million dollars increase.

At the same time, the LDWP has also identified opportunities provided by climate change, such as the increase in energy sales brought by the increased electrification of transportation, increase in return on investments produced by low-emission technologies for the grid, increase in demand for energy efficiency buildings driven by the new law requirements (SB 350) and reduced costs derived from moving to more efficient premises.

Contrarily to SMUD and LDWP, the PAS is in the early stages of implementing the Sustainability Management Plan and Climate Adaptation and Resilience Plan (CARP) to address acute and chronic physical risks posed by climate change and integrate climate resilience into its operations.

While a hydraulic and hydrology study is being undertaken as flooding has been identified as a major threat to the PAS operations, climate change-related risks have not yet been identified nor their potential costs to the organization.

In conclusion, the assessment of climate change-related risks and their integration into organizational risk management processes varies among the three utilities – LWDP, SMUD, and PAS. The frequency, depth and sophistication of risk assessments reflect different levels of maturity in embedding sustainability considerations into their operations.

In essence, the three utilities exemplify diverse levels of readiness and strategic foresight in addressing climate-related risks. As climate change continues to pose uncertainties, the varying degrees of preparedness underscore the importance of a proactive and integrated approach to climate risk management across sectors.

### *5.5.3 The role of competence and decision-making autonomy*

Certainly, for both the LWDP and the SMUD, a crucial driver of their climate change strategies is represented by the California regulatory framework, which is very advanced in mandating public authorities to invest in renewable resources. The California "Clean Energy and Pollution Reduction Act" (Senate Bill no. 350/2018) together with the "100 Percent Clean Energy Act" (Senate Bill no. 100/2018) have set escalating renewable energy procurement targets for the state procurement, mandating P.A. to procure 60% of electricity from renewable sources by 2030 and complete reliance on carbon-free resources for electricity by 2045. The California Public Utilities Commission (CPUC) enforces RPS compliance rules for retail electricity providers, while the California Energy Commission (CEC) certifies renewable energy facilities. This largely explains why the two PAs located in California have been already considering climate change into their procurement strategies and risks.

California's regulatory framework provided legitimacy to both SMUD and LDWP decision-making bodies to adopt climate change-related governance strategies. In fact, to this external incentive, both the SMUD and the LDWP have corresponded internal organizational features that are conducive to building climate change resilience in the organizations' operations.

Top management support is likely to have reinforced the organizations commitments in adapting their procurement governance to account for climate change-related uncertainties (Table 5.3). In fact, SMUD's ambitious green procurement targets and commitments came from a Board Climate Emergency Declaration (SMUD, 2021) and have been cascaded across the organizations' departments, which are rewarded for exceeding the organizations' performance targets, including environmental ones.

On the contrary, the emerging climate change strategy being adopted by PAS appears to be derived less from a top-down approach, as there is no mandating law requiring it, and governance of the climate change strategy is being set up after its development. The PAS is planning to establish a Sustainability Steering Committee to "engage the C-Suite on the implementation of sustainability initiatives". The absence of top-down incentives might entail a longer adaptation process of the organizations' procurement governance, as decisions to change are more linked to the entity of climate change risks that the organization needs to face and the business opportunities that can arise from this shift, which will take time to materialize.

On the other hand, all the investigated PAs present or are building in-house knowledge and specific competences to manage climate change-related risks. All

*Table 5.3* Comparative table showing the role of competence and decision-making autonomy in the three U.S. public authorities and their drivers

| | *LDWP* | *SMUD* | *PAS* |
|---|---|---|---|
| COMPETENCE | Chief Sustainability Manager, Senior Assistant General Manager for climate change risks oversight, Study in Partnership with research agencies | Chief Carbon Zero Officer and Chief Strategy Officer | Sustainability Manager, study on hydrogeological risks |
| DECISION-MAKING AUTONOMY | Top management support | Board Climate Emergency Declaration | Planning to establish a Sustainability Steering Committee |
| DRIVERS | Normative pressure + competitive advantage | Normative pressure + competitive advantage | Competitive advantage |

*Source:* Own compilation.

three PAs have established a managerial-level sustainability function with oversight on the organization climate plan and related risks. In the LDWP case, there is also a dedicated Senior Assistant General Manager in charge of managing climate-related risks and opportunities in supply chain services. Whereas the Zero Carbon Plan in SMUD resulted in the creation of new executive positions, such as the Chief Carbon Zero Officer and the Chief Strategy Officer, reflecting the human resources investments that the PA made to increase its abilities to manage these new risks and strategy. In PAS, investments in building-related competence are reflected in plans to undertake climate change-related studies to inform decision-making and risk management strategies.

In conclusion, the evidence from the three cases confirms that both decision-making autonomy and competence are essential ingredients for the adaptation of public procurement governance strategies to the increased uncertainties resulting from climate change-related events. However, external incentives, such as normative pressures, can provide further legitimacy to PA for undertaking changes in their procurement strategies and organizational settings to adapt to external shocks.

## 5.6 Conclusions

This chapter emphasizes the imperative for public authorities to continually adapt and innovate their procurement governance and supply chain strategies to navigate the challenges posed by climate change in a globalized world and enhance resilience. Procurement has a crucial role to play in strengthening supply chain resilience and sustainability for both public and private sector organizations.

Recognizing the impact of climate change on business continuity, public and private sector organizations are adopting crisis prevention and preparedness strategies in their procurement processes (De Marchi & Gereffi, 2023). Both public and private sector buyers can employ a variety of strategies, ranging from policy integration and engagement with suppliers to risk assessment, to address climate change-related disruptions in their global supply chains. However, as shown by our case-study analysis, the extent to which they do so is a matter of internal capacities, risk awareness and decision-making autonomy.

Employing TCE as theoretical lenses, the analysis of three PAs in the United States shows how public authorities considered transaction attributes to tailor their procurement strategies (governance) for mitigating climate change risks, ultimately enhancing their supply chains sustainability and resilience.

Overall, the analysis of three U.S. PAs' responses to climate change risks underscores the interplay of regulatory influence, organizational competence and procurement governance strategies in building resilience against climate-change-induced uncertainties.

The pressure exerted by the California regulatory framework mandating renewable energy procurement targets marks a difference among the two California-based public authorities and the Philadelphia Airport is that posed by the California regulatory framework by mandating renewable energy procurement targets, showing its role in influencing the more advanced climate change procurement strategies of SMUD and LADWP. This regulatory obligation has increased top management support, further reflected in the ambitious renewable energy procurement commitments of both organizations.

Thus, rather than solely relying on decision-making autonomy, it appears that top management commitment driven by mandatory regulatory requirements has fostered the adaptation of the PA procurement strategies.

Moreover, as predicted by the TCE framework developed by Rokkan and Haugland (2022), to face higher complexity and uncertainty, all the three PAs invested in establishing a dedicated sustainability function, reflecting an effort to build internal competences. Organizational structures were also adapted in all the three PAs following the adoption of the climate plans to ensure their enforcement.

In the same way, the procurement governance strategies were adapted to the anticipated increases in transaction costs due to climate change-related events and varied based on their knowledge about climate change-related risks. For instance, SMUD's whole-supply-chain approach to risk assessment accounted also for risk "velocity", capturing the frequency challenge posed by climate change-related shocks, which further motivated the adoption of a more hands-on procurement governance strategy. Whereas the LADWP's risk assessment focused on downstream supply chain changes due to climate change, estimating increased procurement costs and identifying opportunities for increased operational efficiency and competitive advantage, resorting to third parties to monitor compliance.

Applying the TCE theory to the case of the three U.S. PAs shows the significance of aligning governance structures with transaction attributes such as asset specificity, frequency and uncertainty. In the face of heightened uncertainty resulting from climate change, for public buyers, the adaptation of governance procurement mechanisms should become a priority.

### *5.6.1 Practical implications*

The study findings show that public sector organizations must continuously adapt and innovate their procurement governance and supply chain strategies to effectively respond to the challenges posed by climate change and globalization.

Public buyers should implement GPP policies, selecting products and services with lower environmental impact, aiming at both stimulating market demand for sustainable offerings and increasing resilience of their supply chains. This can be done only if they take a holistic look at their supply chains, identifying and monitoring risks beyond their direct suppliers.

To improve their supply chain resilience and sustainability, public buyers should also reduce rigidity in their supply chain configurations, prioritizing sourcing from local suppliers and those committed to sustainability. However, public buyers should also pay attention to competitiveness and equal treatment of suppliers, motivating the preference for shorter supply chains through a thorough risk-informed strategy and cost-benefit analysis.

As the chapter shows an anticipated increase in procurement transaction costs due to climate change uncertainties and impact, public buyers should take a proactive approach and adopt climate-change scenario planning analysis to enhance preparedness to potential threats.

Finally, the chapter's findings show that public sector organizations should invest in human capital and build internal competences to best equip their procurement functions, thus increasing the organization's abilities to respond to external shocks.

Establishing dedicated sustainability functions and revising organizational structures to enforce climate plans appear to be essential for effective procurement responses.

### *5.6.2 Policy implications*

This study confirms the driver role that mandatory regulations play in increasing public procurement strategic function, particularly on sustainability matters. At present, several countries are discussing changes in their regulatory frameworks introducing obligations for supply chains due diligence and reporting on GHG emissions.

To compare climate change policies and regulations is beyond the aims of this chapter, but here it should be briefly mentioned the most recent regulatory changes adopted by some countries that will likely drive public procurement efforts in embracing a whole of supply chain considerations in the near future.

The State of California is at the forefront of these regulatory efforts, having just passed two climate-related bills: the Senate Bill 253 (Climate Corporate Data Accountability Act[3]) and Senate Bill 261[4] (Greenhouse Gases: Climate-Related Financial Risk). These bills would require large companies doing business in the state, both private and public, to publicly disclose and receive independent third-party verification of their greenhouse gas emissions across Scope 1, Scope 2 and Scope 3 and provide climate-related financial risk reports, potentially impacting businesses' compliance efforts and expenses.

In Europe, the European Commission is discussing a proposal[5] for mandatory corporate human rights and environmental due diligence to promote sustainable and responsible corporate behaviour across global value chains, requiring companies, from the EU or operating in Europe, to identify and address adverse impacts on human rights and the environment.

Some European countries like Germany and France have already integrated obligations for due diligence. The German Supply Chain Act[6] ("Lieferkettensorgfa ltspflichtengesetz" or LkSG) mandates companies operating in Germany with over 3,000 employees (lowering to 1,000 in 2024) to conduct supply chain due diligence, including risk identification, management, mitigation and annual reporting, aiming to protect human rights and minimize environmental harm, with non-compliance potentially incurring penalties of up to 2% of the company's annual turnover (European Coalition for Corporate Justice, 2023). France's Duty of Care Law[7] ("Devoir de Vigilance"), effective from 2017, applies to companies established in France employing more than 5,000 people in France or 10,000 people worldwide, requiring them to follow the UN Guiding Principles on Business and Human Rights[8], establish supply chain due diligence processes, conduct risk mapping, due diligence assessments and mitigation and develop annual plans to prevent human rights and environmental violations, with non-compliance potentially resulting in civil liability following a formal complaint for inadequate diligence or adherence to reasonable care standards (EcoVadis, 2023).

It is thus important for countries, particularly in the EU and United States, to stay ahead of these regulatory changes and reconsider public sector risk management approaches to embed a whole of supply chain approach.

### *5.6.3 Limitations*

This study also presents limitations as the case analysis is based on secondary data and documental review; thus, saturation of information and evidence can be enhanced by conducting interviews and data triangulation. However, the data gathered through the CDP Public Authorities Programme questionnaire represent a very important effort to advance research on this very emerging topic.

## Notes

1 This work received funding from the SAPIENS project, European Union's Horizon 2020 research and innovation program, Marie Skłodowska-Curie grant agreement No. 956696.
2 CDP operates as a no-profit worldwide environmental disclosure system, assisting companies, cities, states and regions in assessing and addressing climate change risks and opportunities in response to requests from their investors, purchasers and city stakeholders.
3 Available at https://leginfo.legislature.ca.gov/faces/billTextClient.xhtml?bill_id=202320240SB253
4 Available at https://leginfo.legislature.ca.gov/faces/billTextClient.xhtml?bill_id=202320240SB261
5 *EU Corporate Sustainability Due Diligence Proposal.* Available at https://commission.europa.eu/business-economy-euro/doing-business-eu/corporate-sustainability-due-diligence_en#what-are-the-next-steps.
6 *Germany Supply Chain Act.* Available at www.bafa.de/EN/Supply_Chain_Act/supply_chain_act_node.html.
7 *France Duty of Care Law.* Available at www.legifrance.gouv.fr/jorf/id/JORFTEXT000034290626/.
8 *Guiding Principles on Business and Human Rights: Implementing the United Nations 'Protect, Respect and Remedy' Framework (Guiding Principles), UN Doc. HR/PUB/11/04 (2011).* Available at www.ohchr.org/Documents/Publications/GuidingPrinciplesBusinessHR_EN.pdf.

## References

Baldus, B. J. and Hatton, L. (2020), 'US chief procurement officers' perspectives on public procurement', *Journal of Purchasing and Supply Management*, 26(1), p.100538.

Bergman, M. A. and Lundberg, S. (2013), 'Tender evaluation and supplier selection methods in public procurement', *Journal of Purchasing and Supply Management*, 19(2), pp. 73–83.

CDP-Carbon Disclosure Project (2023), *Scoping Out: Tracking Nature across the Supply Chain, Global Supply Chain Report 2022*. Available at www.cdp.net/en/research/global-reports/scoping-out-tracking-nature-across-the-supply-chain [Accessed 31 August 2023]

Cheng, W., Appolloni, A., D'Amato, A., and Zhu, Q. (2018), 'Green public procurement, missing concepts and future trends–A critical review', *Journal of Cleaner Production*, 176, pp. 770–784.

Coase, R. H.. (1937), 'The nature of the firm', *Economica*, 4(16), pp. 386–405.

Correia, F., Howard, M., Hawkins, B., Pye, A., and Lamming, R. (2013), 'Low carbon procurement: An emerging agenda', *Journal of Purchasing and Supply Management*, 19(1), pp. 58–64.

Coveri, A. and Zanfei, A. (2023), 'The virtues and limits of specialization in global value chains: analysis and policy implications', *Journal of Industrial and Business Economics*, 50(1), pp. 73–90.

Dahlmann, F. and Roehrich, J. K. (2019), 'Sustainable supply chain management and partner engagement to manage climate change information', *Business Strategy and the Environment*, 28(8), pp. 1632–1647.

Davis, K. F., Downs, S., and Gephart, J. A. (2021). 'Towards food supply chain resilience to environmental shocks', *Nature Food*, 2(1), pp. 54–65.

den Butter, F. A. and Linse, K. A. (2008), 'Rethinking procurement in the era of globalization', *Sloan Management Review*, 50, pp. 76–80.

De Marchi, V. and Gereffi, G. (2023), 'Using the global value chain framework to analyse and tackle global environmental crises', *Journal of Industrial and Business Economics*, 50(1), pp. 149–159.

EcoVadis (2023), *Duty of Care Law (Devoir de Vigilance)*. Available at https://ecovadis.com/regulations/duty-of-care/ [Accessed on 31 August 2023]

Erridge, A. and McIlroy, J. (2002). 'Public procurement and supply management strategies', *Public Policy and Administration*, 17(1), pp. 52–71.

European Coalition for Corporate Justice (2023), *German Supply Chain Law Comes into Force*. Available at https://corporatejustice.org/news/german-supply-chain-act-comes-into-force/ [Accessed on 31 August 2023].

Flynn, A. and Davis, P. (2014), 'Theory in public procurement research', *Journal of Public Procurement*, 14(2), pp. 139–180.

Gereffi, G. (2020), 'What does the COVID-19 pandemic teach us about global value chains? The case of medical supplies', *Journal of International Business Policy*, 3(3), pp. 287–301

Jira, C. and Toffel, M.W. (2013), 'Engaging supply chains in climate change', *Manufacturing & Service Operations Management*, 15(4), pp. 559–577.

Kara, M., Ghadge, A. and Bititci, U.S. (2021), 'Modelling the impact of climate change risk on supply chain performance', *International Journal of Production Research*, 59(24), pp. 7317–7335.

Knight, L., Harland, C., Telgen, J., Thai, K. V., Callender, G., and McKen, K. (eds.). (2012), *Public Procurement: International Cases and Commentary*. Routledge, London.

Koala, K. and Steinfeld, J. (2018), 'Theory building in public procurement', *Journal of Public Procurement*, 18(4), pp. 282–305.

Lian, P. C. and Laing, A.W. (2004), 'Public sector purchasing of health services: A comparison with private sector purchasing', *Journal of Purchasing and Supply Management*, *10*(6), pp. 247–256.

Mariotti, S. (2022), 'A warning from the Russian–Ukrainian war: avoiding a future that rhymes with the past', *Journal of Industrial and Business Economics*, 49(4), pp. 761–782.

New, S., Green, K., and Morton, B. (2002), 'An analysis of private versus public sector responses to the environmental challenges of the supply chain', *Journal of Public Procurement*, 2 (1), pp. 93–105.

OECD (2021), 'Size of public procurement', in *Government at a Glance 2021*. OECD Publishing, Paris. Available at https://doi.org/10.1787/18dc0c2d-en.

Panwar, R., Pinkse, J., and De Marchi, V. (2022). 'The future of global supply chains in a post-COVID-19 world', *California Management Review*, 64(2), pp. 5–23.

Petrella, R. (2005), *Globalization and Internationalization: The Dynamics of the Emerging World Order. States against Markets*. Routledge, London.

Preuss, L. (2011), 'On the contribution of public procurement to entrepreneurship and small business policy', *Entrepreneurship & Regional Development*, 23(9-10), pp. 787–814.

Rainville, A. (2017), 'Standards in green public procurement–A framework to enhance innovation'. *Journal of Cleaner Production*, 167, pp.1029–1037.

Rokkan, A. I. and Haugland, S. A. (2022), 'A transaction cost approach for public procurement', *Journal of Business & Industrial Marketing*, 37(2), pp. 341–352.

Sarkis, J., Dewick, P., Hofstetter, J.S., and Schröder, P. (2020), 'Overcoming the arrogance of ignorance: Supply-chain lessons from COVID-19 for climate shocks', *One Earth,* 3, pp. 9–12.

Sheffi, Y. and Rice Jr, J. B. (2005), 'A supply chain view of the resilient enterprise', *MIT Sloan Management Review*, 47, pp. 41–48.

SMUD (2021), *2030 Zero Carbon Plan*. Available at www.smud.org/-/media/Documents/Corporate/Environmental-Leadership/ZeroCarbon/2030-Zero-Carbon-Plan-Technical-Report.ashx [accessed on 31 August 2023].

Sönnichsen, S. D. and Clement, J. (2020), 'Review of green and sustainable public procurement: Towards circular public procurement', *Journal of Cleaner Production*, 245, p. 118901.

Subramanian, A. and Kessler, M. (2013), 'The hyperglobalization of trade and its future' in *Towards a Better Global Economy: Policy Implications for Citizens Worldwide in the 21st Century.* Oxford University Press, Oxford, pp. 216–276.

Volcker, P.A. (2016), *Doing the People's Business: Key Competencies for Effective Public Procurement*. The Volcker Alliance, *New York, NY.*

Wang, S.L. (2023), 'Digital technology-enabled governance for sustainability in global value chains: A framework and future research agenda', *Journal of Industrial and Business Economics*, 50(1), pp. 175–192.

Williamson, O.E. (1985), *The Economic Institutions of Capitalism*. Free Press, New York.

Williamson, O.E. (1996), *The Mechanisms of Governance*, Oxford University Press, Oxford.

Williamson, O. E. (1998), 'Transaction cost economics: How it works; where it is headed,' *De Economist*, 146, pp. 23–58.

# 6 Sustainable public procurement of school meals in Europe

*Orsolya Diófási-Kovács and Anna Freund*

## 6.1 Introduction

Our topic focuses on a small but potentially impactful field of supply networks, namely sustainable school food systems. In the case of school food systems, sustainability impacts include both environmental and socio-economic aspects.

The environmental impacts arise from (1) the choice of raw materials, seasonality, location of production, farming and trade practices of food products; (2) the distribution practices with the mode of transport and warehousing; and (3) processing in forms of energy and water use, and waste generation. All these elements effect the impact of school food systems on our climate and need special attention on all levels of planning.

The group of socio-economic impacts includes short supply chains, indirectly supporting the economy through relationships with suppliers, job creation, food culture, healthy eating and support for disadvantaged people.

Within the school food systems, public procurement plays a very important role and is among the strongest determinants of sustainability impact. Public procurement is relevant in the field of school food networks because it can determine the upstream of the supply chain (suppliers, ingredients and all the related emissions and sustainability aspects) in the case of food procurement. In the case of catering procurement, the upstream of the supply chain, food production along with related operations and services (sustainability impacts connected to cooking and transporting the food, even reverse logistics of food waste) can be affected, made more sustainable by careful choices made in public procurement.

Based on our literature review, sustainable school food systems seem to be an important but underrepresented topic among academic papers. We aim to fill this gap and contribute to the research field. In our understanding, food systems encompass the full range of activities, components and actors involved in the production, processing, distribution, preparation, serving, consumption and waste management of food, as well as the spaces and environments in which these processes take place (SchoolFood4Change project – EU Horizont, 2020; Franco & Fajó-Pascual, 2022). School food systems or networks also include associated educational practices.

In our study, we use data from school food network mapping done in the SchoolFood4Change project running in 12 European countries between January

DOI: 10.4324/9781032631721-9

2022 and December 2025. The project aims for furthering sustainable and healthy public food networks through innovative public procurement, training of cooks for planetary diets and improving school food environments through the holistic 'WholeSchoolFoodApproach'.

Our work is based on analyzing the different school food networks, their public procurement models from the environmental, social and economic sustainability point of view.

As a result of the analysis, we can distinguish and describe different public procurement models along with possible impacts on the climate and sustainability. The two extremes include centralized and decentralized models (Tátrai & Vörösmarty, 2023). The results of this current paper should contribute both to the academia and the practitioners and seek to support the goals of the European Farm2Fork Strategy (EU Green Deal, 2020) .

## 6.2 Literature review

In the literature review, we focus on the sustainable school food systems. To obtain as many relevant papers as possible, the search engines of Web of Science (WoS) and Scopus were used (see details in Methodology subchapter 3.1.). Food systems can relate to various processes from farm to fork (Dimitri & Effland, 2020; Miller et al., 2021; SchoolFood4Change project – EU Horizont, 2020; Franco and Fajó-Pascual, 2022). European regulations highlight the following actions related to food systems: (1) ensuring sustainable food production and food safety – handled at all levels of the food supply network, from food processing, wholesale, retail, until hospitality and food services; (2) healthy and sustainable diets must be incorporated into the routine of food consumption; (3) reducing food loss and waste must appear throughout food systems; and (4) finally, it is also stated that food fraud must be combated throughout the food supply chain (EU Green deal, 2020).

In the scope of the literature, there are school food systems that can contribute to sustainability goals, in terms of social, environmental and economic responsibility. The centralized and controlled nutrition of young generations might have a dominant impact on their lifelong health conditions (Miller et al., 2021), which can also serve the establishment of their relationship with food consumption. Studies emphasize that school food systems might have a positive impact on the lives of students (Capper et al., 2019). In addition, school food systems focus on nutrition intake policies that support a healthy food environment (McIsaac et al., 2019; Manson et al., 2021). According to experts, not only the supply of food should be managed by school food systems, but also a wider range of activities belong to this task. Capper et al. (2019) consider school food systems as complex ones. Similarly to this, Gilbert et al. (2018) state that 'school food systems contain teachable spaces within schools to introduce students to healthy eating, fresh food and the (in)equitable economies of the larger community food system' (Gilbert et al., 2018, p. 96). Based on the study of Jones, Ruge, and Jones (2022), activities like practical cooking education, practical food-growing education, farm, community and food business links education, food health and sustainability education, school mealtime experience and engagement, co-production and policy change characterize mostly integrated school food systems (Jones et al., 2022, p. 549). SchoolFood4Change (SchoolFood4Change project – EU Horizon 2020) project states that developments towards sustainability shouldn't only be done within schools while educating children and changing the food consumption behaviour of them, but also training cooks, caterers and public procurers at city level might contribute to a comprehensive change in the school food systems. Sustainable public food systems can be defined as school food systems that promote the health of children and young adults in a way that is profitable for all actors in the food value chain, respects the social and cultural environment and considers natural resources and ecological processes, while respecting the limits of the planet. Sustainable school food systems are governed in a democratic and participatory way by all stakeholders, including farmers, purchasers, cooks, teachers, students, parents, municipal and school administrators, researchers, other professionals and policy makers (SchoolFood4Change project – EU Horizont, 2020). The interesting side of school food systems is the different structure of them, varying country-by-country (Ahmed et al., 2022).

Since the above-mentioned definition of sustainable school food systems applies an integrative approach (SchoolFood4Change project – EU Horizont, 2020; Jones et al., 2022), procurement (in most cases, public procurement) has very high relevance in the form of requirements related to sustainability aspects throughout the supply network of school food. Public food procurement aims to exploit the potential of government purchasing power and is often used as a policy instrument to reach sustainability goals, namely more sustainable food systems and healthy diets (Swensson et al., 2021). Public procurement (PP) of food products includes all types of institutional food procurement, including meals for hospitals, schools, elderly homes, universities and other social programmes. For this reason, we reviewed the most recent literature on public procurement of food, with interest in school food system-relevant findings.

The most relevant paper for our research is that of Tregear et al. (2022), who seek to identify the effects of different procurement approaches on sustainability in the case of school food provisions. They also aim to identify which activities and parts of food supply chains have the greatest environmental impacts (Vidergar et al., 2021; Tregear et al., 2022) and which procurement solutions contribute to the economic, social and environmental sustainability goals of contracting authorities. They highlight the role of procurement professionals in setting sustainability criteria and complying with policy-level goals in sometimes resource-poor environments. They identify two different types of procurement approaches using the case study method, analyzing a pair of school food supply chains from five European countries. The procurement approaches in the paper are called 'models of public food procurement', and the differentiation of the models is based on the localization of procurement. Local model service (LOC) cases and low cost (LOW) procurement model cases are described and analyzed from the carbon footprint, nutrition value and economic impacts point of view. Their results suggest that in terms of carbon footprint reduction, the composition of meals, for example, reducing the amount of meat and increasing organic content, is more relevant than local sourcing since transportation accounts for a relatively small range of emissions. The nutritional quality does not show a significant correlation to local sourcing either; only the economic impacts of local sourcing models can provide clearer benefits. The authors suggest that reducing the negative sustainability impacts of public school food procurement can be done most efficiently by introducing sustainable menus (e.g., effects on carbon emissions and nutrition value) and improving the prestige of school food provision overall, along with the appreciation of catering staff since they have an influence on the cooking methods, menu innovations, school food environments that support less waste and even educational activities.

Filippini et al. (2018) focus on organic ingredients in public school food procurement in Italy, where national guidelines are in place for school catering and a minimum environmental criteria set is part of their regulatory framework. The questionnaires were distributed in Lombardy among 1546 municipalities. Their findings include that urbanized areas are more likely to include certified organic products: due to the physical distance from the farms and lack of trust, a third-party certification is expected (Filippini et al., 2018). They also conclude that it is more likely to have more organic products among food procured if local is not among the purchasing criteria. Big catering companies are also mentioned as providers of organic produce, despite somewhat higher prices. The role of parents and teachers in food education and the improvement of sustainability aspects is also mentioned. (Filippini et al., 2018)

In the paper of Neto (2020), 21 green public procurement schemes from 11 European countries are analyzed for the food product and catering service public procurement subjects. This paper dives into a PP-specific differentiation, as the paper provides an overview of the types of criteria used by contracting authorities. The criteria present in more than 50% of the schemes are organic produce, seasonal and fresh produce, staff training and environmental aspects, transportation criteria, menu planning, packaging, waste management and seafood-related criteria. The criteria present in a smaller number of tenders include cutlery and crockery, environmental management systems, catering equipment, cleaning products, energy and water management, vending machines, paper products, carbon footprint of products and avoidance of palm oil. Other criteria include animal welfare, food safety and traceability, GMO-free, hormone-free meat, fair trade products, the encouragement of SME and micro-suppliers to tendering, cooperation with suppliers, staff training and workers' rights. The public school food procurement-related papers we worked with do not mention the question of centralization or decentralization (Ferraresi et al., 2021) of public procurement; however, we find it as an important aspect to be considered.

As mentioned by Filippini et al. (2018) and Tregear et al. (2022) as well, a dominant factor of school food systems are the stakeholders, who in some specific cases seem to be difficult to map (Filippini et al., 2018; Johnson et al., 2020; Woodside et al., 2021; Diófási-Kovács & Freund, 2022; Tregear et al., 2022). Students are identified as having an important role in the regulation of the system and could also be fundamental representatives of potential change. In general, kitchen staff are also important, besides teachers. The school community may be involved in regulating the system. Principals, and thus the school management, seem to play an important role in this issue (McIsaac et al., 2019). Alongside the above, doctors and nurses can also be stakeholders (Harper et al., 2017), so the representatives of the healthcare sector, highlighting the importance of views of diabetics. Studies show that the role of the decision-maker is not negligible in the management of school food systems, thereby making them a prominent stakeholder (Gilbert et al., 2018). School food systems can be specified from a financing perspective. In general, school meals can be provided on a self-financed basis or with state funding. In addition, some school food systems allow food to be brought into the school from home, whereby the regulator has less influence on sustainability efforts (Lucas et al., 2017).

According to our knowledge, the topic of school food systems has not been researched comprehensively yet (a modest amount of academic papers from the Scopus database report on projects from practice), but practitioners have already started several projects to develop the quality and sustainability of school food systems worldwide. For example, the University of British Columbia in Canada released the result of the project 'Think&EatGreen@School' (Think&EatGreen@School Website, 2019), which concentrated on public schools (Rojas et al., 2011). School citizens seem to be the best targets of research because, due to compulsory education, a dominant number of pupils appear in this central stakeholder group. Connected to the statements of Miller et al. (2021) about the lifelong impacts of school food systems, Rojas et al. (2021) add that participating in well-structured and sustainable school food systems can lead students and the school staff too to see food as a fundamental link between nature and humans. Their project emphasizes that food procurement processes in schools have an ecological, environmental and social impact not only on the local communities but also on the food industry, which serves the food for the consumers (Rojas et al., 2011; Weiler et al., 2015). The Think&EatGreen@School project considered the sustainable school food systems, based on results of the UC Sustainable Agriculture Research and Education Programme (SAREP) (UC SAREP Website, 2020), as 'a collaborative effort to build more locally based, self-reliant food economies—one in which sustainable food production, processing, distribution and consumption is integrated to enhance the economic, environmental and social health of a particular place' (Feenstra, 2002; Rojas et al., 2011).

Another project aiming to develop school food systems was conducted by the research group of Ilić (2022) as a part of the framework 'Horizon 2020' project 'Strengthening European Food Chain Sustainability by Quality and Procurement' (Strength2Food Website, 2023). Through the intervention, they tried to incorporate fruit and vegetable consumption into the daily food intake of the age group studied, and hence tried to use methods that included parental education through websites, visual supports, such as posters in classrooms and the integration of new meals into school food systems (Ilić et al., 2022). This research deals mostly with the nutrition intake part of sustainability regarding both the social and environmental impacts using the tools of the change of the habits of students and their parents.

Experts additionally highlight that school food systems must be built on pillars that don't increase food waste (Capper et al., 2019), and this is considered as an environmental impact of sustainability. The general aim of interventions is to provide healthy and environmentally sustainable food for students (Black et al., 2015), which supports both the social and environmental characteristics of sustainability.

## 6.3 Methodology

### *6.3.1 Methodology of secondary data analysis*

To gather data for the literature review, the search engines of Web of Science (WoS) and Scopus were used, where the keywords were tested in more combinations. First, the phrase 'sustainable school food system' was searched, which gave only two findings in the case of Scopus and zero using WoS. An interestingly low number of publications appeared after having searched for this combination of keywords: "ALL=((("school food system") AND ("sustain*" OR "respons*" OR "social*" OR "enviro*" OR "econom*" OR "develop*" OR "improv*"))). A maximum number of 17 papers remained via Scopus and 11 papers via WoS. We used R Studio's bibliometrix package to merge the obtained papers, and the number of 22 publications build the basics of the literature review. After having analyzed the papers, we decided to complement the first literature search. The second part of the searching process covered the literature review of sustainable public procurement of food and catering. The search resulted in only one paper with the exact keywords, then we separated the keywords into two parts. 46 is the number of findings when using 'public food procurement' and adding 'school' with an 'AND' operator halved the list of matches. Some of the findings have already appeared within the first search too.

### *6.3.2 Methodology of empirical data analysis*

In our paper, we analyze different school food systems from the 17 European cities participating in the SchoolFood4Change project with a focus on their public procurement models. These cities are: Budapest (HU), Copenhagen (DK), Dordogne (FR), Essen (DE), Gent (BE), Leuven (BE), Lyon (FR), Malmö (SE), Milan (IT), Nuoro (IT), Nuremberg (DE), Tallinn (EE), Umeå (SE), Valencia (ES), Vienna (AT), and Viimsi (EE).

Our research questions are:

RQ-1: What kind of school food system models exist within the analyzed cities?
RQ-2: What are the characteristics of these school food system models?
RQ-3: What are the effects and potentials of the different models from the sustainability point of view?

A questionnaire was compiled by the SF4C consortium based on preliminary, in-depth interviews with the stakeholders of school food systems. Based on the preliminary interviews, we built a mapping methodology, which consists of 6 steps. The first 3 steps represent the data sourcing activity: (1) identification of stakeholders, (2) process mapping (identification of material flows), and (3) analyses of legal and economic environment. The second 3 steps deal with the analysis of the exact cases: (4) selection of the focal company, identification of business relationships (power relations, financing and information flows), (5) visualization of the school food system map, and (6) analysis and identification of problem areas (Diófási-Kovács & Freund, 2022). To gain a comprehensive view and to reach responses from all SF4C project participants, the decision was made to prepare a questionnaire based on the first three data sourcing steps of the methodology. The questionnaire contains mostly open-ended questions, where respondents have the possibility to give detailed answers similarly to an interview situation. The data we analyze in this paper originates from the questionnaire completed by the city representatives.

The structure of the questionnaire can be divided into two main categories. First, the National Lead Partner (hereinafter: NLP) level was asked about the basics of their school food systems. The second level of the analysis is built on data coming from the city level, with cities providing detailed information about their school food systems and procurement practices. Table 6A.1 (to be found in the annex) lists the questions asked from the NLPs and cities. Based on the questions and answers given by the different cities, we created a school food system matrix, which can be analyzed horizontally and vertically. The vertical story line provides a description of the local school food system, a city-level case study can be derived and leaves room for individual in-depth analyses of their school food system (Mapping methodology steps 4-5-6) (Diófási-Kovács & Freund, 2022).

The paper introduces two cases, which represent the two extremes of the procurement models found. The centralized case is from Hungary and the decentralized case introduced is from France. In these two presented cases, all 6 steps of the mapping methodology of the authors (Diófási-Kovács & Freund, 2022) were applied. The cases are presented because they allow a more comprehensive view about the operations and the decisions made by the interviewees (Yin, 2012), and highlight the reasons for applying these extreme public procurement models. In the SF4C project, this analysis will be done for each city with the aim of further developing their school food systems towards sustainability.

The horizontal analysis of the school food system matrix is the subject of the current paper and provides space for overall, general findings, introduced in the following section.

## 6.4 Analysis

The aim of our work isn't to compare the different countries within the SF4C project, but to recognize patterns and different models and solutions of the countries to provide school meals for children.

On the municipality/regional level, most of the cities have reported about existing food and sustainability policies; only 2 cities do not have either of the two policy types. Two cities mentioned project-based best practices without an explicit policy framework, and 2 mentioned policies under development.

The local public procurement landscape differs quite a lot, although the EU public procurement law is the basic legal framework in all responding cities. There are centralized (Ferraresi et al., 2021) procurement solutions, where the procurement takes place outside of the schools (this is the majority of the cases), and the decentralized solution when schools prepare tenders and procurement procedures individually. The decentralized solution is usually under the national public procurement threshold in value, so the public procurement law does not directly apply to these organizations. However, the basic principles of Public Procurement are mentioned and applied by all cities: principles of economic efficiency, transparency, equality and non-discrimination vis-à-vis bidders, using municipal financial resources (i.e., ultimately taxpayers' money) economically. Procuring healthy, organic or local meals is also mentioned as a principle in some cases. Guidelin,es and, in some cases, mandatory criteria are typically created by a central body about sustainability, which has to be followed by the contracting authorities. The existence of guiding information about sustainable food/catering is used irrespective of centralized or decentralized procurement solutions.

In the case of centralized procurement solutions, an interdisciplinary team is responsible for demand analyses, criteria setting, tendering and contracting, where sustainability experts, public procurement managers, legal experts and representatives of the procuring organization work together.

Some municipalities (e.g. the city of Milan) own catering companies that provide meals for educational institutions; some contract private catering companies (e.g., city of Vienna) or apply the combination of these (e.g., city of Budapest). Some cities have educational institutions with kitchens where food is cooked and served, and usually these institutions provide catering for other schools or kindergartens nearby that only have infrastructure for serving food. The criteria used for the procurement of food or catering services are to serve good, healthy, climate-smart and customized meals, increase organic volume and local meals and reduce GHG emissions originating from food procurement, animal welfare and regional products. Through the public meal, the cities aim to contribute to good public health and sustainable development. However, they have no information on the supplier's supply chain beyond the procurement requirements. The health and nutrition-related requirements are in all cases provided by national law or mandatory guidelines.

Both the decentralized and centralized procurement solutions buy food and catering services as well, or some combination of these. Most municipalities use e-procurement platforms.

The meals vary by each city; most of them serve hot meals, meaning soup and main dish, even salad, but some cities only serve cold snacks. The price of the meals is typically divided between the municipality and the parents. The cost of ingredients and the labour costs are mentioned separately in some cases (e.g., parents pay for the cost share of ingredients, and the municipality provides resources for the labour costs of providing meals). The prices range between 1 and 8 euros/meal. Subsidies are typically given based on the socio-economic status of families and vulnerability.

## 6.5 Example cases

The examined municipalities represent two differently built school food and catering systems, which are explained through the factors of Table 6.1. Two municipalities – a Hungarian (Case 1) and a French (Case 2) one – provide a different methodology when organising their public procurement steps regarding their school food systems. Case 1 is responsible for supplying about 100 school units

*Table 6.1* Different characteristics of public procurement in school food systems

| | | |
|---|---|---|
| Factor (1) Policy framework | | |
| Existing food and sustainability policy | Only sustainability policy | No policies |
| Factor (2) Legal framework | | |
| Mandatory sustainability criteria | Suggestions, guidelines about criteria | |
| Factor (3) Subject of procurement | | |
| Food | Catering service | both |
| Factor (4) PP threshold | | |
| Under PP threshold | Above PP threshold | |
| Factor (5) Organization of PP of school food provision | | |
| Centralized | Decentralized | |
| Factor (6) Personnel involved in the procurement process | | |
| Interdisciplinary team | Food provision expert (single responsible) | |
| Factor (7) Digital solutions in PP | | |
| e-Procurement | Paper-based process | |
| Factor (8) Kitchen types (physical activities of school food provision) | | |
| Cooking kitchen | Warming kitchen | |
| Factor (9) Meals provided | | |
| Warm meals | Snacks and sandwiches | |
| Factor (10) Subsidies of meals | | |
| Fully subsidized | Partially subsidized | Meals paid by the parents |

*Source:* Own compilation, based on data from (SchoolFood4Change project – EU Horizont, 2020).

(kindergarten, elementary and secondary schools), which is a huge challenge for them to operate both in a sustainable, economically returnable and effective way. In contrast, Case 2 is responsible for catering only in junior high schools, in 35 school units. Two side characteristics (centralized and decentralized) of public procurement organizations are introduced through the cases of a French and a Hungarian municipality. Due to the different public procurement approaches, the school food and catering systems in the examined cases are structured in different ways. While Case 1 needs to organize its supply based on various upstream services, Case 2 is serving the 35 units as much as possible on their own capacity.

### *6.5.1 Policy framework of public food procurement – Factor (1)*

Case 1 has only a sustainability policy, which is rather general and does not focus on food-related questions. Thus, the Hungarian municipality is committed to extending their policies in the direction of food. In order to support this goal, Case 1 is participating in the FOODCLIC project (FoodCLIC Website, 2024), whose objective is to develop a food policy for their municipality. Case 2 has both food policy and sustainability policy, and their further introduced system shows the manifestations of the effects of these policies.

### *6.5.2 Legal framework of public food procurement – Factor (2)*

While Case 1 shows a strong compliance with the EU and Hungarian (partly derived from the EU directives) regulations regarding public food procurement, Case 2 does not seem to build only on these directives. In September 2015, Hungary adopted the Act 2015/143 on Public Procurement (PPL), which defines national rules on public procurement procedures and concessions as well as implements the EU Public Procurement Directives (EU PP Directives, 2014). This act is valid in all parts of the country. Case 1 has its own PP rules, but it does not specify food-related issues. Case 2 rather focuses on its local policy, aiming at 100% organic, 100% local and 100% homemade meals. The examined French municipality has so far 8 units that run under this policy, and according to them, all of them will be in line as soon as 2026. This difference in the emphasis on the legal framework compliance might be led back to the number of students who must be supplied by the municipalities. The dimensional diversity (Case 1 – 100 units, Case 2 – 35 units) may require a different approach. In a community with a larger student population, there is a strong reliance on legal compliance (adherence to rules), while a municipality serving smaller units may have the capacity to develop rules that require stricter compliance than the mandatory EU rules.

### *6.5.3 School food and catering service system – Factor (3–10)*

The subject of the PP (3) at Case 1 is both food and catering, while Case 2 focuses rather only on food procurement. The French municipality aims to produce the food coming from reliable suppliers on their own, and it also contributes to monitoring their school food and catering system. When talking about meeting the PP threshold (4), both examined municipalities have their PPs above the threshold. Only in smaller, unpredictable cases is the system of OTC (this platform is used for smaller procurement requirements) used by Case 2, e.g., for replacing a smaller missed order because of bad weather conditions. The organizational structure (5) of PP of school food provision differentiates in the two examined cases. The Hungarian municipality implements a centralized solution, while the French case is decentralized. This dominant difference is the reason for introducing the school food and catering service systems of these two municipalities. Personnel/organizations involved in the procurement process (6) are different in both cases. At the Hungarian municipality, Catering Service Provider (CSP) is owned and maintained by the examined Hungarian municipality. This CSP and its employees are responsible for the provision of the educational institutions in Case 1. The French municipality rather acts as an information provider because the schools are individually responsible for the PP process. Both cases use e-procurement as a traceable solution (7), and digitalization mainly appears in this aspect of their operations. The kitchen types (8) in Case 1 show a shared solution. There are cooking kitchens, cooking&warming kitchens and only warming kitchens available in the served school units. This can be derived from the types of activities applied within the school units. The examined Hungarian case consists of cooking, serving meals and also procuring catering services for the supply. In contrast to it, in the French case, there are multifunctional (cooking&serving) kitchens only. Case 2 does a joint activity: cooking&serving and, in some cases, neighbouring schools share their capacity, e.g., butcher. Both municipalities are committed to high-quality and healthy meals (9), and in order to provide it, they cook (or, in the Hungarian case, cook and procure catering) warm meals. Finally, the subsidies of meals (10) differentiate in the two examined cases. Case 1 enables all three solutions (fully subsidized, partially subsidized and meals paid by the parents), while Case 2 operates with a partially subsidized solution.

It is seen that both in the case of the centralized and decentralized sample, there are different solutions but the same goals when organising the school food and catering system. It took years for Case 2 to build the system. A key element to operate decentralized efficiently is to involve stakeholders in the progress, and therefore the commitment to the provision of sustainable and healthy food plays an important role. In contrast, shortages (regarding capacity or capital) can lead to work at the level of compliance, which is not more or less than aiming for high-quality goals because the regulations also describe an appropriate requirement for the school food and catering provision.

## 6.6 Discussion

As we analyzed the questionnaires according to the 6-step methodology (Diófási-Kovács & Freund, 2022) used, the descriptions of the processes within the school food systems/networks showed that the school food environment has a significant role in shaping the whole network. Some schools have kitchens suitable for providing meals for the students, and some schools only have serving kitchens on site and require catering service to have food delivered for the students. These infrastructure-related determinants originate from historic building design, ownership structures of school buildings and the location of the schools. These endowments and the personal commitment of the employees have an impact on the procurement strategies applied. Reaching to the public procurement-related phrases of 'centralized' and 'decentralized' (Tátrai & Vörösmarty, 2023), we introduce two theoretical, extreme school food system models. These categories are determined by the available infrastructure of schools, meaning that the respondents described that their procurement models were dependent on the available infrastructure for food provision at the schools. Based on the extremes of the different solutions, we can say that there can be two types of theoretical school food systems: (1) centralized school food systems and (2) decentralized school food systems. Based on the two models, we can show the basic characteristics of the different school food system designs:

*Centralized school food systems:*

- the municipality is directly responsible for the PP of the school food provisions
- the subject of the procurement is catering service – the service is outsourced since schools only have warming kitchens on site
- the procurement volumes are high in amount and value as well – over the PP threshold

*Decentralized school food systems:*

- schools are directly responsible for the food provisions
- the subject of procurement is food – the schools have their own kitchens where they prepare the food, with their own cooks, personnel and know-how
- the procurement volumes are relatively low; the value is below the PP threshold

To answer our first research question "What kind of school food system models exist within the analyzed cities?" we can say that hybrid models are used; some kind of combination of the described two models are in place.

The second and third research questions are about the characteristics of the models (RQ2: What are the characteristics of these school food system models? RQ3: What are the effects and potentials of the different models from the sustainability point of view?) To answer these questions, we will highlight the procurement-related solutions, since besides the infrastructure, the procurement models have system-shaping potential.

The sustainable school food system-related studies Filippini et al. (2018) and Tregear et al. (2022) highlighted procurement criteria (local, lowest price, organic characteristics) and, to our understanding, did not differentiate between the public procurement process based on legal aspects (e.g., under or above threshold procurement). These are important differentiators since above PP threshold procurement has to be done in a legally binding environment, which provides less flexibility for the contracting authorities.

The subject of public procurement is also relevant in terms of criteria setting (Neto, 2020): in the case of food/raw material provision, different sustainability criteria can be applied (supply chain traceability, organic certification, farming methods, location, seasonality, etc.), which focuses more on the upstream side of the supply chain, then in the case of catering service procurement (energy efficiency of provision, sustainable menu, cooking methods, delivery options, etc.) which has a stronger downstream focus. According to the study of Neto (2020), typical criteria of food product procurement: organic produce, seasonality, packaging (recycled content and recyclability of the material) and certified fish products. Typical criteria for service provision are connected to staff training, waste management, menu planning and transportation (Neto, 2020).

In the case of (1) centralized school food systems, the municipality is directly responsible for the provision of schools, meaning that the public procurement process is delivered by the municipality and the efficiency aspect is very strong – usually the provision of many schools is part of the tendering. Respectively, in most cases, an interdisciplinary team is working on the criteria set for the PP of catering services, meaning at least legal experts, procurement managers and food experts. If the city has a sustainability or food strategy, the municipality might even implement mandatory sustainability criteria and work in a policy-supported environment – sending clear signals for the market, requesting sustainable services. The advantages of this setup might be that the municipality, due to the higher volumes, has significant purchasing power, the potential to shape the market and a better bargaining position. The resource intensity of this food system design is lower since the maintenance of the kitchen and the related equipment, the catering, cooking equipment and personnel are outsourced. The disadvantage of this solution is that the needs are expressed very far from the actual customers of the supply network (namely the children and the school). Also, in the case of the procurement of catering services, the criteria are typically addressing the catering processes, and the downstream side of the supply chain, the upstream side, the sources of the ingredients and the length of the supply chain might not be so transparent, and the farm-to-caterer route can be out of sight.

In the case of (2) decentralized school food systems, the school is directly responsible for the provision of the children, meaning that the procurement of ingredients, the maintenance of the kitchen, the responsibility about staff and so on are within the area of competence of the school. In this case, usually an individual is responsible for the food supply; his/her expertise and motivation determine the sustainability aspects of procurement; and the city- or municipality-level sustainability and food-related policies might only serve as guidelines or ideas for sustainable procurement, with a lot of flexibility. They procure smaller volumes, so there can be a possibility to partner with farmers, significantly shorten supply chains and buy regional and seasonal products.

As a conclusion, we can say that both procurement models have advantages and disadvantages in terms of sustainability, and since they are theoretic in nature, we can say that real-life solutions need to combine and use the most advantageous elements of the two systems in order to create sustainable and resilient school food systems. Each school food system needs their individual assessment (which will be done in the framework of the SF4C project), and based on their special characteristics, the improvement solutions can be discovered. For example, the question of supporting the local economy might be a great challenge for a centralized school food system, while the transition to organic ingredients would not be achievable for all product types in a decentralized, local sourcing-focused system. The actual environmental and socio-economic impact assessment of the different school food systems and their procurement models still needs to be done, which is planned within the SF4C project. It must be highlighted that the two extreme models are not better than one another from the sustainability point of view; both models have the potential to support sustainability if managed carefully.

## 6.7 Conclusion

School food systems are important, and have great potential for transformation towards sustainability and reducing the climate impact. Sustainable school food systems need the power of all stakeholders to build a healthier, more sustainable future from an economic, social and environmental point of view. In general, it is seen that without policy-level commitment, school food systems won't change. In the praxis, sustainable public procurement of food can lead to more sustainable operation if there is a strong motivation of the decision-makers.

Due to the high number of children, adolescents and their parents, it seems to be worth to intervene at school food systems regarding sustainability. A wide range of people can be reached using the school as a main platform for changing and maintaining healthy eating habits within the limits of our planet.

## Acknowledgments

This work was supported by NKFIH through Grant K 137794.

## References

Ahmed, D. I., Trent, R., and Koch, P. (2022), 'Creating the scratch cooked school food framework: Qualitative data analysis of a scratch cooking pilot', *Health Promotion Practice*, 23(6), pp. 963–972. doi: 10.1177/15248399211038942.

Black, J. L., Velazquez, C. E., Ahmadi, N., Chapman, G. E., Carten, S., Edward, J., Shulhan, S., Stephens, T., and Rojas, A. (2015), 'Sustainability and public health nutrition at school: Assessing the integration of healthy and environmentally sustainable food initiatives in Vancouver schools', *Public Health Nutrition*, 18(13), pp. 2379–2391. doi: 10.1017/S1368980015000531.

Capper, T. Brennan, S., Woodside, J., and McKinley, M. (2019) 'The EIT food school network: Integrating solutions to improve eating habits and reduce food wastage in secondary schoolchildren', *Nutrition Bulletin*, 44(4), pp. 356–362. doi: 10.1111/nbu.12406.

Dimitri, C. and Effland, A. (2020) 'From farming to food systems: The evolution of US agricultural production and policy into the 21st century', *Renewable Agriculture and Food Systems*, 35(4), pp. 391–406. doi: 10.1017/S1742170518000522.

Diófási-Kovács, O. and Freund, A. (2022), 'Exploring the relationship between sustainable public catering and short supply chains – developing and presenting a supply chain mapping methodology through a Hungarian case study', in *Proceedings of the 22nd International Scientific Conference Business Logistics in Modern Management*, Osijek, Croatia, pp. 141–154. https://blmm-conference.com/wp-content/uploads/BLMM2022_Conference_Proceedings.pdf. Osijek, Crotia.

EU Green deal (2020) *Farm to Fork Strategy, European Comission*. Available at https://food.ec.europa.eu/system/files/2020-05/f2f_action-plan_2020_strategy-info_en.pdf

EU PP Directives (2014) *EU Directives 2014/23/EU, 2014/24/EU, and 2014/25/EU*. Available at https://kozbeszerzes.hu/kozbeszerzesek-az/europai-jogi-hatter/kozbeszerzesi-iranyelvek/.

Feenstra, G. (2002) 'Creating space for sustainable food systems: Lessons from the field', *Agriculture and Human Values*, 19(2), pp. 99–106. doi: 10.1023/A:1016095421310.

Ferraresi, M., Gucciardi, G., and Rizzo, L. (2021), 'Savings from public procurement centralization in the healthcare system', *European Journal of Political Economy*, 66(February 2020), p. 101963. doi: 10.1016/j.ejpoleco.2020.101963.

Filippini, R. De Noni, I., Corsi, S., Spigarolo, R., and Bocchi, S. (2018) 'Sustainable school food procurement: What factors do affect the introduction and the increase of organic food?', *Food Policy*, 76(February), pp. 109–119. doi: 10.1016/j.foodpol.2018.03.011.

FoodCLIC Website (2024) *FoodCLIC project*. Available at https://foodclic.eu/.

Franco, M. and Fajó-Pascual, M. (2022), 'School food systems', *Reference Module in Food Science*, pp. 1–9. https://schoolfood4change.eu/wp-content/uploads/2023/07/SchoolFoodSystems_Chapter_HumanNutritionEncyclopaedia.pdf

Gilbert, J., Schindel, A., and Robert, S. (2018), 'Just transitions in a public school food system: The case of Buffalo, New York', *Journal of Agriculture, Food Systems, and Community Development*, 8(October), pp. 95–113. doi: 10.5304/jafscd.2018.08b.011.

Harper, K. Sands, C., Angarita Horowitz, D., Totman, M., Maitín, M., Rosado, J. S., Colon, J., and Alger, N. (2017), 'Food justice youth development: using Photovoice to study urban school food systems', *Local Environment*, 22(7), pp. 791–808. doi: 10.1080/13549839.2016.1274721.

Igarashi, M., De Boer, L., and Michelsen, O. (2015), 'Investigating the anatomy of supplier selection in green public procurement', *Journal of Cleaner Production*, 108, pp. 442–450. doi: 10.1016/j.jclepro.2015.08.010.

Ilić, A. Rumbak, I., Brečić, R., Barić, I. C., and Bituh, M. (2022), 'Increasing fruit and vegetable intake of primary school children in a quasi-randomized trial: evaluation of the three-year school-based multicomponent intervention', *Nutrients*, 14(19). doi: 10.3390/nu14194197.

Johnson, B. J. Zarnowiecki, D., Hutchinson, C. L., and Golley, R. K. (2020), 'Stakeholder generated ideas for alternative school food provision models in Australia using the nominal group technique', *International Journal of Environmental Research and Public Health*, 17(21), pp. 1–12. doi: 10.3390/ijerph17217935.

Jones, M., Ruge, D., and Jones, V. (2022), 'How educational staff in European schools reform school food systems through "everyday practices"', *Environmental Education Research*. Routledge, 28(4), pp. 545–559. doi: 10.1080/13504622.2022.2032608.

Lucas, P. J. Patterson, E., Sacks, G., Billich, N., and Evans, C. E. L. (2017), 'Preschool and school meal policies: An overview of what we know about regulation, implementation, and impact on diet in the UK, Sweden, and Australia', *Nutrients*, 9(7), pp. 1–20. doi: 10.3390/nu9070736.

Manson, A.C., Johnson, B.J., Zarnowiecki, D., Sutherland, R., and Golley, R.K. (2021), 'The food and nutrient intake of 5- To 12-year-old Australian children during school hours: A secondary analysis of the 2011-2012 National Nutrition and Physical Activity Survey', *Public Health Nutrition*, 24(18), pp. 5985–5994. doi: 10.1017/S1368980021003888.

McIsaac, J. L. D., Spencer, R., Stewart, M., Penney, T., Brushett, S., and Kirk, S. F. L. (2019), 'Understanding system-level intervention points to support school food and nutrition policy implementation in Nova Scotia, Canada', *International Journal of Environmental Research and Public Health*, 16(5).doi: 10.3390/ijerph16050712.

Miller, G. D. Kanter, M., Rycken, L., Comerford, K. B., Gardner, N. M., and Brown, K. A. (2021), 'Food systems transformation for child health and well-being: The essential role of dairy', *International Journal of Environmental Research and Public Health*, 18(19), pp. 1–14. doi: 10.3390/ijerph181910535.

Neto, B. (2020), 'Analysis of sustainability criteria from European public procurement schemes for foodservices', *Science of the Total Environment*, 704, p. 135300. doi: 10.1016/j.scitotenv.2019.135300.

Rojas, A., Valley, W., Mansfield, B., Orrego, E., Chapman, G. E., and Harlap, Y. (2011), 'Toward food system sustainability through school food system change: Think & eatgreen at school and the making of a community-university research alliance', *Sustainability*, 3(5), pp. 763–788. doi: 10.3390/su3050763.

SchoolFood4Change project – EU Horizon (2020), *Grant number: 101036763.*

Strength2Food Website (2023), *Strengthening European Food Chain Sustainability by Quality and Procurement Policy Project.* Available at: https://cordis.europa.eu/project/id/678024.

Swensson, L. F. J. Hunter, D., Schneider, S., and Tartanac, F. (2021), 'Public food procurement as a game changer for food system transformation', *The Lancet Planetary Health*, 5(8), pp. e495–e496. doi: 10.1016/S2542-5196(21)00176-5.

Tátrai, T. and Vörösmarty, G. (2023), 'Comparative analysis of the European centralised public procurement', *Central European Journal of Public Policy*, 17(1), pp. 1–15. doi: 10.2478/cejpp-2023-0007.

Think&EatGreen@School Website (2019) *Think&EatGreen@School (TEGS) project.* Available at https://thinkeatgreen.ca/.

Tregear, A. Aničić, Z., Arfini, F., Biasini, B., Bituh, M., Bojović, R., Brečić, R., Brennan, M., Colić Barić, I., Del Rio, D., Donati, M., Filipović, J., Giopp, F., Ilić, A., Lanza, G., Mattas, K., Quarrie, S., Rosi, A., Sayed, M., Scazzina, F., and Tsakiridou, E. (2022), 'Routes to sustainability in public food procurement: An investigation of different models in primary school catering', *Journal of Cleaner Production*, 338(March 2021). doi: 10.1016/j.jclepro.2022.130604.

UC SAREP Website (2020), *Sustainable Agriculture Research & Education Program.* Available at https://sarep.ucdavis.edu/.

Vidergar, P., Perc, M., and Lukman, R. K. (2021), 'A survey of the life cycle assessment of food supply chains', *Journal of Cleaner Production*, 286. doi: 10.1016/j.jclepro.2020.125506.

Weiler, A. M. Hergesheimer, C., Brisbois, B., Wittman, H., Yassi, A., and Spiegel, J. M. (2015), 'Food sovereignty, food security and health equity: A meta-narrative mapping exercise', *Health Policy and Planning*, 30(8), pp. 1078–1092. doi: 10.1093/heapol/czu109.

Woodside, J. V. Adamson, A., Spence, S., Baker, T., and McKinley, M. C. (2021), 'Opportunities for intervention and innovation in school food within UK schools', *Public Health Nutrition*, 24(8), pp. 2313–2317. doi: 10.1017/S1368980020004668.

Yin, R. K. (2012), *Applications of case study research*. SAGE Publications Inc., Thousand Oaks, California.

## Annex

*Table 6A.1* Introduction of the structure of the questionnaire serving as the data source

| *Description of the question* | *NLP level* | *City level* | *Number of valid answers* | *Described area of the question* |
|---|---|---|---|---|
| Description of the national (or regional) food policy/strategy in place, if relevant for the procurement process. Please mention (if relevant): key responsible public institutions and their roles, nutrition/food standards, hygiene and food safety requirements, environmental considerations, social responsibility considerations, etc. | x | | 12 | Process mapping and identification of national food and sustainability policies (2) |
| Description of the national (or regional) legal framework in which you operate (procurement law/regulations, mandatory environmental/social criteria – if any in force), national health dietary guidelines. Please mention the general requirements and other relevant aspects for (school) food procurement. Please add the current status of implementation of GPP in food and catering services (if possible). | x | | 11 | Legal framework of school food systems (3) |

(*Continued*)

*Table 6A.1* (Continued)

| *Description of the question* | *NLP level* | *City level* | *Number of valid answers* | *Described area of the question* |
|---|---|---|---|---|
| Description of the school food and especially sustainable school food related initiatives and projects in your country (these covering the whole country or bigger regions. You can only focus on your region). | x | | 11 | Legal and economic framework of school food systems (3) |
| Does your municipality/ Region have a sustainability/ food policy in place? | | x | 16 | Legal and economic framework of school food systems (3) |
| Please provide a short overview of the local public procurement landscape (local policy/strategy, basic principles and institutions, local public procurement legislation/rules). | | x | 15 | Process mapping and identification of national food and sustainability policies (2) |
| Please provide a short overview of the school food and catering service system at the local/level (local policy/strategy, key responsible public institutions, basic principles, and issues regulated legally at the local level, any reference to sustainability in the general food policy, etc.). | | x | 15 | Process mapping and identification of stakeholders (1-2) |
| Please describe the school food/catering service procurement process and the participants of the process. | | x | 15 | Process mapping and identification of stakeholders (1-2) |
| Please describe the school food and especially sustainable school food related initiatives and projects in your municipality. | | x | 15 | Legal and economic framework of school food systems (3) |

*Table 6A.1* (Continued)

| *Description of the question* | *NLP level* | *City level* | *Number of valid answers* | *Described area of the question* |
|---|---|---|---|---|
| What is the average actual cost (price) of a main school meal (e.g., lunch)? Please specify what it includes – only a hot meal or also a cold meal (snacks, sandwiches), if relevant. | | x | 14 | Economic framework of school food systems (3) |
| What does the meal cost entail? | | x | 16 | Economic framework of school food systems |
| What is the financing/cost model for school meals in your municipality? | | x | 17 | Economic framework of school food systems (3) |
| Comments (please specify, if applicable, who subsidizes (state, municipality), at what rate or amount, for whom it is subsidized – all or only vulnerable groups, etc. | | x | 17 | Economic framework of school food systems (3) |
| What is the operational structure of school catering in your municipality? | | x | 17 | Process mapping (2) |
| To what extent is your procurement digitalized (e-procurement, e-forms)? | | x | 15 | Process mapping (2) |
| Do you have information on the sustainability of your suppliers' supply chain? (both in terms of environmental and social responsibility) | | x | 15 | Process mapping (2) |
| Where do you think SF4C should focus the most on in your municipality? Answer from the perspective of the city project team as a whole, considering your needs and priorities | | x | 17 | Process mapping (2) |

*Source:* Own compilation, based on data from SchoolFood4Change project – EU Horizont (2020).

# PART III

# Preferences and political economy in public procurement

# 7 Colloquium

*Geo Quinot and Benjamin V. Rosa*

## 7.1 Geo Quinot – Introductory remarks

The practice of preferences in public procurement has a long history. In his magisterial work on procurement linkages, McCrudden (2007) records local preferences in U.S. federal procurement legislation from as early as 1844, and there will undoubtedly be earlier examples of such practices around the globe. Current use of preferences in public procurement dates back almost a century, with the basic Buy American policy that is still in use today having been introduced by the Buy American Act in 1933 (Golub & Fenske, 1987; McCrudden, 2007). It is a widespread phenomenon, and there are today very few (if any) modern public procurement systems that do not include some form of preferences.

At its simplest, the practice refers to granting some form of comparative advantage to particular suppliers (either directly or on the basis of their goods or services) in the procurement process. There is tremendous variation in both the design and purpose of these mechanisms within and between procurement systems. However, the one common denominator between them is that they all serve to leverage public procurement for distinct public policy purposes. That is, a policy purpose beyond the mere acquisition of goods or services. Arrowsmith and Kunzlik (2009) have labelled such policy objectives as "horizontal policies", i.e. a policy objective horizontal to that of acquiring the goods or services (and the eventual public policy objective to be served by such goods and services once acquired). A preference in public procurement, in whatever form, is thus always an attempt by a public entity to use its market power as a buyer to pursue a particular public policy objective. And to be clear, that power is not insignificant. The global procurement market is valued at over $13 trillion annually, or over 15% of global GDP (UNEP, 2022). The power to steer that amount of spending in one direction or another is accordingly a potentially impactful power.

### *7.1.1 Scepticism in global policy perspective*

Debate on the use of public procurement preferences in the recent past has played out in the tension between the local and the global in the post-World War II economic integration and globalization agenda. Within the economic integration,

DOI: 10.4324/9781032631721-11

free-trade perspective, procurement preferences have often been framed as protectionist (Warner, 2011; Davies, 2011; Linarelli, 2011). As a result, procurement preferences are viewed as inherently problematic and only to be tolerated in narrow terms as exceptions to the norm.

The World Trade Organization's Agreement on Government Procurement (the GPA) is a good example of this perspective. Under the GPA, preferences are only allowed within a very narrow scope, subject to the national treatment principle informing the agreement. Any form of procurement preference by a GPA member state that would (either directly or indirectly) favour local suppliers over suppliers of other GPA member states, would fall foul of this principle and thus potentially the GPA (depending on whether the procurement falls within the coverage of the GPA in the particular state) (Linarelli, 2011; Bolton & Quinot, 2011). These could include any preferences to local suppliers or local content, preferences to suppliers from particular regions, preferences for suppliers from certain identified groups within the country (e.g. specific minority or historically disadvantaged groups) or preferences for suppliers registered under specific support programmes, such as a national industrial development programme or small business development programme.

### *7.1.2 A shift in policy perspective*

In the wake of the United Nation's millennium development goals and now the United Nation's Agenda 2030 with its Sustainable Development Goals (SDG), sustainable development has gained significant force as an increasingly dominant global policy agenda. Alongside growing public policy resolve around climate change, sustainable development has, in my view, brought a shift in global perspectives on public procurement preferences. A turn to sustainability in public procurement mediates the policy tension experienced in procurement preferences between the global and local. It does so by recognizing that the pursuit of local sustainability priorities, for which a mechanism like preferences is ideally suited, serves the global sustainability objective. SDG 12.7 makes this clear by stating, as a target, to promote public procurement practices that are sustainable, *in accordance with national policies and priorities.* Within this paradigm, a procurement preference scheme that targets local food production, for example, does not elicit an inherent suspicion, as in the free-trade paradigm. Rather, it becomes an indicator of the achievement of a leading global policy objective, contributing to the number of countries implementing sustainable public procurement policies and action plans (SDG indicator 12.7.1).

South Africa provides a good illustration of this shift. As the most unequal society globally (at least according to the Gini coefficient index (World Bank, 2021)), South Africa has relied heavily on public procurement preferences to pursue wealth redistribution, promote historically disadvantaged groups, and generally, realize substantive equality (Quinot, 2019). This is done through the extensive, formal system of preferential procurement as explicitly mandated in Section 217(2) of the Constitution of the Republic of South Africa, 1996 and implemented via the Preferential Procurement Policy Framework Act of 2000. In brief, the scheme entails a mandatory price preference in public procurement ranging between 10% and 20% for suppliers meeting specific criteria, mostly relating to their participation in the government's overarching broad-based black economic empowerment policy, using factors such as level of black (South African) ownership and management of the supplier. This preference scheme undoubtedly narrows down competition in favour of specific domestic suppliers, has a protectionist effect and accordingly presents a challenge to South Africa's participation in the GPA (Bolton & Quinot, 2011). It thus stands to be viewed with scepticism from a free-trade perspective. However, substantive equality is probably the highest national priority in South Africa. Accordingly, procurement practices such as the preferential procurement scheme fall squarely within SDG target 12.7 in aiming to achieve wealth redistribution and counter the poverty that accompanies the massive wealth inequalities in the country. In a sustainability paradigm, South Africa's preferential procurement scheme is thus a fine example of the use of procurement for sustainable development (Stoffel et al., 2019; Shai, Molefinyana, & Quinot, 2019). This is not to suggest that the South African scheme is without challenges, there certainly are many, but my argument is that they are challenges of design, not of principle.

The important point around the policy-perspective shift is that the nature of the relevant preference schemes has not changed. They remain protectionist in nature. What has changed is the policy framework within which preferences are viewed. The (unfolding) shift in policy framework within which procurement is globally conceived from a hegemonic free-trade policy framework to a sustainable development one results in a change in our normative judgement of preferences.

### *7.1.3 An incomplete, evolving, but revealing policy shift*

Despite evidence of a shift in policy perspective, we are still a far way off from squaring the free-trade, economic integration paradigm that continues to be a strong influence in global public procurement policy thought (if no longer hegemonic) with the sustainable development paradigm as far as preferences are concerned. That is, in policy development, we are nowhere near squaring preferences as protectionists (bad) with preferences as sustainability instruments (good).

One way in which this debate has (perhaps) become more difficult than in the past relates to quantification. Before, one could attempt to quantify the impact of preferences on efficiencies in public procurement and construct arguments about the rationality (and perhaps wisdom) of using procurement preferences for the particular policy objective based on the outcome of such quantifications (e.g., Marion, 2007; Nakabayashi, 2013). The quantification could, for example, show the increased costs of acquisitions because of preferences, allowing one to ask whether that price tag is justifiable in pursuing the stated policy goal. However, the argument becomes more difficult if those increased costs must be compared to value in sustainability objectives. How much more are we willing to pay to save the planet for future generations, to put it in stark terms? In the public procurement debate, this exercise is perhaps nothing different from the eternal quest for value for money. But value has now become considerably more complicated. Or, perhaps, it always was. It may just be that a dominant policy agenda has privileged one conception of value above others.

A closer look at value in earlier debates about preferences in public procurement shows that those assessments had strong ideological undertones. This may perhaps explain the tenacity of procurement preferences despite the efficiency arguments against them during a period when neoliberal hegemony should have led to the triumph of efficiency over preferences. The use of procurement preferences in the context of unemployment policy provides a good example. Early accounts of favouring preferences in public procurement as a policy strategy to counter unemployment above other relief instruments such as grants, reveal the ideological agenda at play. Commenting on the strategy of using procurement preferences linked to contractors' use of unemployed labour in public procurement of public works, the International Labour Office stated in 1931: '[T]he object of such a policy is to provide a definite stimulus to the economic system as a whole … providing employment for labour which would otherwise be idle – providing it, be it noted, through ordinary economic channels, not through relief organisations' (McCrudden, 2007). Likewise, Howenstein noted in 1965 with reference to the historical use of procurement of public works as employment policy, 'it was socially unacceptable that able-bodied men should receive direct relief during long periods of time for doing nothing; at the same time, there was a feeling that an effort should be made to preserve, and if necessary rehabilitate, the moral fibre of the individual who was unemployed' (McCrudden, 2007). The underlying theme in linking procurement to unemployment policy, often through preferences, in these examples is that it is more acceptable to create work through procurement than to pay out grants. That is, a market-based policy response to unemployment is better than a social one. Thus, even though preference in public procurement may undermine efficiency and distort the market, i.e. artificially limit the free market in public procurement, it is still to be preferred on ideological grounds above alternative policy instruments such as grants.

Returning then to where we are today, the only difference may be that our policy perspective has now drastically shifted with the ascension of a new, equally powerful policy agenda, opening up new conceptions of value, which in turn allows us to judge preferences differently.

### *7.1.4 Where to from here?*

While the global policy framework within which public procurement generally and preferences specifically operate is shifting (or has shifted), I do not think that global public procurement policy itself has sufficiently shifted to keep up. I think there is currently a mismatch between global policy instruments in public procurement in this respect, which will continue to fuel the tension between the paradigms. In crude terms, pitching the WTO GPA against the SDGs. Somehow, we will have to align these policy agendas. Procurement preference is a key, real-world site where this debate is playing out. Figuring out how to deal with preferences between these competing policy perspectives may greatly assist us in reframing our mantra of value for money. And upon that reframing, we can start to construct a new set of global public procurement policy instruments to guide international procurement reform, fully responsive to current global policy priorities.

## 7.2 Benjamin V. Rosa – Introductory remarks

Public procurement accounts for roughly 30% of government expenditures in Organization for Economic Co-operation and Development (OECD) countries – 30 cents for every dollar or euro spent (OECD, 2023). This spending is often administered by bureaucrats overseen by elected officials, linking politics to the public procurement process. This spending may also be subject to various distributional objectives, and governments may grant preferences to meet those objectives. For example, the United States aims to award 23% of all procurement spending to small businesses and will set aside smaller projects for small businesses only to meet this goal. In this chapter, I explore the economic impact of these preferential policies and the political economy surrounding public procurement contracting.

### *7.2.1 Economic theory*

I begin with an overview of the economic theory linking procurement incentives to specific contracting outcomes. When contractors seek to maximize profits, one can decompose the price offered into a strategic markup over the cost of completing the required work. In the standard competitive bidding process, for example,

$$Bid = Cost + Markup.$$

The markup component then dictates how far above costs contractors are willing to bid and the final cost to the government as a result. Governments would need to incentivize contractors to lower either costs or markups (or both) to reduce procurement costs.

Costs generally depend on how efficiently a contractor completes the work requested on a contract. Costs may decline as contractors gain more experience or form better professional relationships with suppliers. Markups usually depend on how competitive a contract is. Indeed, the markup represents a tradeoff between the likelihood of winning and a contractor's profit if they were to win. Contractors will then reduce their markups in response to more competition because the probability of winning decreases with more competitors.

By instituting discretionary preferential policies, governments can influence which contractors win specific contracts *and* the cost of procurement contracting more generally. In some cases, preferences increase the cost of procurement, but there are other situations where they can work to lower procurement costs.

### *7.2.2 Set asides*

Now consider the various preferences awarded in public procurement. One such preference is set-aside contracting, where governments restrict the set of eligible contractors to those belonging to their preferred group. In the United States, for example, there is a goal to spur economic growth in Historically Underutilized Business Zones, so the U.S. government will set aside contracts for firms in those areas. Canada also sets aside contracts for indigenous firms when the good or service would affect mainly indigenous populations.

The theory on how set-aside contracting affects procurement costs is mixed. On the one hand, limiting the set of eligible contractors may increase bidder markups due to reduced competition and increase bidder costs if the preferred firms are less efficient. On the other hand, set asides may lower procurement costs if the preferred firms can lower costs through experience and if they start to compete on contracts without set asides.

Consequently, empirical set aside studies are also mixed. Using data from U.S. Small Business Administration (SBA) set asides, Cappelletti and Giuffrida (2022) find that set asides attract roughly 14% more bidders than comparable contracts without set asides but result in 12% higher extra costs and an increase in delays of 5.7%. Using data from Japanese public procurement, where nearly half the budget is set aside for small and medium enterprises (SMEs), Nakabayashi (2013) finds that 40% of SMEs would not bid absent set asides, resulting in higher overall procurement costs due to less competition.

### *7.2.3 Bid preferences*

Governments can also apply preferences in price evaluation, known as bid preferences. With bid preferences, governments lower the price preferred firms offer for comparison purposes but pay the full price to the winning contractor. A preferred contractor may then win a contract despite not offering the lowest price, even when the price is the primary evaluation factor. Some procurement in the United States has bid preferences for small businesses, and the Inter-American Development Bank (IDB) uses bid preferences for domestic firms to promote domestic development.

At first glance, bid preferences appear to increase procurement costs, as governments might award contracts to preferred firms at a higher price than firms that do not have preferences. However, preferences may also make preferred firms more competitive, decreasing markups and procurement costs by extension. Indeed, a foreign firm bidding on an IDB contract would understand that domestic firms have a preference and would lower their markup to compensate. Whether bid preferences increase or decrease costs depends on the preference's size and the number of competing preferred and non-preferred firms.

Empirical studies highlight this ambiguity. Krasnokutskaya and Seim (2011) find that the small business bid preferences in California highway procurement ranged from decreasing procurement costs by 0.9% to increasing them by 2.3%, depending on the type of work requested by California and the number of large and small firms eligible to bid. Small firms were up to 20% more likely to bid due to preferences. Rosa (2019) finds that the resident bid preferences in New Mexico reduced procurement costs by 0.4% and increased the probability resident firms submitted bids.

### 7.2.4 Subcontracting requirements

Another type of preference governments use in procurement are requirements on the firms utilized as subcontractors. For example, a 5% subcontracting requirement on a project would require that at least five cents per every dollar or euro spent on a contract go to subcontracting firms in the preferred group. In the United States, some projects use subcontracting requirements for individuals historically disadvantaged in contracting – such as ethnic minorities, women, and military veterans – who own and control small firms.

Subcontracting requirements tend to increase procurement costs whenever the preferred group of subcontractors is more costly. However, competition for subcontractors can lower markups enough to mitigate higher subcontractor costs in the short run, and in the long run, preferred subcontractors may become more efficient through the formation of professional networks and experience.

Empirically, Marion (2009) finds that increasing the subcontracting requirement for disadvantaged firms by 10 percentage points increased procurement costs by 3.1% in California. In contrast, Rosa (2024) and De Silva et al. (2012) find subcontracting requirements do not affect procurement costs in New Mexico and Texas, respectively. Using numerical simulations, Rosa (2020) finds that subcontracting requirements can eventually lower procurement costs if they promote strong business relationship formation. These studies generally find that preferred subcontracting increases in line with the requirement.

### 7.2.5 Political economy

Finally, there is evidence that public procurement is affected by the political environment in which procurement officials operate. In the United States, procurement officers are civil servants that political appointees may oversee. When the political ideologies of the officers and appointees are misaligned, contract outcomes can be negatively impacted. Using voter registration and procurement data, Spenkuch, Teso, and Xu (2023) find that this misalignment led to an increase in cost overruns of about 6% relative to the mean overrun, while contracts assigned to aligned officers were completed 1.8% faster. This effect was most prevalent in high-value and high-uncertainty projects. Spenkuch, Teso, and Xu (2023) attribute this result to a "morale effect", where misaligned officers are less motivated.

Political changes may also affect public procurement by altering the rules governing contracting officer discretion. Hungary is a prime example. When Hungary initially joined the EU, open auctions were its primary procurement method but were considered slower and more costly. As Hungary became more conservative following the 2010 elections, it granted contracting officers more leeway in choosing procurement procedures for contracts below a value threshold, allowing them to select potential applicants. Szucs (2024) finds that this discretionary power led to a 6 percentage point increase in contract price, a decrease in the number of bidders by one, and 28% less productive contracts. In contrast, Coviello, Guglielmo, and Spagnolo (2018) find that similar discretionary power in Italy did not substantially change procurement outcomes, although there was an increase in the probability of the same firm winning multiple contracts. These results suggest that the effect of increased discretion will likely depend on the institutional setting in which it is granted.

### *7.2.6 Conclusion*

This chapter explores how preferences and political economy shape public procurement outcomes. Although preferential policies may appear more costly, there are situations where they may lower procurement costs either immediately or in the future. Political forces may create misalignments in ideologies or increase discretionary power, affecting procurement outcomes consequently. This complex relationship between preferences, politics, and public procurement is fascinating, and I look forward to discussing it further in the debate.

## 7.3 Geo Quinot – Response to Paper 2

The central point of Benjamin Rosa's opening remarks is to show the economic impact of preferences in public procurement. By way of his economic analysis, Rosa shows how different forms of preferences may impact both the cost and markup elements that typically constitute the bid price. He thus makes a strong argument that preferences do not necessarily result in higher procurement costs. Under particular circumstances, preferences may result in lower procurement costs by reducing costs of contract completion, the supplier's markup or both. Along this route, Rosa suggests that preferences may not only serve horizontal policy purposes, but may indeed serve the core (vertical) procurement purpose of optimally acquiring the required goods and services to optimally deliver the public function served by such goods and services (sometimes labelled as value for money in narrow terms in public procurement). Rosa's argument, and the empirical evidence it relies on, thus support Quinot and Arrowsmith's (2013) qualitative claim that 'value for money may in the long run benefit from certain social policy objectives, such as support for SMEs and domestic industries when the pool of competing bidders is extended by these policy objectives, leading to more competition and lower prices'.

Rosa's analysis provides an alternative explanation for the tenacity of procurement preferences during much of the latter half of the previous century. During this period, the neoliberal hegemony dominating international perspectives on public procurement, primarily under a free-trade banner, may have been expected to purge preferences from procurement practice. If one can show that preferences may reduce costs, there is no tension between the use of preferences and the narrow conception of value for money. As a result, a neoliberal perspective should at least tolerate preferences (if somewhat reluctantly). The key to this argument is the circumstances under which preferences reduce costs. That is, preferences would only be acceptable under those circumstances where they can reduce costs in a narrow value for money perspective. This then accounts for why empirical studies are viewed as mixed on the impact of preferences in public procurement.

The mixed results are linked to the circumstances under which preferences were implemented in a given context. Where a study found a reduction in costs, it implies that preferences were allocated under appropriate circumstances and *vice versa*. One logical outcome of this line of reasoning is to identify the circumstances that would lead to reduced costs and restrict preferences to those circumstances.

There are some limitations to this approach, especially when viewed through a broader political economy lens. The first limitation is that the analysis seems to rely quite heavily, although seemingly not exclusively, on supply-side reduction of costs. The formula, *Bid* = *Cost* + *Markup*, seems to situate the analysis primarily within the supply side of the procurement relationship. As Rosa explains in his opening remarks, 'Governments would need to incentivize contractors to lower either costs or markups (or both) to reduce procurement costs'. An analysis of the impact of preferences on this formula thus focuses on the effect of preferences on supplier behaviour and resultant cost implications. The desirability of the use of preferences accordingly depends on shifting the supplier's behaviour vis-à-vis costs. However, cost can, of course, also be viewed from the demand side. That is, what is the impact of preferences on the cost of the procurement process itself? In this perspective, an analysis of increasing or lowering procurement costs does not focus (narrowly) on price (or the supplier's *bid* as depicted in the formula above), but on process costs.

In differentiating between these dimensions of procurement costs, terminology tends to be somewhat vague and thus muddies the analytical waters. This is especially evident in the use of the term "efficiency" in this context. There is a fair degree of inconsistency between different scholars when pointing to efficiency as an objective of public procurement systems. While some refer to efficiency as depicting value for money in the sense of obtaining the best quality goods and services on the best terms (Kelman, 1990; Dekel, 2008), others combine this conception with process costs in a single meaning of efficiency (Trepte, 2004), while yet others only focus on process costs (Schooner, 2002; Albano & Nicholas, 2016). The latter is perhaps best labelled as *process efficiency*. In referring to this conception of efficiency, Schooner (2002) notes that 'a procurement system is efficient when it spends the least amount of resources in the *process* of purchasing what is needed'. When one focuses on process efficiency, procurement preferences can quite quickly become less palatable because of increased procurement costs 'in the form of more complex procurement procedures and more scope for supplier challenges' (Quinot & Arrowsmith, 2013). While focusing largely on the supply side, Rosa does acknowledge these process costs when noting the findings of Cappelletti and Giuffrida (2022) in respect of increased procurement delays in U.S. Small Business Administration preferences, that is, a demand-side cost increase.

A second, and perhaps more significant, limitation to the focus on procurement costs when debating procurement preferences is the limited attention to value. Expressing a view on the desirability of preferences based on procurement costs when one holds value fixed seems logical and persuasive. However, it is in my view exactly in the variability of value that the most challenging aspects of debate on the use of procurement preferences lie within shifting political and economic perspectives. If value within any public procurement transaction is limited to the quality of the acquired goods and services, the movement in costs (whether supply side or demand side or both) can be quantified based on the impact of preferences. Consequently, conclusions can be readily drawn on the use of preferences. Such an approach becomes a little more difficult when value is extended beyond the quality of the goods and services procured to also include the value of the public function served by the goods and services, sometimes captured by the notion of client (or end-user) satisfaction (Schooner, 2002). Despite the increased difficulty, value arguably remains computable. However, when a much broader approach to value is adopted within a new paradigm, such as sustainability, the complexity of value drastically problematizes a cost-based analysis of preferences. Without effective ways of quantifying value when a preference is introduced in a procurement transaction to pursue environmental or social objectives within a sustainability paradigm, it becomes increasingly difficult, if not impossible, to analyse the impact of the preference with reference to cost. While one may still be able to determine the movement in costs, the intangibility of the value, including its moral and normative dimensions, may call into question the usefulness of the exercise.

It is of interest to note that this challenge in measuring value when procurement preferences are evaluated within a sustainability paradigm is echoed in the findings of the UNEP's (2022) *Sustainable Public Procurement Global Review*. The study found no material increases in the proportion of entities monitoring sustainable public procurement impact between the 2017 and 2022 reports and the aspects that are monitored remain based on output, rather than value (UNEP, 2022). The report suggests that this trend is probably due to the difficulty in quantifying outcomes as opposed to outputs.

To conclude, Rosa's analysis makes the important point that preferences are not necessarily more costly. In fact, they may reduce costs. Within a traditional, neoliberal conception of value for money as a guiding principle of public procurement system design, these findings show that procurement preferences are not inherently good or bad. The focus should rather be on the circumstances under which preferences are implemented in order to evaluate the particular impact of preferences in a particular context. Despite the clear usefulness of such an analysis, there is a risk that it may limit the evaluation of procurement preferences taking into account a shift towards a sustainability paradigm in public procurement. It seems important to complement analyses of cost with those of value in evaluating procurement preferences within a sustainability framework. This, however, is a particularly challenging endeavour given the arguable incommensurability of cost and value within this paradigm.

## 7.4 Benjamin V. Rosa – Response to Paper 1

In his opening remarks on preferences and political economy in public procurement, Geo Quinot explores many issues related to procurement preferences, including their history, recent scepticism, and various policy shifts. This comment examines several of Quinot's arguments, primarily from an economic perspective.

### *7.4.1 Horizontal policies*

Quinot writes that preferences grant advantages to certain suppliers in furtherance of alternative policy objectives horizontal to the primary goal of acquiring goods and services. As such, Arrowsmith and Kunzlik (2009) label these other objectives as "horizontal policies". The United States' procurement preference for businesses from historically underutilized business zones (HUBZones) would therefore have a horizontal policy objective of developing HUBZone businesses.

I argue that, although these policies may appear horizontal at face value, many horizontal policies are indeed complementary to procurement's functional objective of acquiring goods and services, particularly development-related policies. In the HUBZone example, granting price-evaluation preferences to HUBZone businesses makes them more competitive and may cause more HUBZone firms to compete on certain contracts – potentially lowering procurement costs. Indeed, the United States' Small Business Administration advertises its 8(a) program – which uses set asides and training to aid small, disadvantaged businesses – as one 'designed to strengthen [disadvantaged firms'] ability to compete effectively in the American economy' (US Small Business Administration, 2020).

Empirical studies have found that such complementary effects can arise in practice. Krasonkutskaya and Seim (2011) find that California's price-evaluation preferences for small businesses lowered procurement costs on various construction contracts. Similarly, Nakabayashi (2013) finds that set-asides, possibly the most stringent form of preference, generated enough entry to lower procurement costs in Japan. He argues that his findings provide an economic rationale for why countries such as the United States and Japan opted small businesses out of the WTO's Government Procurement Agreement. Consequently, there can be cases where a buyer who cares only about competition and acquiring goods and services at the lowest possible price would want to consider preferences in procurement.

### *7.4.2 Preferences and sustainable development*

In his argument for a shift in policy perspective, Quinot uses South Africa as an example of how procurement preferences can promote sustainable development goals. Although I concur with the view that preferences can promote development in principle, I note that challenges can arise in implementation that may undermine any development objectives.

In the South African case, Noon (2009) highlights several challenges. He writes that one of the most common criticisms of South Africa's preference program is that it favours wealthy and politically connected Black firms. This favouritism likely contributed to the increase in poverty and income inequality South Africa experienced post-apartheid, despite preferences leading to increased participation of Black firms. Noon (2009) also writes about other challenges specific to South

Africa's preferences – including corruption, lack of monitoring, confusion and using preferred individuals as fronts to qualify for preferences.

Similar challenges can arise in other contexts too. Rosa (2023) finds that subcontracts awarded to disadvantaged firms in New Mexico are concentrated, even on projects with subcontracting preferences. He finds that certain types of work have as much as 98.6% of all subcontract dollars awarded to three firms (and as much as 98.1% on contracts with preferences). Moreover, preferences can fail to stimulate development and disadvantaged awards entirely if they are not sufficiently generous. Indeed, Rosa (2022) explores how spectrum awards for very small businesses respond to various price-evaluation preferences, while Krasnokutskaya and Seim (2011) examine how small business awards respond to different small-business preferences in price evaluation. As such, one must take care when using preferences for sustainable development objectives.

### *7.4.3 Policy debate and quantification*

Quinot mentions that quantifying the value of sustainability objectives presents a challenge in the debate on public procurement preferences. While one could use outcomes such as the final cost and distribution of contracts as one measure, the value of attaining sustainable development through procurement is often difficult to measure.

The contingent valuation literature may provide a solution to this issue. Contingent valuation studies often rely on surveys to elicit valuations and willingness to pay for environmental services – which, like developmental sustainability, would otherwise be difficult to measure (see Carson & Hanemann (2005) for an overview). This methodology may provide a basis for valuing other procurement objectives too, either supporting the shift that Quinot describes or potentially refuting it.

### *7.4.4 Conclusion*

Quinot's opening remarks document the history and change in policy perspectives on preferences in public procurement. In my comment, I explore some of his points further, primarily from an economist's point of view. Regardless of the direction of where the debate may turn, I hope that these perspectives contribute to the overall discussion on procurement preferences.

## 7.5 Geo Quinot – Conclusions

In our exchange of ideas on preferences and political economy in public procurement, Benjamin Rosa and I seem to largely agree on most points.

### *7.5.1 Upside*

On the upside of using preferences as a tool in public procurement, we agree that preferences can serve both the core, vertical function of public procurement in acquiring goods and services and a range of horizontal policy objectives. In fact, one of the key points emerging from our exchange is that what may, at first blush, appear to be horizontal to the core objective of public procurement may indeed not be horizontal at all but simultaneously facilitate procurement's core acquisition objective. Rosa points to several empirical studies that show the beneficial impact on procurement costs of preference schemes that facilitate new entrants to the procurement market. I fully agree with this view.

I would, however, go further and argue that even where no such impact on competition and thus cost/price can be shown, the so-called horizontal policy objectives can still be viewed as supporting procurement's core acquisition objective if one frames that objective as achieving value for money in the acquisition of goods and services. In my view, the objective of a public procurement regime cannot be viewed as *only* the acquisition of goods or services. One would not need a distinct public procurement system if the aim is limited to acquisition. I take this point to be a key differentiator between private and public acquisition. If the objective is purely to acquire, one arguably needs nothing more than a contract. Yet, public procurement is considered much more than mere contracting. I would argue that it is exactly the additional qualifier attached to the function of acquisition that is the *raison d'etre* for the existence of a public procurement system. Accordingly, in a very traditional perspective, a public procurement system exists to bring value for money to the acquisition function. In this view, preferences will thus be complimentary to procurement's core purpose, and thus not be horizontal, if they enhance value for money. By subsequently interrogating the meaning of value in this qualifier, we can bring a large range of preference schemes into the core function of a procurement system by recognizing the policy objective pursued by the preference scheme as part of the value statement, apart from the scheme's impact on price/cost. For example, we may argue that a preference for electrical vehicles in fleet procurement contributes to the value of countering climate change and thus feeds into the value for money qualifier independent of price/cost implications.

### *7.5.2 Downside*

On the downside, Rosa and I also seem to agree that much depends on the specific design of a preference scheme in order to harness its potential in the political economy. That is, the most important question is not whether procurement preferences should be used or not *per se*, but rather what the most appropriate design of a preference scheme should be under given circumstances. This includes an interrogation of favourable circumstances vis-à-vis particular policy objectives to be pursued by preference schemes. Such schemes will face challenges familiar to most regulatory regimes, such as unintended consequences, gaming of the system, path dependencies and policy drift, all of which will have to be considered in the design.

Returning to preferences and value for money in procurement, one of the key considerations in the design of a procurement preference scheme will be an analysis of the scheme's impact on value versus its impact on costs. As I have argued above, a preference scheme can be viewed as complimentary to procurement's core objective based on its contribution to value, independent of its impact on costs. Rosa's suggestion of turning to the contingent valuation (CV) literature to deal with the value complexity in this context is very interesting and certainly worth exploring. There have been very few studies using CV methods in the context of public procurement generally and even fewer in respect of preferences relating to sustainability. One notable exception in this direction is the study of Lerusse and Van De Walle (2021) of municipal procurers' choices in waste procurement in Belgium, Norway, Estonia and Germany. This study assessed and quantified procurers' stated preferences in relation to a range of sustainability criteria. I remain somewhat sceptical on whether these methods will get us where we need to go. I wonder whether the classic difficulties around principal-agent problems in public procurement fundamentally undermine valuations premised on individual willingness-to-pay measures. I wonder whether the highly dispersed nature of the various values at stake here allows for the construction of trade-off choices at the individual level, particularly when we are trying to gauge values at the global level. And given the normative dimensions of this debate, I am particularly worried about social desirability bias and hypothetical bias in the scenario construction here, especially given that we are dealing with 'valuing distant, complex, and unfamiliar goods and services' (Lerusse & Van De Walle, 2021), where these biases are particularly common. None of this is to reject these methods. Contingent valuation has quite clearly contributed much to our understanding of policy choices beyond readily quantifiable cost-benefit analyses, especially in relation to environmental policy. However, I think this merely illustrates the added dimension of complexity in the context of public procurement and preferences in pursuit of sustainability. And I think there is a real risk that the ostensible incommensurability of cost and value within a sustainability paradigm of procurement preferences may lead to the avoidance of dealing with value as an important dimension of this debate.

In my view, despite these challenges, we are making progress in engagement with preferences in public procurement system design when we at least recognize the independent role of value in the analysis of what public procurement preferences often seek to achieve. From that recognition flows interesting and potentially fruitful further debate. This includes debate about potential valuation mechanisms in the context of procurement preferences such as contingent valuation noted by Rosa. It also includes debate about the continued utility of value for money as public procurement's holy grail.

## 7.6 Benjamin V. Rosa – Conclusions

In my closing remarks, I would first like to thank Geo Quinot for his insightful comments on my opening remarks. There, he argues that one should consider the costs of the entire procurement process, which includes supply-side costs (which were the primary focus of my chapter) *and* costs from the demand side. Quinot also contends that the limited attention to value further complicates an analysis of preferences and that value is changing and can be difficult to measure.

Regarding Quinot's points on the procurement process, I believe we are mostly in agreement: a full analysis of preferences in procurement should consider supply-side costs, demand-side costs, and the value generated through preferences. My opening remarks focused more on the supply side for two reasons. First, buyers often use preference programs to address supply-side issues in procurement, such as allocating contracts to firms with preferences. Second, there is a paucity of studies on demand-side costs and values, whereas there are many more studies on supply-side costs.

Nevertheless, some reports consider the economic value of preferences, which one can contrast against operating budgets for a more complete picture of the procurement process. Those reports often find that the value generated through preferences far exceeds operating costs. For example, the HUBZone program, which is a program that grants preferences to firms located in underdeveloped areas, cost the U.S. government \$8.2 million in the 2021 fiscal year (SBA, 2022). However, that program allocated \$2.5 billion in contract dollars to HUBZone firms – generating \$5.9 billion in gross output, \$1.9 billion in personal income, and 25.4 thousand jobs (Optimal Solutions Group, 2023). Thus, it is possible that an analysis of demand-side benefits vastly underestimates the true value of preferences. Note, though, that a limitation of this type of evaluation is that it does not consider what would have happened absent preferences.

Moreover, those reports do not include the more abstract notion of the value Quinot mentions in his comment. While measuring the value people have for preferences is by no means trivial, there are well-established methods that might provide some insight. Namely, contingent valuation studies – which use survey methods to construct people's willingness to pay for non-market goods, such as the environment – may provide a way to measure value in these more abstract cases.

In conclusion, I would again like to thank Quinot for his opening remarks and comment. I would also like to highlight once more the potential economic implications of preferences – which have the potential to lower supply-side costs and generate economic value, depending on how buyers implement them.

## References

Albano, G.L. and Nicholas, C. (2016), *The Law and Economics of Framework Agreements.* Cambridge University Press, Cambridge.

Arrowsmith, S. and Kunzlik, P.F. (2009), *Social and Environmental Policies in EC Procurement Law: New Directives and New Directions.* Cambridge University Press, New York.

Bolton, P. and Quinot, G. (2011), 'Social policies in procurement and the Agreement on Government Procurement: A perspective from South Africa, in Arrowsmith, S. and Anderson, R.D. (eds.), *The WTO Regime on Government Procurement: Challenge and Reform.* Cambridge University Press, Cambridge, pp.459–480.

Cappelletti, M. and Giuffrida, L.M. (2022), *Targeted Bidders in Government Tenders.* ZEW – Centre for European Economic Research Discussion Paper No. 22-030.

Carson, R.T. and Hanemann, W.M. (2005), 'Contingent valuation', in Mäler, K. and Vincent, J.R. (eds.), *Handbook of Environmental Economics*, Elsevier, Amsterdam, pp. 821–936.

Coviello, D., Guglielmo, A., and Spagnolo, G. (2018), 'The effect of discretion on procurement performance'. *Management Science,* 64(2), pp. 715–738.

Davies, A. (2011), 'The national treatment and exceptions provisions of the Agreement on Government Procurement and the pursuit of horizontal policies', in Arrowsmith, S. and Anderson, R.D. (eds.), *The WTO Regime on Government Procurement: Challenge and Reform.* Cambridge University Press, Cambridge, pp.429–443.

De Silva, D.G., Dunne, T., Kosmopoulou, G., and Lamarche, C. (2012), 'Disadvantaged business enterprise goals in government procurement contracting: An analysis of bidding behavior and costs', *International Journal of Industrial Organization*, 30(4), pp. 377–388.

Dekel, O. (2008), 'The legal theory of competitive bidding for government contracts', *Public Contract Law Journal*, 37, pp. 237–268.

Golub, M.J. and Fenske, S.L. (1987), 'US government procurement: Opportunities and obstacles for foreign contractors'. *George Washington Journal of International Law and Economics,* 20, pp. 567–598.

Kelman, S. (1990), *Procurement and Public Management.* The AEI Press, Washington DC.

Krasnokutskaya, E. and Seim, K. (2011). 'Bid preference programs and participation in highway procurement auctions'. *American Economic Review,* 101(6), pp. 2653–2686.

Lerusse, A. and Van de Walle, S. (2021), 'Public managers' valuation of secondary policy objectives in public procurement – results from a discrete choice experiment'. *Journal of Behavioral Public Administration,* 4, pp. 1–22.

Linarelli, J. (2011), 'The limited case for permitting SME procurement preferences in the Agreement on Government Procurement', in Arrowsmith, S. and Anderson, R.D. (eds.), *The WTO Regime on Government Procurement: Challenge and Reform.* Cambridge University Press, Cambridge, pp.444–458.

Marion, J. (2007), 'Are bid preferences benign? The effect of small business subsidies in highway procurement auctions'. *Journal of Public Economics*, 91(7-8), pp. 1591–1624.

Marion, J. (2009), 'How costly is affirmative action? government contracting and California's proposition 209', *Review of Economics and Statistics,* 91(3), pp. 503–522.

McCrudden, C. (2007), *Buying Social Justice,* Oxford University Press, Oxford.

Nakabayashi, J. (2013), 'Small business set-asides in procurement auctions: An empirical analysis'. *Journal of Public Economics,* 100, pp. 28–44.

Noon, C.R. (2009), 'The use of racial preferences in public procurement for social stability'. *Public Contract Law Journal,* 38(3), pp. 611–632.

OECD. (2023), *OECD Government at a Glance.* Available at www.oecd.org/publication/government-at-a-glance.

Optimal Solutions Group (2023), *Fiscal Year 2021 Economic Impact Study – Small Business and Type of Set-aside Procurement Programs.* Available at https://optimalsolutionsgroup.com/2023/02/13/fy-2021-economic-impact-study-small-business-and-type-of-set-aside-procurement-programs/.

Quinot, G. (2019), 'Constitutionalising public procurement through human rights: lessons from South Africa, in Martin-Ortega, O. and Methven O'Brien, C. (eds.), *Public Procurement and Human Rights.* Edward Elgar Publishing, Cheltenham.

Quinot, G. and Arrowsmith, S. (2013), *Public Procurement Regulation in Africa.* Cambridge University Press, Cambridge.

Rosa, B.V. (2019), 'Resident bid preference, affiliation, and procurement competition: Evidence from New Mexico', *The Journal of Industrial Economics,* 67(2), pp. 161–208.

Rosa, B.V. (2020), 'Affirmative action subcontracting regulations in dynamic procurement auctions', *International Journal of Industrial Organization,* 72, p.102657.

Rosa, B.V. (2022), 'Bid credits in simultaneous ascending auctions', *Games and Economic Behavior*, 132, pp. 189–203.

Rosa, B.V. (2023), *Diversity versus Equity in Government Contracting*. Institute for the Study of Free Enterprise, Lexington, Working Paper 51.

Rosa, B.V. (2024), 'Subcontracting requirements and the cost of government procurement', *RAND Journal of Economics,* 55(1), pp. 3–32.

Schooner, S.L. (2002), 'Desiderata: Objectives for a System of Government Contract Law'. *Public Procurement Law Review,* 11, pp. 103–110.

Shai, L., Molefinyana, C., and Quinot, G. (2019), 'Public procurement in the context of Broad-Based Black Economic Empowerment (BBBEE) in South Africa—Lessons learned for sustainable public procurement, *Sustainability*, 11(24), pp. 1–27.

Spenkuch, J.L., Teso, E., and Xu, G. (2023), 'Ideology and performance in public organizations, *Econometrica,* 91(4), pp. 1171–1203.

Stoffel, T., Cravero, C., La Chimia, A., and Quinot, G. (2019), 'Multidimensionality of Sustainable Public Procurement (SPP)—Exploring concepts and effects in Sub-Saharan Africa and Europe, *Sustainability*, 11(22), pp. 1–23.

Szucs, F. (2024), 'Discretion and favoritism in public procurement', *Journal of the European Economic Association*, 22(1), pp. 117–160.

Trepte, P. (2004), *Regulating Procurement: Understanding the Ends and Means of Public Procurement Regulation.* Oxford University Press, Oxford.

United Nations Environment Programme (UNEP) (2022), *Sustainable Public Procurement: 2022 Global Review.* UNEP, Paris. Available at www.oneplanetnetwork.org/knowledge-centre/resources/sustainable-public-procurement-2022-global-review-parts-i-and-ii.

U.S. Small Business Administration (SBA) (2020), *8(a) Business Development Program.* Available at www.sba.gov/federal-contracting/contracting-assistance-programs/8a-business-development-program.

U.S. Small Business Administration (SBA). (2022), *FY 2023 Congressional Budget Justification and FY 2021 Annual Performance Report*. Available at www.sba.gov/document/report-congressional-budget-justification-annual-performance-report.

Warner, M. (2011), *Local Content in Procurement.* Greenleaf Publishing Limited, Sheffield.

World Bank. (2021), *GINI Index (World Bank Estimate) | Data.* Available at https://data.worldbank.org/indicator/SI.POV.GINI?most_recent_value_desc=true.

# 8 Preferences and Unilateral Measures Relating to Public Procurement

*Jean Heilman Grier*

## 8.1 Introduction

Governments have always used their purchasing power to achieve certain social and political purposes. In the United States and other countries, governments have adopted many forms of protectionism for a wide range of purposes (Qiao et al., 2009). A key European Union (EU) procurement official, Lucian Cernat (Cernat, 2023, p. 89), observed the continuing prevalence of such practices: ‘Although some procurement barriers have been in place for decades, the current geopolitical and economic environment is conducive to a record number of protectionist and discriminatory measures affecting international public procurement’.

New policy directions are unfolding against several major shifts in domestic economic policy and global economic governance. One shift is the United States’ pivot towards industrial policy driven by major legislation, including a 2021 infrastructure law that imposed a broad domestic preference on infrastructure projects and legislation that extended preferences beyond procurement. Another factor is the ‘dramatic turnabout in global attitudes toward supply chain management and the balance between efficiency, resilience, and security in cross-border trade’ (Sutton & Williams, 2023). Reactions in the West to China’s ascendancy, its extensive industrial policies and protection of its domestic markets, especially in technology, are another factor. Finally, there is the urgent need to respond to climate change (*Economist*, 2023a).

In public procurement, governments often use preferences to favour their own industries and discriminate against foreign suppliers. One common approach is preferential margins that provide domestic firms with a specific level of preference. Another is domestic content requirements that call for procurement to be sourced locally (Gourdon & Messent, 2017, p. 6). A third tactic is to reserve certain contracts for domestic suppliers. In addition, some countries impose discriminatory qualification or technical evaluation requirements, such as mandating prior experience in the country, using technical standards or licensing conditions that favour domestic producers or limiting key experts to nationals (Cernat, 2023).

Two organizations have attempted to quantify and address the extent to which ‘home bias’ and discriminatory measures are detrimental to international

DOI: 10.4324/9781032631721-12

procurement. In 2017, the Organization for Economic Cooperation and Development (OECD) established a global taxonomy of public procurement barriers that is comparable across countries and aligned with the World Trade Organization's (WTO) procurement agreement and the United Nations Commission on International Trade Law's Model Law on Public Procurement (Cernat, 2023, p. 89). Based on the OECD taxonomy, the Global Trade Alert (GTA) project monitors policies affecting global trade, including public procurement (GTA, 2022). The GTA database has revealed 'a worrying upward trend in the number of restrictive and discriminatory measures against international procurement' (Cernat, 2023, p. 89). The GTA data collection effort illustrated that during the 2009–2017 period, market-liberalizing measures nearly disappeared, in contrast to a steady increase in the number of protectionist measures. These measures quadrupled to nearly 700 between 2017 and 2022.

When industrial policy encourages domestic production of goods or favours locally made products over those of foreign origin, trading partners may challenge it as running afoul of the long-standing principle of national treatment at the centre of the WTO and other international agreements (Sutton & Williams, 2023). It can also prompt countries to adopt similar measures.

## 8.2 International Disciplines on Domestic Preferences

The first international disciplines on government procurement entered into force in 1981 under the General Agreement on Tariffs and Trade's (GATT) Code on Government Procurement (GATT Code). The 40th anniversary of that milestone was celebrated in 2021, along with the 25th anniversary of its successor, the WTO's plurilateral Agreement on Government Procurement (GPA) (for background on the GPA, see Grier, 2022a, Part One). Over the decades, the GPA has expanded to cover the procurement of 49 WTO members, with North Macedonia becoming the most recent addition in 2023 (Grier, 2023f).

Under the GPA, as under the GATT Code, parties have specified the procurement that they promise to conduct in accordance with the agreement's principles and procedures. The fundamental principle underlying the GPA is non-discrimination with two prongs. One is national treatment, in which the parties agree to treat the goods and services of the other parties the same as their own goods and services and to not apply domestic preferences to that procurement. The second prong is most-favoured-nation (MFN) treatment, where the parties commit to not treat the goods and services of another party better than those of other parties. Notwithstanding the MFN principle, many parties derogate from that principle to achieve reciprocity, withholding certain of their GPA-covered procurement from parties that do not open comparable procurement.

The GPA does not prohibit its parties from applying domestic preferences to procurement not covered under the agreement. Parties such as the United States have explicitly excluded certain procurement subject to domestic preferences from their GPA commitments. For example, the United States excludes the Department of Defense's procurement of products covered by the Berry Amendment from the GPA (Grier, 2022a, Ch. 7.3.2). In addition, its coverage of infrastructure projects undertaken by non-federal entities is limited (Grier, 2022a, Ch. 6.3.2). When parties impose new domestic preferences on procurement outside the GPA, they can do so without violating the plurilateral agreement. This limits the role of the GPA as a moderating influence on preferences.

## 8.3 U.S. Domestic Preferences

Domestic preferences in government procurement 'are deeply embedded in US politics and law', observe Yukins and Green (2018, p. 3) 'and, once in place, are difficult to erase'. For example, a policy favouring U.S. businesses existed during the Civil War, and a current preference for small businesses dates to at least 1941. The Buy American Act of 1933[1] has roots that may 'go back to 1844 legislation that required agencies to purchase domestically' (Qiao et al., 2009, p. 371). The Buy American Act is the primary domestic preference law that governs the procurement of goods by the federal government. It was enacted during the Great Depression to foster American industry by protecting it from foreign competition in federal government procurement and preserve jobs for Americans. The Buy American Act is one of a plethora of U.S. laws that impose domestic preferences with the aim of limiting the purchase of foreign goods. During the 1970s, Congress began extending preferences beyond direct federal procurement to infrastructure projects undertaken by state and local governments with federal funds, especially in the transportation sector (Grier, 2022a, Ch. 7).

In its negotiations to open government procurement under the GPA and free trade agreements (FTAs), the United States has had to take its domestic purchasing restrictions into account in crafting commitments. It pursued two strategies to reconcile the conflict between these restrictions and agreements' national treatment obligations. It either waived the domestic preference for its trade agreement partners or excluded the restricted procurement from its commitments, depending on whether Congress had given the president the authority to waive the requirement (Grier, 2022a, Ch. 7.4.1).

### *8.3.1 U.S. Pivot to Protectionism in Public Procurement*

Beginning with President Donald Trump's 'America First' agenda (2017–2021) and accelerating under the administration of President Joe Biden, U.S. trade and industrial policies have prioritized relocating manufacturing production back to the United States and applying domestic preferences to encourage domestic manufacturing, rather than liberalizing trade and opening its procurement market (Posen, 2023).

#### *8.3.1.1 Trump's 'America First' Agenda*

President Trump made 'Buy American' directives a centrepiece of his 'America First' policy to protect the domestic procurement market from foreign products.

He implemented that policy through orders to federal agencies to maximize the purchase of goods produced in the United States in both direct procurement and funding of sub-federal infrastructure projects (Grier, 2022a, Ch. 8.2).

Under a Trump directive to tighten the application of the Buy American Act (White House, 2019), the Federal Acquisition Regulatory Council (FAR Council)[2] revised federal procurement rules to increase the domestic content required for a product to be treated as American-made from 50% to 95% for iron and steel products and to 55% for all other products (FAR Council, 2021). That means, for example, that iron and steel end products are considered of foreign origin when they incorporate as little as 5% foreign iron and steel.

Trump also mandated the increase of price preferences applied to the price of a foreign product from 12% to 30% when the lowest domestic offer is from a small business and from 6% to 20% when such an offer is from other businesses (White House, 2019). Federal agencies may purchase a foreign product if they determine that it is less costly (and the cost of a domestic product is unreasonable). Using a comparative price evaluation test, agencies add a price evaluation factor or price preference of 20% to the price of the lowest acceptable foreign offer if the lowest domestic offer is from a large business or 30% from a small business.

#### *8.3.1.2 Biden Administration's 'Made in America' Policies*

President Biden set the direction of his administration's government procurement policy with an executive order, '*Ensuring the Future Is Made in All of America by All of America's Workers*' (Order) (White House, 2021), at the beginning of his presidency in 2021. His aim was to maximize the use of American goods and services by federal agencies and recipients of federal funding. To further that aim, he sought to curtail the use of waivers of domestic preferences and strengthen 'Buy American' preferences. (The Biden administration used 'Made in America' to describe policies that are otherwise known as 'Buy American' or 'Buy America'.)

The Buy American Act and other domestic preference laws allow waivers of the domestic purchasing requirement in certain circumstances. They include the non-availability of U.S. goods, the unreasonableness of the cost of domestic goods, and when application of the domestic preference would be inconsistent with the public interest. To reduce the use of waivers, Biden centralized waiver review in a newly created Made in America Office within the Office of Management and Budget (OMB) (White House, 2021), making it the final authority on waiver requests for all procurement using federal funds (Watson, 2021).

In accordance with the presidential directive, the administration strengthened the enforcement of the Buy American Act by increasing the U.S. content required for a product to be considered a domestic product – from 55% of the cost of all components in three stages: to 60% in 2022, 65% in 2024, and 75% in 2029 (FAR Council, 2022).

President Biden's order also called for an increase in the price preferences applied to determine whether a domestic product's price is unreasonable and thus eligible for a waiver. In response, the FAR Council created a framework for applying higher (or enhanced) price preferences to critical products and construction materials and critical components in 2022. It defined 'critical items' as domestic construction material or domestic end products deemed critical to U.S. supply chain resiliency, and 'critical components' as components mined, produced, or manufactured in the United States and deemed critical to the U.S. supply chain. However, the FAR Council deferred establishing a definitive list of critical items and critical components and their associated enhanced price preferences to a subsequent rulemaking (FAR Council, 2022). (As of February 2024, it had not been initiated.) In recognizing that price preferences would likely require the federal government to pay higher prices for critical domestic products and components, the administration asserted they were essential to create a steady source of demand to 'catalyze domestic production and bolster thin supply chains' (White House, 2022a). It was also considering the possible first-time application of preferences to critical services (Grier, 2022a, Ch. 12.2.1.2).

#### *8.3.1.3 Infrastructure Investment and Jobs Act of 2021*

The Biden administration significantly expanded procurement subject to a domestic preference in implementing a major bipartisan infrastructure law, the Infrastructure Investment and Jobs Act (Infrastructure Act).[3] Its massive investment in domestic infrastructure included the most far-reaching domestic content requirements that had been applied to infrastructure projects in the United States (Grier, 2022a, Ch. 12.2.1.3).

The Build America, Buy America Act (BABA Act), incorporated into the Infrastructure Act, prohibits the use of federal funds on any infrastructure project undertaken by a non-federal entity unless all the iron, steel, manufactured products, and construction materials used in the project are produced in the United States. This requirement supplanted a 'soft' domestic preference instituted by the Trump administration (Grier, 2022a, Ch. 8.2.3). The BABA Act allows waivers for the nonavailability of U.S. goods, unreasonableness of the cost of domestic goods, and the public interest.

In implementing the BABA Act, the Biden administration sought to close what it characterized as a 'giant loophole' that had allowed infrastructure projects to be built with products 'sourced from anywhere in the world' (White House, 2023a). The Act broadly defines 'infrastructure' to include 'at a minimum' the structures, facilities, and equipment for roads, highways, and bridges; public transportation; dams, ports, harbours, and other maritime facilities; intercity passenger and freight railroads; freight and intermodal facilities; airports; water systems, including drinking water and wastewater systems; electrical transmission facilities and systems, including electric vehicle charging; utilities; broadband infrastructure; and buildings and real property.[4]

In determining whether a particular construction project constitutes 'infrastructure', OMB urged broad application and directed agencies to consider whether the project serves a public function. It further instructed them to apply the preference to any federal financial assistance program under which an award might be issued for an infrastructure project, regardless of whether infrastructure is the primary purpose of the award (OMB, 2022). It did, however, allow that the domestic preference would not apply to any non-infrastructure spending under an award.

One of the most significant additions of the BABA Act was its first-time application of a domestic purchasing requirement to construction materials. Previously, domestic preferences for infrastructure projects had been limited to iron, steel, and manufactured products (Grier, 2022b).

To facilitate implementation of the BABA Act preference, OMB issued three sets of guidance: initial guidance in April 2022 (OMB, 2022), final guidance in August 2023, following public comments on proposed guidance (OMB, 2023a), and supplemental guidance in October 2023 (OMB, 2023b). OMB's last guidance rescinded and replaced its initial guidance (OMB, 2023b; Grier, 2023g).

In its guidance, OMB defined key terms such as construction materials and specified the domestic manufacturing process standards for each construction material covered by the Act. It also directed that manufactured products must be manufactured in the United States as well as at least 55% of their components (by cost).

Before OMB issued its final guidance, it allowed public comments on its proposed guidance. An element of its proposed guidance of particular concern to foreign suppliers was its omission of any reference to the BABA Act's directive that its domestic preference be applied in a manner consistent with U.S. obligations under international agreements (Grier, 2023d). In comments to OMB on its proposed guidance, the EU contended that '[t]he lack of reference to international obligations in the guidance document could lead to incorrect application of the [Infrastructure Act] by the U.S. public agencies and misunderstandings of the requirements by bidders' (EU Delegation to the US, 2023). As a remedy for this deficiency, the EU recommended that the final guidance explicitly state 'that "Buy America" requirements do not apply to government procurement covered by the United States' obligations under international agreements'. Similarly, in its comments, Canada encouraged the agency to provide further guidance to ensure that the 37 U.S. states covered by the GPA comply with the Infrastructure Act's provision for international agreements (Government of Canada, 2023a).

In issuing its final guidance, OMB acknowledged the concerns with the lack of an explicit statement relating to the application of the Buy America preference to procurement covered by international agreements (Grier, 2023d). Stating that 'the BABA provisions apply in a manner consistent with United States obligations under international agreements', OMB concluded there was no reason to address this issue in the final guidance. Rather, it relied on its initial guidance's requirement that a public interest waiver would be needed to purchase foreign goods covered by an international agreement (OMB, 2023a, p. 57785).

In its supplemental guidance, issued two months later, OMB rescinded its initial guidance and addressed the concern raised by the EU, Canada, and others by including a section on Consistency with International Agreements, which stated: 'Pursuant to Section 70914(e) of BABA, this guidance must be applied in a manner consistent with the obligations of the United States under international agreements' (OMB, 2023b).

OMB continued to insist that a public interest waiver is required for a sub-federal entity to purchase a foreign product covered by an international agreement. However, there is no certainty that a public interest waiver will be issued when an agreement applies. OMB's latest guidance maintained that: 'If a recipient is a State that has assumed procurement obligations pursuant to the Government Procurement Agreement or any other trade agreement, a waiver of a Made in America condition to ensure compliance with such obligations *may be in the public interest* (emphasis added)' (OMB, 2023b). And, even if it is in the public interest, the granting of a waiver is not a simple or straightforward process, as detailed in the guidance. The burden will be on foreign suppliers to demonstrate that a particular project is covered by a trade agreement and persuade sub-federal entities to seek a public interest waiver. Even if a waiver is requested, it must be approved by the federal granting agency and OMB (Grier, 2023g).

OMB's 2023 treatment of projects covered by international agreements contrasts sharply with the Obama administration's implementation of a domestic preference applied to infrastructure under the American Recovery and Reinvestment Act of 2009. In 2009, OMB developed rules to provide assurances to trading partners that the United States would implement the requirement in a manner that would ensure compliance with its obligations under agreements. That included incorporating in the CFR an appendix that detailed the procurement covered under trade agreements (Grier, 2023a).

### 8.3.2 Domestic Preferences Extend Beyond Procurement

The Infrastructure Act, together with the Inflation Reduction Act and the CHIPS and Science Act, form the core of U.S. industrial policy championed by President Biden. Through a combination of domestic preferences, direct subsidies, tax incentives, and support for research and innovation, these laws seek to restructure the American economy and boost U.S. manufacturing (Sutton & Williams, 2023).

#### *8.3.2.1 Inflation Reduction Act*

The U.S.'s enactment of the Inflation Reduction Act[5] (IRA) was heralded as the single largest climate investment in U.S. history, putting the nation on a path to reduce its carbon emissions by roughly 40% by 2030 (Hamilton & Quinlan, 2023). The initial enthusiasm for the Act was tempered when a closer look revealed that its subsidies and tax credits would discriminate against other countries unless they had an FTA with the United States.

While welcoming the IRA's climate investment, European officials criticized its discriminatory local content provisions and its manufacturing subsidies amid fears that the incentives might induce European firms to shift their production to the United States (Hamilton & Quinlan, 2023; Reinsch & Denamiel, 2023). Of particular concern was the IRA's tax credit of up to $7,500 for buyers of new electric vehicles (EVs) if the vehicle is assembled in a North American plant and meets certain domestic content requirements relating to critical minerals and battery components. Materials such as critical minerals for EV batteries must be sourced in either the United States or one of its FTA partners. The EU, along with other trading partners, including Japan, South Korea, and Britain, also asserted the IRA's local content provisions may violate WTO rules by favouring U.S.-based producers and suppliers (Grier, 2023b; Rashish, 2023).

Half of the tax credit is available if a certain percentage by value (beginning at 40% in 2023, increasing incrementally to 70% by 2027) of the EV battery's critical minerals are extracted or processed in the United States or in one of the 20 countries with which the United States has an FTA[6] or recycled in North America. Another $3,750 of the tax credit is available if the battery components are manufactured or assembled in North America.

In contrast to its stringent implementation of the Infrastructure Act's domestic preference, the Biden team took a more flexible approach with respect to the IRA (Grier, 2023b). The administration took several steps to assuage European and other foreign country concerns. For example, at the end of 2022, it 'quietly announced what may turn out to have been an economic bombshell', according to Chad Bown of the Peterson Institute for International Economics (Bown, 2023): it was allowing subsidies for 'commercial clean vehicles' produced by European and other foreign carmakers – if the vehicle is leased and not purchased. Currently, half of German electric vehicles in the United States are leased (Hamilton & Quinlan, 2023). That meant U.S. consumers who lease (rather than purchase) electric vehicles could qualify for the IRA's $7,500 tax credit for 'commercial vehicles' that do not have to meet the IRA's stringent North American requirements (IRS, 2022; Rashish, 2023). Used vehicles, comprising 70% of the market, are not subject to local sourcing requirements and thus benefit from tax credits (Hamilton & Quinlan, 2023).

Bown has pointed out that almost none of the constraints that had applied to the tax credit, including caps on the price of the EV and the income of the consumer, apply when U.S. consumers lease vehicles. The consequence was that '[e]xpensive European-assembled models from Porsche, BMW, and Mercedes – and the high-income consumers who can afford them – suddenly became eligible for US tax credits' (Bown, 2023, p. 22).

The Internal Revenue Service (IRS) and Treasury Department made a further concession to foreign supplies in proposing regulations to implement the IRA requirement that critical minerals for EV batteries must be sourced in either the United States or one of its FTA partners (IRS, 2023). They proposed a broader definition of FTAs than had been used traditionally. (While 'free trade agreement' is not defined in the IRA or any other law, it has to date been used to refer to comprehensive agreements negotiated under Trade Promotion Authority and implemented after approval by Congress (Grier, 2023b).) The agencies proposed to define countries with which the United States has FTAs as countries with which the United States has comprehensive FTAs (agreements covering substantially all trade in goods and services between the parties, including trade in critical minerals), as well as countries that meet certain criteria. Those criteria include whether the United States has agreements with them on critical minerals that provide for reducing, eliminating, or refraining from the imposition of trade barriers or export restrictions or establishing high-standard disciplines in key areas affecting trade, such as core labour and environmental protections.

In support of the IRS's proposed expansion of pacts considered to be an FTA for purposes of the IRA, the U.S. Trade Representative delineated two types of FTAs. One lists 20 countries with comprehensive FTAs with the United States. The other, added in 2023, are countries with 'an agreement focusing on free trade in critical minerals', listing only Japan (USTR, 2023a; Grier, 2023b).

Japan's listing was based on a United States–Japan Critical Minerals Agreement (CMA) that was signed and implemented on 28 March 2023 (USTR, 2023b). It aims to strengthen, secure, and diversify critical minerals supply chains and promote the adoption of EV battery technologies. It obligates the two countries to:

- refrain from imposing export duties on critical mineral exports to the other country;
- consult on domestic measures to address non-market policies and practices of other countries affecting critical minerals trade and global supply chains;
- consult on best practices regarding the review of critical mineral investments within their territories by foreign entities;
- advance robust labour and environmental standards; and
- expand cooperation in efforts to ensure secure, sustainable, and equitable critical minerals supply chains (Grier, 2023b).

In its proposed regulations, the IRS cited the United States–Japan CMA as an agreement that it expected to consider an FTA for the purpose of the tax credit as it contains 'robust obligations to help ensure free trade in critical minerals' (IRS, 2023, p. 23376).

The United States and EU are engaged in negotiations on a similar deal. On 10 March 2023, the presidents of the United States and European Commission announced their intention to begin negotiations on a targeted critical minerals agreement that would allow EU vehicles to be eligible for the tax credit despite the lack of a traditional FTA (White House, 2023b). The Commission adopted its negotiating mandate to provide the necessary authority for it to negotiate a CMA with the United States in June 2023 (European Commission, 2023b). The Council of the EU approved the mandate the following July, allowing negotiations to commence (Council of the EU, 2023). The two sides had been expected to complete a CMA before the end of 2023 (Reuters, 2023), but they had not reached agreement by February 2024.

In June 2023, as part of an Atlantic Declaration for a Twenty-First Century U.S.–UK Economic Partnership, the United States and the United Kingdom announced that they would also negotiate a critical minerals trade agreement to enable five critical minerals for EVs that are extracted or processed in the United Kingdom to count towards EV tax credit requirements (White House, 2023c; Akhtar, 2023). Other countries, including Indonesia, Argentina, and the Philippines, have signalled interest in similar pacts. Even South Korea, which already has an FTA with the United States, wants more critical mineral concessions (Dabbs, 2023).

#### *8.3.2.2 The CHIPS and Science Act*

Another legislative measure that is part of the Biden industrial policy is the 2022 Creating Helpful Incentives to Produce Semiconductors and Science Act (CHIPS and Science Act).[7] It provides funding to boost domestic research and development (R&D) and manufacturing of semiconductors in the United States. It includes subsidies for chips manufactured in the United States and funds for semiconductor research and workforce training, with the primary aim of countering China (White House, 2022b). The CHIPS and Science Act directs $280 billion towards scientific R&D and semiconductor production to encourage advanced technology manufacturing to move to the United States and away from China (Siripurapu & Berman, 2022).

#### *8.3.2.3 Federally Funded R&D*

President Biden extended his 'Buy America' policies to R&D funded by the federal government in July 2023, when he signed an '*Executive Order on Federal Research and Development in Support of Domestic Manufacturing and United States Jobs*' (White House, 2023e). It sets out the administration's policy that new technologies and products developed with U.S. government support 'will be manufactured in the United States whenever feasible and consistent with applicable law'. The order seeks to boost the incentive to manufacture in the U.S. inventions developed with federal funds.

A White House Fact Sheet outlined four core objectives of the R&D funding order:

- Improve transparency, cut red tape, and streamline reporting requirements in the Federal R&D process to better track progress towards domestic manufacturing goals.
- Boost the incentive to manufacture new inventions in the United States when those inventions are developed using Federal funds.
- Encourage the expansion of domestic production for critical industries while maintaining flexibility to build strong international R&D partnerships.
- Make the domestic manufacturing waiver process clearer, timelier, and more consistent, including when production is not commercially feasible (White House, 2023d).

The order encourages agencies to factor domestic manufacturing of inventions into their R&D award solicitations and to consider using the broad range of their authorities to purchase or invest in leading-edge technologies to support domestic production. In addition, to emphasize the importance of domestic manufacturing and encourage potential federal funding recipients to build that consideration into their long-term planning to commercialize inventions, the White House Office of

Science and Technology Policy will seek to add domestic manufacturing to the government's technology R&D roadmaps (White House, 2023e).

With the order, the White House is also seeking to address the limited scope of the domestic manufacturing requirement in the Bayh-Dole Act of 1980. That law is one of various mechanisms established by Congress to encourage the commercialization of technology and research resulting from the use of federal funds. When federal contractors license federally funded inventions to private businesses for commercialization, the Bayh-Dole Act imposes a U.S. manufacturing preference. It prohibits contractors from licensing the exclusive right to use or sell a covered invention in the United States unless the licensee agrees it will be 'manufactured substantially' in the United States. Federal agencies may waive the requirement 'when domestic manufacture is not commercially feasible' (Blevins & Gallo, 2022). The Bayh-Dole requirement does not apply to organizations with a non-exclusive license, federal funding awardees themselves, or organizations that take an invention developed with U.S. federal funding to market to sell solely overseas (White House 2023d). To remedy that deficiency, the Biden order encourages agencies to expand the domestic manufacturing requirement beyond exclusive licensees for critical and emerging technologies.

This latest iteration of Biden's 'Buy America' policies is a softer requirement than the broad 'Buy America' mandate in the Infrastructure Act and the 'Buy America' requirements in the Inflation Reduction Act (Grier, 2023e).

## 8.4 Canada's Approach to Domestic Preferences

In response to the expansion of U.S. protectionist measures, Canada has sought exemptions for its firms. It successfully lobbied the U.S. government for special treatment of North American production under the Inflation Reduction Act. However, it has not been able to convince the Biden administration to exclude Canadian products from other 'Buy America' policies, prompting Canada to consider adoption of its own 'buy local' policies.

When the United States was developing the IRA legislation, Canadian officials expressed serious concerns with its proposed U.S. content and assembly requirements for EV tax credits (Meyer, 2023). That led the Canadian government to undertake 'a relentless advocacy and outreach effort to ensure that the tax credits would apply to Canadian production, given the integrated nature of Canada-U.S. supply chains in the auto sector' (Government of Canada, 2023b, p. 71). Its efforts were rewarded when, in the final legislation, Congress expanded the U.S. content and assembly requirements to include North American partners, largely addressing concerns with the negative impacts on Canada and the integrated North American auto sector (Meyer, 2023). Canada emphasized that the IRA's 'Buy North American' provisions for critical minerals and electric vehicles will create opportunities for its suppliers (Government of Canada, 2023b, p. 83).

Canada has adopted its own made-in-Canada plan centred on 'federal financial incentives that will attract new investment, create good middle class jobs, and build Canada's clean economy' (Government of Canada, 2023b, p. 73). The incentives include a Clean Technology Investment Tax Credit (first announced in Canada's 2022 budget) that will support domestic companies adopting clean technologies and a Clean Technology Manufacturing Investment Tax Credit to support Canadian companies that manufacture or process clean technologies, as well as their precursors (Government of Canada, 2023b).

### *8.4.1 Canada's Proposed Reciprocal Preferences*

Canada has long been annoyed with U.S. protectionism and domestic preferences that exclude Canadian goods and suppliers (Government of Canada, 2022b). In 1994, it refused to cover its provinces under the GPA because its firms were excluded from U.S. small business set-asides and 'Buy American' waivers (Dawar, 2017, p. 117). Its provinces remained outside the GPA until the two countries negotiated a bilateral procurement agreement in 2010 that exempted Canadian firms from a 'Buy American' provision in the 2009 American Recovery and Reinvestment Act, and the two neighbours exchanged access to the procurement of their states and provinces under the GPA (Grier, 2022a, Ch. 5.5.2).

When the North American Free Trade Agreement (NAFTA) was renegotiated in 2017–2018, Canada registered its strong objection to the Trump administration's proposal to cap the country's access to the U.S. procurement market at the value of the procurement it opened to the United States. It refused to be bound by the procurement provisions in NAFTA's replacement, the United States–Mexico–Canada Agreement (Grier, 2022a, Ch. 8.3.2.3).

Canadian officials urged the Biden administration to exempt Canada from the BABA Act's 'Buy America' requirements for infrastructure projects, 'pointing to tightly integrated U.S.-Canada supply chains, with Canadian finished products containing U.S. components and vice versa' (Meyer, 2023, p. 18). The United States' refusal to exempt its goods and suppliers has prompted Canada to reconsider access to its essentially open procurement system. For the first time, it is exploring the adoption of unilateral reciprocity measures that would allow it to close its procurement to countries that do not open equivalent procurement. It is particularly considering measures that would generally mirror U.S. restrictions that adversely affect Canadian suppliers. Canada would ensure compliance with its international obligations and would not apply any such measures to procurement covered by trade agreements (Grier, 2022a, Ch. 12.3).

After President Biden issued a 'Made in America' executive order at the beginning of his presidency, the Canadian House of Commons formed a special committee in February 2021 to study the nation's economic relationship with the United States. It directed the committee to examine 'current and proposed "Buy America" procurement rules, requirements, and policies' and make recommendations to safeguard Canadian interests (Government of Canada, 2022b, pp. 3–4). In a June 2021 report, the committee recommended that the Canadian government seek exemptions from the application of existing and future 'Buy American' policies (Government of Canada, 2022b).

The 2021 Canadian budget included a commitment to ensure that its federal government only purchased from countries that grant its businesses similar access (Government of Canada, 2021). Based on that commitment, Canada began a consultation process in March 2022 to explore the adoption of reciprocal procurement policies. It outlined three potential approaches. Its first proposal would limit access to Canada's federal procurement (except defence purchases) 'to what is strictly required by Canada's government procurement obligations'. That strategy would permit Canada to provide preferential access, such as awarding 'extra points in the bid evaluation process for bidders who meet prescribed content requirements', preventing certain foreign suppliers, goods, and services from competing in Canadian federal procurement, or limiting access based on their origin (Government of Canada, 2022a).

Canada reflected U.S. restrictions on federally funded infrastructure projects in its second proposal. Like the United States, it would place conditions on its financial assistance to provinces and territories for infrastructure projects. That approach could authorize Canada to impose domestic content requirements, 'whereby foreign content would only be considered alongside Canadian content if that foreign content originates from a country that provides reciprocal access to infrastructure projects for Canadian suppliers, goods, and services' (Government of Canada, 2022a). A third proposal would establish a small business set-aside program that would permit Canada to exclude foreign suppliers (except those from the EU and the United Kingdom under their respective FTAs with Canada (Grier 2022a, Ch. 11.4.2)) from federal procurement set aside for Canadian small businesses (Government of Canada, 2022a). (The United States has long maintained a small business set-aside program that applies to nearly a quarter of U.S. federal procurement dollars (Grier, 2022a, Ch. 7.3).) In 2024, Canada was still considering the adoption of reciprocal procurement measures that could exclude U.S. companies (Clark, 2023).

### *8.4.2 Canadian Provincial Protectionist Legislation*

The Canadian province of Ontario followed the global trend of procurement policies with its passage of new protectionist legislation intended to favour local businesses (McCarthy Tetrault, 2023). The Ontario Government launched a Building Ontario Businesses Initiative[8] (BOBI) in March 2022 to reduce barriers and provide companies in the province with greater access to public procurement opportunities. The BOBI's central plank is the Building Ontario Businesses Initiative Act, 2022 (BOBI Act). After that legislation enters into force (at a date to be determined), it will require Ontario's public sector entities to give a preference to Ontario businesses when procuring goods and services under trade agreement thresholds (Ontario, 2022b).

In accordance with the legislation, Ontario will require businesses seeking provincial contracts valued at or above CDA$10 million to contribute to economic growth through an Industrial Regional and Technology Benefit (IRTB) requirement. To maximize the local economic impact of the province's large procurement, the IRTB would incorporate economic development considerations into the procurement process. Under the BOBI Act, the Ontario government targets awarding at least $3 billion in contracts to Ontario businesses annually by 2026 (Ontario, 2022a).

The BOBI Act sets out a broad goal of giving preferences to Ontario businesses, in accordance with regulations to be issued by the Lieutenant Governor in Council. Although the content and scope of the regulations are unknown, they are expected to provide key information, including the threshold amount under which the Act will apply, the goods and services subject to preferences, the definition of an Ontario business, and the way a preference will be given to Ontario businesses. It is generally expected that Ontario will set the value threshold at a level below Canadian obligations under the Canada Free Trade Agreement (Grier, 2017) and other trade agreements. A Canadian law firm has observed that: 'Even if the BOBI Act is ultimately of limited application, it provides a strong signal that the Ontario Government intends to take a more protectionist bent with its public procurement strategy into the future' (McCarthy Tetrault, 2023, p. 5).

### *8.4.3 Canadian Court Rejects a Procurement Preference*

In an unexpected development, and in contrast to the advancement of domestic preferences, a Canadian court has struck down the application of a domestic preference as violating a trade agreement. On 1 June 2022, the Ontario Divisional Court issued a decision that demonstrated courts could quash a domestic preference that would not be consistent with Canada's obligations under trade agreements. The case, Thales DIS Canada Inc. v Ontario (Ministry of Transportation), dealt with a challenge by Thales DIS Canada of the Ontario Ministry of Transportation's application of a local preference in an identity card procurement (Thales, 2022). The procurement was for card production and photo comparison technology services related to nine million drivers' licenses, health cards, and other identity cards issued annually by the Government of Ontario. The case was brought by a bidder in the procurement, a security technology company that is part of the French multinational Thales Group (Thales) (LaLonde, 2023).

The procurement under review began in September 2021 when the Government of Ontario issued a Request for Bids (RFB) for the design, processing, manufacturing, and personalization of Ontario identification cards. The RFB required the card stock to be produced at a single facility located in Canada. Thales was able to meet all the technical and security requirements of the RFB, except for its proposed production of card stock at a secure facility in Poland (not Canada) (LaLonde, 2023).

When the Ontario government rejected its bid, Thales objected and sought judicial review of the decision. It claimed that the RFB and the rejection of its bid were procedurally unfair and contrary to applicable trade agreements. In June 2022, the Court allowed Thales' application for judicial review and quashed the RFB. It found that the terms of the RFB were contrary to the obligations of the Government of Ontario under the non-discrimination rules of the procurement chapter of the

Canada-European Union Comprehensive Economic and Trade Agreement (CETA). According to Paul LaLonde, a Canadian lawyer, 'This is likely the first time a court in Canada has concluded that a government decision must be quashed on the basis that it violates a trade agreement' (LaLonde, 2023, p. 74).

The Thales case considered whether Ontario breached the non-discrimination provisions in CETA's procurement chapter when it required bidders to produce card stock in a secure facility in Canada. In arriving at its decision, the Court found 'that there is a strong public interest in ensuring that Ontario's public procurements are conducted in a manner consistent with Canada's obligations under international trade agreements'. The decision of the Ontario Superior Court of Justice is now under appeal. If the Court's decision is upheld, it may generate similar challenges to discriminatory bids in Ontario and other provinces (LaLonde, 2023, p. 74).

## 8.5 EU's Trade Defence Measures

The *Economist* has characterized the EU 'as in essence the deepest and most comprehensive free-trade agreement in the world' and relatively open to trade and investment from the outside world (Economist, 2023b). The EU has generally encouraged the progressive abolition of restrictions on international trade. Over the past decade, it has negotiated FTAs with extensive provisions that open foreign public procurement markets to EU suppliers (Grier, 2022a, Ch. 11.4 and 11.5). While the EU pursued an ambitious trade agenda, the bloc's leaders worried that its openness had left it exposed to America's protectionism and China's rising assertiveness. Many argued that the EU needed to take a more interventionist role (Economist, 2023b).

These concerns led the EU to shift 'towards a more assertive commercial policy relying on the development of new geoeconomic instruments designed to level the playing field and deal with the increasing blurriness between economy and national security' (Basedow et al., 2023). European Commissioner for Internal Market Thierry Breton pointed out in a September 2023 speech that 'We have equipped ourselves with new trade defence instruments' to safeguard the bloc's interests. They include a Foreign Subsidies Regulation, an International Procurement Instrument, and an Anti-Coercion Instrument (European Commission, 2023c). These initiatives demonstrate the EU's 'willingness to safeguard its economy against third-country trade policy measures that are perceived as unfair competition' (Friton, 2023). They also illustrate the important role of its large public procurement market, which accounts for an estimated 16% of the bloc's gross domestic product.

The EU adopted two legislative instruments in 2022, one to ensure equal access for EU companies in third countries' public procurement markets and the other to protect the EU internal market from bids of companies receiving foreign subsidies. These initiatives demonstrate the EU's willingness to act against third-country measures that are perceived as resulting in unfair competition (Friton, 2023). In 2023, the EU added a third trade defence measure that will allow it to retaliate against countries trying to coerce it or its member states to take certain action (Grier, 2023c).

### *8.5.1 EU Framework Relating to Treatment of Third Countries*

In considering how the EU may use access to its procurement market as a tool for tempering the actions of third countries, it is useful to examine the ability of EU member states to restrict access to their procurement. Through its procurement directives, the EU sets the parameters for the conduct of procurement by its member states (EU, 2014a; EU, 2014b; EU, 2014c). Within those parameters, each member state establishes its own procurement system based on its national laws.

The GPA and FTAs obligate the member states to not discriminate against the goods and services of the agreement partners in covered procurement. However, the states are not obliged to give preference to bidders from the EU or GPA or FTA parties over bidders from third countries. Generally, they have allowed third countries outside trade agreements to participate in their procurement even if they do not provide reciprocal access to EU suppliers. Similarly, most member states allow GPA and FTA parties to participate in procurement to which they have no legal rights under agreements. As an example, even though U.S. suppliers are denied rights to specific EU procurement under reciprocity conditions in the GPA, including the procurement of services by subcentral entities, they 'often have de facto access to the excluded procurement' (Woolcock & Grier, 2015, p. 312).

In 2019, the European Commission clarified the member states' authority to reject bids from non-EU suppliers without a GPA or FTA right to participate in a particular procurement. That extends to both suppliers from a country without an EU procurement agreement and suppliers from a country with an EU agreement in procurement not covered by the agreement (European Commission, 2019b). While the Commission acknowledged the authority of the states to reject such bids, it did not require their rejections even where bidders lack legal rights to participate in a procurement.

The Commission's third-country guidance does not apply to procurement by utilities, which are subject to a Utilities Directive with its own penalties (EU, 2014c).[9] This Directive permits utilities in the water, energy, transport, and postal sectors to reject tenders with more than 50% content from a country that does not have the right to participate in EU procurement. Instead of rejecting such a tender, the utility may include it in its evaluation of tenders, provided it gives preference to equivalent tenders with less than 50% third-country content. This provision does not apply to EU FTA and GPA partners that provide reciprocal access to their procurement in the same utility sector.

Notwithstanding the Commission's guidance, a member state can exclude third-country bidders from its procurement only if its national law authorizes such an exclusion (Baciu, 2021). Among their differing domestic legal systems, only a few member states have such authority (outside of the utilities sector). Belgium and Italy forbid third-country bids unless they are subject to international commitments (the GPA or FTAs). Spain requires symmetric reciprocity, while Austria, Estonia, and Hungary allow their procuring authorities at their discretion to reject bids (Szczepański, 2022). Hungary's Public Procurement Act (143/2015) authorizes its procuring entities to exclude suppliers that are not entitled to national treatment under the GPA or another international agreement and tenderers who offer a product not eligible for national treatment due to its place of origin. In Romania, a 2021 law provides for the automatic exclusion from the award procedures of suppliers that do not reside or are not established in an EU member state or other listed country. The listed countries include GPA parties with rights under the EU's coverage schedules, third countries in EU accession negotiations, and parties to other international agreements. Romania's adoption of this law was the result of an 'active campaign' by the European Commission to persuade member states to take concrete measures restricting the access of suppliers without rights to participate in EU procurement (Baicu, 2021).

In contrast, Germany requires equal treatment of bidders regardless of their nationality, applying the principle of non-discrimination to tenderers from third countries. Its Higher Regional Court of Düsseldorf, the court with jurisdiction over federal public procurement, ruled in a December 2021 decision[10] that unequal treatment of bidders based on their origin would be illegal as a matter of national and EU law (Friton, 2023).

### *8.5.2 International Procurement Instrument*

The EU implemented the first of the three trade defence measures, the International Procurement Instrument (IPI) in August 2022 (EU, 2022a). The regulation was adopted to respond to mounting concerns with the disparity between the openness of EU public procurement and the growing number of protectionist measures that restrict access by European suppliers in foreign procurement markets. According to the Council of the EU, '[f]ewer than half of the world's public procurement markets are currently open to European companies' (Council of the EU, 2022). Moreover, as Cernat points out, the vast majority of WTO members have not undertaken international procurement commitments (Cernat, 2023).

The IPI was designed to promote greater reciprocity in access to international public procurement markets and improve market access for EU suppliers, goods, and services. It provides the EU with leverage to negotiate the opening of public procurement markets in third countries by authorizing the European Commission to restrict or block access to EU procurement by countries that restrict participation in their home procurement markets and refuse to negotiate an opening of their procurement. Under this Instrument, EU member states can continue to implement their national measures (EU, 2022a).

The EU's decade-long pursuit of a means of promoting reciprocity with third countries began in 2012 when the European Commission proposed a procurement reciprocity measure that could have closed its procurement to suppliers from non-EU countries discriminating against EU suppliers in their own procurement (European Commission, 2012). When it failed to garner sufficient member state support, it was put on hold (Grier, 2022a, Ch. 12.4.1).

In 2016, the Commission offered a revised proposal that would have imposed penalties of up to 20% on the price of tenders from countries restricting access to their procurement (European Commission, 2016). That proposal drew criticism from the business community for not effectively addressing issues with participation by state-owned enterprises (SOEs) in EU procurement. BusinessEurope urged the exclusion of SOEs from any country that did not commit to opening its procurement to the EU and maintained discriminatory policies and practices (BusinessEurope, 2020). In addition, the European Parliament considered the proposal too weak and sought a reinstatement of the initial proposed exclusions from the EU market (Dreyer, 2017).

When 14 member states withheld their approval, the discussions were put on hold (Dreyer, 2021). In 2021, a revised IPI proposal that included both the threat of market exclusion and the price adjustment mechanism received member state support and provided the basis for negotiations between the EU's co-legislators (the European Parliament and the Council of the EU), leading to adoption of the IPI in June 2022 (Cernat, 2023).

The IPI authorizes the Commission to investigate alleged restrictions in third-country procurement markets, engage in consultations with the country concerned on opening its procurement, and, if all attempts fail, to impose proportionate restrictions in the EU procurement market against those countries. The Commission may initiate an investigation based on a substantiated complaint by an EU interested party or a member state or as an *ex officio* investigation. If the Commission concludes that an IPI measure should be adopted, it will determine the thresholds, the sectors, type of goods and services, contracting authorities, and companies to which the IPI measure must be applied. The Commission may adopt a price and score adjustment measure or exclude the third-country's suppliers from EU tenders (Cernat, 2023). In designing the IPI measure, the Commission must consider the principles of proportionality and effectiveness as well as the effects on EU contracting authorities, such as the availability of alternative sources of supply for the goods and services concerned (Friton, 2023).

The IPI applies to procurement of at least €15 million for public works and concessions and €5 million for goods and services. It excludes least developed countries unless they are involved in the circumvention of an IPI measure such as transshipment. The IPI also does not apply to parties to the GPA or other EU trade agreements in procurement covered by the agreement. However, such parties could be subject to an IPI measure if the EU finds they discriminate against EU suppliers in procurement not covered by an agreement. The U.S. Trade Representative raised concerns with the EU relating to the potential application of the measure to the United States (USTR, 2022).

### *8.5.3 Foreign Subsidies Regulation*

A second trade defence measure adopted by the EU, a Foreign Subsidies Regulation (FSR), empowers the Commission to prevent state-subsidized companies from bidding on public procurement contracts in the EU (EU, 2022b). The FSR also applies to concentrations (mergers and acquisitions and joint ventures). While the rule was principally targeted at China, it could impact U.S. companies that receive state subsidies under the Inflation Reduction Act or related legislation (Hamilton & Quinlan, 2023).

The FSR was intended to close a perceived regulatory gap. While subsidies granted by EU member states are subject to a rigorous EU state aid regime, in accordance with the Treaty on the Functioning of the European Union (TFEU),[11] subsidies granted by countries outside the EU to foreign operators active in the EU were unregulated. That meant third countries could, in principle, support their own companies to a much greater extent than could member states. A further concern was that the EU's existing public procurement rules were not sufficient to address and remedy distortions caused by foreign subsidies (Friton, 2022).

The importance of this regulation to the EU is reflected in the speed with which it was adopted. In contrast to the decade-long development of the IPI, the EU moved expeditiously regarding the FSR. Two years after the European Commission issued a white paper proposing a remedy for distortions resulting from subsidies (European Commission, 2020), and a year after it proposed a regulation (European Commission, 2021a), the European Parliament and the Council of the EU reached a political agreement on the FSR in mid-2022 (European Parliament 2022). Following their formal adoption of the Regulation in December 2022, it entered into force on 12 January 2023 and became directly applicable across the EU six months later. Its notification requirement applied from 12 October 2023.

The application of the FSR to procurement was prompted by concerns that foreign subsidies can provide foreign firms with an unfair advantage in EU public procurement by enabling bidders receiving such subsidies to win contracts with bids below market price or even below cost, to the disadvantage of European firms (European Commission, 2020). The FSR gives the Commission the power to investigate financial contributions or subsidies granted by non-EU governments to companies active in the EU.

The FSR requires notification of financial contributions received by suppliers from foreign governments. The notification requirement applies to companies participating in large public tenders in EU countries (the value of the procurement is at least €250 million), and the bid involves a foreign financial contribution of at least €4 million per third country. In such cases, the supplier must notify the contracting authority of all foreign financial contributions it received in the prior three years (or a declaration it had not received any). The Regulation specifies the timing for the submission of notifications. In open tendering, the supplier must submit the notification (or declaration) with its tender. In procurements with multiple stages, the supplier is obligated to submit two notifications: one with the request to participate in the procurement and the other as an update with the tender or final tender.

The FSR defines very broadly the financial contributions that must be notified. They include: (i) any transfer of funds or liabilities such as capital injections, grants, loans, loan guarantees, fiscal incentives, and debt forgiveness; (ii) tax exemptions or other tax benefits; and (iii) the provision or purchase of goods or services to public entities. The FSR defines 'foreign subsidies' as a financial contribution by a third country that confers a selective benefit on a company engaging in an economic activity in the EU internal market. While the FSR's definition of foreign subsidies differs from the definition of state aid according to the TFEU, the recitals to the FSR suggest that the criteria are essentially the same. Yet, 'it remains to be seen whether the Commission will interpret the concept of foreign subsidies under the FSR fully in line with the notion of aid under EU state aid law' (Friton, 2023, p. 67).

The FSR provides the Commission with broad powers to investigate foreign subsidies and adopt remedial measures. The first step is a preliminary review of notifications and, then if warranted, an in-depth investigation to determine whether a subsidy distorts a procurement. During investigations, the procurement procedures can continue, except the contract cannot be awarded. If the Commission finds that financial contributions constitute distortive subsidies, it can impose measures to remedy the distortion (Grier, 2022a, Ch. 12.4.2).

An investigated bidder cannot be awarded the contract until cleared by the Commission. Upon a finding that a bidder received a foreign subsidy that distorted the internal market, the Commission can prohibit the award of a contract to the subsidized bidder unless the bidder commits to remove the distortion of the internal market.

The Commission acknowledged that the exclusion of bidders under the FSR would have to be compatible with the EU's commitments under the GPA and FTAs. The EU has included provisions related to subsidies in government procurement in FTAs with several GPA parties (Japan, Singapore, and the United Kingdom). Those FTAs allow a procuring entity to enquire whether an abnormally low tender is the result of a subsidy, but only the Singapore FTA allows the exclusion of a supplier in such cases (Grier, 2022a, Ch. 11.4).

### *8.5.4 Anti-Coercion Instrument*

In October 2023, the EU's co-legislative institutions approved an Anti-Coercion Instrument (ACI), its third trade defence instrument, which entered into force on 27 December 2023 (EU, 2023). The development of the ACI began with a European Commission proposal in 2021 in response to third countries' targeting deliberate economic pressure against the EU and its member states (European Commission, 2021b). While the EU has indicated that the new measure is not directed at any specific country, *Borderlex* labelled China's blockade of trade with Lithuania in response to its opening of a Taiwan representative office in its capital, Vilnius, as 'a perfect scene-setter' for the regulation (Borderlex Editor, 2021). (For a discussion of the primary and secondary sanctions imposed by China on Lithuania, see Reynolds & Goodman, 2022.)

The EU describes the ACI as 'first and foremost' a deterrent against economic coercion, defining such coercion 'as a situation where a third country attempts to pressure the EU or a Member State into making a particular choice by applying, or threatening to apply, measures affecting trade or investment against the EU or a Member State' (European Commission, 2023a). If the new regulation does not deter coercion, it allows the Union to formally identify instances of economic coercion and to respond, first through dialogue and engagement with the coercing country. If that is not successful, the EU can retaliate against it.

The ACI authorizes the adoption of a variety of anti-coercion measures. The Commission can place restrictions on access to the EU public procurement market, as well as on the import and export of goods and services, intellectual property rights, and foreign direct investment. It could also remove market authorizations for chemicals and food products under EU sanitary and phytosanitary rules (European Commission, 2021c).

If it invokes the procurement remedy, the Commission may suspend any international obligations providing for participation in EU procurement and exclude the goods, services, or suppliers of the coercing country or tenders with more than a specified percentage of goods or services from that country. It may also impose a mandatory price evaluation weighting penalty on the third country's tenders, thus increasing the price of its goods or services.

The anti-coercion instrument joined the IPI and the FSR as 'defensive trade and investment instruments enacted by the EU against perceived encroachments against the integrity of its single market' (Dreyer, 2023). These measures illustrate the value of access to the large EU procurement market and the hope and expectation that threats of denial of such access will affect actions of third countries (Grier, 2023c).

## 8.6 China's Challenges to Foreign Participation in Procurement

China has long had a state-directed economy despite some market-oriented reforms beginning in the late 1970s. In recent years, Beijing has embraced an aggressive industrial policy in the form of its 'Made in China 2025' strategy. It outlines China's ambition to achieve global dominance in ten high-tech industries, including electric vehicles, advanced rail and shipbuilding, and artificial intelligence. The Chinese government has provided massive subsidies for the development of these industries (Siripurapu & Berman, 2022).

With its 'Made in China 2025' program, Beijing was explicit in its aim to free China from dependence on Western technologies and to make the country a world-beater in critical sectors. Despite some adjustments, China's basic goals remain the same. Its current five-year plan emphasizes industrial strategies with the intent of catching up with the West and leading in critical technology. U.S. Secretary of State Antony Blinken portrayed Beijing's plan as making 'China less dependent on the world and the world more dependent on China' (Hamilton & Quinlan, 2023, p. 38).

China maintains 'buy local' policies and practices that obstruct foreign firms' participation in its procurement market (Grier, 2022a, Ch. 13.5.2). Its primary procurement law, the Government Procurement Law, implemented at the beginning of 2003, includes a 'Buy China' mandate in Article 10 that requires government entities to purchase domestic goods, construction works, and services (except when they are not available in China, cannot be acquired on reasonable commercial terms, or are for use outside China).

In 2022, China implemented a Foreign Investment Law (FIL) with commitments to allow participation by foreign firms in its government procurement (Grier, 2020).

It guaranteed foreign-invested enterprises' (FIEs) participation in government procurement activities through fair competition and equal treatment. It defined an FIE as an enterprise incorporated under Chinese laws within the territory of China and wholly or partly invested by a foreign investor.

The FIL and its implementing regulations (promulgated on 1 January 2020) require government authorities to treat goods produced by FIEs and services provided by them in China the same as those of domestic enterprises. The authorities may neither discriminate against foreign firms in the procurement process nor restrict a supplier's participation in procurement based on its ownership, organizational form, shareholding structure, the nationality of its investors, or the brand of the product or service it offers. The FIL's implementing regulations provide that government authorities must not apply differential or discriminatory treatment to FIEs in procurement activities, including in the publication of procurement information, determination of conditions for suppliers, examination of supplier qualifications, and bid evaluation criteria (Grier, 2020).

The U.S. government and business community, such as the United States–China Business Council and the American Chamber of Commerce in China, have long complained of the obstacles to the participation of U.S. and other foreign firms in China's government procurement, including its use of domestic preferences (USTR, 2021, p. 13). In assessing China's compliance with its WTO obligations, President Biden's administration concluded that 'China continues to implement policies favoring products, services, and technologies made or developed by Chinese-owned and Chinese-controlled companies through explicit and implicit requirements that hamper foreign companies from fairly competing in China' (USTR, 2021, pp. 43–44). For example, even though China committed, when it joined the WTO in 2001, to provide equal opportunities for foreign firms to participate in its procurement, U.S. companies continued to report cases in which domestic brands and indigenous designs were required in tendering documents.

For years, Europe did not join the United States in complaints about China's trade behaviour to avoid being seen 'as ganging up on Beijing' (Chase, 2020, p. 11). However, the EU now generally shares the United States' concerns. As the EU considered the adoption of the IPI to allow it to penalize countries that do not offer reciprocal access to their procurement, it identified barriers to China's procurement market. They included lack of transparency, 'Buy Chinese' requirements, exclusion of certain projects from procurement rules, and requirements that EU firms establish joint ventures with local companies (European Commission, 2019a).

Major European business organizations, including BusinessEurope and the EU Chamber of Commerce in China, have detailed their complaints and concerns relating to participation by foreign firms in China's procurement markets. In a 2020 report, BusinessEurope called on the EU to rebalance its relationship with China to address systemic challenges arising from its state-led economy that were leading to market distortions within China, the EU, and third-country markets (BusinessEurope, 2020). The business group pointed out numerous investment and trade barriers, arguing that China's state domination of all aspects of the economy produces discrimination and market distortions that include a disparity in market access between Chinese and foreign firms. They include a closed government procurement market in which EU firms are often prohibited from bidding, while the EU's procurement market is open to Chinese suppliers (BusinessEurope, 2020, pp. 4 and 37; Chase, 2020, p. 18).

China poses a unique challenge to the international procurement system. As the world's second-largest economy, its government procurement is significant, particularly when purchases by its state-controlled entities are included (BusinessEurope, 2020; Grier, 2022a, Ch. 13.2). Yet, foreign governments and foreign firms have no legal recourse to challenge China's procurement practices because it has not undertaken any binding international obligations to allow foreign firms to participate in its procurement on the same basis as its domestic firms.

Although China applied to join the GPA in 2007, based on a commitment it made when it became a WTO member in 2001, its GPA negotiations have been protracted. They entered their 17th year in 2024 and have already taken at least as long as China's negotiations to accede to the WTO. While it has offered to open procurement under the GPA that is commensurate in many respects with the coverage of existing GPA parties, China has not made a market access offer acceptable to the GPA parties (Grier, 2022a, Ch. 13.5.1). Moreover, with growing tensions between China and the West, especially the United States, the prospects for its accession to the GPA are in question.

## 8.7 Conclusion

Preferences in public procurement are creating tensions and divisions in the international trading system. Forty years ago, the implementation of the first international procurement agreement bound a core group of countries to common public procurement obligations. While that core has grown to 49 WTO members, the international procurement system is facing pressures. This threat can be seen in the increasing resort to preferences and unilateral measures to address deficiencies in the international system and to advance domestic priorities.

Beginning with the 'America First' policies of the Trump administration and pursued with even more vigour by President Biden, the United States is pivoting away from its support of liberalization. Biden has gone farther than his predecessor in incorporating industrial policy into laws. The 2021 Infrastructure Act significantly expanded the application of domestic preferences. The Inflation Reduction Act extended 'Buy America' requirements into non-procurement areas with its provision of tax credits for purchases of electric vehicles that contain critical minerals from the United States or FTA partners and that are assembled in North America.

The U.S. protectionist policies are reverberating among its trading partners, leading Canada to consider the adoption of its own 'made-in-Canada' policies. Recently, the EU has adopted trade defence measures aimed at safeguarding its interests. These measures allow the EU to restrict access to its large public procurement market in response to actions of third countries.

Finally, there is China with a huge procurement market and broad 'buy local' policies that continue unchecked as it has yet to undertake any international procurement obligations.

## Notes

1 Buy American Act of 1933, Public Law 72–428 (1933).
2 The FAR Council consists of the Administrator of the Office for Federal Procurement Policy, the Secretary of Defense, the Administrator of General Services, and the Administrator of National Aeronautics and Space. Federal Acquisition Regulatory Council. Available at www.acquisition.gov/far-council.
3 Infrastructure Investment and Jobs Act, Public Law 117-58 (2021).
4 Infrastructure Investment and Jobs Act, sec. 70912(5).
5 Inflation Reduction Act, Public Law 117-169 (2022).
6 The United States has FTAs with Australia, Bahrain, Chile, Colombia, Costa Rica, the Dominican Republic, El Salvador, Guatemala, Honduras, Israel, Jordan, South Korea, Mexico, Morocco, Nicaragua, Oman, Panama, Peru, and Singapore.
7 Creating Helpful Incentives to Produce Semiconductors and Science Act (CHIPS and Science Act), Public Law 117-167 (2022).
8 Building Ontario businesses initiative. Available at https://news.ontario.ca/en/backgrounder/1001730/building-ontario-businesses-initiative.
9 The Utilities Directive provides rules on procurement by entities operating in the water, energy, transport, and postal services sectors.
10 Higher Regional Court of Düsseldorf, decision of 1 December 2021, VII-Verg 55/20).
11 The Treaty on the Functioning of the European Union is one of two treaties forming the constitutional basis of the European Union. It was known previously as the Treaty Establishing the European Community (or Treaty of Rome). The other is the Treaty on European Union. The Consolidated Version of the Treaty on the Functioning of the European Union.

## References


Akhtar, S.I. (2023), 'U.S.-UK trade relations', *Congressional Research Service*, 17 August. Available at https://crsreports.congress.gov/product/pdf/IF/IF11123.

Baciu, I. (2021), 'The exclusion of third-country suppliers from EU public procurement procedures: The Romanian case', *European Procurement & Public Private Partnership*, 16(2), pp. 151–157.

Basedow, R., Meunier, S., and Roederer-Rynning, C. (2023), 'Fair play?: The politics of evaluating foreign subsidies in the European Union', *European University Institute*. Available at https://cadmus.eui.eu/bitstream/handle/1814/75630/RSC_2023_41_GGP.pdf?sequence=1&isAllowed=y.

Blevins, E.G. and Gallo, M.E. (2022), 'U.S. technology made in China: The role of federal technology licensing policies', *Congressional Research Service*, Report No. IN12019, 20 September. Available at https://crsreports.congress.gov/product/pdf/IN/IN12019#:~:text=96%2D480)%20and%20the%20Bayh,research%20resulting%20from%20federal%20funds.&text=One%20mechanism%20involves%20licensing%20federally,to%20private%20businesses%20for%20commercialization.

Borderlex Editor (2021), 'Week ahead: EU anti-coercion trade tools, DIT goes to Washington, UK, Australia', *Borderlex* 6 December. Available at https://borderlex.net/2021/12/06/week-ahead-eu-anti-coercion-trade-tools-dit-goes-to-washington-uk-australia/?utm_source=mailpoet&utm_medium=email&utm_campaign=the-last-newsletter-total-posts-from-borderlex_2.

Bown, C.P. (2023), 'Industrial policy for electric vehicle supply chains and the US-EU fight over the Inflation Reduction Act', May. *Peterson Institute for International Economics*, 22. Available at www.piie.com/publications/working-papers/industrial-policy-electric-vehicle-supply-chains-and-us-eu-fight-over.

BusinessEurope (2020), 'The EU and China: Addressing the systemic challenge', 6 January. Available at:www.businesseurope.eu/sites/buseur/files/media/reports_and_studies/2020-01-16_the_eu_and_china-addressingthesystem-icchallenge-fullpaper.pdf.

Cernat, L. (2023), 'The International Procurement Instrument (IPI): Promoting a level playing field around the world', *Información Comercial Española (ICE), Revistas de Economia*, 930, 31 March.

Chase, P. (2020), 'The missing partnership: The United States, Europe, and China's economic challenge', *The German Marshall Fund of the United States*, September.

Clark, S.P. (2023), 'North American business summit speech', *U.S. Chamber of Commerce*, 15 May. Available at www.uschamber.com/assets/documents/North-American-Business-Summit-As-Prepared-5.15.23.pdf.

Council of the EU (2022), 'International Procurement Instrument: Council gives green light to new rules promoting reciprocity', 17 June. Available at www.consilium.europa.eu/en/press/press-releases/2022/06/17/international-procurement-instrument-council-gives-final-go-ahead-to-new-rules-boosting-reciprocity/.

Council of the EU (2023), 'Trade with the United States: Council authorises negotiations on EU-US Critical Minerals Agreement', 20 July. Available at www.consilium.europa.eu/en/press/press-releases/2023/07/20/trade-with-the-united-states-council-authorises-negotiations-on-eu-us-critical-minerals-agreement/.

Dabbs, B. (2023), 'Biden's latest climate minefield: EV mineral deals', *EnergyWire, E&E News*, 9 May. Available at www.eenews.net/articles/bidens-latest-climate-minefield-ev-mineral-deals/.

Dawar, K. (2017), 'The government procurement agreement, the most-favored nation principle, and regional trade agreements', in: Georgopoulos, A., Hoekman, B., and Mavroidis, P. (eds.), *The Internationalization of Government Procurement Regulation*, Oxford University Press, Oxford.

Dreyer, I. (2017), 'Procurement reciprocity: Caspary report calls for return to full market access suspension', *Borderlex*, 12 July. Available at https://borderlex.net/2017/07/12/procurement-reciprocity-caspary-report-calls-for-return-to-full-market-access-suspension/.

Dreyer, I. (2021), 'IPI: Council finds compromise, paves way for trilogue', *Borderlex*, 2 June. Available at https://borderlex.net/2021/06/02/international-procurement-instrument-council-finds-compromise-paves-way-for-trilogue/.

Dreyer, I. (2023), 'The EU's anti-coercion instrument's final fine print', *Borderlex*, 6 June. Available at https://borderlex.net/2023/06/06/the-eus-anti-coercion-instruments-final-fine-print/?utm_source=mailpoet&utm_medium=email&utm_campaign=the-last-newsletter-total-posts-from-borderlex_2.

Economist (2023a), 'What America's protectionist turn means for the world', 9 January. www.economist.com/finance-and-economics/2023/01/09/what-americas-protectionist-turn-means-for-the-world

Economist (2023b), 'The battle for Europe's economic soul', 23 March. Available at www.economist.com/finance-and-economics/2023/03/23/the-battle-for-europes-economic-soul.

European Commission (2012), 'European Commission levels the playing field for European business in international procurement markets', 21 March. Available at http://trade.ec.europa.eu/doclib/press/index.cfm?id=788.

European Commission (2016), 'Amended proposal for a regulation of the European Parliament and of the Council on the access of third-country goods and services to the Union's internal market in public procurement and procedures supporting negotiations on access of Union goods and services to the public procurement markets of third countries, COM(2016) 34 final', 29 January. Available at http://trade.ec.europa.eu/doclib/docs/2016/january/tradoc_154187.pdf

European Commission (2019a), 'International Procurement Instrument, fact sheet'. Available at https://trade.ec.europa.eu/doclib/docs/2019/march/tradoc_157728.pdf.

European Commission (2019b), 'Guidance on the participation of third-country bidders and goods in the EU procurement market', 24 July. Available at https://eceuropa.eu/docsroom/documents/36601.

European Commission (2020), 'Commission adopts White Paper on foreign subsidies in the Single Market', 17 June. Available at https://ec.europa.eu/commission/presscorner/detail/en/ip_20_1070.

European Commission (2021a), 'Proposal for a regulation of the European Parliament and the Council on foreign subsidies distorting the internal market, COM/2021/223 final', 5 May. Available at https://eur-lex.europa.eu/legal-content/EN/TXT/PDF/?uri=CELEX:52021PC0223&from=EN.

European Commission (2021b), 'Proposal for a regulation of the European Parliament and of the Council on the protection of the Union and its Member States from economic coercion by third countries', 8 December. Available at https://eur-lex.europa.eu/resource.html?uri=cellar:9f3b1699-58d9-11ec-91ac-01aa75ed71a1.0001.02/DOC_1&format=PDF.

European Commission (2021c), 'Annexes to the proposal for a regulation of the European Parliament and of the Council on the protection of the Union and its Member States from economic coercion by third countries', 8 December. Available at https://eur-lex.europa.eu/resource.html?uri=cellar:9f3b1699-58d9-11ec-91ac-01aa75ed71a1.0001.02/DOC_2&format=PDF.

European Commission (2023a), 'Political agreement on new Anti-Coercion Instrument to better defend EU interests on global stage', 6 June. Available at https://ec.europa.eu/commission/presscorner/detail/en/IP_23_3046.

European Commission (2023b), 'EU moves forward with Critical Minerals Agreement negotiations with the US', 14 June. Available at https://ec.europa.eu/commission/presscorner/detail/en/IP_23_3214.

European Commission (2023c), 'A Europe that protects, transforms and projects: Industrial policy the European way – Speech by Commissioner Thierry Breton at the Bruegel Annual Meeting', 6 September. Available at https://ec.europa.eu/commission/presscorner/detail/en/speech_23_4369.

European Parliament (2022), 'Provisional agreement resulting from interinstitutional negotiations: Regulation of the European Parliament and of the Council on foreign subsidies distorting the internal market', 11 July. Available at www.europarl.europa.eu/meetdocs/2014_2019/plmrep/COMMITTEES/INTA/DV/2022/07-13/1260231_EN.pdf.

European Parliament (2023), 'MEPs adopt new trade tool to defend EU from economic blackmail', 3 October. Available at www.europarl.europa.eu/news/en/press-room/20230929IPR06122/meps-adopt-new-trade-tool-to-defend-eu-from-economic-blackmail.

European Union (EU) (2014a), 'Directive 2014/23/EU of the European Parliament and of the Council of 26 February 2014 on the award of concession contracts', *Official Journal of the European Union*, 94/1, 28 March.

EU (2014b), 'Directive 2014/24/EU of the European Parliament and of the Council of 26 February 2014 on public procurement and repealing Directive 2004/18/EC', *Official Journal of the European Union*, 94/65, 28 March.

EU (2014c), 'Directive 2014/25/EU of the European Parliament and of the Council of 26 February 2014 on procurement by entities operating in the water, energy, transport, and postal services sectors and repealing Directive 2004/17/EC', *Official Journal of the European Union*, 94/243, 28 March.

EU (2022a), 'Regulation (EU) 2022/1031 of the European Parliament and of the Council of 23 June 2022 on the access of third-country economic operators, goods and services to the Union's public procurement and concession markets and procedures supporting negotiations on access of Union economic operators, goods and services to the public procurement and concession markets of third countries (International Procurement Instrument – IPI)', *Official Journal of the European Union*, 65, 30 June, 173/1. Available at https://eur-lex.europa.eu/legal-content/EN/TXT/PDF/?uri=CELEX:32022R1031&from=EN.

EU (2022b), 'Regulation (EU) 2022/2560 of the European Parliament and of the Council of 14 December 2022 on foreign subsidies distorting the internal market', *Official Journal of the European Union*, 330, 23 December. Available at https://eur-lex.europa.eu/legal-content/EN/TXT/?uri=CELEX%3A32022R2560.

EU (2023), 'Regulation (EU) 2023/2675 of the European Parliament and of the Council of 22 November 2023 on the protection of the Union and its member states from economic coercion by third countries', 2023/2675, 7 December. Available at https://eur-lex.europa.eu/legal-content/EN/TXT/PDF/?uri=OJ:L_202302675.

EU Delegation to the US (2023) [European Union Delegation to the United States (2023)], 'Comments by the European Union to the Office of Federal Financial Management, Office of Management and Budget, Request for comments: Proposed rule: Revision of the Office of Management and Budget Guidance for Grants and Agreements (88 FR 8374)', 13 March.

FAR Council (2021) [Federal Acquisition Regulatory Council (2021)], 'Federal acquisition regulation: Maximizing use of American-made goods, products, and materials', *Federal Register*, 86(11), p. 6180, 19 January. Available at www.govinfo.gov/content/pkg/FR-2021-01-19/pdf/2021-00710.pdf.

FAR Council (2022) [Federal Acquisition Regulatory Council (2022)], 'Federal acquisition regulation: Amendments to the FAR Buy American Act requirements', *Federal Register*, 87(44), p. 12780, 7 March. Available at www.govinfo.gov/content/pkg/FR-2022-03-07/pdf/2022-04173.pdf.

Friton, P. (2022), 'European procurement developments in 2021: The EU's persistent (and sometimes a little desperate) pursuit of a resilient economy', *2021 Thomson Reuters' Government Contracts Year in Review Conference Briefs*, 102.

Friton, P. (2023), 'EU and Germany: The influence of growing unilateralism and the Russian aggression against Ukraine on public procurement procedures', *2022 Thomson Reuters' Government Contracts Year in Review Conference Briefs*, pp. 61–65.

Gourdon, J. and Messent, J. (2017), 'How government procurement measures can affect trade', *OECD Trade Policy Papers*, 199, 12 April, OECD Publishing, Paris. Available at http://dx.doi.org/10.1787/d1ab07b8-en.

Government of Canada (2021), 'Budget 2021, Part 2, Creating jobs and growth', Available at www.budget.gc.ca/2021/report-rapport/p2-en.html#68.

Government of Canada (2022a), 'Consultations on reciprocal procurement policies in Canada', March. Available at www.international.gc.ca/trade-commerce/consultations/RP-AR/index.aspx?lang=eng.

Government of Canada (2022b), 'Buy America Procurement Policies: An Interim Report, Report of the Special Committee on the Economic Relationship between Canada and the United States', *House of Commons*, 3 June. Available at www.queensu.ca/sps/sites/spswww/files/uploaded_files/QITP%20pdfs/2021/7%20-%20House%20of%20Commons%20Report%20on%20Buy%20America%20Procurement%20Policies.pdf.

Government of Canada (2023a), 'Comments from the Government of Canada to the United States Office of Management and Budget', 13 March.

Government of Canada (2023b), 'Budget 2023, a made-in-Canada plan: Strong middle class, affordable economy, healthy future', 28 March. Available at www.canada.ca/en/revenue-agency/programs/about-canada-revenue-agency-cra/federal-government-budgets/budget-2023-made-canada-plan-strong-middle-class-affordable-economy-healthy-future.html.

Grier, J.H. (2017), 'Canada's New Internal Agreement: Backgrounder', *Perspectives on Trade*, 2 May. Available at https://trade.djaghe.com/canadas-new-internal-trade-agreement-backgrounder/.

Grier, J.H. (2020), 'China's Investment Law: Opens procurement', *Perspectives on Trade*, 30 January. Available at https://trade.djaghe.com/chinas-foreign-investment-law-open-procurement/.

Grier, J.H. (2022a), *The International Procurement System: Liberalization & Protectionism*, Dalston Press, Washington.

Grier, J.H. (2022b), 'US Transportation Department's construction materials waiver', *Perspectives on Trade*, 31 May. Available at https://trade.djaghe.com/transportation-departments-waiver-for-construction-material/.

Grier, J.H. (2023a), 'Trade agreements ignored in new 'Buy America' rules', *Perspectives on Trade*, 13 February. Available at https://trade.djaghe.com/trade-agreements-ignored-in-new-buy-america-rules/,.

Grier, J.H. (2023b), 'Domestic content requirements: Contrasting treatment', *Perspectives on Trade*, 3 May. Available at https://trade.djaghe.com/domestic-content-requirements-contrasting-treatment/.

Grier, J.H. (2023c), 'EU gains new trade tool: Anti-coercion instrument', *Perspectives on Trade*, 11 July. Available at https://trade.djaghe.com/eu-gains-new-trade-tool-anti-coercion-instrument/.

Grier, J.H. (2023d), 'Final infrastructure guidance: No trade agreement provisions', *Perspectives on Trade*, 21 August Available at https://trade.djaghe.com/final-infrastructure-guidance-no-trade-agreement-provisions/.

Grier, J.H. (2023e), 'Buy America extended to federally funded R&D', *Perspectives on Trade*, 29 August. Available at https://trade.djaghe.com/buy-america-policies-extended-to-federally-funded-rd/.

Grier, J.H. (2023f), 'North Macedonia implements WTO Procurement Agreement', *Perspectives on Trade*, 1 November. Available at https://trade.djaghe.com/north-macedonia-implements-wto-procurement-agreement/.

Grier, J.H. (2023g), 'GPA parties criticize OMB infrastructure guidance', *Perspectives on Trade*, 14 November. Available at https://trade.djaghe.com/gpa-parties-criticize-omb-infrastructure-guidance/.

GTA (2022), ' Global Trade Alert Database'. Available at www.globaltradealert.org/data_extraction.

Hamilton, D.S. and Quinlan, J.P. (2023), 'The Transatlantic Economy 2023: Annual survey of jobs, trade and investment between the United States and Europe', *Foreign Policy Institute*, Johns Hopkins University. Available at https://transatlanticrelations.org/wp-content/uploads/2023/03/Transatlantic-Economy-Report-2023-Summary.pdf.

IRS (2022) [Internal Revenue Service (2022)], 'Frequently asked questions related to new, previously-owned and qualified commercial clean vehicle credits', RS:FS-2022-42, December.

IRS (2023) [Internal Revenue Service (2022)], 'Proposed regulations, Section 30D New Clean Vehicle Credit', *Federal Register*, 88(73), p. 23370, 17 April. Available at www.govinfo.gov/content/pkg/FR-2023-04-17/pdf/2023-06822.pdf.

LaLonde, P.M. (2023), 'Canada: year of transition: Post-pandemic hang-over, inflation and changing attitudes to defense procurement and a ground-breaking local preference case', *Thomson Reuters' Government Contracts Year in Review Conference Briefs*, pp. 72–78.

McCarthy Tetrault (2023), 'Public Procurement 2022 year in review', January. Available at www.mccarthy.ca/sites/default/files/2023-01/Public_Procurement_2022_Year_in_Review.pdf.

Meyer, P.J. (2023), 'Canada: Background and U.S. relations', *Congressional Research Service*, Report No. R47620, 11 July. Available at https://crsreports.congress.gov/product/pdf/R/R47620#:~:text=The%20United%20States%20and%20Canada,Aerospace%20Defense%20Command%20(NORAD).

OMB (2022) [Office of Management and Budget (2022)], 'Memorandum for heads of executive departments and agencies, initial implementation guidance on application of Buy America preference in Federal Financial Assistance Programs for Infrastructure, M-22-11', 18 April. Available at www.whitehouse.gov/wp-content/uploads/2022/04/M-22-11.pdf.

OMB (2023a) [Office of Management and Budget (2023)], '2 CFR Parts 184 and 200, Guidance for grants and agreements', *Federal Register*, 88(162), p. 57750, 23 August. Available at www.govinfo.gov/content/pkg/FR-2023-08-23/pdf/2023-17724.pdf.

OMB (2023b) [Office of Management and Budget (2023)], 'Memorandum for the heads of executive departments and agencies, implementation guidance on application of Buy America preference in Federal Financial Assistance Programs for Infrastructure, M-24-02', 23 October. Available at www.whitehouse.gov/wp-content/uploads/2023/10/M-24-02-Buy-America-Implementation-Guidance-Update.pdf.

Ontario (2022a), 'Province launches building Ontario businesses initiative', 2 March. Available at https://news.ontario.ca/en/release/1001729/province-launches-building-ontario-businesses-initiative.

Ontario (2022b), 'Building Ontario businesses initiative', 9 March, *Backgrounder*. Available at https://news.ontario.ca/en/backgrounder/1001730/building-ontario-businesses-initiative

Posen, A. (2023), 'America's zero-sum economics doesn't add up', *Foreign Policy*, 24 March. Available at https://foreignpolicy.com/2023/03/24/economy-trade-united-states-china-industry-manufacturing-supply-chains-biden/#.

Qiao, Y., Thai, K.V., and Cummings, G. (2009), 'State and local procurement preferences: A survey', *Journal of Public Procurement*, *9*, p. 371.

Rashish, P.S. (2023), 'The IRA and the meaning of free trade', *American Institute for Contemporary German Studies, Johns Hopkins University*, 6 February. Available at https://aicgs.org/2023/02/the-ira-and-the-meaning-of-free-trade/.

Reinsch, W.A. and Denamiel, T. (2023), 'The CHIPS and Science Act guardrails' implications for the U.S. Trade Agenda', *Center for Strategic International Studies*, 13 April. Available at www.csis.org/analysis/chips-and-science-act-guardrails-implications-us-trade-agenda.

Reuters (2023), 'U.S. should reach minerals deal with EU this year, U.S. official says', 10 July. Available at www.reuters.com/markets/commodities/us-should-reach-minerals-deal-with-eu-this-year-us-official-2023-07-10/.

Reynolds, M. and Goodman, M. (2022), 'China's economic coercion: Lessons from Lithuania', *Center for Strategic and International Studies*, May. Available at www.csis.org/analysis/chinas-economic-coercion-lessons-lithuania.

Siripurapu, A. and Berman, N. (2022), 'Is industrial policy making a comeback', *Council on Foreign Relations*, November. Available at www.cfr.org/backgrounder/industrial-policy-making-comeback?utm_source=dailybrief&utm_medium=email&utm_campaign=DailyBrief2023Apr19&utm_term=DailyNewsBrief.

Sutton, T. and Williams, M. (2023), 'A new horizon in U.S. trade policy: Key developments and questions for the Biden administration', *Center for American Progress*, 14 March. Available at www.americanprogress.org/article/a-new-horizon-in-u-s-trade-policy/.

Szczepański, M. (2022), 'EU international procurement instrument', *European Parliamentary Research Service*, March. Available at www.europarl.europa.eu/RegData/etudes/BRIE/2020/649403/EPRS_BRI(2020)649403_EN.pdf.

Thales (2022), 'Thales DIS Canada Inc. v Ontario (Ministry of Transportation) (Thales), 2022 ONSC 3166'. Available at www.canlii.org/en/on/onscdc/doc/2022/2022onsc3166/2022onsc3166.html.

USTR (2021), [Office of the U.S. Trade Representative], 'Report to Congress on China's WTO compliance', 13 February. Available at https://ustr.gov/sites/default/files/enforcement/WTO/2021%20USTR%20Report%20to%20Congress%20on%20China's%20WTO%20Compliance.pdf.

USTR (2022), [Office of the U.S. Trade Representative], 'National Trade Estimate report on Foreign trade barriers', 204. Available at https://ustr.gov/sites/default/files/2022%20National%20Trade%20Estimate%20Report%20on%20Foreign%20Trade%20Barriers.pdf.

USTR (2023a), [Office of the U.S. Trade Representative], 'free trade agreements'. Available at https://ustr.gov/trade-agreements/free-trade-agreements.

USTR (2023b), [Office of the U.S. Trade Representative], 'Agreement between the Government of the United States of America and the Government of Japan on strengthening critical minerals supply chains', 28 March. Available at https://ustr.gov/sites/default/files/2023-03/US%20Japan%20Critical%20Minerals%20Agreement%202023%2003%2028.pdf.

Watson, C.D. (2021), 'Congress expands Buy America requirements in the Infrastructure Investment and Jobs Act (P.L. 117-58)'. *Congressional Research Service*, Report No. IFI1989C. Available at https://crsreports.congress.gov/product/pdf/IF/IF11989.

White House (2019), 'Executive Order 13881 of July 15, 2019, maximizing use of American-made goods, products, and materials', *Federal Register*, 84(138), 18 July, p. 34257. Available at www.govinfo.gov/content/pkg/FR-2019-07-18/pdf/2019-15449.pdf.

White House (2021), 'Executive Order 14005 of January 25, 2021, ensuring the future is made in all of America by all of America's workers', *Federal Register*, 86 (17), p. 7475, 28 January. Available at www.govinfo.gov/content/pkg/FR-2021-01-28/pdf/2021-02038.pdf.

White House (2022a), 'The Biden-Harris plan to revitalize American manufacturing and secure critical supply chains in 2022', 24 February. Available at www.whitehouse.gov/briefing-room/statements-releases/2022/02/24/the-biden-harris-plan-to-revitalize-american-manufacturing-and-secure-critical-supply-chains-in-2022/.

White House (2022b), 'Fact sheet: CHIPS and Science Act will lower costs, create jobs, strengthen supply chains, and counter China', 9 August. Available at www.whitehouse.gov/briefing-room/statements-releases/2022/08/09/fact-sheet-chips-and-science-act-will-lower-costs-create-jobs-strengthen-supply-chains-and-counter-china/.

White House (2023a), 'Fact sheet: The Biden economic plan is working', 6 February. Available at www.whitehouse.gov/briefing-room/statements-releases/2023/02/06/fact-sheet-the-biden-economic-plan-is-working/.

White House (2023b), 'Joint statement by President Biden and President von der Leyen', 10 March. Available at www.whitehouse.gov/briefing-room/statements-releases/2023/03/10/joint-statement-by-president-biden-and-president-von-der-leyen-2/.

White House (2023c), 'The Atlantic declaration: A framework for a twenty-first century U.S.-UK economic partnership', 8 June. Available at www.whitehouse.gov/briefing-room/statements-releases/2023/06/08/the-atlantic-declaration-a-framework-for-a-twenty-first-century-u-s-uk-economic-partnership/.

White House (2023d), 'Fact sheet: Amidst manufacturing boom, President Biden will sign an executive order on federal research and development in support of domestic manufacturing and United States jobs to encourage "invent it here, make it here" in industries of the future', 28 July. Available at www.whitehouse.gov/briefing-room/statements-releases/2023/07/28/fact-sheet-amidst-manufacturing-boom-president-biden-will-sign-an-executive-order-on-federal-research-and-development-in-support-of-domestic-manufacturing-and-united-states-jobs-to-encourage/?eType=EmailBlastContent&eId=5748aa22-60f7-4a4e-acfb-1b58b2015715.

White House (2023e), 'Executive order on federal research and development in support of domestic manufacturing and United States jobs', 28 July. Available at www.whitehouse.gov/briefing-room/presidential-actions/2023/07/28/executive-order-on-federal-research-and-development-in-support-of-domestic-manufacturing-and-united-states-jobs/.

Woolcock, S. and Grier, J.H. (2015), 'TTIP and public procurement', in: Hamilton, D. and Pelkmans, J. (eds.), *Rule-makers or Rule-takers? Exploring the Transatlantic Trade and Investment Partnership*, Rowman & Littlefield International, London.

Yukins, C.R. and Green, A. (2018), 'International trade agreements and US procurement law', in: Felix, E.L. and Peterson, M. (eds.), *The Contractor's Guide to International Procurement*, American Bar Association, Chicago, pp. 148–177.

# 9 Defence procurement as industrial policy

## From domestic to European procurement in a global market

*Andrea Truppo*

### 9.1 Introduction

Why defence procurement matters?

> *Whether we like it or not, after decades of relaxation we are now back to an era of confrontation.*[1]

This clear and concise statement invites us to delve deeper into the role of defence during a significant historical moment marked by the rapid acceleration of European integration in the defence sector while in Ukraine Europeans are fighting each other in a high-intensity conventional war.

The world seems to be abandoning the idea of true global integration, which was hoped for after the fall of the Berlin Wall and initiated with the opening of the World Trade Organization (WTO). The search for stability through mutual economic and commercial interdependency on a global scale, which excited so many, has unfortunately had a very short life.

In this new context where the planet's superpowers are confronting each other in search of new geostrategic balances, the concept of defence assumes a central role and, at the same time, a dimension that definitively abandons the domestic boundaries and logics of the last century. The challenges we face are no longer within the reach of each individual European country. This requires us to conceive of defence at the European level and to take concrete actions to consolidate and give substance to a true EU Common Defence.

> *There is no State without Defence, but also no Defence without State.*[2]

This thought-provoking statement prompts us to contemplate the concept of sovereignty and its crucial connection to defence, thus highlighting the primary paradox in the EU: the aspiration for a unified defence while retaining national sovereignty. This statement calls for a closer examination of the complexities and challenges associated with the pursuit of a common defence strategy within a diverse and sovereign European landscape.

DOI: 10.4324/9781032631721-13

As a result of this inherent contradiction, which is often deemed too intricate to address, the ongoing efforts to unify defence in Europe remain stuck at the proclamation stage. EU is fighting against itself, locked in a state of internal conflict, hindered by a 'strategic immobility' that makes progress extremely challenging.

Certainly, there are many reasons that explain this inefficiency; however, one of the main causes is the fact that the European Union has not yet resolved one of its main conflicts: whether to proceed from a supranational or intergovernmental perspective. During this very long dispute, which began together with Europeanism itself, a third vision has effectively been consolidated: neo-functionalism, which we could define as the logic of 'the cart ahead of the horse'. In summary, an inverted process is observed in which it is not from politics that regulations are derived but rather the opposite: common policy actually derives from regulations approved downstream of long and difficult negotiations, where it is often difficult, if not impossible, to extract a simple and shareable principle from the articulate and controversial compromise reached.

This paper instead addresses the topic of Defence Industrial Policy with a top-down approach: from generic principles to specific and detailed initiatives.

All the issues that will be addressed below are intrinsically interconnected; however, to facilitate reading, they will be treated individually, starting from the more general ones to the more specific ones. We are in the context of human sciences, concepts that find their raison d'être to the extent that they help us interpret the present to better orient ourselves towards an uncertain future that is evolving at an increasingly accelerated pace. In this perspective, given the geopolitical context in which we live, the challenges that emerge from this scenario, the best way to face them, and the role that defence plays in this context, we will focus our attention on defence procurements, its peculiarities, the necessary investments, and the objectives that policy aims to achieve and how these objectives can migrate from a domestic dimension to a European one.

## 9.2 How defence procurement works and why is it different?

When we talk about defence procurement, we are referring to the specific stage of the entire defence acquisition process. It is a crucial stage that connects the government, typically the military, with the market.

The Defence Capability Acquisition process is a continuous loop that can be simplified with the following sequential phases:

- Threat Analysis. Intelligence information is used to hypothesize operational scenarios where the military capabilities of potential adversaries are thoroughly examined. This includes the analysis of their military equipment, the performance of individual weapon systems, doctrines of use, training of troops, and logistical capabilities for the supply and deployment of weapons. The purpose of this analysis is to better understand the strengths and weaknesses of potential adversaries and to inform the development of strategies for defence and deterrence.

- Gap Analysis. This process aims to highlight areas in which the operational capabilities of our armed forces show deficiencies or criticalities compared to the military capabilities that emerge from the previous 'threat analysis' phase.
- Operational Needs. Once gaps have been identified, government expert officials define the operational needs within the Capability Development Planning process with the purpose of filling those gaps in the most effective way.
- Requirements: The operational needs (scenario-based and capability-driven) are translated into operational requirements to qualify the specific performance of military equipment to be developed and/or procured.
- Procurement. In this phase, government experts engage with the market and define the most suitable methods for acquiring the capabilities that meet the operational requirements. It is determined whether to acquire systems that are already available (off the shelf) or to develop new ones. In the latter case, procurement takes on a much broader significance than the former. The procurement action takes on the characteristics and dimensions of a Defence Investment Programme, with costs, timeframes, and implications that are entirely different. In this case, operational requirements are translated into technical specifications to support the contractual action. Given the peculiarity of the market, the various contractual models are an important topic that deserves further discussion, which we will address later. The contract can be considered concluded upon delivery of the product after the acceptance phase, in which the customer verifies that (in accordance with a negotiated acceptance test manual) the final product meets the technical specifications contracted, in compliance with the agreed-upon design (which may undergo modifications and/or restrictions during the development phase).
- Operational Test and Evaluation Units (OT&E). Unlike the previous phase, where the product is accepted based on contractual documents (correspondence to technical specifications and design), OT&E verifies the actual capability (testing the system in a realistic, complex operational environment) to meet the final operational needs aimed at eliminating the identified gaps. Once the real capabilities/limitations of the newly acquired systems are demonstrated, these highly qualified and valued (OT&E) units provide two essential outputs:

  1. Recommendations to operational units for the development of effective tactics and procedures to maximize strengths and mitigate limitations identified;
  2. Recommendations to industries to develop new technological solutions that address the identified shortfalls. This activity is usually defined as the Future Capture Requirement Process that enters the contractual phase within the so-called spiral development.

The process described above is meant to maximize the effectiveness of the military instrument remaining within the Capability domain. However, the Capability domain is shaped by a complex process that is articulated on several dimensions that gradually reduce downstream the 'manoeuvring space'.

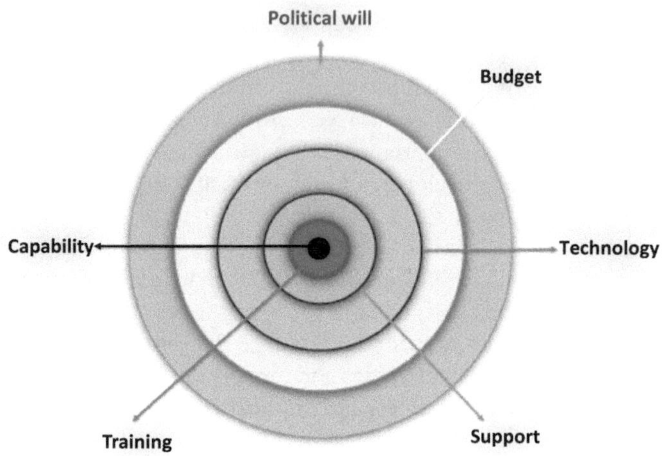


*Figure 9.1* Defence capability dimensions.

*Source:* Own compilation.

Figure 9.1 illustrates, in a conceptual way, how the variables at play steadily reduce, in fact restrict, the overall military capacity that a nation or a coalition could potentially express.

Each of these variables can be represented by a coefficient (expressed from zero to one) that progressively restricts, or rather constrains, the subsequent area. The area of the final inner black circle, produced by all the restrictions, represents the real military capacity.

This graphic, in its simplicity, allows us to tackle a complex subject in a clear and more aware fashion. The first and perhaps obvious consideration is that the military capacity of a nation or collection of nations depends on underlying political will. Political will is an expression and synthesis of the history of a nation (or more than one), as well as what we have called the culture of security of a population. It encompasses the logic of consensus, the media, political lobbies, the stability and strength of governments, the standing of ruling classes, and many other factors that directly or indirectly influence political decisions and can rapidly change priorities, especially in moments of economic crisis or environmental disaster.

For the purpose of this paper, it is necessary to delve into the first domain, the outermost one, and understand what are the drivers that impact political will.

The composition of these drivers and their specific weight depend on the country and, above all, on the industrial fabric present in the territory.

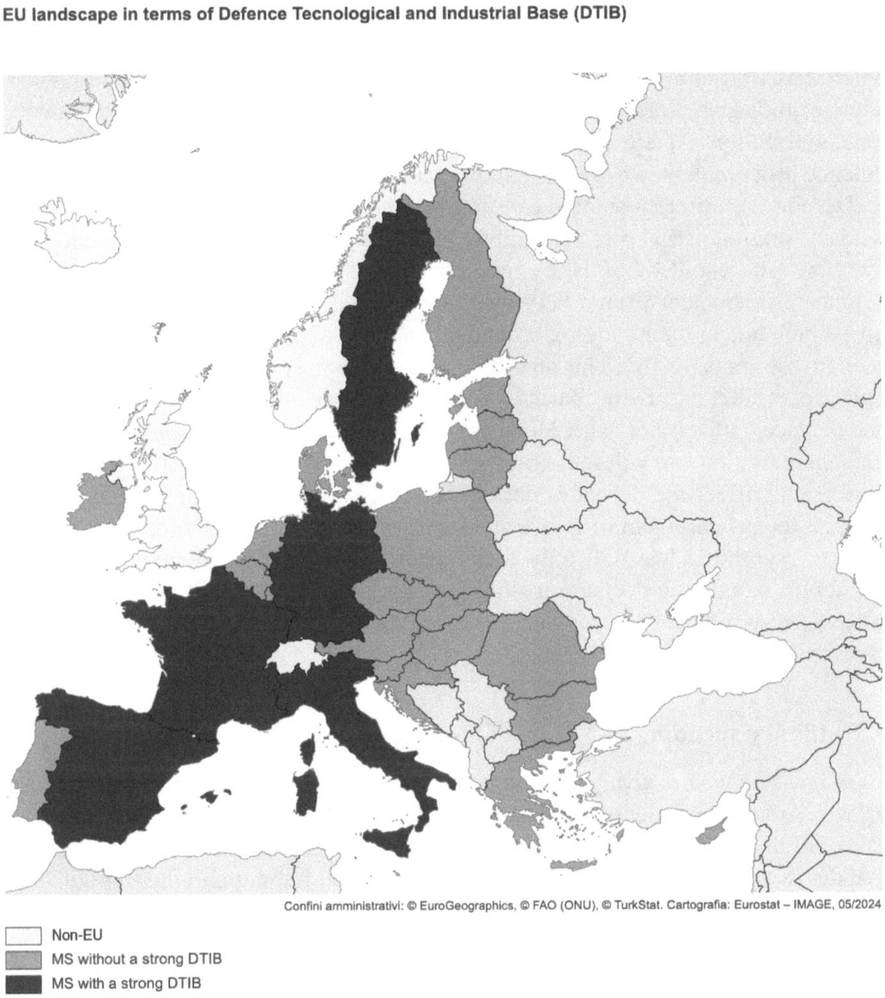


*Figure 9.2* EU landscape in terms of Defence Technological and Industrial Base DTIB.

*Source:* Own compilation.

As shown in Figure 9.2, among the 27 EU member states, there are 5 countries with a strong presence of large defence industries (highlighted in dark grey: FR, IT, DE, SP, and SE), while in the remaining countries (in light grey), the production capacity in the defence sector is mainly made up of SMEs.

This clarification is necessary to understand the difficulties that the Union is facing and will have to face in converging the different Defence Industrial Policies, even before the market, through targeted initiatives to promote joint forms of procurement and incentives to support the European Defence Technological and

Industrial Base (EDTIB). In this perspective, defence ministries, which, among other things, are responsible for Defence Industrial Policy, play two roles. On the one hand, they represent demand, which, unlike other markets, in the case of defence is only a government demand, and on the other hand, they are responsible for Industrial Policy. Both functions (at least for those countries with a strong industrial footprint) are implemented through procurement. For these reasons, defence procurement is different and particularly relevant.

Despite the different stances of European member states, both for the countries with a strong industrial presence and for all the others as members of the Union and therefore 'shareholders' of the Common Industrial Policy, it is necessary to address defence procurement from a very wide perspective, where spending is seen as an investment and as such requires a detailed analysis of all the expected returns over such investments (ROIs). This analysis can be extremely complex as there are multiple aspects that intertwine, partially overlap, reinforce each other on the one hand, and balance on the other hand. However, while working on developing an effective predictive model,[3] we will focus on the main elements that characterize the defence market and affect the decision-making process, which ultimately manifests itself through the procurement of goods and services. For the sake of simplicity and the need for synthesis, we will only focus on the aspects that have demonstrated a greater impact on the decision-making process in the recent past. We will neglect other equally relevant aspects that, however, have a minor impact on defence procurement choices.

## 9.3 Military spending as a source of innovation and economic growth

Economy science has always questioned about the factors influencing the economy growth. Adam Smith defined economy as a science that enquires into the nature and causes of the wealth of a nation (Smith, 1776). The early economic theories identified the two main factors influencing production: the Labour and the Capital. This model has remained (almost) unchanged for nearly two centuries. Despite different perspectives of prominent nineteenth-century economists like Ricardo, Marx, and Walras, the analytical framework has not been subject to significant changes.

Starting from the immediate post-war period, new schools of thought emerged that, in less than half a century, reached a level of maturity significant enough to impact economic theories. Thanks to the genius of figures such as Robert Solow (Nobel 1987), Paul Samuelson (Nobel 1970), Kenneth Arrow (Nobel 1972), and others equally renowned, the Knowledge Economy was born, with Paul Romer's (Nobel 2018) elegant and rigorous formulation serving as a cornerstone.

In the 1950s Robert Solow introduced, as an additional variable to the productivity function, the 'stock of ideas'. He understood that the standard economic model was not only unable to correctly predict the level of growth but also that the growth would eventually stop. Adding the 'stock of ideas' variable will boost instead.

Solow, for the first time, understands that economies depend on innovation (Solow, 1956). However, he considers the set of ideas an exogenous factor because new discoveries cannot be predicted by economists. Such a new variable became so important that it launched a new intellectual stream of activity named 'the knowledge economy'.

The father of this new field of economy is Ken Arrow, who considers knowledge as both an economic good and an economic process (Arrow, 1962). He, as well as Solow, recognizes the concept of 'idea' to be an exogenous feature that possesses both positive and negative externalities. The positive ones are represented in the so-called spillovers due to the concept of non-rivalry of ideas, while the negative ones originate in the appropriability.

As these brilliant economists had realized, the creation of wealth is primarily the result of works of genius that generate innovation. Unlike capital that tends towards concentration, where the strongest prevails and absorbs the weakest, genius is instead the outcome of a distributive phenomenon of knowledge that is intrinsically collaborative. This is a particularly complex distributive phenomenon, which paradoxically is also fuelled by an inherent weakness of innovation, the so-called 'appropriability issue', or the difficulty of protecting new ideas that are by nature a non-rival good.

From an economic standpoint, the non-rivalry of a good is a serious defect, so serious as to make ideas a non-economic good, lacking in marginal value. The first anti-tumour pill costs pharmaceutical companies billions of euros, but producing the second one costs only a few cents. The cost associated with the first unit of the product is composed of the production's standard costs plus the cost necessary to generate the idea (in this case, the chemical formula). The (low) cost of the second pill made possible by the now-established knowledge of the formula effectively nullifies its value. Therefore, an idea is intrinsically lacking in marginal value on the one hand, and difficult to protect on the other. For this reason, rules are needed to protect intellectual property. These protections act on the excludability of the good, which compensates, at least initially and from an economic standpoint, for the lack of scarcity, or non-rivalry.

This implies that the economy alone, in the absence of appropriate regulations, would not be able to economically exploit the most precious good. The Knowledge Economy not only suggests an adequately (not excessively) regulated market but goes beyond modelling the role of institutions, highlighting how some parameters act on the growth curve. Parameters that are correlated with a plethora of virtuous institutional mechanisms complementary to the economic mechanisms of the free market and necessary to correct the serious market failure of the lack of incentives to produce innovative ideas are the result of a long, extremely costly, and equally uncertain process that does not justify an investment. Concepts that will mature with Paul Romer's famous paper in 1990.

With Paul Romer (1990), the Theory of Endogenous Growth assumes a complete and rigorous formulation. The core of the theory, which frees the Solow model from the threat of steady states due to the diminishing returns to scale, is the concept of non-rival goods that produce increasing returns with scale. If we duplicate a company to produce exactly twice as much, we won't need to duplicate the research and development centre because its production of ideas can satisfy both companies. Therefore, innovative products valued by a new idea allow for greater returns as volumes increase because the idea that enriches them always adds the same value regardless of total quantity with an impact on unit costs that progressively decreases.

A fundamental passage in Romer's theory is conceiving market imperfections as an essential variable in the model. Innovation has two important externalities that we could consider two sides of the same coin, namely non-rivalry (the ability to satisfy a large audience both directly and through spill-over effects), which, however, generates an appropriability problem that discourages entrepreneurs from investing.

Romer (1990) states that, under particular circumstances, where the role of institutions creates the right conditions, the overall beneficial effects of spill-overs amply justify private investments even in the presence of 'imperfect competition'. The entrepreneur understands that it will never be possible to maintain their competitive advantage by insisting on protecting their invention, preferring instead to increase their innovative capacity to maintain and edge over their competitors. Everyone, albeit with some delay, can benefit from the novelty introduced by a competitor and propose further optimizations based on that innovation, with the hope of anticipating a particularly innovative new release to reduce or overturn the competitive advantage. This triggers a real Innovation Race (Systemic Competition). The armament race during the Cold War was mainly fuelled by industrial espionage. However, such a pervasive and fast race has been able to radically modify the rules of the game, it generated explosive effects not only in the purely economic dimension but also in the social, political, ethical, and global scales.

It becomes comprehensible that, in this regard, the role of governments and the many interactions among the various institutions is directly connected to the production of new ideas and innovation.

> New impetus must be given to research in our country; such new impetus can come only from the government.........In the future we must pay increased attention to discovering this knowledge for ourselves particularly since the scientific applications of the future will be more than ever dependent upon such basic knowledge.....
>
> (Bush, 1945, p. 21)

Since innovation is not a predictable feature, and thus, on the commercial side, it can be unsafe to fulfil it, it is important that the governments fill the gap by generating strong funding activities under proper agencies with the aim of producing a strong innovation culture and the right knowledge through highly skilled people who share ideas and who will eventually collaborate in a network with universities, research centres and industries.

In the landscape of many institutions that interact in order to make innovation possible, it is fundamental to underline that public procurement for high-technology goods and services is extremely relevant.

The great 'machine' of the economy that goes from needs to wealth is fuelled by new ideas that require governmental institutions and processes to be able to develop and carry on. Public procurement, in this respect, is an essential gear of this complex machine. Based on these considerations, the modern economies of the most advanced countries are defined as innovation-driven economies, where the human capital engaged in research is the driver behind technology innovation. This new growth theory also introduces the fundamental role of institutions that, as previously said, allow all the ideas to be generated. The factors of production are the direct result of a great number of continuous interactions among institutions.

In summary, in the prospector theory Paul Romer asserts (Romer, 1990) that the positive effects generated by spillover events are much higher than the negative ones generated by the non-appropriability under the condition that on the institutional side some mechanisms are created to increase the production factors with the intention of creating the above-mentioned parameters of a profitable environment.

In light of the considerations mentioned above, it is clear that defence investments play a crucial role in driving innovation and promoting economic growth with high multipliers. This is largely due to the fact that defence investments involve high levels of innovation, which can lead to the creation of non-rivalrous new ideas that can satisfy a wide range of needs when they are properly extracted and applied to other products for different functions, adding value multiple times without incurring significant additional costs.

Consider a few well-known defence investments that led to highly innovative technologies such as satellites, internet, and touch screens. These technologies were developed with the help of government funds to meet very specific and narrow 'operational needs', such as intelligence, surveillance, and reconnaissance (ISR); secure communication; and human-machine interface (HMI). The U.S. Department of Defense (DoD) undoubtedly made significant investments for these narrow needs. However, the knowledge gained from these innovative technologies remained trapped in them and, over time, has served thousands of different needs through many other products in a much larger market. This has multiplied the return on investment by several orders of magnitude, attracted additional R&D private and public funds, and generated additional new ideas and innovative products in response to private and public needs, fuelling an increasingly larger market and a self-strengthening virtuous cycle.

> *Silicon Valley is in the US and not in EU because is a consequence of the Pentagon......* [4]

Certainly, this slogan is too simplistic. However, while there are many factors that contributed to the growth of Silicon Valley, it is undeniable that defence investments played a crucial role in the development of the region's innovative technological sector. The Pentagon's support for research and development, particularly during the Cold War, helped to establish a strong defence industry presence in the region, which in turn provided a steady stream of talent and investment that fuelled the growth of the technology sector. This symbiotic relationship between defence and technology continues to this day, with many defence contractors and technology companies working closely together to develop cutting-edge products and technologies.

Someone could object by noting that in 2022 Amazon invested $73 billion in R&D (Statista, 2022). A huge figure that stands up well to public investments in most OECD countries where defence investments would represent just a marginal fraction. However, these private investments are to be considered a consequence of public investments; therefore, they add up to public investments (Moretti et al., 2019) and above all focus on those areas where institutional and para/institutional infrastructures dedicated to training, research, and development are most pronounced. Hence the creation of districts.

Silicon Valley aggregates particularly innovative homogeneous industrial realities that prefer to coexist in a sort of osmosis rather than isolate themselves to protect their secrets. Born around Stanford University, it is home to HP, founded by two recent graduates in 1949. The area has been affected by a progressive and effective aggregation of talents, initiatives, and infrastructure. An entire ecosystem that revolves around the Stanford Research Park, which today hosts the main Big Companies in High Tech,[5] accelerators of start-ups, Venture Capital, specialized law firms, and fuels a local economy with very high added value, so much to position itself at the top of the list of geographic areas with the highest per capita income.

This phenomenon is justified by the fact that innovation is the result of a recombination process, in which the greater the number of combinations, the greater the probability of success, while isolation and protectionism inevitably lead to a slowdown in innovative capacity.

In summary, when procurement is part of a broader Defence Investment Program for the development, production, and acquisition of military capabilities that require highly innovative technologies, it is necessary to reflect on:

- Analysis and mapping of the entire value chain, where it is in the Design phase (including the previous pre-concept and concept phases) that the know-how is concentrated, i.e. the most valuable component.
- Intellectual property: Whoever holds design authority holds intellectual property. Intellectual property must be properly managed. On the one hand, it must be defended to guarantee those who have generated it and as an incentive to invest in R&D; on the other hand, it must not become an obstacle to collaboration.
- Industrial and technological districts: These represent the place where a real ecosystem is formed in which industries, SMEs, universities, and research centres coexist. Places where virtuous paths of training and specialization of new skills are triggered, talents are attracted, and a high value-added economy is fuelled.
- Competitiveness: Defence market is global, where export is an important piece of the puzzle and competitiveness is key. Aggregated demand allows to increase investments (non-recurrent costs) for Research and Development of

cutting-edge technologies needed to reach the highest level of performance with a reasonable impact of unit price. Competitiveness relies on leveraging all the best available technologies the market can offer, even if they come from third countries.

## 9.4 Effective military equipment to support armed forces

The defence market exists to provide weapon systems that offer a competitive advantage to the Armed Forces of the countries that fuel and support it as government clients and policymakers. In this logic, it seems appropriate to start from the demand to which the supply reacts by configuring itself in the most suitable way. The latter statement deserves further exploration in the defence sector, where one often witnesses inverted logics fuelled by strong and effective lobbying activities. However, for the sake of clarity and simplicity, we will intentionally overlook this dysfunction.

On the demand side, the European scenario is as complex as critical. As a direct expression of national sovereignty, in light of a rather diversified historical legacy, defence has always been a national prerogative.

Due to such a nationalist approach, demand is extremely diversified, resulting in market fragmentation. This fragmentation has a negative impact both on the cost and on the effectiveness fronts. Before describing the fragmentation of the demand, it is necessary to focus on the capability aspects. Therefore, we will quickly review, in a simplified manner, the main operational, technological, and organizational trends.

Technological evolution has recently transformed military tools at an unprecedented speed in history. The close-quarters combat with thousands of men fighting on the same battlefield ended with World War I. Since then, thanks to technology, weapons have evolved to become increasingly effective at a greater distance from the enemy. This trend applies to both surface and aerial forces and has been fuelled by and, at the same time, benefitted from the development of 20th-century electronics. Electronics have given rise to sensors such as radars, highly accurate navigation systems, and missiles capable of neutralizing the adversary well beyond the visual range.

In this context, the quality of military tools has proven to be more relevant than mere quantitative factors. Observing, identifying, and engaging the enemy from a long distance are capabilities (i.e. Information Superiority) that matter much more than the number of assets. The race towards increasingly sophisticated technologies has had significant repercussions. In particular:

- The increase in the level of specialization, both among military personnel and designers. In almost the entire Western world, conscription is being phased out or suspended, with a transition to an entirely professional system. The armed forces are becoming more specialized and reduced in size.

- The exponential growth of non-recurring costs: Scientific research becomes the cornerstone for achieving a competitive advantage, where significant investments are required to expand the technology frontier.
- The proliferation of multinational programs: To cope with the enormous development costs and contain the impact on unit costs, multinational programs are necessary, promising:
  - Significant orders: The defence industry falls under the category of industries with decreasing costs to scale. The size of contracts determines the financial availability and therefore the level of technological ambition, which, when accompanied by effective management, generates a virtuous process benefiting competitiveness that quickly characterizes the market and establishes the roles of industries and countries.
  - Stable and long-lasting commitments: Current armament programs require consistent and stable decision-making processes that involve multiple legislations. Intergovernmental agreements for multinational programs are essential constraints to ensure stability and management of such complex and costly projects in the long term.
- New operational requirements: As described in the introduction, operational requirements are defined within a continuous cycle of activities that conceptually start with threat analysis. With the fall of the Berlin Wall, which many (erroneously) referred to as the end of history, the scenario has become extremely volatile and uncertain. This characteristic of the scenario itself becomes a threat. Consequently, gaps arise due to static systems designed for specific functions and purposes, which are inflexible and have high operational costs. These closed weapon systems were designed to be employed in a particular context, where any modifications may be requested to the Design Authority and obtained with long lead times and exorbitant costs. Hence, the need arises for flexible and scalable systems capable of adapting to the volatility of the real operational context. This need, commonly referred to as Freedom of Modification (FoM) and Freedom of Action (FOA), has generated new requirements that go beyond mere performance but relate to cooperation models, aiming to have unrestricted access to qualified support from the Design Authority to enable the necessary synergy between users and producers within a collaborative international framework to share and hence reduce costs.

Regarding purely technical requirements, the historical trend of increasing integration continues. If we observe the evolution of combat aircraft systems, which encompass the most sophisticated technologies, this phenomenon is particularly evident. The very first aircraft of World War I were equipped with rifles mounted on the wings. During World War II, guns were integrated into the fuselage, and aiming systems and additional ballistic weapons were added. The next generation was characterized by sensors that enhanced the capabilities of detection, targeting, and guiding increasingly sophisticated weapons, enabling engagement even beyond visual range. With the third generation, armament and sensors were integrated into a single human-machine interface. Avionics integration paved the way for what is known as Sensor Fusion, enabling the reconstruction of a comprehensive and accurate Air Picture. In the fifth generation, Sensor Fusion extends beyond individual aircraft to the entire fleet. From there, the ambition arises to expand this fusion of raw data from sensors to a wide range of systems (air, surface, space) in the sixth generation, forming what is known as a system of systems.

In this context, the Lead System Integrator assumes relevance. This is the company responsible for the overall system-level design and development of the software that enables the integration of all systems and subsystems. This trend will have a ripple effect on the entire industrial organization. Sensors will be streamlined in their functions, primarily serving as hardware components within an open architecture managed by a single software (likely divided into modules for mission-critical and safety-critical aspects). This strong shift towards software is accompanied by the transition towards the creation of the so-called Digital Environment. This involves the implementation of a digital twin model that allows, on the manufacturer's side, the virtual execution of all development, qualification, and certification phases, saving time and cost. On the user's side, it enables the definition of requirements (through war gaming), development of operational procedures, training of crews and operators, as well as remote control through appropriate simulators.

These technological challenges are extremely ambitious. To have reasonable chances of success, enormous investments are required, as well as expertise and consolidated experience across a wide range of sectors.

In this context, cooperation is both a necessity (no European country can reasonably expect to develop these technologies alone) and an opportunity to leverage existing diverse skills and harness diversity as an amplifier of innovation capacity.

As shown by the data collected and published by the European Defence Agency (EDA Defence data, 2022), there is a significant increase in overall expenditure (+ 8% from €198 billion to €214 billion) compared to 2021. This increase is observed both in investments (+16% from €45 billion to €52 billion) and in the Research and Technology (R&T) share (+44% from €2.5 billion to €3.6 billion). Despite a perceived increase in propensity for collaboration, the absolute numbers still indicate a market strongly dominated by national interests, still far from the objectives set by the member states themselves in 2017.[6]

The €214 billion expenditure of the European Union – still very far from the United States that was by far the largest defence spender in 2021 (€686 billion) – may seem reasonable compared to China (€241 billion) and Russia (€56 billion); however, this number is undermined by the significant market fragmentation, which diminishes its effects.

The gap, which has further increased since 2022, as evidenced by the data collected by the International Institute for Strategic Studies (IISS) published in the Military Balance (2023, p. 14), where the top 15 defence budgets are listed as follows:

Absolute value
1. United States: 766.6 bln $
2. China: 360 bln $
3. Russia: 192 bln $
4. United Kingdom: 70 bln $
5. India: 66.6 bln $
6. France: 54.4 bln $
7. Germany: 53.4 bln $
8. Japan: 48.1 bln $
9. Saudi Arabia: 45.6 bln $
10. Iran: 44 bln $
11. Soth Korea: 43 bln $
12. Australia: 33.8 bln $
13. Italy: 31.1 bln $
14. Canada: 24.6 bln $
15. Brazil: 23 bln $

As percentage of GDP
1. Oman: 5.9%
2. Kuwait: 5.0%
3. Algeria: 4.8%
4. Jordan: 4.8%
5. Saudi Arabia: 4.5%
6. Mali: 4.5%
7. Marocco: 4.5%
8. Israel: 4.3%
9. Armenia: 4.2%
10. Russia: 4.1%
11. UAE: 4.0%
12. Qatar: 3.8%
13. Azerbaijan: 3.8%
14. Greece: 3.5%
15. Cambogia: 3.5%

The global spending comparison clearly highlights how irrelevant the effort of each individual EU country is if it remains confined within national boundaries and logics. Even France, the top spender in the EU, does not reach 7% of the United States. From this perspective, the need for convergence towards a common defence is both a collective requirement and an unavoidable necessity for individual member states. Community interest and national interest are conceptually aligned in the sense that national interest is better protected when appropriately embedded within a community framework. However, we must recognize that such convergence is by no means simple, primarily due to the EU decision-making processes and the heterogeneity of interests, sensitivities, threat perceptions, industrial fabric, and political visions among the member states.

The following graphs show the contribution of each member state (except for Denmark, which has recently joined the defence sector) in both absolute terms (see Figure 9.3) and as a proportion of their GDP (see Figure 9.4). These graphs highlight the heterogeneous nature of the European context. Ireland, Malta, and Luxembourg allocate less than 0.5% of their GDP to defence, while Greece spends over 3.5% of its GDP.

Figure 9.5 presents a different perspective on the contributions of the member states, highlighting that in absolute values, the first 4 contributors (FR, DE, IT, PL) account for (almost) 75% of the defence spending of the entire European Union.

This percentage is significantly surpassed when Spain is included. Despite spending slightly less than Poland, Spain possesses an industrial fabric that is sufficiently modern and technologically advanced, much more akin to that of the top three contributors. This observation also applies to Sweden, which, despite being the eighth contributor, preceded by Greece, boasts a highly prominent defence industry. This achievement is the result of an industrial policy that, although

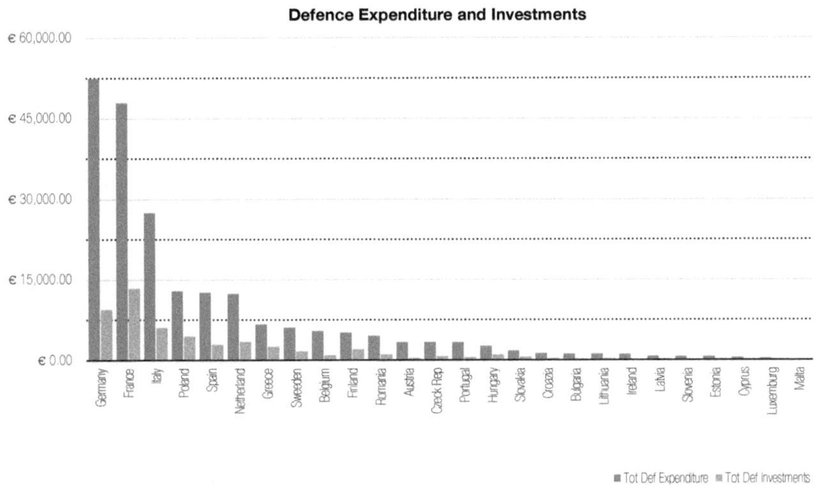


*Figure 9.3* Defence expenditure and investments.

*Source:* Own compilation.

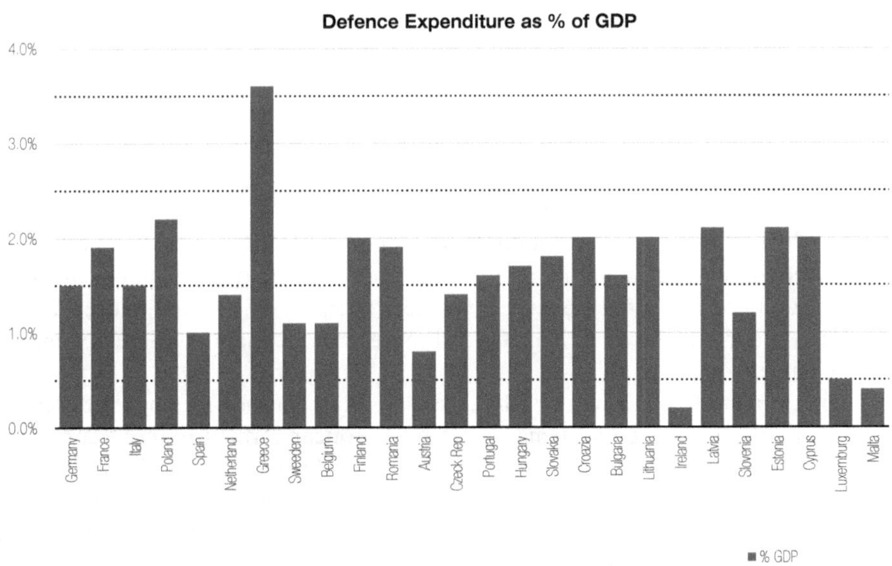


*Figure 9.4* Defence expenditure as percentage of GDP.

*Source:* Own compilation.

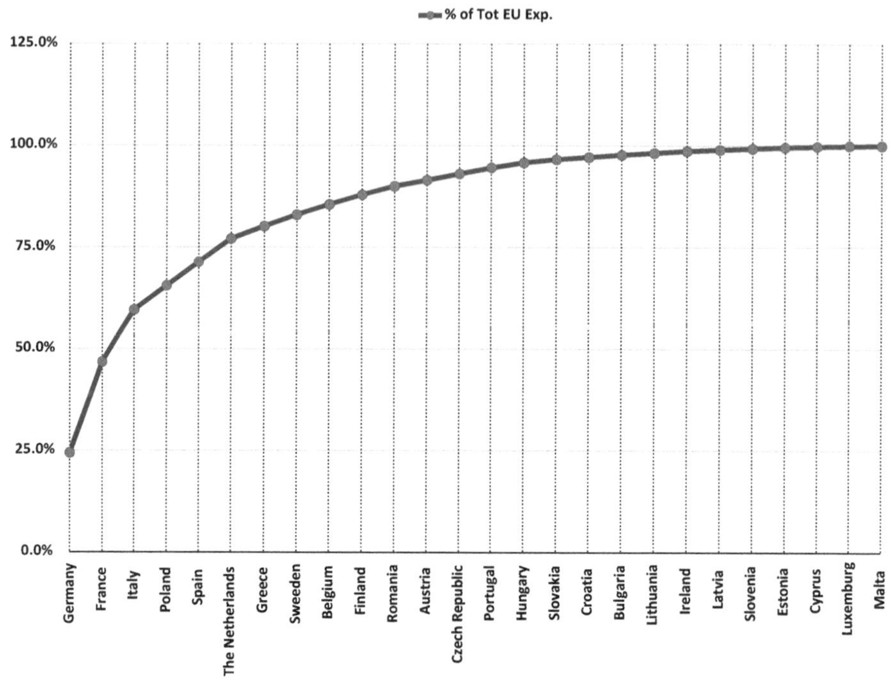


*Figure 9.5* MS contribution to total EU defence expenditure.

*Source:* Own compilation.

predominantly focused on the domestic market, has proven to be effective and forward-thinking in the last decades.

The algebraic sum of these multiple and significant differences of a political, social, economic, and industrial nature delineates the contours of highly diverse national defence industrial policies. This heterogeneity is the root cause of the extremely fragmented overall demand and represents the main obstacle to market convergence.

The recent study published by McKinsey (2024, p. 5) shows a huge difference in the number of weapon systems in use by European Armed Forces compared to those of the United States. This divergence is a factor of 1:6 (178 in the EU versus 30 in the United States). Based on similar (even less critical) assumptions, a study carried out in 2013 (Briani, 2013) estimated that the average annual cost of deploying a single European soldier in operations outside national borders is around 310,000 € higher than the cost of an American soldier, due to the excessive fragmentation of the forces that does not allow the interoperability of assets.

It must be recognized that behind the 178 weapon systems there are just as many contracts, projects, production and assembly lines, suppliers of raw materials, semi-finished products, and maintenance support equipment. This objective loss of efficiency is largely the picture of an industrial system that is particularly fragmented, with a very broad industrial base that relies on the domestic market to survive. Therefore, if one wants to hypothesize a path of defence integration to generate a European military force supported by a strong, resilient, and competitive EDTIB, we must first converge the different National Industrial Policies. In this respect, the aforementioned fragmentation is certainly a cause of inefficiency and ineffectiveness, but it is in turn an effect of deeper causes that lie within individual member state, where defence procurement does not end with the mere acquisition of a weapon system according to the logic of the best cost-effectiveness ratio but rightly takes into account all the additional elements previously described that still have solid roots within national borders. From this perspective, to solve these objective critical issues, it is necessary to develop appropriate models of cooperation that recognize all the expected returns on investments and distribute them fairly and honestly among all stakeholders involved in different capacities. The inability to develop these cooperation models is the reason for the duplication of projects with very high strategic and technological value such as the Future Combat Air System.

An additional significant element is represented by the contractual forms adopted. When procurement is directed towards the supply of specific equipment that responds to very strict operational requirements, the entire acquisition process is unable to remain within the boundary of a competitive market. By its very nature, given the significant R&D investments required to develop and produce the required system, the defence market operates mainly in a non-competitive regime. In this context, fixed-price contracts and cost-plus contracts still generate an imbalance in favour of the industry, which shifts all risks to the customer (in this case, the government). In summary, the business risk that in a competitive context requires a continuous optimization of processes, in this case, passing through unsuitable contractual instruments, becomes an opportunity for profit at the expense of efficiency.

In a global competitive market that (only) rewards champions, defence procurement is necessary to train the best national athletes.

In the early 1990s, following the collapse of the Berlin Wall, the global landscape began to shift. Defence spending decreased by approximately one-third in real terms in less than a decade. The radical change in the geopolitical scenario occurred simultaneously with significant technological revolutions that transformed military tools at a speed unprecedented in history.

As warfare changed, there was a move away from traditional large weapon stockpiles to innovative new weapon systems that prioritized rapid deployment and precision.

Significant recurring costs required for the mass production of weapon systems have been redirected and multiplied towards non-recurring investments for the research and development of unprecedented operational capabilities.

To mitigate and share risk associated with such technological challenges, strategic alliances, ranging from consortia to joint ventures, gained in popularity. This change caused the defence industry to undergo significant evolution. By 1998, 24 of the 100 largest defence companies in 1990 had exited the industry, and those that remained grew larger through a series of consolidating mergers.

Starting from the late 1980s (with the Reagan administration), a radical consolidation of the defence market began in the United States, which lasted until the end of the 1990s. This consolidation, desired by the U.S. DoD (which still today is the subject of debate on the validity of public spending in light of strong U.S. lobbying), produced the famous big 5 (1. Lockheed Martin, 2. Raytheon, 3. Boeing, 4. Northrop Grumman, 5. General Dynamics), which also became the undisputed leaders on the world market. It should be noted, however, that the attempted M&A between the two giants Lockheed Martin and Northrop Grumman in 1998 was denied by American antitrust (*New York Times*, 1998) for potential excessive dominance. From these observations and the reading of extensive literature on the subject, we can extract three main pillars of the American Defence Industrial Policy:

1. Competition in the early development phase (up to prototype)
2. Global Balance
3. Synergy user-producer in the (continuous) development phase

In fact, this new reality has completely altered the market's logic, products, and processes. If the European industry continues to trail behind, adhering to the same approach imposed by the United States, it will be extremely challenging to narrow the current gap. There is nothing convincing enough to confidently invest in.

The U.S. Defence Industry's global market dominance implies that only a disruptive approach, albeit risky, holds some potential for success.

The defence market is far from perfect, both in Europe and the rest of the world. However, in the United States, the major groups (Boeing, Lockheed Martin, and Northrop Grumman) are well-coordinated by the American government, which directly manages procurement programs, promoting both competition in the early prototyping stages of pre-selection and collaboration in the contractual phase. The Joint Strike Fighter (JSF) program for the development of a fifth-generation multirole fighter, for example, initially saw strong competition between Boeing and Lockheed Martin, each proposing their own solution. Immediately after Lockheed Martin's victory, a broader consortium was formed that includes Northrop Grumman and BAeS, to which many other second- and third-tier suppliers refer with a more or less significant share, both in financial and technological terms. In summary, a unique program that brings together the engineering skills of the major aerospace industries of the West.

In 2018, few were surprised when the giant Boeing, defeated in the multi-billion-dollar competition for the JSF contract, won (in partnership with the Swedish SAAB) the T-X advanced Trainer Competition, winning an initial contract (only from the U.S. Air Force) worth $9.2 billion.

This process of consolidation in Europe has been followed only at the national level, where the absorption of many industrial realities has created national groups that, however, operate at least in the domestic market in a monopolistic regime.

Exceptions are AIRBUS, born mainly to counter the dominance of the civil aircraft market by Boeing, and MBDA to reduce the fragmentation of the missile market and avoid definitive marginalization.

## 9.5 Defence investments to reduce technology dependency towards 'strategic autonomy'

Defence is inherently connected to the concept of sovereignty. Throughout history, military tools have always been used and kept at the national level. However, the technological and industrial collaborations initiated during World War II among the allied countries gradually strengthened during the Cold War. The defence market progressively assumed a global dimension driven by the United States and Russia.

On the Western front, NATO has certainly been an effective enabler of the expansion of the arms market by promoting standardization and cooperation. As a security provider, NATO has been the ideal framework to allow Americans to offer arms and equipment to all alliances. This market expansion has made the United States the undisputed leader in the market, which, like in all other countries, has appropriately accompanied the export of arms with government regulations aimed at maintaining strict control over the use, transfer, and subsequent export of each individual weapon, including its components and related information.

In the past, countries jealously guarded their own military technology, both to keep their capabilities secret and to prevent weapon systems from being used improperly or transferred to hostile groups or countries. However, over time, this concept has evolved. Thanks to technology, it is possible to maintain control over the actual use of weaponry and protect technological advantage. Therefore, the export of arms is seen by many Western countries as part of their defence strategy in the context of alliance politics. Along this line, the export and import of weapons assume a strategic value that goes beyond simple market considerations related to the concept of best value for money.

The governments' ability to freely dispose of their own weapons, where these are intended as an essential tool for the full exercise of sovereignty, contradicts industrial cooperation even if limited to a few components in light of the constraints imposed by national export control regulations.

Despite the EU's (re)direction of the Common Foreign and Security Policy towards the goal of EU Strategic Autonomy, which implies reducing external dependencies and seeking European sovereignty, export control laws from which such restrictions derive are still national. While numerous initiatives have been observed, starting from the Global Strategy (2016) up to the most recent Strategic Compass for Security and Defence (2022), which clearly indicate the objective of greater independence from third countries' technologies, including the United States, the United Kingdom, and Israel, there is not as much emphasis on reducing or even eliminating internal dependencies within the Union's countries.

Moreover, the concept of strategic autonomy, if not contextualized to specific and concrete objectives, moves in parallel with other strategic objectives that travel in the opposite direction. In summary, an ideological approach to strategic autonomy (and technology) can have negative consequences on:

1. Level of industrial competitiveness. As described in the previous point, innovation is the result of a combinatory process; the wider and more diverse the context, the greater the chances of developing innovative technologies. Many European industries achieve an adequate level of competition by benefiting from external technologies or establishing strategic partnerships with highly specialized industries, even if located in third countries (where appropriate political conditions exist) in order to (hyper) specialize themselves in particular sectors. Giving up external excellences by closing the market with protectionist logic would immediately have negative repercussions for numerous national 'champions' located in the various member states. It is important to note that this impact would be different from country to country: more pronounced for Italy, Germany, Sweden, and Spain; less pronounced for France, which has tended to maintain a more nationalist approach in recent decades and therefore less dependent on external technologies.
2. Market size. On the one hand – initially and regardless of the pending issue of intra-European dependencies – the closure/protection of the European market could generate (eventually) an increase in domestic demand. On the other hand, there would be a contraction in external demand due to the effect of the loss of competitiveness.
3. International stability. Cooperation agreements, especially in the defence sector, strengthen international relations for the benefit of geopolitical stability. Closing markets and reducing cooperation would have negative impacts on global stability. On the contrary, mutual dependencies require shared and therefore more measured and stable approaches.

In summary, with a practical and non-ideological approach, it is absolutely acceptable to invest in enabling and particularly strategic technologies exclusively for the benefit of the EDTIB so that it can develop highly competitive products, thus effectively overcoming external dependencies. However, it is essential, in the logic of avoiding the negative effects described earlier, to broaden forms of industrial cooperation in the context of the alliance's (political and industrial) policy, seeking legitimately appropriate forms of freedom commonly named Freedom of Modification (FOM), Freedom of Action (FOA), and Freedom of Export (FOE), through appropriate business constructs where valuable removable mutual dependencies are accepted.

## 9.6 Where to go

European countries have no choice but to converge towards an 'effective' common defence that, beyond political proclamations, establishes the conditions for a common market and the establishment of increasingly integrated armed forces, enabling a progressive transfer of sovereignty for the benefit of European defence.

Not an easy game, which is unlikely to produce tangible effects with a continuous cycle of trial and error. Continuing to do something (whatever it may be) together risks generating disaffection towards the Union and further slowing down the process of integration. The challenge is instead to do the 'right thing' together, so that all member states can have tangible evidence of the value of facing at EU level the challenges that lie ahead for the future. To do this, a top-down approach is necessary. In this perspective, the main topics to address are provided below:

1. *What kind of market do we envision?*
2. *How to promote government and industrial collaboration?*
3. *Which cooperation model to adopt?*
4. *How to seek efficiency through best or innovative practices?*

## 9.7 The future EU defence market

In the European Union, there are five member states with a significant industrial footprint. Undoubtedly, a market transformation cannot occur without a shared vision among these five countries. If we project ourselves into the future, we can envision three main scenarios:

0. *Do nothing.* The market continues to strengthen national dynamics and remains predominantly domestic.
1. *Specialization.* The process moves towards aggregating the demand, followed by a gradual adjustment of the industry, which will emerge after a lengthy and challenging struggle in establishing European champions that will assume leadership in specific sectors. In this scenario, the government's role is primarily focused on the demand side (as a customer) rather than the supply side (as a policymaker).
2. *Collaboration.* The demand aggregates under the condition of creating industrial collaboration models that aim at establishing Joint Ventures (structured or programmatic). In this scenario, the dual role of governments (as customers and policymakers) is well balanced.

Intermediate options are certainly possible and perhaps even the most likely. Nonetheless, it is worth continuing the analysis on these hypotheses in a clear manner for the sake of simplification. Here are some initial considerations:

- The 'do nothing' scenario is extremely dangerous. It would result in an overall loss of competitiveness for the entire sector on a global scale, leading to a progressive marginalization of the industry and complete dependence on the American market.
- Scenario 1 may appear as the simplest or the only viable option, but it hides significant pitfalls. In the absence of shared agreements at the governmental level, which are difficult to achieve, this scenario can easily shift towards scenario 0.

- Scenario 2 is potentially very appealing for two reasons: it facilitates the convergence of industrial policies along with the convergence of demand and supply, and it proposes greater sharing of expertise and know-how, which can have positive repercussions on the sector's overall innovative capacity and competitiveness. However, it requires highly qualified and strongly motivated governmental leadership to establish appropriate cooperation models to overcome the inherent obstacles related to sharing know-how and intellectual property in innovative ways.

From an implementation perspective, scenario 1 is primarily in the hands of the industry, with governments and EU institutions attempting to develop regulatory interventions to indirectly facilitate or hinder the establishment of European champions, benefiting some and disadvantaging others, likely resulting in a zero-sum game with a win-lose logic.

Regarding scenario 2, which requires greater institutional activism, it will be necessary to develop concrete proposals that facilitate the establishment of Joint Ventures through appropriately structured collaboration models. Considering this scenario – acknowledging its probability of occurrence – as the most innovative and attractive, it is useful to envision a possible implementation path and define key enablers necessary to maximize the likelihood of success.

## 9.8 Collaborative models

Industrial cooperation models within the European context have always been based on the concept of balancing (to a more or less flexible extent) between government cost-sharing and industrial work-sharing, where, within acceptable limits, a partner country's financial contribution should be proportional to the quantitative and qualitative work-share of its industry. This model worked very well in the 1980s, as seen with the Tornado programme and the early stages of the Eurofighter programme (Piga et al., 2017), but it started showing some limitations with the evolution of technology towards software-driven capabilities. This technological evolution, known as open architecture, has made it challenging to divide the work-share equally (along the entire lifecycle and predominantly from a qualitative perspective).

In the United States, with the JFS programme, under the direction of the DoD and in conditions completely different from those in Europe, a collaboration model open to non-U.S. partners was conceived, known as 'lead nation/best athlete'. In this model, within the same country, a leading role is assigned to the government and the reference industry, with participation from other countries, as tier 2 or tier 3, based on the best athlete logic. Although this model has proven to be sufficiently effective, it requires the recognition of strong leadership by the prime contractors from all partners, as well as significant differentiation on the funding and ordering fronts by the reference government. This condition is very challenging to replicate in a European context. The duplication, if not the triplication, of 6th generation Future Combat Air Systems can be attributed to the difficulty of imposing this model by France.

If the path towards lead-nation cooperation models appears unconvincing and even less effective in generating aggregation, the path towards parity-based collaborative models is no less challenging. To make it viable, it is necessary to develop an analytical model that outlines all the expected returns from defence investment across the dimensions discussed in Part 1, in order to foresee a **fair and equitable distribution** of these returns among all partner countries.

The Italian government has launched an interesting project in support of the Global Combat Air Programme (GCAP) for the development of an International Value Model (IVM). Although it has only completed Phase 1, it has already provided very promising results and insights.

## 9.9 Best practices

The numerous defence cooperation programmes have provided extremely valuable lessons. Based on these lessons observed and learned, some very interesting proposals have been developed.

- **IPR toolbox**. Innovation and creativity is a key driver in the modern economy. Appropriability and zero marginal value make innovation a very complex subject. Institutions promote innovation and creativity through a balanced and effective Intellectual Property System. When dealing with industrial collaboration, IPR is essentially related to the protection of know-how rather than patents or trademarks.

  Governments are responsible for enhancing collaboration and sharing of know-how. In this regard, they should elaborate tools to help industries to cope with appropriability issues so that the benefit of sharing knowledge ('trade secret') overcomes risks. Those tools should create the condition so that Intellectual Property is properly rewarded. A potential effective line of actions could be fencing right to use; generating royalty mechanisms for the following phases (production, export, and future enhancements); elaborate non-competition agreements such as market segmentation, export strategies, and others.
- **From a 'contract-driven environment' to a 'capability-driven environment'.** The Industry is contracted to achieve a bundle of capabilities and functionalities against a defined technical specification, through a given Qualification & Certification process, by a time limit. Whenever they fail to reach the target either in terms of performances or time (which is extremely likely in an advanced capabilities development where technology challenges are significant), the customer can apply contractual remedies like rework or price abatements.

  As a matter of fact, the relationship between the customer and the contractor is managed in a framework of commercial monopoly for the industrial actors, which leads them to build the price just in order to cope with a ministerial price investigation rather than a market challenge. The price charged to the customer is therefore broadly composed by the bare costs to be sustained for the required activity along the scheduled time, plus the profit, plus the risk to be impacted by the remedies. In other words, more strict are the customer demands in terms of remedies against the required performances and time constraints, and higher is the price applied.

The result is that the Customer actually bears all the risk, and there is no real incentive on the contractor to be efficient and competitive. This has been the commercial construct behind almost all defence programs.

It is interesting to see how, in the real cases, running most of the defence contracts, nations managed the significant shortfalls in delivery of the expected development packages without applying price abatements but asking Industry to keep on working until the room of the contractor liability for rework was exhausted, so getting at the end just what was achievable: a delayed package with reduced performance but at full price, inflated by the original commercial risk.

Remaining shortfalls have been regularly spilled over to the following development package, reinforcing the contractor attitude to grant the financial sustaining for the extant industrial base by just adding new development tasks and collecting 'assumed' new operational requirements to justify the continuity of the customer commitment and funding. This can be defined a 'contract-driven environment'.

During the first Eurofighter contractual revision, it was introduced a different approach to cover the In-Service Support engineering services. The sizing of assets and teams to be maintained in the 4 industries has been mainly defined upon the long term (5 years) affordability constraints of the core Partner Nations. To properly manage the throughput obtainable from this industrial base, the contract has been provided with specific tools to assess the resource utilization and a clear tasking priority discipline shared amongst the nations. Resources and assets have been contracted for 5 years, and the specific engineering services are provided against the Engineering Support Demands raised by the Customer that tracks the industry performances related to the single task in a context free of any commercial or funding risk on both parties. This 'fixed resources – flexible outputs' contractual construct has been commonly adopted by all four Partners and extended by some Nations, like Italy, to sustain additional spare engineering resources of the national Eurofighter Partner Company concentrating the effort on what were deemed as key capabilities within the scope of the Italian Industry System Design Responsibility.

These teams and assets have been successfully employed for very challenging and complex developments. Obviously, this approach implies a close technical control of the Customer on the activities by applying the 'measure and declare' principle on time-bounded maturity gates. Some of the outputs, like Drops, only when mature enough, have been offered for insertion in the common international baseline (the 'internationalization').

- **Horizontal Competition.** In consideration of these satisfactory results, Italy has undertaken a further exploitation of this method, by sustaining specific teams and assets at the major Supplier level, tasked with achieving well-identified improvements on some equipment.

The commercial commitment is just the sustainment of the team itself for a given period of time. The technical task assigned, again, is not a contractual object, but rather a target to check how much fruitful the investment made is or not.

The time-bounded maturity gates are intended to be no longer than 1 or 2 years; after that, whatever has been produced is delivered to the customer, and the investment is confirmed or reallocated to different equipment in the same company or to a different supplier, generating a sort of 'horizontal competition' among all Joint Development Teams involved or even between different departments of the same company. In this way, the synergistic effort of the industry and the government is fully focused on achieving technological solutions that effectively meet operational requirements without commercial influences.

## Notes

1 Quote from Ambassador G. Massolo (President Istituto per gli Studi di Politica Internazionale: ISPI).
2 Quote from Lucio Caracciolo extract from the introduction of Piga et al. (2017).
3 Within the framework of the programme GCAP (Global Combat Air Programme, Italy, UK, Japan), Italy is developing an International Value Model to map, analyse, and assess all the Expected Return Over the Investments in all the different Countries. Phase 1 has already been completed with a very promising result.
4 Meads W.R. (2017), Presentation in Rome of the book 'Difendere l'Europa'.
5 Among the biggest: 3Com, Abobe, AMD, Amazon (HW division), Apple, Cisco Systems, eBay, Electronic arts, Facebook, Fairchild Semiconductor, Google, HP, Intel, LinkedIn, Loochkeed Martin, Microsoft (HW division), Netflix, Nvidia, Oracle, PayPal, SunDisk, Square, Sun Microsystems, Symantec, Tesla, Texas Instruments, Visa, VMWare, Xerox, Yahoo, Zoom Video Communication.
6 Equipment procurement (including R&D/R&T): 20% of total defence spending; European collaborative equipment procurement: 35% of total equipment spending; Defence R&T: 2% of total defence spending; European collaborative defence R&T: 20% of total defence R&T spending.

## References

Arrow, K.J. (1962), 'The economic implications of learning by doing', *The Review of Economic Studies* 29(3), 155–173.
Briani V. (2013), 'I Costi della Non-Europa della Difesa, Centro Studi sul Federalismo e Istituto Affari Internazionali, aprile 2013'. Available at www.iai.it/sites/default/files/CSF-IAI_nonEuropadifesa_aprile2013.pdf.
Bush, V. (1945), *Science, the Endless Frontier: A Report to the President*, US Government Printing Office, Washington, D.C.
EDA Defence data (2022). Available at https://eda.europa.eu/docs/default-source/brochures/2022-eda_defencedata_web.pdf.
Global Strategy (2016), 'Shared vision, common action: A stronger Europe. A global strategy for the Union's Foreign and Security policy'. Available at https://eeas.europa.eu/archives/docs/top_stories/pdf/eugs_review_web.pdf

Kenneth, A.J. (1962), 'The economic implications of learning by doing', *The Review of Economic Studies*. Technical Report no.101.

McKinsey (2024), Innovation and efficency: Increasing Europe's defence capabilities. Available at www.mckinsey.com/industries/aerospace-and-defense/our-insights/innovation-and-efficiency-increasing-europes-defense-capabilities.

Military Balance (2023), The annual assessment of global military capabilities and defence economics. Available at www.iiss.org/press/2023/02/military-balance-2023.

Moretti, E., Steinwender, C., and Reenen J.V. (2019), 'The intellectual spoil of war? Defence R&D, productivity and international spillovers'. Available at www.nber.org/papers/w26483.

*New York Times* (1998), Lockheed cancels Northorp merger. Available at www.nytimes.com/1998/07/17/business/lockheed-cancels-northrop-merger-citing-us-stand.html.

Piga, G., Pecchi, L., and Truppo, A. (2017), 'Difendere l'Europa, 2017 Chiarelettere'. Available at https://art.torvergata.it/handle/2108/238731

Romer, P.M. (1990), 'Endogenous technological change', *Journal of Political Economy*, 98, S71–S73.

Smith, A. (1776), *The Wealth of Nations*. W. Strahan and T. Cadell, London.

Solow, R.M. (1956), 'A contribution to the theory of economic growth', *The Quarterly Journal of Economics*, 70(1), 65–94.

Statista (2022), Ranking of the companies with the highest spending on research and development worldwide in 2022. Available at www.statista.com/statistics/265645/ranking-of-the-20-companies-with-the-highest-spending-on-research-and-development/.

Strategic Compass for Security and Defence (2022), European Union. "For a European Union that protects its citizens, values and interests and contributes to international peace and security". Available at www.eeas.europa.eu/sites/default/files/documents/strategic_compass_en3_web.pdf.

# PART IV

# Defence procurement

# 10 Colloquium

*Keith F. Snider and Martin Trybus*

## 10.1 Keith Snider – Introductory Remarks

Defence procurement, like any state activity, requires regulation; how much is the issue. I argue here that, where defence procurement is concerned, less regulation is to be preferred. American defence procurement, likely the most regulated among industrialized nations, is examined. Two main points are made: first, that most important decisions and actions, as well as a substantial portion of defence contract awards, are made outside of the regulatory framework, thus making extensive regulation unnecessary; and second, that excessive regulations have hampered defence procurement in years past, a finding long recognized by American lawmakers and procurement officials and evidenced in their recent actions to reduce regulatory burden.

Some background is necessary to introduce defence procurement in the United States. In 2022, the United States spent just over $750 billion on defence, about 11% of all national spending. Of that total, about one-third was spent on contracts for research and development (R&D) and purchases of major weapons (e.g. F-35 fighter, Patriot air defence system) and information systems.[1] While most who read this paper would characterize these actions as 'public procurement', most in the United States would not use that term, using 'defence acquisition' instead. Far from just a matter of translation, the United States' view and treatment of defence acquisition as more expansive than and distinct from public procurement has had major effects on how expensive and technologically advanced systems are developed and purchased.

The U.S. Department of Defense (DoD) also spends about a third of the defence budget on routine purchases and contracts (e.g. for fuel, food services, and administrative support), but it is the high-tech major systems that attract the lion's share of attention and external scrutiny. The all-too-common cost growth and schedule slippages in R&D for these systems provide impetus for Congressional and media critique and oversight. Thus, the acquisition of these major systems shapes the United States' perspective on defence procurement to a much greater extent than routine purchases and contracts.

In the U.S. parlance, defence acquisition entails a broad range of activities necessary to realize a material solution to satisfy an identified capability shortfall

DOI: 10.4324/9781032631721-15

or to take advantage of emerging technology for a military advantage. These activities go well beyond contracting processes to encompass both need determination (that is, the definition, analysis, and refinement of requirements to be met by a materiel solution) and the budgeting of financial resources to fund contracts to satisfy the need.

Because these diverse activities must be integrated effectively for success in acquiring highly complex weapon and information systems, project (or programme) management concepts and tools have been central to defence acquisition since the mid-twentieth century. Each acquisition programme (e.g. the F-35 programme) has a designated project/programme manager (PM) who leads by planning and coordinating all relevant activities, including requirements development, budgeting, R&D, engineering, manufacturing, and contracting, to achieve successful deployment of a defence system. Considerations to be addressed in programme planning and execution are myriad: logistics, testing, new equipment training, facilities (e.g. aircraft hangars), and environmental impacts, to name but a few.

While a PM leads all aspects of an acquisition programme, a PM does not have authority to award contracts; that falls under the purview of a warranted contracting officer. Ideally, a PM and a contracting officer work together to develop a contracting strategy that best supports the programme's particular features while also satisfying U.S. public procurement requirements expressed in the Federal Acquisition Regulation (FAR).

Acquisition programmes in the United States are typically structured into phases (e.g. preliminary development, full-scale development, and production), with separate contracts awarded for each phase. Higher level acquisition executives in the DoD conduct progress reviews for each phase and grant approval to begin subsequent phases. Programme life cycles of 10–15 years are not uncommon. Following deployment, supply and support activities and contracts sustain a system throughout its service life.

This lengthy background helps one to understand how, for any major acquisition programme, many critical decisions regarding its initiation, key features, continuance, and perhaps termination, are taken outside the scope of the FAR. These decisions are key in shaping how contracts are structured and awarded under the FAR; contracts under the FAR simply implement the decisions taken outside its scope.

Two brief illustrative examples from U.S. helicopter programmes:

- In the early 2000s, the U.S. Marine Corps faced an ageing fleet of CH-53E heavy-lift helicopters. Instead of opening a competition for a new replacement helicopter, the Marine Corps chose to define its need as an upgrade to the existing fleet. This decision enabled the award of a non-competitive contract to Sikorsky Aircraft, which had produced the CH-53E, for new-build CH-53K helicopters under one of the FAR's exceptions to full and open competition, namely, only one responsible source.[2]

- Again, in the early 2000s, the Marine Corps determined a need for a more technologically advanced helicopter for short-range air transportation for the U.S. President. The VH-71 programme was subsequently initiated under full and open competition. It soon experienced major cost overruns between March 2008 and March 2009, and programme cost estimates rose by $2 billion. During this same period, President Obama publicly criticized the programme, stating that the existing fleet of Presidential helicopters seemed 'perfectly adequate' to him. Only a few weeks later, funding for the VH-71 was stripped from the defence budget, and shortly thereafter, the programme was formally cancelled (Colvin, 2009).

These examples highlight the greater importance of actions and decisions in the managerial realm of defence acquisition than in its regulatory realm. It follows that defence acquisition policy should focus, pragmatically, on the managerial rather than the regulatory, and a reduced set of rules tailored specifically for defence acquisition should govern.

Another pragmatic argument in favour of reduced regulation concerns the facility by which defence acquisition contracts are awarded outside the regulatory regime for competition. While full and open competition in solicitations is the general rule in U.S. public law and the FAR, several exceptions allow for non-competitive contract awards; note the 'one responsible source' exception mentioned above. Other exceptions include cases of unusual and compelling urgency, the need for industrial mobilization, and when information disclosed in a solicitation may compromise national security. These exceptions present DoD with a range of alternatives for avoiding the costs of competition when national defence priorities can be invoked. The extent to which DoD has used these exceptions, compared to other U.S. departments, is shown in Table 10.1.

Compared to other Departments, DoD competes a large percentage of its contract actions, but it awards many high-value contracts, particularly those pertaining to major systems in the defence acquisition domain, outside the competitive regime. The absence of public outcry and opposition to this situation suggests that it is at least tolerable to the nation. If so, one must ask: Why retain a regulatory preference for competition in defence acquisition when it is so easily and frequently bypassed?

*Table 10.1* Use of exceptions to competition in contracting by selected U.S. federal departments

| *US Federal Department* | *% competed awards* | *% competed dollars* |
|---|---|---|
| | *2016–2020* | *2016–2020* |
| Defence | 98.3% | 53.1% |
| Transportation | 71.4% | 83.6% |
| Health and Human Services | 64.9% | 85.1% |

*Source:* System for Award Management[3].

Arguments for reduced regulation have been made for many years. Almost forty years ago, an acquisition reform commission found that the workforce operated under the burden of 'inefficient, confusing regulations that are often inconsistent with sound business practices' (Greenwalt, 2013). While numerous reform measures were enacted during the next few decades, a 2010 independent review found that these initiatives 'produced more structure and more process but have not produced notable improvement in delivering required capabilities when needed at the expected cost' (Greenwalt, 2013, citing the 2010 Quadrennial Defense Review).

The irony of trying to adopt business-like approaches through regulation is illustrated by the regulatory implementation of the Federal Acquisition Streamlining Act (FASA). Congress enacted FASA amid the mid-1990s waves of New Public Management and 'Reinventing Government', the aim of which was to create a government that 'works better and costs less' (Gore, 1995). FASA sought to make acquisition more business-like through preferences for commercial products, services, and processes. In implementation, however, FASA led to a new section of the FAR (Part 12), that is, more regulations specifying how the government is to be more commercial.

The continual accretion of regulations,[4] all enacted in the pursuit of reform, has led to high transaction costs in compliance and reporting requirements. In addition to increasing the workload for an already overburdened government workforce, these requirements lead to increased contract prices from defence vendors. They also present barriers to entry into the defence market for potential new suppliers, which limits DoD's access to commercial innovation. (Greenwalt, 2013).

On a promising note, however, the rapidly evolving technological front has led DoD to adopt new approaches to retain technological superiority over global competitors. In years past, DoD essentially pulled high-tech development from industry through its definition of and investments in beyond-state-of-the-art weapons performance requirements. Now, however, the commercial sector leads in innovations in cloud computing, AI, cyber, and other areas, the military applications of which DoD is only beginning to explore. In this new environment, Congress and the DoD have recognized the need to lower barriers – like excessive regulations – which in the past have distanced the DoD from the private sector. For example, DoD is now making use of new legislative authority, which allows for rapid development and fielding of promising products outside of the traditional programme management framework.[5] Additionally, it has in recent years significantly expanded its use of 'Other Transactions Authority' (OTA), which allows suppliers to perform R&D work for DoD without a FAR-based contract. OTA projects, which in 2015 accounted for only 3% of DoD's R&D portfolio, now account for almost 25%. In granting expanded OTA to DoD, Congress noted the intention to 'support Department of Defense efforts to access new source of technical innovation' by making OTAs 'attractive to firms and organisations that do not usually participate in government contracting due to the typical overhead burden and "one size fits all" rules' (McCormick, 2020).

A final note is made on reducing regulations with respect to the conflict in Ukraine. Congress has granted DoD regulatory relief in the procurement of munitions in consequence of United States' support to Ukraine. This relief takes the form of multi-year procurements,[6] which in the past were used only for major systems like ships and aircraft. Allowing DoD to award multi-year procurements for munitions is intended to replenish stockpiles that have been drawn down as munitions were shipped to Ukraine, as well as to ensure continued health of the industrial base for munitions.

## 10.2 Martin Trybus – Introductory Remarks

Defence procurement regulation aims to meet the same objectives as any other form of public procurement (Arrowsmith et al., 2000; Schooner, 2002; Arrowsmith et al., 2011). The government, in this case the ministry or department of defence, buys its armaments, munitions, and war material from the private sector defence industries rather than producing these themselves 'in-house'. Being able to deploy defence materiel when it is needed is the primary objective of defence procurement. Connected to this centrality of efficiency is the objective of value for money: like any other part of the public or private sectors, defence procurement agencies aim to procure defence material at the best possible terms – the highest possible quality at the lowest possible price with the best possible contract terms and at the earliest possible delivery date. In most markets this can only be achieved through competition: prices only go down while quality is going up when the bidders know that they are not the only option, that high prices and bad quality might be punished by missing out on business opportunities. Competition is often only created through transparency in the form of advertising contract notices on defence purchases. Transparency also discourages corruption. The appropriate procedure depends on the type of materiel or services to be procured. For certain simple purchases, for example, ammunition or uniforms, open or restricted procedures can be used, even framework agreements or dynamic purchasing systems. For many complex procurements that require the input of the private defence industries, negotiated procedures, including the competitive dialogue, are more appropriate. Technical specifications, qualification and selection criteria, and award criteria can be regulated in *almost* the same way as for any other public contract award.

However, defence procurement operates in a context and within a market that differs substantially from other procurement contexts and markets. While there are specific economic characteristics of defence procurement, such as monopsony, monopolies, duplication, high costs, state ownership and/or control, and inefficiency (Trybus, 2014), the context is dominated by national security objectives. On the one hand, that only enhances the importance of the primary efficiency and value for money objectives when procuring weapons and ammunition: national security makes the timely and efficient delivery of the best possible product or service even more important. On the other hand, national security makes the defence industries an important element of the defence effort of any country, whether these industries are domestic or not. If a country has a substantial domestic defence industry, then at least in theory this is the most reliable supplier of the ministry of defence of that country. This is because in such a case the ministry of defence would be largely independent of the priorities of any other government and could, as a last resort, take direct control of these companies to ensure security of supply. As only a few countries have defence industries extensive enough to have domestic competition for major weapons systems, that makes the government somewhat responsible for the economic survival of any defence industrial capacity on their territory. This would frequently lead to direct awards to the domestic defence industries without competition and predicable consequences for price and quality. Countries with only limited domestic defence industries will still aim to protect whatever capabilities they have and often require the involvement of these domestic companies in the supply chains of foreign suppliers through offsets and similar arrangements, which are also difficult to reconcile with a competitive procurement procedure. Even in the context of deeply integrated free trade agreements such as the EU, the trade in armaments, munitions, and war material is subject to extensive limitations in the form of transfer licences, export licences, foreign military sales requirements, and often short-term foreign and security policy changes – affecting all the above – and thus compromising security of supply. The cutting-edge technology that can win wars requires extensive research and development efforts and the investment that goes with it. Since the industries are dependent on the government as buyers and export licence authority to an extent that the 'civilian' industries are not, their investment needs some guarantee regarding the later contract for the eventual product or service. Even in the context of the larger Member States of the EU, for example, larger weapons systems can often only be developed in collaboration with other Member States, leading to complex collaboration projects that can often not be reconciled with competitive procurement procedures. Finally, when procuring from outside the jurisdiction, requirements of the exporting nation, such as the U.S. Foreign Military Sales regime, require going through another government, thereby eliminating competition unless that other government is imposing it.

Nevertheless, defence procurement should be regulated to ensure the objectives of efficiency and value for money through competition and transparency. Moreover, defence procurement can be regulated. It is argued here, first, that certain requirements of the ministries of defence that have no specific military application, such as food, medication, ambulances, and even boots or uniforms, should be procured according to the same regime that other parts of the government use for their procurement.[7] The fact that the contracting entity is the ministry of defence represents no reason for exclusion from that regime.

Second, it is argued that the procurement of goods and services with a specific military application, such as armaments, munitions, and other war material and related services, can be regulated if the specific context of the defence sector outlined above is fully accommodated. This will require a special defence procurement regime adapted from the regular public procurement regime. The prime example of such an adapted regime is the EU Defence Directive (2009), which used the old 2004 Public Sector Procurement Directive and adapted it through limitation, flexibility, description, and substitution to produce a 'tailor-made' procurement regulation for defence (Trybus, 2013). EU Defence Directive (2009) was then transposed into the laws of the 27 Member States and is used by their ministries of defence. Limitation involves the exclusion of certain types of defence procurement from the scope of the regime that would be too complex or politically sensitive to include so that the potential problems of their inclusion cannot compromise the effectiveness of the legislation in its entirety. In the EU Defence Directive (2009), this limitation concerns government-to-government contracts (Article 13f EU Defence Directive, 2009; Butler, 2017), including U.S. Foreign Military Sales, collaborative projects between several Member States with or without third countries involving research and development (Article 13c EU Defence Directive, 2009; Heuninckx, 2016), intelligence services (Article 13b EU Defence Directive, 2009), and procurement involving secrecy (Article 13a EU Defence Directive, 2009). Flexibility involves the (in comparison to the 'civilian' public sector regime) less restrained use of the less competitive procedures involving negotiation. In the EU Defence Directive (2009), this flexibility involves the non-inclusion of the open procedure (where all economic operators are allowed to bid for a contract without pre-selection), the free availability of the restricted procedure (which involves pre-selection), the free use of the negotiated procedure with competition (which in the civilian regime is limited to expressly stipulated situations), and the provision of additional stipulated situations that allow the use of the negotiated procedure without competition (Article 28 EU Defence Directive, 2009; Trybus, 2014). Description involves the expressly permitted use of numerous security of supply and security of information requirements at various stages of any procurement procedure, such as the finalization of the technical specifications and contract performance conditions (Article 18 EU Defence Directive, 2009; Trybus, 2014), qualification (Articles 39–43 EU Defence Directive, 2009; Trybus, 2014), or selection and award criteria (Article 47 EU Defence Directive, 2009; Trybus, 2014). Substitution involves first the prohibition of offsets on the one hand and their substitution with an elaborate subcontracting regime on the other hand.[8]

Third, it is argued, that the national security context in which defence procurement operates requires an 'emergency break' for situations in which national security concerns can no longer be accommodated within the defence procurement regime. Such a provision would allow governments to derogate from the defence procurement regime in such situations and award the contracts in question without legal constraints as they see fit. Such an emergency break would have to apply in national jurisdictions but also in free trade agreements that include procurement regimes, Article 346(1)(b) of the Treaty on the Functioning of the EU-TFEU (Trybus, 2014; Koutrakos, 2009; Pourbaix, 2011)[9] being a prime example. As such a provision may be abused with the result that the larger part of defence procurement is conducted outside the defence procurement regime, the emergency break requires some kind of independent oversight, ideally through judicial review as that provided under Article 348 TFEU for Article 346 TFEU.[10]

## 10.3 Keith Snider – Response to Paper 2

Trybus argues that defence procurement should be regulated and can be regulated in a special regime adapted from the regular public procurement regime. Here

I argue that a special regulatory regime is not necessary and, in the United States' experience, has not been effective and indeed has had deleterious effects. An alternative is to reduce regulation while increasing capacity in the professional procurement workforce.

On 21 May, the American TV news magazine *60 Minutes* aired a 13-minute segment on 'price gouging' by U.S. defence contractors (CBS News, 2023). The segment focused on what it called 'exploitive prices' charged by firms for major weapon systems (e.g. F-35 Joint Strike Fighter, Patriot air defence system) and for spare parts for systems like the Apache helicopter. While failing to delve deeply into reasons for high arms prices, the segment cited reduced competition resulting from industry consolidation[11] and downsizing of the Federal contracting workforce[12] as two major factors. Such sensationalistic reports call to mind the 'horror stories' of seemingly vastly overpriced parts in the United States in the mid-1980s,[13] which attracted Congressional scrutiny and media attention and which led President Reagan to form the Blue Ribbon Commission on Defense Management ('Packard Commission'). The Commission's report, however, countered popular notions that industry fraud and abuse were the main causes of U.S. procurement problems, finding instead that 'the truly costly problems are those of overcomplicated organization and rigid procedure' (Thomas, 1986). Yet, as Schwartz (2007) describes, 'efforts to reform the procurement system, advertised as simplifying the procurement process, taken in aggregate, have produced a system that is significantly more complex than its predecessors'. Yukins (2017) agrees, citing 'strong countervailing forces, whether born of inertia or bureaucratic self-interest, that resist any wholescale dismantling of what is, in fact, a startlingly complex regulatory regime'. So, from the United States' experience of the 1980s and subsequent 'reform' initiatives, we can see that regulations might not achieve their intended outcomes but rather may make matters worse. It remains to be seen whether the recent *60 Minutes* report will lead to increased U.S. procurement 'regulatory bulk' (Yukins, 2017) to fight perceived industry profiteering.[14]

Regarding a special regime for military procurement, the rationale is presumably based on objectives that are uniquely tied to national security and that those national security objectives are so important that they outweigh other objectives of public procurement and deserve special treatment. Other domains of procurement, however, may be equally critical for national security; pandemics and natural disasters are obvious examples of large-scale threats to national security for which special procurement procedures would be appropriate. Such non-military domains would also qualify for the 'emergency break' that Trybus says is needed for defence acquisition. From this perspective, a special regime is not needed specifically for military items; rather, what is needed are procedures and processes that are tailored for procurements in any domain essential for national security. As for the objectives of defence procurement, Trybus asserts that they are the same as for any other domain of public procurement.[15] The 'value for money' objective is interpreted in terms of contributions to national security, but of course the same interpretation will apply for any other procurement domain (e.g. health, infrastructure) with links to national security.

In the United States, however, defence has been treated as a unique procurement regime, in terms of both its regulatory and administrative aspects, with adverse consequences. This condition arose during the Cold War years in the segregation from the broader commercial sector of a specialized defence industry focused on developing and producing unique high-tech weaponry (Dunn, 2020). Reinforcing defence firms' differentiation were the multitude and variety of laws and regulations that imposed government-unique requirements and practices, compliance with which entailed what Nagle (2012) has called 'a sea of paperwork'. The high cost of compliance inhibited, and continues to do so, defence firms' abilities to diversify into the commercial marketplace and gain access to emerging commercial technologies with potential defence applications (Dunn, 2020).

Emerging along with the specialization and regulation of U.S. defence industry was the government perspective of 'defence acquisition' as predominantly focused on managing and contracting for major weapon systems (e.g. aircraft, tanks, missiles) to be developed and produced by defence firms, with little emphasis on commercial practices or acquisition of commercial items. Evidence of this view is the content of the present Federal Acquisition Regulation, which is heavy on government-unique procedures for major systems contracting (reflecting influence from its Cold War-era predecessor, the Armed Services Procurement Regulation), but which is light (only one chapter, Part 12) on acquisition of commercial items. Additionally, the professional development orientation of the U.S. defence acquisition workforce has been dominated by an emphasis on major weapon system development and procurement, with little attention given to acquiring items from commercial sources. Internal DoD policies reinforce the workforce's orientation with a long-standing policy focus on templates for managing full life-cycle acquisition programmes for the types of major weapon systems that specialized defence firms would develop and produce, with only passing mention of commercial buys as an alternative.[16] This treatment has dampened the workforce's capacity for innovation and flexibility, traits which are increasingly critical in today's dynamic defence acquisition environment.

Alternatives are possible, though, as Dunn (2020) suggests, improvements may be possible only incrementally in a system that has taken 70 years to create. We in the United States might envision a FAR devoted mainly to procuring commercial items and to commercial practices, with perhaps only a single chapter on complex weapon system acquisition. We might also envision an industrial base guided by a regulatory 'light touch' with minimal compliance costs as well as robust incentives to pursue technological advances for military applications. An essential element of such reform would be enhanced administrative capacity in the form of a larger and more professional procurement workforce, with members who are trained to have business and public administration acumen, to be technologically savvy, and who are given sufficient administrative discretion to make sound decisions in the public interest. Knowledge of regulations is important, but by itself will not lead to innovation, flexibility, and improvements in defence procurement.

## 10.4 Martin Trybus – Response to Paper 1

While the title of Snider's first section suggests he is making the case against the regulation of defence procurement, he is really arguing for reduced regulation, which while being *reduced* is still an argument *for* regulation. He cites examples of armaments projects that were either procured outside the competitive regime because they were subject to one of its exemptions or had to be cancelled because of cost overruns or other problems he attributes to them being awarded within the competitive regime. Moreover, he differentiates between armaments contracts and other contracts awarded by the U.S. DOD and points to the large proportion of armaments contracts being exempt from the competitive regime as they are subject to one of the exemptions. His vision of 'reduced regulation' entails a regime based on commercial practices. It should be noted that the background to his examples and arguments is characterized by defence acquisition in the unique U.S. context, in which a single defence procurement agency blessed with the largest peacetime defence budget in history procures armaments from the world's most comprehensive domestic defence industrial base and from nearly nobody else. The rest of the world, and notably Europe, simply does not compare; they have (much) smaller defence budgets and defence industrial capabilities and, consequently, need to cooperate with one another. With the need to cooperate across borders comes the necessity to regulate that cooperation, adding another argument and layer for regulation, which could only be dispensed of once the cooperating countries trust each other completely.

This section continues the case *for* regulation, although Snider's arguments will fully be considered. First, the authors agree that there are contracts of an MoD or DoD that do not differ from the same kind of contract being awarded by the (U.S.) General Services Administration,[17] the City of Cagliari, or the University of Birmingham. This will cover all contracts other than the procurement of armaments and related services but for the armed forces, such as food, medical supplies, office furniture, cleaning services, or gym equipment. Here, as in for all contracts for the armed forces, the devil is in the detail. The EU, for example, has a detailed list of what counts as 'arms, ammunitions, and war material', leaving everything not on the list within the 'normal' or 'civilian' regime.[18] In the EU, uniforms and boots are off their list, a solution that might be decided differently in other jurisdictions. The bottom line is that a large proportion of purchases for the armed forces are not subject to a special but the regular public procurement regime, FAR or Directive 2014/24/EU, for example, unless other exemptions from these regimes apply.

Second, the authors agree that there are contracts that, for different reasons, cannot be awarded based on a competitive procurement procedure and which therefore need to be exempt from even a specialized defence procurement regime. In the EU contracts relating to large collaborative projects with other Member States involving research and development, government-to-government contracts, including Foreign Military Sales (FMS) from the United States, contracts awarded by international organizations, or intelligence services, are all exempt from the regime of the Defence Procurement Directive 2009/81/EU and the 27 Member

State laws transposing it into their respective domestic laws. This will often involve the strategically most important, financially most extensive, and politically and diplomatically most sensitive projects. Moreover, it represents a large percentage of the purchases of any defence procurement agency and normally most armaments – defence procurement in the narrow sense – contracts often by number and always by value. This is what this author calls 'limitation', and Snider names 'reduction': there is a competitive procurement regime specifically designed for the acquisition of defence goods, but it is reduced or limited by excluding a considerable number or share of contracts from that regime. Again, the devil is in the details, and jurisdictions will differ regarding their preferences. The United States will need the exemption for government-to-government contracts less as it is the seller rather than the buyer, and collaborative projects are less important for them than they are for Europe.

An aspect of this second point is that all the situations and conditions behind the exemptions from the regime discussed in the previous paragraph are occurring regularly and can therefore be accommodated in specifically drafted exemptions in the legal framework, which can then be facilitated by guidance notes. However, there will also be less foreseeable situations where national security concerns rule out a competitive procedure without being already accommodated in one of the specific exemptions. This requires additional and more general national security exemptions from the regime, such as Article 346(1)(a) – secrecy, 346(1)(b) – armaments, and 347 – war TFEU. However, these can never be blank checks; their use needs to be justified, the situation proven, and subject to administrative and judicial review.

Exemption from the competitive regime does *not* mean that there are no legal requirements, no regulation at all, for the relevant contracts. The use of exemptions needs to be controlled, audited, and reviewed to prevent abuse. In the EU, for example, the decision to exempt a contract can be and should be documented, and in many cases even advertised as it can be challenged in the courts. The decision to exempt a contract must be subject to judicial review, like any other decision of the government in a jurisdiction under the rule of law.

Third, there are contracts on weapons, ammunition, and other warlike materials and related services that can be awarded based on a competitive regime, which could be an adapted version of the competitive regime used for public procurement. As outlined above, adaptations should take the special character and needs of the defence sector into account, provide for flexibility, allow for less competitive procedures inside the regime where specific conditions of armaments contracts so require, accommodate security clearances and generally security of information, safeguard security of supply, and even adapt the review and remedy system (bid protests) to the national security context. This is the approach of the EU Defence and Security Procurement Directive 2009/81/EU discussed above.

In summary, the argument *for* regulation of this author divides the procurement of defence ministries or departments into three broad categories: (1) the procurement of non-military goods and services which should be conducted based on a competitive regime that is *not* adapted to the defence sector, (2) the procurement of specifically military goods and services that can be subjected to a competitive procurement regime that is in various ways adapted to the defence sector, and (3) the procurement of specifically military goods and services that for various reasons rooted in national security, the complexity of large projects, or specific trans-national procurement practices can*not* be subjected to a competitive procurement regime and should therefore be excluded from such a regime on the basis of clearly defined exemptions. The question of whether this approach can be called 'reduced' regulation depends to an extent on what share of the budget is attributed to the three categories, specifically the share that is completely excluded. The dividing lines between the three categories outlined here are contested battlegrounds. The decision of whether a regime applies at all to a procuring entity, or a contract, is always an important legal problem.

An important question is *why* procurement procedures based on a competitive regime run into difficulties and need to be cancelled, as Snider reports. Is that always due to the regime or is that at times an excuse and has entirely different reasons, such as lack of training, experience, or rigour?

## 10.5 Keith Snider – Conclusions

Trybus claims that my argument for *reduced* regulation of defence acquisition is still an argument *for* regulation. Of course, it would be silly to argue that such an important state activity should have no regulation, so the real issue is its proper extent. My position is against regulation in the sense that it should be held to the minimum necessary extent. Reduction and simplification of acquisition rules, together with enhancements in workforce professionalism and capacity, should lead to better outcomes.

Poor outcomes – cost overruns, schedule slips, and quality shortfalls – have substantially shaped the U.S. regulatory environment for defence acquisition, yet after decades of increased regulation, outcomes have not improved. As I noted earlier, past Congressionally chartered studies laid blame for these problems not on contractor fraud or corruption by procurement officials but rather on a system of excessive, complex, and burdensome procurement rules. Of course, the problems plaguing United States' acquisition are not unique to it; poor outcomes are not uncommon in complex defence projects undertaken by the United Kingdom, Germany, and other industrialized nations.[19]

Trybus has not addressed problematic acquisition outcomes. An argument for regulation should explain either how it leads to better outcomes or why it does not contribute to poor ones. But perhaps he is not so enthusiastic a regulatory advocate. The second two of his three categories of defence procurement (from p. 2 of his Part II) envision adaptation to or exclusion from the usual competitive regime, which implies reduced regulation. So, in arguing for *reduced* regulation, he argues *against* regulation.

There is, however, a more insidious outcome of excessive acquisition regulation, that is, degradation of a nation's combat capabilities. In 2016, Congress commissioned the 'Section 809' panel,[20] a group of senior acquisition experts from both government and industry, to review the U.S. acquisition system out of national security concerns that it 'could not maneuver inside the turn of the nation's near-peer competitors and nonstate actors, which are not bound by the same acquisition rules as [the US]'. The panel validated this concern, calling for U.S. defence acquisition to adopt a 'mission first' approach in which 'rapidly and effectively acquiring warfighting capability … takes precedence over achieving other public policy objectives'. It cited 'rigid, bureaucratic rules [and] overly prescriptive regulations' as factors that promote 'adherence to process and procedure instead of creativity and innovation' within the procurement workforce.[21] The panel proposed 98 reform recommendations, including many to repeal or amend current regulations and statutes, to streamline and improve the efficiency and effectiveness of the acquisition process[22] (Advisory Panel, 2018b). The top-ranking U.S. Air Force general summed up this mission-first orientation, 'If we are to beat our competitors in conflict, we must also beat them in development and fielding of capability' (Brown, 2020).

The present German government would agree with this approach. Recent reporting describes the intent of Germany's defence minister, motivated by the Ukraine's exigency, to restore the Bundeswehr's fighting capabilities by cutting procurement regulations, streamlining approval processes, and promoting creativity, flexibility, and initiative among members of the defence procurement workforce (Glucroft, 2023; Vad, 2023).

Trybus notes that I argue mainly from the U.S. experience. For better or for worse, where defence acquisition is concerned, what happens in the United States has worldwide consequences. Other nations have a big stake in the outcomes of the U.S. defence acquisition system. To cite only a few examples: The armed forces of sixteen nations use or will use the F-35 strike fighter, the Apache attack helicopter, and the Patriot air defence system. Twenty-five nations have the Hellfire air-to-ground missile. The air forces of 25 nations fly the F-16 fighter, which will continue in service into the 2070s.[23] These nations rely on the United States to provide superior weaponry to meet their defence needs and surely hope, for the sakes of their own national security, that the United States can achieve its acquisition reform goals.[24]

## 10.6 Martin Trybus – Conclusions

Defence procurement needs to be regulated. It is argued here that not regulating defence procurement at all, leaving all the decisions and procedures to the discretion of the procurement officers, trusting in their training and experience alone, is not an option for the following reasons:

First, no government activity that impacts individuals or legal persons, also in their business interests, can ever be left unregulated. The rule of law, often enshrined in the Constitution, such as for example in the fundamental Article 20 Basic Law (the German Constitution), requires all government activity to be authorized by law and thus normally by the elected parliament and then to be conducted in a lawful manner, subject to judicial review. Defence procurement represents an important government activity, spending considerable funds of the taxpayer and serving essential interests of national security. Therefore, in a state under the rule of law, defence procurement needs to be regulated; it is far too important to be left unregulated.

Second, if there is a case that the flexibility offered by a regulated system is insufficient to satisfy the demands of national security or extreme urgency, such as that brought about a natural disaster or pandemic, that case has not been made. A regulated defence procurement regime is, as explained in the previous sections contributed by this author, capable of addressing flexibility requirements – by excluding certain types of contracts, by reducing participation requirements, by allowing more negotiation, by reducing competition, or by providing procedures and approaches that are tailor-made for the defence sector. Reducing and adapting regulation, rather than completely removing it, has been the approach so far – an approach that can still be improved, but the right approach.

Third, the idea that national security is a concern that should allow categorical exclusion from regulated procurement regimes is not convincing. Yes, the executive needs to be given wide margins of discretion when taking measures to protect national security, including, if necessary, derogation from a defence procurement regime. Yes, courts reviewing such decisions will apply a certain degree of deference respecting these margins of discretion. Yes, defence contractors might be given wider discretion than their 'civilian' colleagues. However, a complete absence of the law from defence procurement is not warranted by national security or similar concerns.

Fourth, when advocating the removal or further reduction of regulation of defence procurement, a concrete proposal on what could replace regulation has to be made. How will value for money be ensured without competition, at least when markets with more than one possible supplier or provider exist? How will competition be ensured when the economic operators who are to compete against each other are not compared in well set-out procedures, procedures the operators trust enough to participate in? How can competition be fostered without transparency, most importantly through the publication of contract opportunities? In an Internal Market with several different states, such as in the EU, how can cross-border tenders be facilitated without rules that prohibit discrimination on grounds of nationality? Less regulation, regulation based on only a few principles, yes, but none at all?

Fifth and finally, Snider advocates better training as an alternative to regulation. This proposal is a double-edged sword. On the one hand, nobody can deny the importance and utility of (better) training for procurement officers; not least, the European Commission has been making recommendations to that effect for a long time. However, training should be continuously improved and updated in addition to good regulation, not as a substitute for it. Moreover, the basis of that training, in addition to experience, technology, research, and common sense, should be regulation produced by the legislator elected by the taxpayers who are funding the very armaments to be procured and who are the citizens whose security and interests they are intended to protect.

## Notes

1 Office of the Under Secretary of Defense (Comptroller)/Chief Financial Officer Defense Budget Overview United States Department of Defense Fiscal Year 2024 Budget Request (2023). Available at https://comptroller.defense.gov/Portals/45/Documents/defbudget/FY2024/FY2024_Budget_Request_Overview_Book.pdf.
2 United States Government Accountability Office (2021), *Heavy Lift Helicopter Program: Navy Should Address Cost and Schedule Risks*, GAO-21-208, March, Washington, DC.
3 Data retrieved from System for Award Management (https://www.SAM.gov), 4 March 2023.
4 Some regulations are patently unnecessary, for example, the FAR's requirement that contracts include a clause prohibiting texting while driving. See FAR 23.1105 and FAR 52.223-18.
5 United States Government Accountability Office (2023), *Middle-Tier Defense Acquisitions: Rapid Prototyping and Fielding Requires Changes to Oversight and Development Approaches*, GAO-23-105008, 7 February, Washington, DC.
6 Multi-year contracts commit the DoD to buying products over a period of usually three to five years, an arrangement that reduces vendor risk.
7 This is the case in the EU Member States where the 27 ministries of defence need to procure these goods and services based on the national laws that transposed the Public Sector Procurement Directive 2014/24/EU.
8 Offsets are not expressly prohibited in the Directive, but see the Commission *Guidance Note on Offsets*, at 1 and *Guidance Note on Subcontracting*, at 1. The subcontracting regime is contained in Articles 21 and 50-4 Directive 2009/81/EC (Trybus, 2014), pp. 429–452.
9 Art. 346(1)(b) TFEU: '… any Member State may take such measures as it considers necessary for the protection of the essential interests of its security which are connected with the production of or trade in arms, munitions and war material; such measures shall not adversely affect the conditions of competition in the internal market regarding products which are not intended for specifically military purposes …'. In 1958, the Council compiled a list of armaments to which Art. 346(1)(b) TFEU applies. See Council Decision 298/58 of 15 Apr. 1958 (not published).
10 The Court of Justice of the EU applies a narrow interpretation to Article 346 TFEU see: Case C-414/97, *Commission* v. *Spain*, EU:C:1999:417. This interpretation was reiterated in Commission, Interpretative Communication on the Application of Article 296 of the Treaty in the field of defence procurement COM(2006)779 final. This position has been confirmed and further refined in subsequent judgments: the *Agusta* judgments (Case C-337/05, *Commission* v. *Italy,* EU:C:2008:203 and Case C-157/06, *Commission* v. *Italy*, EU:C:2008:530); the *Military Exports* judgments (Case C-284/05, *Commission* v. *Finland*, EU:C:2009:778; Case C-294/05, *Commission* v. *Sweden*, EU:C:2009:779; Case C-387/05, *Commission* v. *Italy*, EU:C:2009:781; Case C-409/05, *Commission* v. *Greece*, EU:C:2009:782; Case C-461/05, *Commission* v. *Denmark*, EU:C:2009:783; Case C-38/06, *Commission* v. *Portugal,* EU:C:2010:108; Case C-239/06, *Commission* v. *Italy*, EU:C:2009:784) and *Finnish Turntables* (Case C-615/10, *Insinööritoimisto InsTiimi Oy*, EU:C:2012:324), and most recently Case C-246/12 P, *Ellinika Nafpigeia*, EU:C:2013:133, and Case C-474/12, *Schiebel Aircraft*, EU:C:2014:2139.
11 Thereby increasing the likelihood of 'hold-up' problems; see Rogerson (1992, p. 7).

12 Resulting in reduced capacity to award and manage contracts.
13 A $435 'price' resulted from the firm using the equal allocation method to assign contract indirect costs equally across all items, whether sophisticated or mundane; see Fairhall (1987).
14 Data compiled by New York University sources suggest that excessive profits are not common in defence industries. 'Aerospace and Defense' ranks in the bottom half of all sectors, with average firm net margins around 8%. See https://pages.stern.nyu.edu/~adamodar/New_Home_Page/datafile/margin.html.
15 Arrowsmith et al. (2011) list these objectives of public procurement: Value for money (efficiency); Integrity (avoiding corruption and conflicts of interest); Accountability; Equal opportunities and equal treatment for providers; Fair treatment of providers; Efficient implementation of industrial, social and environmental objectives; Opening public markets to international trade; Efficiency in the procurement process.
16 Several iterations of the 'DoD 5000'-series regulations have been issued in the past four decades. Because these are meant as policies to guide internal DoD acquisition procedures, they do not have the same force of law as do provisions of the Federal Acquisition Regulation. While various versions of the full development and production program management template have dominated in the past, the most recent issuance gives more weight to flexible and commercially oriented approaches.
17 US federal centralised procurement agency for all federal departments and agencies other than the DoD.
18 The list according to Article 346(2) TFEU was compiled in 1958.
19 See, for example, Sabbagh (2021).
20 Named after the section of the legislation that chartered the panel: Section 809 of the Fiscal Year 2016 National Defense Authorization Act (Public Law 114-92).
21 Advisory Panel on Streamlining and Codifying Acquisition Regulations (2018a).
22 Advisory Panel on Streamlining and Codifying Acquisition Regulations (2018b).
23 Data sources: F-35, see 'International Participation' at https://www.jsf.mil/aboutus; Apache, Hellfire, Patriot, see https://asc.army.mil/web/weapon-systems; F-16, see Tirpak (2021).
24 I gratefully acknowledge the thoughtful critiques and helpful suggestions given by my colleague, Dr. Rene Rendon, in the preparation of the case against regulation.

## References

Advisory Panel on Streamlining and Codifying Acquisition Regulations (2018a), *Report of the Advisory Panel on Streamlining and Codifying Acquisition Regulations*, Vol. 2, Defense Technical Information Center, p. 62. Available at https://discover.dtic.mil/section-809-panel/.

Advisory Panel on Streamlining and Codifying Acquisition Regulations (2018b), *Report of the Advisory Panel on Streamlining and Codifying Acquisition Regulations*, Defense Technical Information Center, p. 1 (Roadmap Report). Available at https://discover.dtic.mil/section-809-panel/.

Arrowsmith, S., Linarelli, J., and Wallace, D. Jr. (2000), *Regulating Public Procurement. National and International Perspectives*, Kluwer Law International, London, chapters 1 and 2, pp. 27–32, 61–63, and 73–98.

Arrowsmith, S., Treumer, S., Fejø, J., and Jiang, L. (2011), S. Arrowsmith (ed.), *Public Procurement Regulation: An Introduction*, University of Nottingham, Public Procurement

Research Group. pp. 4, 1–23, Nottingham, Available at: www.nottingham.ac.uk/pprg/documentsarchive/asialinkmaterials/publicprocurementregulationintroduction.pdf

Brown, C.Q. (2020), 'Accelerate change or lose', Office of the Chief of Staff of the Air Force, 22 August, p. 6. Available at www.af.mil/Portals/1/documents/csaf/CSAF_22/CSAF_22_Strategic_ Approach_Accelerate_Change_or_Lose_31_Aug_2020.pdf

Butler, Luke R. A. (2017), *Transatlantic Defence Procurement: EU and US Defence Procurement Regulation in the Transatlantic Defence Market*, Cambridge University Press, Cambridge.

CBS News (2023), 'ICYMI: A look back at Sunday's 60 Minutes', 22 May. Available at www.cbsnews.com/news/icymi-60-minutes-pentagon-price-gouging-digital-theft-jeff-koons-2023-05-22/

Colvin, R. (2009), 'Obama questions presidential helicopter project', *Reuters*, 23 February. Available at www.reuters.com/article/us-obama-weapons-idUSTRE51M6UM20090223

Dunn, R.L. (2020), 'Defense industry needs new way of doing business', *National Defense*, November, p. 18. Available at https://digital.nationaldefensemagazine.org/publication/?m=46185&i=678993&p=20

EU Defence Directive (2009) Directive 2009/81/EC of the European Parliament and of the Council of 13 July 2009 on the coordination of procedures for the award of certain works contracts, supply contracts and service contracts by contracting authorities or entities in the fields of defence and security, and amending Directives 2004/17/EC, 2004/18/EC and [2009] OJ L216/76

EU Public Sector Directive (2004) Directive 2004/18/EC of the European Parliament and of the Council of 31 March 2004 on the coordination of procedures for the award of public works contracts, public supply contracts and public service contracts [2004] OJ L 134/114

EU Public Sector Directive (2014) Directive 2014/24/EU of the European Parliament and of the Council of 26 February 2014 on public procurement and repealing Directive 2004/18/EC [2014] OJ L94/65

Fairhall, J. (1987), *The Case for the $435 Hammer*. The Free Library. Available at www.thefreelibrary.com/The+case+for+the+%24435+hammer.-a04619906.

Glucroft, W.N. (2023), *Germany: Defense Minister Battles Bundeswehr Bureaucracy*, Deutsche Welle, 18 May. Available at www.dw.com/en/germany-defense-minister-battles-bundeswehr-bureaucracy/a-65661438.

Gore, A. (1995), *National Performance Review: Introduction*. 7 September. Available at https://govinfo.library.unt.edu/npr/library/nprrpt/annrpt/comsen95/228e.html.

Greenwalt, W. (2013), *Five Factors Plaguing Pentagon Procurement*, 13 December. American Enterprise Institute, Washington, DC.

Heuninckx, B. (2016), *The Law of Collaborative Defence Procurement in the European Union*, Cambridge University Press, Cambridge.

Koutrakos, P. (2009), 'The application of EC law to defence industries: Changing interpretations of Article 296 EC', in: Barnard, C. and Odudu, O. (eds.), *The Outer Limits of European Union Law*, Hart Publishing, Oxford, Portland, Oregon, pp. 307–328.

McCormick, R. (2020), *Department of Defense Other Transaction Authority Trends: A New R&D Funding Paradigm?* Center for Strategic and International Studies, Washington, DC, 8 December.

Nagle, J.F. (2012), *A History of Government Contracting—Vol. II* (3rd ed.), Government Training Inc., ISBN: 978-1-937246-37-2.

Pourbaix, N. (2011), 'The future scope of application of Article 346 TFEU', *Public Procurement Law Review*,1, pp. 1–8.

Rogerson, W.P. (1992), 'Contractual solutions to the hold-up problem', *The Review of Economic Studies*, 59(4), pp. 777–793. Available at https://doi.org/10.2307/2297997.

Roque, A. (2023), '"Up our game": The Pentagon's 3 strategies to shore up munitions stockpiles', *Breaking Defense*, 23 January. Available at https://breakingdefense.com/2023/03/up-our-game-the-pentagons-3-strategies-to-shore-up-munitions-stockpiles/.

Sabbagh, D. (2021), 'MoD procurement disasters, delays and overspends', *The Guardian*, 2 November. Available at www.theguardian.com/uk-news/2021/nov/03/mod-procurement-disasters-delays-and-overspends.

Schooner, S. (2002), 'Desiderata: Objectives for a system of government contract law', *Public Procurement Law Review*, 11, p. 103.

Schwartz, J.I. (2007), *Regulation and Deregulation in Public Procurement Law Reform in the United States*, p. 179. Available at www.ippa.org/IPPC2/BOOK/Chapter_9.pdf.

Thomas, E. (1986), 'Defensive about defense', *Time*, 3 October.

Tirpak, J.A. (2021), 'F-16s could still be flying into the 2070s', *Air & Space Force Magazine*, 23 May.

Trybus, M. (2013), 'The tailor-made EU Defence and Security Procurement Directive: limitation, flexibility, description, and substitution', *European Law Review*, 1, pp. 3–29.

Trybus, M. (2014), *Buying Defence and Security in Europe*, Cambridge University Press, Cambridge.

Vad, E. (2023), *Ukraine War Compels Bundeswehr to Refocus and Rebuild, but at Too Slow a Pace. Russia Matters*, Harvard Kennedy School, 20 April. Available at www.russiamatters.org/analysis/ukraine-war-compels-bundeswehr-refocus-and-rebuild-too-slow-pace-0.

Yukins, C.R. (2017), 'The U.S. federal procurement system: An introduction', Public Law Research Paper No. 2017-75. George Washington University Law School, Washington, DC, p. 79. Available at https://ssrn.com/abstract=3063559.

# 11 'Zeitenwende' (new era) for defence procurement

## The role of speed and symbiotic collaboration by investigating combination versus separation in defence supply chains

*Andreas H. Glas and Michael Eßig*

### 11.1 Setting the frame: defence procurement around the world

The cooperation and interrelations between the military and defence industry has been a subject of economic research for decades focusing on diverse topics such as the 'military–industrial complex', 'arms/capacity conversion', 'outsourcing', or 'strategic alliances/preferred relations' as well as 'collaboration under performance-based contracts' (see e.g. Glas, 2017).

Reflecting research on defence economic research, the impression arises that the discussion developed from a focus on military effectiveness to a discussion about mainly cost-focused economization of resources spent for the military (e.g. Arena, 2006). That discussion finally reached a point in which research analysed how the military and the defence industry together master the challenges of scarce budgets and resource constraints, what more or less resulted in efficiency-centric relations between both sides.

In February 2022, Russia started its aggression and war on Ukraine which led to a strategic turnaround in the understanding of defence and armament. For all European states this war was a significant turning point, in Germany branded as 'Zeitenwende' following a quote from the German chancellor – mainly because traditional frameworks of security and defence policy have changed dramatically (Major & Mölling, 2023). However, Russia's war against Ukraine is not the only crisis. On the contrary, one can get the impression that the current situation in 2023 is characterized by overlapping and simultaneous crises, conflicts, and serious events (Lorentz et al., 2021). Referring only to some recent crises – climate crisis, pandemic crisis, migration crisis, financial crisis, energy crisis – one can imagine how explosive and risky the situation can be as perceived by defence analysts (Gürtlich & Lampl, 2022). Adding other threats to this, only as examples one might think about the Gaza-conflict in 2024, the Suez Canal congestion due to shipwreck in 2021, or many others like forest fires, lack of water, the Taiwan–China issue, raw material bottlenecks for rare earths, etc.[1] – then it becomes obvious that 'Zeitenwende' may generally mark a turning point in the security and defence discussion.

DOI: 10.4324/9781032631721-16

The situation is even more serious, because European armed forces evaluate themselves extremely critically in terms of their performance and the deficient state or deficits they face (for an indicative overview, see Stern, 2023, or for a single country, see Bundesministerium der Verteidigung, 2022). For example, the Bundeswehr in Germany is described as being 'more or less defenceless (blank)' (General Alfons Mais, Inspector of the German Army in Spiegel.de, 2022). The British armed forces are described as being 'in a dire state' (Tobias Ellwood, Chairman Defense Committee in Skynews, 2023). There is no doubt that the military has a huge demand for material, equipment of any kind.

The changed situation is already affecting defence procurement and the relation between the defence acquisition agencies on the one hand and the suppliers from the defence industry on the other. First of all, many countries increased defence budgets significantly. In Germany, a special fund of around 100 billion EUR has been provided only a couple of days after the beginning of the Russian attack.

But referring to a controversial paper on defence procurement, money is important, but not the sole or the most important factor for an efficient and effective defence procurement system (Brzoska et al., 2023). This points to factors aside of financial resources that hinder a procurement execution that satisfies demand in time, budget, and quality. Especially because even defence procurement relies heavily on the interconnection between defence and 'commercial' supply chains, e.g. by being dependent on raw material dependencies from outside its own home base (e.g. Girardi et al., 2023).

As a result, defence procurement needs a much more strategic approach, developing an integrated defence acquisition management approach (see e.g. Ekström, 2010; Wright, 2010; Glas & Eßig, 2017) addressing the triangle of availability/quality, cost, and time simultaneously.

This chapter addresses two of these factors. The first one refers to the procurement process time. One prominent claim is to accelerate procurement processes, what is typically demanded by industry. For example, the speaker of the German Association of Defence Industry expressed that production would be possible on the short run by the industry and claimed that the bottleneck is slow procurement management. He called for a far more rapid ordering by the defence procurement agency (Deutschlandfunk, 2023).

The second factor refers to the business environment and its uncertainties. One typical perspective from defence industry on this is that defence industry requires support, reliable and stable framework conditions for their capacity management, and long-term financing and strategic planning security (see e.g. Eßig et al., 2014). All this can be seen as protectors against a number of contingency uncertainties, e.g. changes in demand quantities and qualities; changes in technologies or supply relations. It seems as if the 'Zeitenwende' increases procurement uncertainty, what then might call for a substantial, symbiotic collaboration ('symbiotic arrangements', e.g. Picot, 1993; Raub and Weesie, 1993; Schanze, 1993) between defence industry and armed forces by building up so-called defence supply networks (e.g. Tatham, 2013) to solve this uncertainty.

This research will address these factors and follows the guiding research aim to explore the effects of procurement uncertainty and procurement acceleration on defence industry. More fine-grained, their effects are analysed considering industrial symbiotic collaboration, order speed, and generally business performance of the defence industry. For this purpose, a structural equation modelling approach is used to analyse data from a focus sample of German defence industry managers. All respondents provided insights into their perceptions about both factors (procurement uncertainty, procurement acceleration) and defence industrial performance.

Therefore, this research is able to contribute to the literature in several ways: First, the very recent topic of the 'Zeitenwende' is analysed on a survey focusing only on defence suppliers. The survey insights are one of very few quantitative empirical views on the supply side at this time. Second, this research focuses on two main propositions to increase procurement performance in defence (acceleration and industrial symbiosis). To the best of our knowledge, both aspects have not been surveyed in comparison before.

This chapter presents the research as follows. The next section presents briefly the theoretical background followed by the development of hypotheses. Then the methodology is presented. Next, the research findings are presented. Finally, a discussion and limitations conclude the chapter.

## 11.2 Background

### *11.2.1 The factor time in defence procurement*

Since the 1980s the issue of fast or adequate 'time-to-market' has been discussed as a competitive advantage in management literature, and research investigated methods how to accelerate in particular new product development (e.g. Mahmoud-Jouini et al., 2004). As such, many scholars investigated 'Speed Management' or 'Rapid' topics, e.g. rapid manufacturing or rapid prototyping (Hague et al., 2006). Acceleration has many aspects, e.g. the use of new, faster technology, like additive manufacturing (Meyer et al., 2022), but also new or changed processes, like simultaneous engineering (Shenas & Derakhshan, 1994). Purchasing can make a significant contribution in improving time-based advantages (e.g. Hendrick, 1994).

It is worth highlighting that the factor time does imply not only 'faster is better' but also the opposite can be true. Another research stream addresses 'postponement' in supply management (Swaminathan & Lee, 2003). Here, it is the aim to stay for the longest time possible in a specific status. One application of postponement is manufacturing supply, in which standard products are individualized as timely to the point of sale as possible. Another example is logistics: to bundle stock in a central infrastructure as long as possible to allow for a maximum of optimized shipping and routing in transport. These brief remarks shall introduce the importance of the factor time in procurement literature in general. More specifically, the topic is also of relevance for defence procurement. Of course, time has similar ambivalent notions in defence: Speeding up supply increases fast capability building and sometimes also increases standardization, as fast procurement often means buying off-the-shelf market-available products. Postponing supply can also have advantages, as long-term solutions might increase capabilities in a far more innovative and, for the military, in a more superior way (Glas & Schnell, 2023). Different time aspects in military logistics literature have been investigated recently (Ekström et al., 2020). Besides, also the evaluation of defence procurement claims on the one hand the high project risks (low quality, low availability, low reliability) but on the other hand calls for acceleration of procurement (see e.g. the evaluation report of BMVg, 2014). Therefore, time is a relevant factor for defence procurement, but it is still not clear how acceleration or postponement of procurement effects industrial performance. As a result, defence procurement has to be re-investigated highlighting in time availability as a central element of defence procurement power (e.g. Ädel et al., 2022).

### *11.2.2 The factor uncertainty and supply integration/industrial symbiosis in defence procurement*

Uncertainty is ubiquitous in supply chain (Flynn et al., 2016). As such, uncertainty is described as a multilevel phenomenon (Carter et al., 2015), existing at individual, group, functional, and organizational levels. Typically, factors of uncertainty are interrelated and refer, for example, to information accuracy, information availability, (in-)stability of demand, organizational (in-)stability, etc. (Flynn et al., 2016). As a matter of fact, uncertainty is a dynamic construct and highly dependent on the situation. As such, uncertainty is a central concept of contingency theory, so an organization's performance is contingent on the fit between its structure, processes, and environment (Lawrence & Lorsch, 1967; Downey & Slocum, 1975; Flynn et al., 2016).

Therefore, supply chain integration is a relevant construct; it is defined as the scope and strength of linkages of supply chain processes across organizations (Leuschner et al., 2013). Supply chain integration can be an effective protector against some origins of uncertainty, by facilitating relations between buyers and suppliers and by fostering close collaboration (e.g. Koufteros et al., 2007; Wong et al., 2015). Integration typically distinguishes between internal, customer, and supplier integration.

A literature stream that is highly related to supply chain integration is referring to 'industrial symbiosis'. Industrial symbiosis has its roots in biology research (see e.g. Penrose, 1952) in which symbiosis represents the 'association of individuals of different species in a relationship where there is mutual benefit' (Schwarz & Steininger, 1997). The term symbiosis was then used in the context of industry branches and/or corporate groups (e.g. Spindler, 1993). It is expressed that industrial symbiosis links traditionally separately analysed entities. Industrial symbiosis expects organizations to behave at least to some extent collectively, e.g. exchanging information, by-products, energy, etc. The analogy to biologic systems (trees and their microbiome of supporting plants and animals; humans and their microorganisms within the body, etc.) is obvious. One can see industrial symbiosis going one step beyond supply chain integration, as industrial symbiosis acknowledges joint business opportunities and often also refers to ecosystem industrial innovations that then foster competitive advantages of each single organization (e.g. Lombardi & Laybournd, 2012).

For this study, industrial symbiosis seems to be a very suitable construct, because the defence sector typically is an industry branch characterized by one (or very few) buyers on a national level and a small and very specialized supply organization which depends more or less directly on the single buyer. Reciprocal dependencies are the consequence, what has been identified in very early works on defence acquisition ('military–industrial-complex' or 'defence supply networks'; see above). However, knowledge on industrial symbiosis is still rare, as it is a quite new construct and concept. Furthermore, it is often referred to as sustainability or green supply chain initiatives. An application to the defence context is at least very rare if it exists at all. This gap is addressed by this work.

## 11.3 Hypotheses development

As already outlined in the introduction, the defence procurement of many countries face the changes following the 'Zeitenwende'. As such, defence procurement might aim to evoke a positive market echo to its changed conditions and activities.

A first important condition is procurement uncertainty. That construct refers to a wider construct on environmental uncertainty (see e.g. Fynes et al., 2004). Uncertainty is often used as an antecedent construct that explains the emergence of protector initiatives such as risk management (Hoffmann et al., 2013). As such, the first hypothesis addresses effects of procurement uncertainty and assumes that a high (low) level of uncertainty leads to a more (less) intense necessity for close cooperation. This is in line with Liu et al. (2022), who showed that management perceptions about the situation impact industrial symbiosis. As the defence market is characterized by bilateral monopoly or at least oligopolistic structures (one/few buyers and one/few suppliers for a product), an increase in uncertainty may result in risks which can only be taken in a joint approach. However, in a phase of low uncertainty the opposite may become true – competitive, non-integrated cooperation could make sense. As such, a higher current procurement uncertainty ('Zeitenwende') leads to a closer and more symbiotic collaboration between defence procurement agency and defence industry.

**H1: Defence procurement uncertainty positively effects symbiotic collaboration.**

The second hypothesis addresses the current procurement acceleration initiative in Germany. It is a law even named 'defence procurement acceleration law'.[2] In this law, a number of acceleration approaches are opened to the procurement agency. Here are some examples: The legal/procedural tendency to procure products in lots can easily be refused. It is eased to enable European-wide acquisition together with partner nations. Obviously non-suitable suppliers can be excluded more easily from the tender process. Market-common products are favoured. Supplier claims and legal actions are canalized so that these do not delay the procurement process. Obviously, these acceleration measures aim to increase the performance in terms of speed. Prier et al. (2020) already addressed decision speed in public procurement markets, especially referring to the European Single Market. Speed refers to orders that are awarded to industry. Overall, the second hypothesis is as follows:

**H2: Procurement acceleration positively effects order speed.**

Next, it is assumed that order speed as the performance measure of fast procurement execution will have an impact on how buyer and supplier collaborate in industrial symbiosis. Symbiosis refers to joint planning and decision-making. Therefore, fast and timely ordering might have positive effects. The third hypothesis is as follows:

**H3: Order speed positively effects industrial symbiosis.**

Finally, the two factors and their effect on the defence supply chain are measured in relation to business performance of the defence industry. It is assumed that both factors have positive effects on the competitive position and future sales and business expectations. It could be assumed that industrial symbiosis has a more long-term cause–effect, while order speed is more short-term. Existing research shows that industries with higher demand variations can lead to different manufacturing strategies addressing reaction speed on additional demand (e.g. Ferdows, 1990). But in the structural equation model, both factors should have a positive relation. Therefore, the fourth and fifth hypotheses are as follows:

**H4: Industrial symbiosis positively effects business performance.**
**H5: Order speed positively effects business performance.**

Figure 11.1 illustrates the research framework and model of this study. The model itself is embedded in a specific context environment of defence. As Figure 11.1 shows, the model assumes, that industrial symbiosis and order speed have a combined effect on business performance ('combination assumption').

## 11.4 Methodology

To test the hypotheses, survey data have been collected with a questionnaire addressed to managers of German defence supply companies in December 2022. Before conducting the survey, pre-tests were performed. In the first pre-test, ten researchers from the author's university faculty received the questionnaire, and responded to it while checking for comprehensibility, structure, and length. Parts of the survey are also included in a longitudinal study; therefore, large parts have been questioned already in five previous survey rounds. This provides indications that the questionnaire is accessible and comprehensive to respondents. After revisions to the questionnaire, the survey was finalized and sent out via the questionnaire

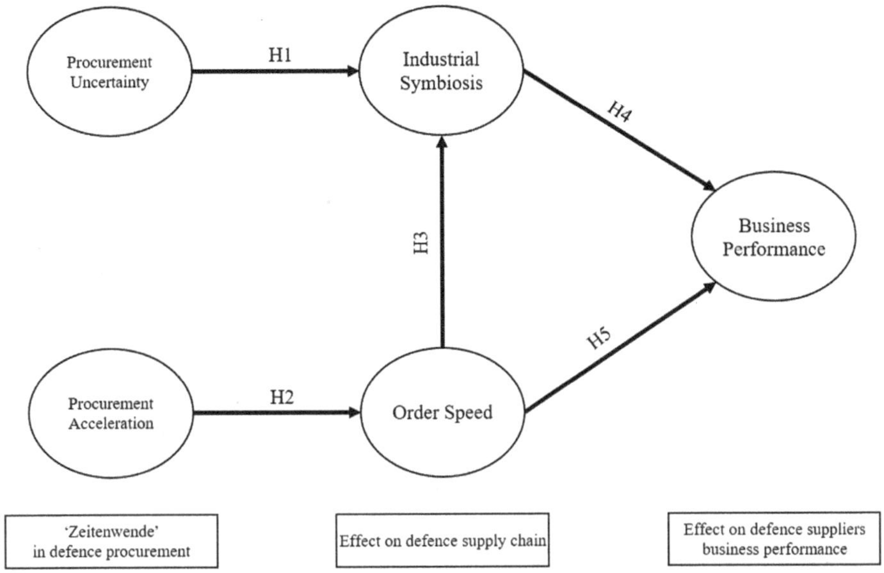


*Figure 11.1* Research model.

*Source:* Own compilation.

platform UniPark from 20 November 2022 to 5 December 2022 (14 days).[3] Each participant received a personalized e-mail from the German Association on Defence Technology.[4]

Using the help of the association, this research uses a purposeful sampling method (Patton, 1990). So, it was assured that sampling results in a homogenous group concerned with the same phenomenon. It was assured that the survey targets respondents who have expert insights into the business and relationship of their company with the defence customer. The expert status is identified through their role in the defence company and the long-term experience with the subject.

Overall, 270 members are included in the database of the German association. Overall, the survey saw a relatively high number of 298 clicks on the survey. This can be explained by re-routing of a survey from a company e-mail address to a specific respondent. One indicator for this is also the number of 142 dropouts on the title page. A number of 156 respondents finalized the survey. This is a response quote (to 270 addressed) of 0.57% or (to 298 clicks) of 0.52%. This is high and can be explained by the small and closely tied community in the association; it implies that the respondents are willing to support the initiatives of the association. A number of 35 questionnaires had at least some missing values in their responses and were excluded from the analysis. So the final sample consisted out of 121 questionnaires.

The sample was analysed with regard to non-response bias. The approach by Armstrong and Overton (1977) was used for this purpose. It tests if relational perceptions are not dependent on the time of response. The parameter-free, two-tailed Mann–Whitney U-test revealed no significant differences at the 5% level for all variables. Also, a comparison of means of early and late respondents, an investigation of the raw data and a search for outliers, however, did not reveal an indication of a structural bias problem.

Table 11.1 shows descriptive statistics. Personnel characteristics of the respondents were gender, position in the company, and previous military career. The majority of respondents were male (88.2%), which is not surprising as there is generally only a very small number of women in management positions in Germany (Holst & Wiemer, 2010).

The sample is more or less split into two halves referring to the company size. Based on the European Union's definition of small- or medium-sized enterprises (SMEs) (<250 employees, <50 million euro turnover, European Commission (EC, 2006), 46.3% of the sample are SMEs, whereas 53.7% are large enterprises. This reflects the traditionally high share of SMEs in German defence industry.

*Table 11.1* Sample characteristics

| *Variable* | *N* | *(%)* |
|---|---|---|
| *Gender of respondent* | | |
| Male | 112 | 92.6 |
| Female | 8 | 6.6 |
| No response | 1 | 0.8 |
| Σ | 121 | 100.0 |
| *Company position of respondent* | | |
| Board member | 24 | 189.8 |
| Division leader | 43 | 35.5 |
| Department leader/leadership position | 26 | 21.5 |
| Expert position | 17 | 14.0 |
| Others | 11 | 9.1 |
| Σ | 121 | 100.0 |
| *Company size* | | |
| Small- and medium-size | 56 | 46.3 |
| Large | 65 | 53.7 |
| Σ | 121 | 100.0 |
| *Defence market relevance for the company* | | |
| Key market | 65 | 53.7 |
| Very important | 27 | 22.3 |
| Important | 18 | 14.9 |
| Less important | 8 | 6.6 |
| No response | 3 | 2.5 |
| Σ | 121 | 100.0 |

*Source:* Own table compilation.

To estimate the structural equation model, the partial least square (PLS) method is used by applying SmartPLS 4.0 software (Ringle et al., 2022). PLS is a variance-based method that offers certain advantages and disadvantages compared with covariance-based methods. Hair et al. (2021) provide a couple of propositions when PLS has advantages. In making the decision to use PLS, the following considerations are of relevance. PLS has advantages when:

- the prediction of a focal variable is sought;
- the analysis is explorative because little confirmed knowledge is available; and
- the sample size is small.

This is the case here, as the topic of interest is of course new and must be addressed in an explorative way. Paths, relations, and even constructs are new and, according to the defence procurement situation, also under researched. This all supports the observation that the model has an exploratory character. Besides, the sample size of this study is below the often-referred threshold of 250 for covariance-based methods of structural equation modelling (e.g. Reinartz et al., 2009). However, the 121 respondent data sets are more than sufficient for exploring effect in variance-based structural equation models. That method provides indicative results already from very small sample sizes as low as around 20 observations (Chin & Newsted, 1999).

The evaluation of the model followed two main steps (Chin, 2010). First, the reflective measurements are evaluated using indicator reliability, which should be higher than 0.7; construct reliability, which should be higher than 0.6; average variance extracted (AVE), which should be higher than 0.5 and Cronbach's alpha, which should be more than 0.7. Furthermore, discriminant validity is assessed by checking if the square root of the AVE is higher than the absolute value of correlation shared between any of the other constructs (Götz et al., 2010).

Second, the structural model is evaluated (Chin, 2010). The statistical significance is evaluated by applying the bootstrap method of individual changes with 5,000 bootstrap drawings (Henseler et al., 2009). As a goodness-of-fit index, the coefficient $R^2$ is used. To confirm the findings, the heterotrait–monotrait ratio of correlations is also calculated (Henseler et al., 2015). In addition, $f^2$ provides information on the relative effect of a variable (Chin, 1998). An $f^2$ value of 0.02, 0.15, and 0.35 indicates that an exogenous variable has a small, medium, or large influence, respectively, on an endogenous variable (Cohen, 1988). In addition, the Stone–Geisser criterion is used to assess the model's predictive relevance, $Q^2$ (Geisser, 1974; Stone, 1974). A $Q^2$ value higher than 0 indicates that the model has predictive relevance.

## 11.5 Construct and item measurement

To measure the latent constructs, we referred to the previous literature and adjusted our context using Likert scales. The questions from the German questionnaire, retranslated into English, can be found in the Appendix. The scale ranged from 'totally disagree' to 'totally agree'.

To measure procurement uncertainty, we used the items from Ponomarov (2012), who refers to it as environmental uncertainty and who adapted the items from Fynes et al. (2004), Chen and Paulraj (2004), and Slater and Narver (1994). To measure industrial symbiosis, this work fully refers to the items used in Liu et al. (2022) building on Vachon and Klassen (2008). The items on procurement acceleration and on order speed have been developed by the authors. This is due to the specific procurement acceleration initiatives that took place in German defence procurement in the wake of the 'Zeitenwende'. Pre-test indicated that items are comprehensive, respondents understand them, and they are consistent. This is why we used them in the survey. Finally, business performance is measured by three items. This follows loosely the findings that business performance is a complex and multi-dimensional construct (Venkatraman & Ramanujam, 1986). As outlined by Abdallah and Ghwayeen (2020), many studies refer business performance to measures for profitability, market share, sales, growth, and customer satisfaction or loyalty, but also market share and competitive position are indicators. In this study, business performance is referred to indicators on the competitive position, sales (expectations), and order backlog/order pipeline.

## 11.6 Findings

After variable measurement, several validity tests were performed. The values for the assessment of the reflective measurement are shown in Table 11.2. Convergent validity is used to identify the extent to which a single measure variable correlates positively with alternative measures of the same construct. Items had to be retained if they did not meet factor sufficient loading thresholds (e.g. PUN3, PUN4, SPE4, SPE5, INDSYMB1, FUSIT3). Item loadings of the final model are sufficiently high (>0.7). In one case (PUN5), the value is slightly below threshold, but we retained the reflective indicator, because a deletion does not increase measures above threshold (Hair et al., 2021). In addition, the AVE measures convergent validity on the construct level with the criteria of 0.50 or higher. The AVE values ranged from 0.629 to 0.790. Internal consistency reliability refers to a form of reliability used to determine the consistency of results across items on the same test. PLS uses composite reliability for this criterion. Composite reliability values over 0.6 are acceptable. The composite reliability values satisfy these thresholds.

Next, the discriminant validity is examined; this is used to measure the extent to which a construct is distinct from other constructs in two ways. As recommended by Fornell and Larcker (1981), the square root of the AVE for each construct should be greater than its highest correlation with any other construct. This is the case for the analysis of this research. In addition, we checked the cross-loadings of the measurement variables. The indicator's cross-outer-loadings are higher than all its cross-loadings. Besides, the variance inflation factor values for all the constructs range from 1.000 to 1.014, which does not point to multicollinearity. Furthermore

*Table 11.2* Measurement parameters of multi-item constructs

| *Construct* | *Item* | *Loading* | *Convergent validity, average variance extracted (AVE)* | *Internal consistency* / *Composite reliability* |
|---|---|---|---|---|
| *Critical values* | | *>0.7* | *>0.5* | *>0.6* |
| Procurement uncertainty | | | 0.629 | 0.834 |
| | PUN1 | 0.783 | | |
| | PUN2 | 0.887 | | |
| | PUN5 | 0.697 | | |
| Procurement acceleration | | | 0.683 | 0.865 |
| | SPE1 | 0.895 | | |
| | SPE2 | 0.857 | | |
| | SPE3 | 0.716 | | |
| Industrial symbiosis | | | 0.790 | 0.919 |
| | INDSYMB2 | 0.882 | | |
| | INDSYMB3 | 0.912 | | |
| | INDSYMB4 | 0.872 | | |
| Order speed | | | 0.695 | 0.820 |
| | SPEPERF1 | 0.788 | | |
| | SPEPERF2 | 0.877 | | |
| Business performance | | | 0.778 | 0.875 |
| | FuSit1 | 0.915 | | |
| | FuSit2 | 0.849 | | |

*Source:* Own compilation.

heterotrait–monotrait ratio is below the critical value of 0.85 with the highest value of 0.664.

## 11.7 Structural model findings

Figure 11.2 depicts the structural model tested by the PLS analysis and Tables 11.3 and 11.4 display the findings in detail. The results, referring to H1, indicate that procurement uncertainty is negatively associated with industrial symbiosis. This means that the more/less uncertain the procurement situation is, the less/more symbiotic industrial collaboration takes place. H1 cannot be rejected. There is an opposed significant relationship with a weak effect size (–0.274, $p = 0.006$, $f^2 = 0.081$). For H2, it could be stated that it is no surprise that this hypothesis cannot be rejected. The procurement acceleration efforts have positive influence on order speed and effect size is medium (0.445, $p = 0.000$, $f^2 = 0.247$). It has been also assumed that order speed would have a positive effect on industrial symbiosis in H3, but this hypothesis must be rejected (0.077, $p = 0.304$, $f^2 = 0.006$).

Referring on the antecedents for business performance, H4 cannot be rejected. Industrial symbiosis is significant with a weak effect size on business performance

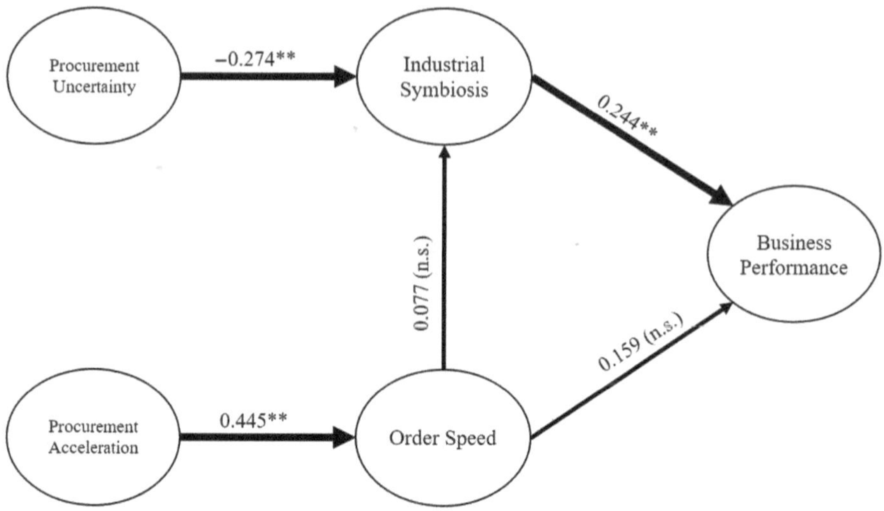


Note: * = p < 0.05; ** = p < 0.01; n.s. = not significant

*Figure 11.2* Results depicted in the research model.

*Source:* Own compilation.

*Table 11.3* Predictive relevance

| *Construct* | $R^2$ | $Q^2$ | *Order speed* $f^2$ | *Industrial symbiosis* $f^2$ | *Business performance* $f^2$ |
|---|---|---|---|---|---|
| Procurement uncertainty | | | | 0.081 | |
| Procurement acceleration | | | 0.247 | | |
| Industrial symbiosis | 0.086 | 0.038 | | | 0.065 |
| Order speed | 0.198 | 0.176 | | 0.006 | 0.027 |
| Business performance | 0.093 | 0.034 | | | |

*Source:* Own compilation.

(0.244, $p = 0.004$, $f^2 = 0.065$). In contrast, order speed is not significantly effecting business performance at the 0.05 threshold and H5 is rejected (0.159, $p = 0.054$, $f^2 = 0.027$). However, it is recognized that a looser threshold of $p < 0.1$ would allow to not reject H5.

Overall, the $R^2$ for order speed ($R^2 = 0.198$; $Q^2 = 0.176$), industrial symbiosis ($R^2 = 0.086$; $Q^2 = 0.038$), and for business performance ($R^2 = 0.093$; $Q^2 = 0.034$) indicate that the model has weak to moderate explanatory power (Cohen, 1988).

*Table 11.4* Results of the path coefficient

| *Path* | *Coefficient* | *Standard error* | *t-value* | *p-value* |
|---|---|---|---|---|
| Procurement uncertainty → Industrial symbiosis | –0.274 | 0.100 | 2.740 | 0.006 |
| Procurement acceleration → Order speed | 0.445 | 0.058 | 7.688 | 0.000 |
| Order speed → Industrial symbiosis | 0.077 | 0.075 | 1.028 | 0.304 |
| Order speed → Business performance | 0.159 | 0.082 | 2.790 | 0.054 |
| Industrial symbiosis → Business performance | 0.244 | 0.087 | 2.902 | 0.004 |

*Source:* Own compilation.

## 11.8 Discussion and conclusions

The results of the analysis are partly in line with the proposed hypotheses, but also some of them had to be rejected. This is of value to develop future theory on the topic and deserves a closer look on both factors and causal chains (uncertainty–symbiosis) and (acceleration–speed).

On a first glance, it seems as if both factors contribute to an industrial echo on changed procurement conditions that improves business performance of the defence industry. As stated earlier, the 'combination assumption' is based on this integration of speed and symbiosis. Following H1, a high level of uncertainty effects a closer and symbiotic collaboration, while a low level of uncertainty calls for looser and maybe more competitive relationship between procurement and industry. This is supported and is plausible. The same is true for H2. Accelerating initiatives are perceived as effective, as these effect positively the speed of orders to the defence industry. To be honest, the support of H2 is by far no surprise.

But data also shows that order speed does not contribute to military–industrial collaboration in terms of industrial symbiosis (H3) and even worse, it does not significantly (at the 0.05 threshold) effect business performance (H5). Only collaboration is able to effect business performance positively and in a significant way. How can this be interpreted?

One attempt is to see faster orders not only as a benefit for the industry but also as advanced consumption of latter sales. Very fast orders also cause a lot of capacity and resource challenges to fulfil the orders. So acceleration is maybe even a factor that positively effects procurement uncertainty, even if it has not been investigated in that way in this research. In this sense, speed is effective with respect to faster orders, but the outcome is not (significantly) related due to hidden or time-delayed drawbacks of acceleration.

As a result, the basic assumption of a combined approach seems not to be true – instead, results show two separate paths for effects on the defence supply chain: One is related to relational collaboration, the other is related to acceleration (only). This does not mean that supply chains should be steered in different ways (going in line with what Choi and Hartley (1996) reported for the automotive industry) – in contrast, the uncertainties of our times ('Zeitenwende') require a closer and more symbiotic decision-making and execution of defence supply tasks. This is a joint, collaborative task. A more collaborative approach bears potential not only on the short-run but it also effects the long-term business performance. In contrast to the 'straw fire' of order speed, industrial symbiosis is a potential contribution to substantially improve defence acquisition situation for procurement and defence industry.

As such industrial symbiosis is a construct that deserves future research to better understand its cause–effects. Furthermore, it is called for a theoretical foundation of industrial symbiosis in supply management in general.

Of course, this study like any other empirical analysis faces several limitations. We see two major limitations: Sample size is high for defence sector analysis, but generally relatively small. Future research could broaden its empirical basis, also to allow the application of different structural equation model instruments (e.g. covariance-based methods). This may include broadening the scope from single key informant per company to multiple informants. Next, we see limitations in the survey situation, as the 'Zeitenwende' is a very dynamic and challenging time for defence. Perceptions may change very quickly, as the situation in Ukraine and in the world also changes in a very dynamic way. Future research should address the topic again to check for situational bias.

## Acknowledgements

This research is part of the Wehrökonomisches Kompetenzzentrum (research center) Defence Acquisition and Supply Management (DASM), supported and funded by the Bundeswehr.

## Notes

1 List is of course only an indicator for a number of heterogenous and recent risks that have an impact on today's risk management.
2 In German: Gesetz zur Beschleunigung von Beschaffungsmaßnahmen für die Bundeswehr, Bundeswehrbeschaffungsbeschleunigungsgesetz.
3 Please see www.unipark.com/.
4 In German: Deutsche Gesellschaft für Wehrtechnik e.V.

## References

Abdallah, A.B. and Al-Ghwayeen, W. S. (2020), 'Green Supply Chain Management and Business Performance: The Mediating Roles of Environmental and Operational Performances', *Business Process Management Journal*, 26(2), pp. 489–512.

Ädel, M., Johnson, A., and Junerfält, T. (2022), *Dealing with Defence-Specific Purchasing Power. A Discussion and Further Development on Current Methodology*, Swedish Defence Research Agency (FOI), Stockholm (Defence Economic Outlook, FOI-R--5209--SE).

Arena, M.V. (2006), *Why Has the Cost of Navy Ships Risen? A Macroscopic Examination of the Trends in U.S. Naval ship Costs Over the Past Several Decades*, RAND National Defense Research Institute, Santa Monica CA.

Armstrong, J.S. and Overton, T.S. (1977), 'Estimating Nonresponse Bias in Mail Surveys', *Journal of Marketing Research*, 14(3), pp. 396–402.

BMVg (2014), *Umfassende Bestandsaufnahme und Risikoanalyse zentraler Rüstungsprojekte*. Available at www.bmvg.de/resource/blob/11644/d5cdd057b87a9a9f84dadeaa72d4ae59/c-06-10-14-download-expertenbericht-zu-ruestungsprojekten-uebergeben-data.pdf [Accessed 5 May 2023].

Brzoska, M. (2023), *It's Not the Money, Stupid! Die Hauptprobleme im Beschaffungswesen der Bundeswehr*. Available at www.greenpeace.de/publikationen/S04011-greenpeace-studie-frieden-beschaffungswesen-bundeswehr.pdf [Accessed 3 May 2023].

Bundesministerium der Verteidigung (2022), '16. Bericht des Bundesministeriums der Verteidigung zu Rüstungsangelegenheiten', *Teil*, 1, Berlin.

Carter, C. R., Meschnig, G., and Kaufmann, L. (2015), 'Moving to the Next Level: Why Our Discipline Needs More Multilevel Theorization', *Journal of Supply Chain Management*, 51(4), pp. 94–102.

Chen, I. J., and Paulraj, A. (2004), 'Towards a Theory of Supply Chain Management: The Constructs and Measurements', *Journal of Operations Management*, 22(2), pp. 119–150.

Chin, W.W. (1998), 'The Partial Least Squares Approach to Structural Equation Modeling', in: Marcoulides, G.A. (ed.), *Modern Methods for Business Research*, Erlbaum, Mahwah, pp. 295–358.

Chin, W.W. (2010), 'How to write up and report PLS analyses', in: Esposito, V.V., Chin, W.W., Henseler, J. and Wang, H. (eds.), *Handbook of Partial Least Squares: Concepts, Methods, and Applications*, Springer, Heidelberg, pp. 655–690.

Chin, W.W. and Newsted, P.R. (1999), 'Structural Equation Modeling Analysis with Small Samples Using Partial Least Squares', in: Hoyle, R.H. (ed.), *Statistical Strategies for Small Sample Research*, Sage, Thousand Oaks, CA, pp. 307–341.

Choi, T.Y. and Hartley, J.L. (1996), 'An Exploration of Supplier Selection Practices Across the Supply Chain.' *Journal of Operations Management*, 14(4), pp. 333–343.

Cohen, J. (1988), *Statistical Power Analysis for the Behavioral Sciences*, 2nd edition, Routledge, New York.

Deutschlandfunk (2023), *Atzpodien: 'Die Produktion ist nicht langsam'*, May, Philipp | 14 February 2023. Available at www.deutschlandfunk.de/ruestungsindustrie-woran-hapert-es-interview-mit-hans-christoph-atzpodien-bdsv-dlf-1e9cd375-100.html [Accessed 4 May 2023].

Downey, H. K. and Slocum, J. W. (1975), 'Uncertainty: Measures, Research and Sources of Variation'. *Administrative Science Quarterly*, 18, pp. 562–577.

Ekström, T. (2010), *The Transformation from Defence Procurement to Defence Acquisition. Opportunities for New Forms of Analytical Support*, North Atlantic Treaty Organization (NATO). Sofia, Bulgaria, 26–28 April 2010.

Ekström, T., Hilletofth, P., and Skoglund, P. (2020), 'Differentiation Strategies for Defence Supply Chain Design', *Journal of Defense Analytics and Logistics*, 4(2), pp. 183–202.

Eßig, M., Mohr, D., and Tandler, S. (2014), An Exposure-Capacity-Portfolio for Defense Supply Chains: The Case of the Military Airlifter A400M, in: *International Journal of Defense Acquisition Management*, 6, pp. 1–20.

European Commission (2006), The new SME Definition: User Guide and Model Declaration. Available at: https://op.europa.eu/en/publication-detail/-/publication/756d9260-ee54-11ea-991b-01aa75ed71a1 [Accessed 4 May 2023].

Ferdows, K. and de Meyer, A. (1990), 'Lasting Improvements in Manufacturing Performance: In Search of a New Theory', *Journal of Operations Management*, 9(2), pp. 168–184.

Flynn, B.B., Koufteros, X., and Lu, G. (2016), 'On Theory in Supply Chain Uncertainty and its Implications for Supply Chain Integration', *Journal of Supply Chain Management*, 52(3), pp. 3–27.

Fornell, C. and Larcker, D. (1981), 'Evaluating Structural Equation Models with Unobservable Variables and Measurement Error', *Journal of Marketing Research*, 18(1), pp. 35–90.

Fynes, B., De Burca, S., and Marshall, D. (2004), 'Environmental Uncertainty, Supply Chain Relationship Quality and Performance', *Journal of Purchasing and Supply Management*, 10(4-5), pp. 179–190.

Geisser, S. (1974), 'A Predictive Approach to the Random Effects Model', *Biometrika*, 61(1), pp. 101–107.

Girardi, B., Patrahau, I., Cisco, G., and Rademaker, M. (2023), Strategic Raw Materials for Defence, in: *Mapping European Industry Needs*. Hague Centre for Strategic Studies (HCSS), Hague.

Glas, A.H. and Eßig, M. (2017), Building a Conceptual Framework for Defense Acquisition Management Based on Service Dominant Logic Theory, in: Kevin Burgess und Peter Antill (eds.), *Emerging Strategies in Defense Acquisitions and Military Procurement*. IGI Global (Advances in Public Policy and Administration), Hershey, pp. 93–108.

Glas, A.H. (2017), Preferential Treatment from the Defense Industry for the Military, *Journal of Defense Analytics and Logistics*, 1(2), pp. 96–119.

Glas, A.H. and Schnell, J. (2023), *Ressourcenmanagement in Streitkräften, Eine Einführung in das Streitkräftemanagement*, SpringerGabler, Wiesbaden.

Götz, O., Liehr-Gobbers, K. and Krafft, M. (2010), Evaluation of structural equation models using the Partial Least Squares (PLS) approach, in: Eposito, V.V., Chin, W.W., Henseler, J. and Wang, H. (eds.), *Handbook of Partial Least Squares: Concepts, Methods, and Applications*, Springer, Heidelberg, pp. 691–711.

Gürtlich, G.H. and Lampl, S. (2022), Resilience and Military Supply Chain Management, in: Kummer, S., Wakolbinger, T., Novoszel, L. und Geske, A. M. (eds.), *Supply Chain Resilience. Insights from Theory and Practice*, Springer (Springer Series in Supply Chain Management, Cham, 17, pp. 337–352.

Hague, R., Dickens, P., and Hopkinson, N. (eds.) (2006), *Rapid Manufacturing: An Industrial Revolution for the Digital Age*, John Wiley & Sons, New York, USA.

Hair Jr., J. F., Hult, G. T. M., Ringle, C. M., and Sarstedt, M. (2021), *A Primer on Partial Least Squares Structural Equation Modeling (PLS-SEM)*, Sage Publications. 3rd Edition, Los Angeles, USA.

Hendrick, T. E. (1994), *Purchasing's Contributions to Time-Based Strategies*. Center for Advanced Purchasing Studies (CAPS), Tempe, Arizona.

Henseler, J., Ringle, C.M. and Sinkovics, R.R. (2009), The Use of Partial Least Squares Path Modeling in International Marketing, in: Sinkovics, R.R. and Ghauri, P.N. (eds), *New Challenges to International Marketing*, Emerald Group Publishing Limited, Leeds, UK, pp. 277–319.

Henseler, J., Ringle, C.M. and Sarstedt, M. (2015), 'A New Criterion for Assessing Discriminant Validity in Variance-Based Structural Equation Modeling', *Journal of the Academy of Marketing Science*, 43(1), pp. 115–135.

Hoffmann, P., Schiele, H., and Krabbendam, K. (2013), 'Uncertainty, Supply Risk Management and Their Impact on Performance'. *Journal of purchasing and supply management*, 19(3), pp. 199–211.

Holst, E. and Wiemer, A. (2010), *On the Underrepresentation of Women in Top Boards of Large Companies, DIW Berlin Discussion Paper No. 1001*,

Koufteros, X. A., Nahm, A., Cheng, T. C. E., and Lai, K.- H. (2007), An Empirical Assessment of a Nomo- Logical Network of organizational Design Constructs: From Culture to Structure to Pull Production to Performance, *International Journal of Production Economics*, 106(2), pp. 468–491.

Lawrence, P. R., and Lorsch, J. W. (1967), 'Differentiation and Integration in Complex Organizations'. *Administrative Science Quarterly*, 12(1), pp. 1–47.

Leuschner, R., Rogers, D. S., and Charvet, F. F. (2013), 'A meta-analysis of supply chain integration and firm performance', *Journal of Supply Chain Management*, 49(2), pp. 34–57.

Liu, Y., Cheng, P., and Hu, L. (2022), 'How Do Justice and Top Management Beliefs Matter in Industrial Symbiosis Collaboration: An Exploratory Study from China', *Journal of Industrial Ecology*, 26(3), pp. 891–906.

Lombardi, D.R., Laybourn, P., (2012), Redefining Industrial Symbiosis: Crossing Academic-Practitioner Boundaries', *Journal of Industrial Ecology*, 16, pp. 28–37.

Lorentz, H., Laari, S., Meehan, J., Eßig, M. and Henke, M. (2021), An Attention-Based View of Supply Disruption Risk Management: Balancing Biased Attentional Processing for Improved Resilience in the COVID-19 Context, *International Journal of Operations and Production Management*, 41(13), pp. 152–177.

Major, C. and Mölling, C. (2023), Zum Zaudern keine Zeit, in: *Internationale Politik Special Rührt Euch! Deutschland und die Zeitenwende*, 2023(2).

Mahmoud-Jouini, S. B., Midler, C., and Garel, G. (2004), 'Time-to-Market vs. Time-to-Delivery: Managing Speed in Engineering, Procurement and Construction projects', *International Journal of Project Management*, 22(5), pp. 359–367.

Meyer, M., Glas, A.H., and Eßig, M. (2022), 'Using Additive Manufacturing in Supply Chains: A Simulation-Based Analysis of Supply Resilience', *International Journal of Integrated Supply Management*, 15(3), pp. 304–328,

Slater, S. F. and Narver, J. C. (1994), Does Competitive Environment Moderate the Market Orientation-Performance Relationship?', *Journal of Marketing*, 58(1), pp. 46–55.

Patton, M. (1990), *Qualitative Evaluation and Research Methods*, 2nd edition, Sage, Beverly Hills, CA.

Penrose, E. T. (1952), 'Biological Analogies in the Theory of the Firm', *American Economic Review*, 42(5), pp. 804–819.

Picot, A. (1993), 'Contingencies of the Emergence of Efficient Symbiotic Arrangements', *Journal of Institutional and Theoretical Economics*, 149(4), pp. 731–740.

Ponomarov, S. (2012), *Antecedents and Consequences of Supply Chain Resilience: A Dynamic Capabilities Perspective*. Dissertation. Available at https://trace.tennessee.edu/cgi/viewcontent.cgi?article=2526&context=utk_graddiss [Accessed 2 May 2023].

Prier, E., McCue, C. and Csaki, C. (2020). 'Evaluating Decision Speed as a Measure of Public Procurement Performance in the European Single Market', *International Journal of Public Administration*, 44(13), pp. 1065–1075.

Raub, W., and Weesie, J. (1993). 'Symbiotic Arrangements: A Sociological Perspective', *Journal of Institutional and Theoretical Economics*, 149(4), pp. 716–724.

Ringle, C. M., Wende, S., and Becker, J.-M. (2022), *SmartPLS 4.0*. Oststeinbek: SmartPLS. Retrieved from www.smartpls.com.

Reinartz, W.J., Haenlein, M. and Henseler, J. (2009), 'An Empirical Comparison of the Efficacy of Covariance-Based and Variance-Based SEM', *International Journal of Research in Marketing*, 26(4), pp. 332–344.

Schanze, E. (1993), 'Symbiotic Arrangements', *Journal of Institutional and Theoretical Economics*, 149(4), pp. 691–697.

Schwarz, E.J., Steininger, K.W. (1997), 'Implementing Nature's Lesson: The Industrial Recycling Network Enhancing Regional Development', *Journal of Cleaner Production*, 5, pp. 47–56

Shenas, D. G. and Derakhshan, S. (1994), '*Organizational Approaches to the Implementation of Simultaneous Engineering*', *International Journal of Operations and Production Management*, 14(10), pp. 30–43.

Skynews (2023), *Senior Tory Tobias Ellwood Admits British Army is in 'Dire State' after US general's Criticism of UK Forces*. Available at https://news.sky.com/story/senior-tory-tobias-ellwood-admits-british-army-is-in-dire-state-after-us-generals-criticism-of-uk-forces-12799032 [Accessed 30 January 2023].

Spindler, G. (1993), 'Symbiotic Contracts and Corporate Groups', *Journal of Institutional and Theoretical Economics*, 149(4), pp. 756–761.

Stern (2023). *Ukraine-krieg-offenbart-gnadenlos-defizite-westeuropaeischer-Armeen*. Available at www.stern.de/politik/ausland/ukraine-krieg-offenbartgnadenlos-defizite-westeuropaeischer-armeen-33188002.html [Accessed 23 March 2023].

Spiegel.de (2022). *Bundeswehr steht aus Sicht von Heeresinspekteur »mehr oder weniger blank da«*, Available at www.spiegel.de/politik/deutschland/ukraine-invasion-bundeswehr-steht-laut-heeresinspekteur-mehr-oder-weniger-blank-da-a-e5bdc1f4-e9d3-472f-9ed7-beed5aa02eb0 [Accessed 24 February 2022].

Swaminathan, J.M. and Lee, H.L. (2003), 'Design for postponement', in: *Handbooks in Operations Research and Management Science, Supply Chain Management: Design, Coordination and Operation*, Vol. 11, pp. 199–226.

Tatham, P. (2013), 'An exploration of trust and shared values in UK Defence Supply Networks', *International Journal of Physical Distribution and Logistics Management*, 43(2), pp. 148–166.

Vachon, S. and Klassen, R. D. (2008), 'Environmental management and manufacturing performance: The role of collaboration in the supply chain', *International Journal of Production Economics*, 111(2), pp. 299–315

Venkatraman, N. and Ramanujam, V. (1986), 'Measurement of business performance in strategy research: A comparison of approaches', *Academy of Management Review*, 11(4), pp. 801–814.

Wong, C. W. Y., Lai, K. H., and Benroidey, E. W. N. (2015), 'The performance of contingencies of supply chain integration: The roles of product and market complexity', *International Journal of Production Economics*, 165, pp. 1–11.

Wright, E. (ed.) (2010), *Defense Acquisition Management. A Reader*, iUniverse, New York.

## Appendix

*Table 11A.1* Constructs and measurement

| *Construct/Item* | *Item text* | *Source* |
|---|---|---|
| *Procurement uncertainty* | | |
| PUN1 | Demand fluctuates drastically. | *Ponomarov (2012), Fynes et al. (2004), Chen and Paulraj (2004), Slater and Narver (1994)* |
| PUN2 | Requirements vary drastically. | |
| PUN3 | Supplier quality is not stable. | |
| PUN4 | Our sub-suppliers change often. | |
| PUN5 | Technology is changing rapidly. | |
| PUN6 | Innovation provides big opportunities in our industry. | |

*Table 11A.1* (Continued)

| *Construct/Item* | *Item text* | *Source* |
|---|---|---|
| *Industrial symbiosis*[a] | | |
| INDSYMB1 | We achieve goals collectively. | *Liu et al. (2022), Vachon and Klassen (2008)* |
| INDSYMB2 | We are working together to increase the impact of our activities. | |
| INDSYMB3 | We conduct joint planning to anticipate and resolve problems. | |
| INDSYMB4 | We make joint decisions about ways to increase outcomes of our products. | |
| *Procurement acceleration*[b] | | |
| SPE1 | Ease use of exemption rules for lot size tendering speeds up defence acquisition. | *Items follow the defence procurement acceleration initiative in Germany in 2022.* |
| SPE2 | Ease use of joint European armament speeds up defence acquisition. | |
| SPE3 | Ability to exclude competitors speeds up defence acquisition. | |
| SPE4 | Lowering sue/claim abilities speeds up defence acquisition. | |
| SPE5 | Focusing on market-available products speeds up defence acquisition. | |
| *Order speed*[b] | | |
| SPEPERF1 | Acceleration instruments already effect tenders in which my firm participated. | *Generally following* |
| SPEPERF2 | Order time in defence procurement is becoming faster. | |
| *Business performance*[b] | | |
| FuSit1 | The competitive position will develop to the better. | *Venkatraman and Ramanujam (1986)* |
| FuSti2 | My expectation is that business will improve in the future. | |
| FuSit3 | My order backlog has increased already. | |

*Source:* Own compilation.

*Notes:*

[a] Measured with a seven-point scale ranging from 1 'totally disagree' to 6 'totally agree'.

[b] Six-point scale ranging from 1 'totally disagree' to 7 'totally agree'. + Inverse/reverse code measurement.

# 12 Lessons from the United States' Articles of Confederation

*Daniel E. Schoeni and Christopher R. Yukins*

## 12.1 Introduction

Defence procurement by EU Member States has the potential to purchase arms that would make the EU, taken together, a formidable fighting force. Collectively, the Member States maintain 1.3 million active-duty soldiers, constituting the fourth largest force in the world, on par with the United States' 1.4 million (Herr & Speer, 2022; Statista, 2023),[1] and even before the Ukraine War (*SIPRI*),[2] the EU Member States' defence outlay was an impressive $225 billion (Herr & Speer, 2022). Yet this money is spent ineffectively. The twin evils of protectionism and fragmentation diminish the Member States' aggregate capacity. As a recent article in the *Washington Post* explained,

> the planning, development and procurement of defense technology by 27 sovereign countries has produced an enormous amount of inefficiency. While the U.S. military uses just 30 weapons systems, the EU's militaries use some 180, six times as many. While the U.S. armed forces use just one main battle tank, the E.U. fields – depending how you count – 11 to 17 different models.
>
> (Herr & Speer, 2022)

For those conversant with defence policy and defence procurement by the EU Member States, these problems are familiar (Sandler & Hartley, 1999; *UNISYS*, 2005; Staples, 2013). Commenting on these facts, then-European Commission President Jean-Claude Juncker said, 'We are spending half of the American budget when it comes to defense, so we should be efficient at 50 percent of the U.S. We are only 15 percent as efficient.' (Herr & Speer, 2022).

It is also clear to anyone who has given these problems much thought that the source of these problems lies neither with the Defence Directive (2009) nor with its procurement regime more broadly, but rather with the EU's very structure. We would submit that these challenges are not technocratic in nature; merely tweaking the next version of the Defence Directive will not solve these problems. The problems that beset European defence procurement are more fundamental; addressing them properly would seem to require deeper constitutional reforms.

DOI: 10.4324/9781032631721-17

In a speech at the University of Zurich in September 1946, only a year after the end of World War II, Winston Churchill looked optimistically towards a 'United States of Europe':

> … [T]here is a remedy which, if it were generally and spontaneously adopted by the great majority of people in many lands, would as by a miracle transform the whole scene and would in a few years make all Europe, or the greater part of it, as free and happy as Switzerland is today. What is this sovereign remedy? It is to recreate the European family, or as much of it as we can, and to provide it with a structure under which it can dwell in peace, safety and freedom. We must build a kind of United States of Europe. In this way only will hundreds of millions of toilers be able to regain the simple joys and hopes which make life worth living. The process is simple. All that is needed is the resolve of hundreds of millions of men and women to do right instead of wrong and to gain as their reward blessing instead of cursing.
>
> (Churchill, 1946)

We should stress, however, that for our part we are not arguing for a constitutional reordering in the EU, in defence or otherwise. The EU's current structures regarding defence, procurement, and the procurement of defence materiel reflect a delicate political, social, and economic balance between Member State autonomy and a tightly bound union, shaped in deep and complex ways by history, political compromise, and a common purpose (Trybus, 1999; Arrowsmith, 2005; Judt, 2005; Kershaw, 2015). What we instead want to share – with apologies for the inevitable oversimplification – are insights from our own history in the United States, when 13 states first sought security by banding together under a loose federation. As we will explain, that initial constitutional experiment disappointed. America's first government was established in order to ensure the 'common defence' (U.S. Articles of Confederation, articles III, VII, and VIII) and in this regard it proved a signal failure. Common security came only when the loosely confederated states were willing to form a closer union under a stronger federal government. Only when mortal threats imperilled the young republic did the states coalesce under the banner of the current constitution. Although a similarly 'federal' Europe may never come together – or at least not in our lifetimes – lessons (good and bad) from the United States' progression to a closer union may prove useful as the EU reassesses how defence procurement is accomplished within the EU's current structure – and how it may be improved.[3]

This chapter proceeds in three parts. First, we argue that a procurement system's broader environment (external matters) may affect its operation as much as or more than its particular rules and regulations (internal matters). Second, we describe the broader environment within which the defence procurement systems (both in the Member States and in the EU itself) function. Finally, we contrast the broader environment in which the U.S. defence procurement system operates – paying special attention to the contrast between America's first and second constitutions, the reasons for which the framers radically changed the U.S. constitutional order, and how all of this bears on defence procurement (both in the EU and in the United States) down to the present.

Before proceeding, we want to make clear that we are mindful of the hazards of the particular comparison we are attempting. The systemic and institutional differences between the United States and EU are extensive, and they may render comparisons complicated if not meaningless (Stein, 1985). For foreign and defence policy, such differences are especially acute (Stein, 1985). We thus proceed with caution. We also acknowledge that the transferability of lessons from the United States may be limited. Nevertheless, we still consider this effort worthwhile.

## 12.2 A Procurement System's Broader Environment

To govern is to choose (Tiersky, 2003),[4] and a similar truism applies to policy choices about the functioning and purpose of a public procurement system. Each system must choose between mutually exclusive desiderata, or 'competing aspirations' (Schooner, 2003). These may include transparency, integrity, competition, efficiency, value for money, customer satisfaction, wealth redistribution, risk avoidance uniformity, and sustainability (Schooner, 2003). Numerous choices must also be made about the how a procurement system will function in furtherance of such goals.[5] But perhaps more important than the nature and make-up of the procurement system itself is the broader legal environment in which it operates. Other elements – social, economic, and historical, for example – may buffet and mark a procurement system, but because the law binds and directs most modern procurement systems from within and without, the legal environment that envelops a procurement system plays perhaps the most decisive role in shaping it (Nash et al., 2023, ch. 16).[6]

We are not the first to observe that procurement systems function within the context of a broader legal environment. Considering procurement systems from a trade perspective, Sue Arrowsmith has argued that such differences in the legal landscape can inadvertently create non-tariff barriers, discouraging foreign suppliers from bidding (Arrowsmith, 2003).[7] Others would agree that unfamiliarity with local legal regimes reduces participation by foreign suppliers (Reich, 1999; Woolcock & Grier, 2015).[8] Still others have written about the effect of the broader environment on the functioning of a procurement system, irrespective of trade (Mashaw, 1991).[9]

For defence procurement, which typically inherits the debates born of the broader procurement and administrative regimes, tension often arises between goals of competition, trade, and economic efficiency on the one side and security goals on the other (Walker & Willett, 1993; Anderton, 1995; Miller, 2009).[10] Free traders favour open markets, even at the expense of military readiness (Savas, 1999)[11]; security hawks favour sacrificing market liberalism to ensure key goods and services (not to mention native industrial capacity) are available domestically, so that a nation does not become too dependent on potential adversaries for such war materiel (Trybus, 2014). Even Adam Smith, the father of modern economics, warned that a nation should not become too dependent on foreign powers for sail cloth, gunpowder, and the like – sound advice on the eve of the Napoleonic wars (Smith, 1776).[12] Though there is a well-known tendency to overstate security needs (Trepte, 2007; Trybus, 2014),[13] the need for some self-sufficiency in defence is surely understandable – and arguably inherent in a procurement regime designed to protect a nation (Trybus, 2014). Defence procurement after all constitutes an integral part of any coherent, full-spectrum defence strategy (Trybus, 2013).

That basic insight – that a defence procurement regime must be focused first on security – carries special meaning for the Member States of the EU, for theirs is in practical terms a collective security. As Aris Georgopoulos has argued with respect to the EU's common defence and security policy, a coordinated defence procurement policy is the sine qua non (Georgopoulos, 2007). That is because, however well generaled or manned, without adequate logistics and support driven by a robust and efficient procurement system, a nation's defence – and by logical extension, the EU's collective defence – risks losing both deterrent and defensive effect.

At the same time, a procurement system's goals and objectives are also determined by its internal laws and regulations. For example, the introduction to the U.S. Federal Acquisition Regulation (FAR)[14] states in simple terms what its goals are – to deliver best value, retain public trust and meet the United States' policy objectives (FAR 1.102). The FAR explains: 'The vision for the Federal Acquisition System is to deliver on a timely basis the best value product or service to the customer, while maintaining the public's trust and fulfilling public policy objectives.' Its signal purposes are to satisfy customers to minimize costs to do business with integrity, fairness, and openness and to fulfil other policy objectives (ibid.).

In like manner, the EU's 2014 Public Procurement Directive's 137 recitals state a series of goals and objectives for Member States' procurement systems, ones grounded perhaps more in European integration goals than in optimal procurement outcomes (Directive 2014/24/EU).[15]

Such internal laws, rules, and regulations are not, however, the only source of a procurement system's administration. A procurement system, as noted, does not operate in isolation but rather functions within a larger political and legal environment. Thus, without further argument, we will proceed under a basic assumption about defence procurement and public procurement law generally – namely, that they operate within a legal and constitutional environment and this external environment is sometimes more important than the internal rules and regulations that govern a procurement system.

## 12.3 The EU's Constitutional Order and Defence Procurement Challenges

One of the single most significant distinctions between the U.S. federal and the EU public procurement systems is their treatment of defence procurement. Yet this variance arises not because of dissimilar internal laws and regulations that govern these two procurement systems but due to the fundamental divide between their external legal, political, and constitutional environments. Whereas the United States is a conventional federal system, the EU constitutes a system that is like no other; it 'is neither a simple free trade area nor a federal community' but 'an original construction with no equivalent in the world' (Verdeaux, 2006, p. 713).

This distinction at so fundamental a level makes comparisons between the two systems hard, whether one is considering just one feature of these two polities (such as their public procurement systems) or their broader characters. Some have argued that such comparisons are impossible, or at least ill advised (Young, 2018). We are wary of making legal or historical comparisons that are inapt or offering suggestions that may sound 'preachy' (to borrow from our own argot) to our European colleagues. Yet we cannot help noticing a parallel between the United States' political and constitutional history that seems apropos to the EU's current conundrum in defence procurement, lessons not from the United States' recent internal divisions but from an earlier time when unity reinforced – indeed, defined over a trajectory of several centuries – our nation's strength. Before turning to that parallel in the next section, we will offer a few words of introduction to the EU's defence procurement system and broader structure – observations of outsiders coloured, of course, by our shared experience as Americans.

From its humble beginning as the European Coal and Steel Community, the EU's primary purpose has been not to prepare for or to deter foreign aggression but to prevent the outbreak of war from within. As one of its architects declared, the EU was created to entangle the European economies such that war between the Member States was 'not merely unthinkable, but materially impossible' (Schuman, 1950). Eight decades later, this cardinal purpose still informs how the EU works.

The aspirational goal of a Common Security and Defence Policy (CSDP) was reinforced with the Maastricht Treaty in 1992 (for a timeline of the CSDP, see European Union). But little came of this policy until the Treaty of Lisbon came into force in 2009, which placed the CSDP on an equal footing with the EU's other three pillars (Koutrakos, 2015). Indeed, the Lisbon Treaty gave the CSDP a broad remit covering all areas of foreign policy. A fact sheet issued by the European Parliament provides a helpful summary:

> On the common security and defence policy (CSDP) … , the Treaty of Lisbon introduces a mutual defence clause which provides that all Member States are obliged to provide help to a Member State under attack. A solidarity clause provides that the Union and each of its Member States have to provide assistance by all possible means to a Member State affected by a human or natural catastrophe or by a terrorist attack. A 'permanent structured cooperation' is open to all Member States which commit themselves to taking part in European military equipment programmes and to providing combat units that are available for immediate action… .
>
> (European Parliament)

Principle, the CSDP lays the foundation for what one day may be a 'European Army' (Trybus, 2014).[16] In practice, however, the use of these authorities has been sparing (Koutrakos, 2015). To date, the mobilization in support of Ukraine has been the EU's most ambitious undertaking, and commentators have suggested that this EU-coordinated military effort constitutes a watershed moment for Europe (Moser, 2022). For example, Carolyn Moser writes,

> European States' reaction to the Russian invasion of Ukraine has triggered both constitutional and statutory reforms which fall into two categories: increased participation in multilateral cooperation forums and alliances (namely the EU's Common Security and Defence Policy and NATO) and increased financial investment and resource acquisition in defence. While diplomacy continues to be the European tool of choice for external action, the realization that security chiefly rests on military capability is profoundly impacting Europe's 'security and defence constitution,' that is the legal, institutional, and political arrangements governing security and defence across European States.
>
> (ibid)

Yet apart from these recent developments, progress towards a muscular CSDP has been modest. This is likely in part the result of insufficient authority, and in part the result of insufficient political will. Member States could unite under a stronger supranational or federal government, but they choose not to.[17] And closer cooperation on defence matters seems unlikely in the near term, in large part because of serious differences in approach among Member States (and their citizens) to the Russian invasion of Ukraine (Meng, 2023).

The nature of this legal, constitutional, and above all political environment has consequences for how defence procurement works within the EU. As noted, the problems with Member States' defence procurement are well documented (Trybus, 1999). The cause is simple, but the cure is hard. Member States (rightly) see defence as a critical vestige of their sovereignty and are thus loath to make concessions (Georgopoulos, 2007).[18] Indeed, there is an 'inherent tension' between Member States' sovereignty and the EU's fundamental purposes (Pourbaix, 2011).

Multiple initiatives have been undertaken to advance a common EU security strategy, resulting in 'institutional congestion' (Georgopoulos, 2007). These have seen only limited success. The fact remains that the EU cannot build a credible defence policy without establishing a coherent procurement strategy – the two go hand-in-hand. We submit that such coordinated defence procurement will prove impossible unless the EU forms a much closer union through constitutional or political change, or can otherwise leverage strategies to make defence procurement in the EU more efficient and effective.

It lies beyond the scope of this chapter either to explain in detail the environment in which Member States' defence procurement operates or to demonstrate the precise connection between the EU's constitutional order and these problems (Trybus, 2014). Nor will we chronicle the many EU initiatives to improve defence procurement, which (as with the root causes of failure in EU defence) have been addressed so ably by our European colleagues (see e.g. Trybus and White, 2014). Instead, we take it as a given that deep problems with EU defence procurement exist and that they are related at least in part to a broader external environment. We posit that whatever the precise cause, EU defence procurement remains too fragmented, production runs are too small, and self-defence is thus imperilled. And while the solution may not lie down the path trodden by the young American republic, whose founders were unsatisfied with the nation's first constitution and specifically its provision for common defence, the inspiration for a stronger, more cohesive EU defence procurement regime, however devised, may lie in the American example.

## 12.4 The First and Second U.S. Constitutions

In France, it is common to speak of the various democratic systems from 1789 down to the present as *republics* preceded by an ordinal number. For example, the current regime is the fifth republic spearheaded by Charles de Gaulle in 1958 (Brown et al., 2018). The United States' political organization could be classified in a similar fashion, with a 'first republic' that operated under the Articles of Confederation, which was instituted during the Revolutionary War in 1781 and lasted until 1789 when the current constitution was ratified.[19] It is this first regime that may provide a useful historical example of uniting under a tighter constitutional order – including a truly unified 'common security and defence policy' and a correspondingly unified defence procurement system.

In this discussion we are indebted to Yale Law's Akhil Reed Amar, whose recent book on U.S. constitutional history reshaped our understanding of both the Articles of Confederation and of America's ensuing 'second republic'. This section tracks not only Amar's book (Amar, 2021) itself but also a review of his book that one of us authored (Schoeni, 2023).[20]

During the American Revolutionary War, which spanned from 1775 to 1783, the 13 British colonies that rebelled against their colonial master operated first under the Continental Congress, which initially lacked a written constitution, and later coalesced into a loose federation under the U.S. Articles of Confederation in 1781. Amar's book breaks new ground by explaining the close connection between the Articles of Confederation and the Constitution of 1789 (Amar, 2021, pp. 162–165, 169–174). This connection, as articulated in the aforementioned review, was mostly about national security (Schoeni, 2023). Americans submitted to a strong federal government only after they had learned from hard experience that a weak central government could not protect them (Amar, 2021).

Ironically, one of the core reasons for the colonies-become-states to unite under the Articles of Confederation was for the national government to provide for the young republic's 'common defence'; in fact, as Amar is at pains to emphasize, the Articles use that phrase three times.[21] This, he argues, was the main reason that the Continental Congress was convened in the first place. The failure of the Articles of Confederation to provide effectively for the states' mutual defence explains the creation of the current constitutional order, which was redesigned to ensure national security 'above all else' (Amar, 2021, p. 536).

The decision to reorganize the U.S. government was not made hastily; lessons leading to this choice came in instalments over the course of a decade or more. Lessons came first to the veterans of the Revolutionary War (1775–1783), who learned firsthand that too much blood and treasure had been wasted and the war lengthened because of a weak central government that was incapable either of decisive action or of providing for the needs of its soldiers. Perhaps more than anyone else, George Washington appreciated the dangers of foreign aggression for a nation incapable of defending itself. The Constitutional Convention of 1787, therefore, met at his behest (Amar, 2021) and the 'fighting constitution' (Hughes, 1917)[22] that they commissioned answered his concerns as to the survival of the young republic.

Further lessons came after the war, when a series of embarrassing military and geostrategic setbacks endangered American peace and safety. First, the nation's founders feared the hegemons of their day (England, France, and Spain) who sought either to limit the nation's westward expansion or, if possible, to retake their territories. Second and relatedly, they feared coalitions forming between European powers and Native Americans (Amar, 2021). Third, they feared the Barbary pirates, who had taken captive three ships full of American sailors shortly before the Convention met.[23]

Each of these fears materialized to some degree, which came at the expense of America's respect abroad (Amar, 2021). The answer to these problems, Amar argues, lay in a stronger central government: 'America had to be able to be capable of fielding an army, equipping a navy, and borrowing money from abroad if needed' (Amar, 2021, p. 187). Notably for purposes of this chapter, two out of three requirements that he mentions are fundamentally defence procurement issues. The deeper solution lay not in designing a better procurement code but in establishing a constitutional structure more suited to defence procurement. To this day, the structure of this second constitution affects how wars are fought and the workings of the U.S. federal procurement system (see generally Schoeni, 2021, contrasting the United States' defence-oriented procurement system with EU Member States' civil-oriented procurement systems).[24] This constitution thus enabled the fledgling nation to purchase what it needed to fight and win – thereby granting the United States 'the power to wage war successfully' (Hughes, 1917, pp. 2, 9).

## 12.5 Conclusion

If the United States' experiment with a weak form of federal government under the Articles of Confederation has anything to teach us, perhaps it is this: If the EU is to develop a strong deterrent to foreign aggression and to effectively further its security interests more generally, it must either unite around a stronger constitutional framework (that would include a better defence procurement system which would curb both protectionism and fragmentation) or it must develop the capacity and unity of purpose to reach those same ends by other institutional means.[25] Hostile forces arrayed on the EU's borders have, as many Europeans have noted, made it essential for the EU to leverage not only its soft power, but also its full economic, technological, and industrial might. Were the EU more united, including in its defence procurement, it would also be stronger; and that, we think, would make the world a safer place.

Because deep unification seems unlikely in the near term given EU Member States' widely divergent security interests and reluctance to relinquish their sovereignty, the next-best alternative is to address the existing obstacles to effective defence procurement by optimizing the current procurement regime, defined by existing laws and regulations. In this interim, public procurement professionals – lawyers, officials, and their counterparts in the broader procurement community – may play an important role. Defence procurement law and its practitioners are, in the parlance of the U.S. policymakers, 'instruments of national power' (Schoeni, 2022). In a world where this expertise is in short supply, such procurement acumen in this highly specialized field can strengthen the defence of the EU, its Member States, and their allies (*Economist*, 2023).[26] May we all do our part.

## Notes

1 Depending on how manpower is measured, the EU's effective fighting force may reach some 2.4 million and constitute the second largest force in the world (Sandler, 2008, p. 407).

2 Since Russia's invasion of Ukraine, defence spending increased markedly with western and central European countries spending reaching $345 billion in 2022 (*SIPRI*).

3 We are not, of course, the first to note a parallel between the EU's current constitutional order and that of the United States under the Articles of Confederation, for example see Thomson. For a lengthier scholarly treatment of this subject, especially as to the conduct of foreign and defence policy, see Stein, especially pp. 6–12, 79–82.

4 This was the motto of Pierre Mendès-France, who was briefly the prime minister of France (1954–1955).

5 For example, one feature of any modern procurement system is a bid protest process, and how that function is organized has a profound impact on the system as a whole (Gordon, 2006, pp. 430–432).

6 Chapter 16 discusses the difficulties of cross-border comparative law because of the inherently different contexts in which nations' laws arise (Nash et al., 2023).

7 In this section, Arrowsmith describes what she calls 'structural restrictions' to free trade in the procurement sector which arise from the 'environment in which purchasing takes place' (Arrowsmith, 2023, pp. 18–19).

8 These three authors also discuss various non-procurement laws and regulations that create indirect barriers to free trade.

9 In this review of Kelman's seminal volume on U.S. federal procurement (Kelman, 1990), Mashaw laments that Kelman says too little about 'the *external* environment within which procurement operates' (Mashaw, pp. 516–518, emphasis added).

10 Miller observes, 'The very benefits of liberalized trade … are inherent threats to self-sufficiency in defense' (p. 104). And Walker and Willet state that 'a very real tension exists between the desire to regulate trade in military related technologies and the counter pressure to liberalise international trade in civil goods' (p. 158).

11 Savas disparages defence procurement as the 'last refuge' of economic illiberalism (p. 303).

12 Smith of course favoured free trade, but he made an exception for war materiel for purposes of national defence because 'it might not always be prudent to depend upon our neighbours for the supply' (pp. 405, 461–462).

13 Indeed, tension between the need for some self-sufficiency in defence and the tendency to use that as an excuse for protectionism has come to a head in disputes about the United States' invocation of the national security exception in disputes before the World Trade Organization (Maruyama & Wolff, 2023).

14 Federal Acquisition Regulation - Available at: www.acquisition.gov/browse/index/far#:~:text=Part%201%20-%20Federal%20Acquisition%20Regulations%20System.%20Part%202%20-

15 This language is wordier than the FAR's statement, carrying on for 27 pages, perhaps making the Directive's goals more explicit. 'A more debatable question', however, 'is whether the directives seek not merely to ensure that contracts are awarded without discrimination, but also to ensure that they are awarded to the best firm' (Arrowsmith, 2005, sec. 3.10).

16 In this passage, Trybus describes a failed attempt in the 1950s to establish a 'unified European Army' (Trybus, 2014, pp. 15–16).

17 For an assessment of potential obstacles to the CSDP written before Russia's February 2022 invasion of Ukraine, see Gotkowska.

18 Georgopoulos aptly calls defence and security matters the 'crown jewel' which Member States are reluctant to part with (ibid.).

19 The United States declared independence from Britain in July 1776, about a year after the war of independence ('Revolutionary War') had commenced in April 1775. A year later, the Continental Congress passed the Articles of Confederation, which came into effect in 1781. This first constitution was operable until 1789, when America's second constitution became the supreme law of the law following its ratification in 1788. Arguably, America entered a 'third republic' with the passage of the Civil War amendments (1865), which fundamentally altered the relationship between states and the federal government. But considering that matter in detail would take us far afield from the subject matter at issue here. That is the subject of a forthcoming book by Akhil Reed Amar, the second in a series on the history of the U.S. Constitution: *The Words That Made Us Equal* (Amar, 2021).

20 We are also deeply grateful to our colleague James Nagle, whose *History of Government Contracting* (1992), newly available in open source, details in chapter 1: The lessons of the Revolutionary War due to failed procurement, and chapter 2: The improvements that came to U.S. federal contracting after the launch of the new constitutional order in 1789.

21 Amar, 2021, p. 182, citing articles III, VII, and VIII and calling 'common defence' their 'thrice mentioned raison d'être'.

22 This law review article republishes a famous speech given by Charles Hughes in 1916 defending his political opponent Woodrow Wilson's exercise of war powers and coining the phrase 'fighting Constitution'. Hughes had previously served on the U.S. Supreme Court (1910–1916), would later serve as Secretary of State in the Harding and Coolidge administrations, and ultimately served as Chief Justice the U.S. Supreme Court (1930–1941).

23 Amar gives short shrift to the outsized role of the Barbary pirates for delegates to the Constitutional Convention; as one historian quipped, 'the brutal Dey of Algiers was a Founding Father of the [U.S.] Constitution' (Bailey, 1958, p. 65). One of us has written two pieces that discuss the influence of the Barbary pirates on the defence-oriented nature of the U.S. constitutional order (Schoeni, 2023, pp. 515–517; Schoeni, 2019, pp. 428–432). Both relied on one source in particular: Michael Oren's, *Power, Faith, and Fantasy*.

24 This piece owes much to our colleague Joshua Schwartz's unpublished essay first presented at the Public Procurement Global Revolution conference at the University of Nottingham in 2003, 'The Centrality of Military Procurement: Explaining the Exceptionalist Character of United States Federal Public Procurement Law'. In that essay he argued, 'it would require a willful blindness to the main currents of United States history to miss the fact that military and defense contracting has played the central role in development of both the United States system of public procurement and the development of a regulatory structure therefor' (p. 52).

25 Stein lists some ways in which the United States' experience may afford ideas for developing legal doctrines (pp. 79–80), serve as a model for allocating power in the institutions of a central government (pp. 80–81), and even provide a cautionary tale in some respects (p. 81).

26 The article from *The Economist* laments the shortage of experts versed in the technicalities of the U.S. defence procurement system and observes that Washington, DC is now the hub for such 'regulation wonks' (pp. 49–50).

## References

Amar, A.R. (2021), *The Words That Made Us: America's Constitutional Conversation, 1760–1840*, Basic Books, New York.

Anderton, C.H. (1995), 'Economics of Arms Trade', in: Hartley, K. and Sandler, T. (eds.), *Handbook of Defense Economics*, Vol. 1. North Holland, Amsterdam, pp. 524–561.

Arrowsmith, S. (2003), *Government Procurement in the WTO*. Kluwer Law International, The Hague.

Arrowsmith, S. (2005), *The Law of Public and Utilities Procurement*, 2nd ed., Sweet & Maxwell, Croydon.

Bailey, T.A. (1958), *A Diplomatic History of the American People*, 6th ed., Appleton-Century Crofts, New York.

Brown, G.W., McLean, I., and McMillan, A. (eds.) (2018), *The Concise Oxford Dictionary of Politics and International Relations*, 4th ed., Oxford University Press, Oxford.

Churchill, W. (1946), 'Speech of September 19, 1946, University of Zurich'. Available at https://perma.cc/W62J-CN82 [Accessed 24 November 2023].

Defence Directive (2009), Directive 2009/81/EC of the European Parliament and of the Council of 13 July 2009 on the coordination of procedures for the award of certain works contracts, supply contracts and service contracts by contracting authorities or entities in the fields of defence and security, and amending Directives 2004/17/EC and 2004/18/EC.

Economist (2023), 'The cost of the global arms race', *The Economist*, 27 May 2023, pp. 49–50.

European Parliament (2023), *Fact Sheet: The Treaty of Lisbon*. Available at https://perma.cc/X4ZP-2YBC [Accessed 24 November 2023].

European Union (2021), *The Shaping of a Common Security and Defence Policy*, European Union External Action. Available at https://perma.cc/2FEX-CUW9 [Accessed 24 November 2023].

Georgopoulos, A. (2007), 'The European Armaments Policy: A conditio sine qua non for the European Security and Defence Policy?' in: Trybus, M. and White, N.D. (eds.), *European Security Law*, Oxford University Press, Oxford, pp. 198–222.

Gordon, D.I. (2006), 'Constructing a bid protest process: The choices that every procurement challenge system must make', *Public Contract Law Journal*, 35, pp. 427–445.

Herr, V.-I. and Speer, M. (2022), 'The European Union needs its own army', *Washington Post*, 18 May. Available at https://perma.cc/B8BF-K3W3 [Accessed 24 November 2023].

Hughes, C.E. (1917), 'War powers under the constitution', *Marquette Law Review*, 2, pp. 1–18.

Judt, T. (2005), *Postwar: A History of Europe Since 1945*, Penguin Press, Westminster.

Kelman, K. (1990), *Procurement and Public Management: The Fear of Discretion and Quality of Government Performance*, AEI, Washington, DC.

Kershaw, I. (2015), *To Hell and Back: Europe 1919–1949*, Viking, New York.

Koutrakos, P. (2015), *The EU Common Security and Defence Policy*, Oxford University Press, Oxford.

Maruyama, W. and Wolff, A.W. (2023), 'Saving the WTO from the National Security Exception, Peterson Institute of International Economics, Working Papers 23-2'. Available at https://perma.cc/37NP-XS62 [Accessed 24 November 2023].

Mashaw, J.L. (1991), 'The fear of discretion in government procurement: A book review of S. Kelman, *Procurement and Public Management: The Fear of Discretion in Public Procurement*', *Yale Journal on Regulation*, 8, pp. 511–519.

Meng, P. (2023), *Europeans Continue to Back Ukraine, But Disagree on the Endgame*, Chicago Council on Global Affairs. Available at https://perma.cc/8NEV-4FRZ [Accessed 24 November 2023].

Miller, D.B. (2009), 'Is it time to reform reciprocal defence procurement agreements?', *Public Contract Law Journal*, 39, pp. 93–111.

Moser, C. (2022), *The War in Ukraine and Its Repercussions on Europe's 'Security and Defence Constitution'*, ConstitutionNet. Available at https://perma.cc/HM6Z-2X37 [Accessed 24 November 2023].

Nagle, J.F. (1992), *A History of Government Contracting*, George Washington University, Washington, DC. Available at https://scholarship.law.gwu.edu/history_gov_contracting/1/ [Accessed 24 November 2023].

Nash, R.C., Cibinic, J., Jr., Yukins, C.R., and Castellano, N.E. (2023), *Formation of Government Contracts*, 5th ed., Wolters Kluwer, New York.

Oren, M.B. (2007), *Power, Faith, and Fantasy: America in the Middle East, 1776 to Present*, W.W. Norton & Company, New York.

Pourbaix, N. (2011), 'The future scope of application of Article 346 TFEU', *Public Procurement Law Review*, 1(3), pp. 1–8.

Public Procurement Directive (2014), Directive 2014/24/EU European Parliament and European Council of 26 February 2014 on public procurement and repealing Directive 2004/18/EC.

Reich, A. (1999), *International Public Procurement Law: The Evolution of International Regimes on Public Purchasing*, Kluwer Law International, The Hague.

Sandler, S.R. (2008), 'Cross-border competition in the European Union: Public procurement and the European defence equipment market', *Washington University Global Studies Law Review*, 7, pp. 373–454.

Sandler, T. and Hartley, K. (1999), *The Political Economy of NATO, Past, Present, and into the 21st Century*, Cambridge University Press, Cambridge.

Savas, E.S. (1999), *Privatization and Public Private Partnerships*, 2nd ed., Chatham House, London.

Schoeni, D.E. (2019), 'On the non-tariff barriers obstructing free trade in the transatlantic defense procurement market', in: Racca, G.M. and Yukins C.R. (eds.), *Joint Public Procurement and Innovation: Lessons Across Borders*, Bruylant, Brussels, pp. 419–469.

Schoeni, D.E. (2021), 'Differing perspectives on defence procurement: The relative composition of purchases as a barrier to Transatlantic understanding and trade liberalisation', *Public Procurement Law Review*, 30, pp. 45–60.

Schoeni, D.E. (2022), 'Government contracts law as an instrument of national power: A perspective from the Department of the Air Force', *Public Contract Law Journal*, 51, pp. 553–576.

Schoeni, D.E. (2023), 'A bellicose founding charter: The U.S. Constitution and providing for the "common defence": A book review of Akhil Reed Amar, *The Words That Made Us: America's Constitutional Conversation 1760–1840 (2022)*', *Journal of National Security Law and Policy*, 13, pp. 509–519.

Schooner, S.L. (2003), 'Desiderata: Objectives for a system of government contract law', *Public Procurement Law Review*, 11, pp. 103–110.

Schuman, R. (1950), 'Declaration of May 9, 1950', reprinted in Weigall, D. and Stirk, P.M.R. (eds.), *The Origins And Development of the European Community*, Leister University Press, Leister, pp. 58–61.

Schwartz, J.I. (2004), 'The centrality of military procurement: Explaining the exceptionalist character of United States Federal Public Procurement Law', *GW Law Faculty Publications & Other Works*, Paper 1077. Available at https://perma.cc/ZW88-NS8Q [Accessed 24 November 2023].

SIPRI (2023), *World Military Expenditure Reaches New Record High as European Spending Surges*. Available at https://perma.cc/MYU7-FAYQ [Accessed 24 November 2023].

Smith, A. (1776), *The Wealth of Nations*, Alfred A. Knopf, New York (1991 ed.).

Staples, M. (2013), *The Future of European Defence: Tackling the Productivity Challenge*, McKinsey & Co. Available at https://perma.cc/TH3W-AURJ [Accessed 24 November 2023].

*Statista* (2023), *Largest Armies in the World Ranked by Active Military Personnel in 2022*. Available at https://perma.cc/JR8F-6F9A [Accessed 24 November 2023].

Stein, E. (1985), 'Towards a European foreign policy: The European Foreign Affairs System from the perspective of the United States Constitution', in: Bermann, G., Seccombe, M., and Weiler, J. (eds.), *Integration Through Law: Europe and the American Federal Experience*, Vol. 3, Book 3, Walter de Gruyter & Co, Berlin.

Thomson, J.A. (2003), 'Why U.S. history holds a lesson for Europe', *Financial Times*, 19 December. Available at https://perma.cc/R4EE-7SXU [Accessed 24 November 2023].

Tiersky, R. (2003), *François Mitterrand: A Very French President*, Roman & Littlefield, Washington, DC.

Treaty on European Union (1992), 1992 O.J. (C 191) 1, 31 I.L.M. 253 (1992) ('Treaty of Maastricht'). https://eur-lex.europa.eu/resource.html?uri=cellar:2bf140bf-a3f8-4ab2-b506-fd71826e6da6.0023.02/DOC_1&format=PDF

Treaty of Lisbon Amending the Treaty on European Union and the Treaty Establishing the European Community (2007), OJ C 306 ('Treaty of Lisbon'). https://eur-lex.europa.eu/legal-content/EN/TXT/?uri=CELEX:12007L/TXT

Trepte, P. (2007), *Public Procurement in the European Union: A Practitioner's Guide*, 2nd ed., Oxford University Press, Oxford.

Trybus, M. (1999), *European Defence Procurement Law: International and National Procurement Systems as Models for a Liberalised Defence Procurement Market in Europe*, Kluwer, The Hague.

Trybus, M. (2013), 'The tailor-made EU Defence and Security Procurement Directive: Limitation, flexibility, descriptiveness, and substitution', *European Law Review*, 38, pp. 3–29.

Trybus, M. (2014), *Buying Defence and Security in Europe: The EU Defence and Security Procurement Directive in Context*, Cambridge University Press, Cambridge.

Trybus, M. and White, N.D. (eds.) (2014), *European Security Law*, Oxford University Press, Oxford.

U.S. Articles of Confederation of 1781 (1781), National Archives. Available at https://perma.cc/2UMP-VVHA [Accessed 24 November 2023].

UNISYS (2005), 'Final report of the study, assessment of community initiatives related to intra-community transfers of defence products' (no longer available online).

Verdeaux, J.-J. (2006), 'Public procurement in the European Union and the United States: A comparative study', *Public Contract Law Journal*, 32, pp. 713–738.

Walker, W. and Willett, S. (1993), 'Restructuring the European defence industrial base', *Defense Economics*, 4, pp. 141–160.

Woolcock, S. and Heilman Grier, J. (2015), 'TTIP and public procurement', in: Hamilton, D.S. and Pelkmans, J. , *Rule-Makers or Rule-Takers?: Exploring the Transatlantic Trade and Investment Partnership*, Center for European Policy Studies, Brussels, pp. 297–340.

Young, E.A. (2018), 'A comparative perspective', in: Schütze, R. and Tridimas, T. (eds.), *Oxford Principles of European Union Law*, Vol. 1, Oxford University Press, Oxford, pp. 142–190.

PART V

# Global and local perspectives to public procurement

# 13 The Future of Procurement

*Enzo de Laurentiis*

## 13.1 Introduction

Public sector procurement affects a substantial share of world trade flows, represents a significant part of national economies (estimated at 10–15% of gross domestic product), and accounts for a considerable share of total government expenditure (around 30% in OECD countries).[1] Public procurement is a key nexus between the financial management system and social and economic outcomes in the community. The public sector is also the largest player in many markets, and thus it is in a strong position to affect the demand for goods and services in the global economy.

Procurement has evolved into a strategic public policy and management function to help deliver on a broad range of socio-economic and environmental objectives, promote economic growth, contribute to improving public investment and expenditures management, and stimulate innovation in markets. Fit-for-purpose and a broader concept of value for money which includes sustainability, quality, and lifecycle cost are key principles guiding modern governments in developing optimal procurement strategies.

The World Bank's (the Bank) Procurement Framework,[2] which became effective on 1 July 2016, is predicated on these principles and helps borrower tailor their procurement approaches to different markets and situations so they can achieve better value for money in delivering sustainable development.

The profound challenges posed by multiple global crises demand further enhancements in this role for public procurement in general and, for the Bank, in the application of our Procurement Framework to help respond to domestic as well as global challenges with greater speed, scale, and impact.

The Procurement Framework has already proven to be a critical tool in supporting the Bank's mission, responding to these crises, and paving the way towards a green, inclusive, and resilient future. Strategic, value-for-money approaches help convert investments into outcomes. Effective procurement also helps to address a wide range of country-, project-, and market-specific risks which may undermine the Bank's and borrowers' ability to achieve these objectives.

Building on core principles and lessons learned over the past several years, the Bank's procurement function is poised to continue evolving rapidly with a laser focus on development impact.

DOI: 10.4324/9781032631721-19

Achieving development results requires countries to engage effectively with markets and power project implementation by incentivizing the best suppliers to participate, knowing that the extra value they bring will be considered in contract award decisions.

This approach creates new opportunities for the Bank such as factoring climate impact in procurement decisions and supporting key commitments including the Evolution Roadmap,[3] alignment of all projects to the Paris Climate Agreement, the Green Resilient and Inclusive Development (GRID) agenda,[4] and several global priority programs under development which will implement a series of projects in replicable and scalable programs to achieve impact at the local, regional, and global level (e.g. renewable energy, agricultural resilience and productivity, and health emergency preparedness). Last but not least, it helps countries develop their capacity to manage public procurement and prepare for future emergencies with a footprint much larger than Bank-financed projects.

To operationalize this new paradigm, project implementation has been strengthened in four fundamental ways: (1) critical impact through value-driven procurement; (2) agile adaptation leveraging a risk-based, fit-for-purpose approach to evolve in response to rapidly changing market conditions; (3) enhanced performance through strengthened contract management, focus on supply chain resilience, proactive market engagement, and strategic sourcing; and (4) scaled-up efforts to build effective institutions, professionalize procurement staff, and leverage partnerships, ensuring that capacity-building programs led by different development partners are complementary.

## 13.2 The First Five Years of the Procurement Framework's Implementation

The Bank carried out a detailed five-year retrospective on the results of the Procurement Framework's implementation and reported to the Bank's Board in April 2022. One of the first objectives of the policy was to change behaviours and culture by realigning procurement resources with Bank strategy, increasing staff skills on modern and complex procurement methods, and ramping up the Bank's efforts to build borrowers' capacity to manage procurement both under Bank projects and using their own systems.

Both Bank and borrower staff needed to better understand and manage a wide range of risks affecting procurement outcomes, expand business and industry engagement, and exercise evidence-based judgement in a more flexible and strategic way when making procurement decisions. Notably, similar improvements across the portfolio including both projects implemented under the old Procurement Guidelines[5] and the new Framework highlight positive trends in the change management process which included significant training and outreach to staff, governments, and the private sector.

A large database of contracts (over 100,000) tracked by a new information system at every step of the procurement process was analysed using proxy indicators which reflect the key commitments made with the Procurement

Framework (i.e. to increase efficiency and effectiveness, build borrower capacity, and better manage transparency and integrity). Data analytics showed a sizable influx of new bidders suggesting increased private sector confidence and better tailoring of procurement strategies to relevant markets. Several indicators measuring administrative and professional implementation capabilities evidenced faster turnaround times, less time and cost overruns during contract implementation, and more efficient handling of complaints. Overall, borrowers began to adopt a more strategic approach to procurement planning, market analysis, and mitigation of a wide range of relevant risks. Equally important was the agile, effective use of fit-for-purpose approaches to adapt procurement processes and contract conditions in response to emerging needs (e.g. to address market and logistic disruptions during the COVID-19 pandemic).

## 13.3 The Bank's Operating Environment – Reshaping Development

Many factors contribute to creating the Bank's complex and dynamic operating environment which:

a. encompasses significantly diverse client segments (geographic regions, sizes, capacity, fragility, stage of economic development, culture, etc.);
b. includes a wide range of country- and project-specific risks, issues, and opportunities;
c. fosters development through a range of cross-cutting themes; and
d. faces increasingly complex intersections through converging global crises and cross-border challenges.

Since 2020, the world has witnessed a decline in growth, increase in poverty, and reversals in hard-won human development. The devastating impacts of climate change, the COVID-19 pandemic, the Russian invasion of Ukraine, persistent high inflation, and increased fragility have injected volatility and uncertainty into the global economy and affected the lives of millions, especially the poor and vulnerable.

These developments prompted new expectations from shareholders that the Bank become even more ambitious in three fundamental directions:

- scaling up impact for good development outcomes for countries
- tackling cross-border global challenges
- preventing, preparing, and responding to crises

The Bank launched on a journey to reshape its mission with greater focus on Global Public Goods[6] (e.g. climate and pandemic preparedness), while evolving its operating and financial models to better support the mission and enable more systematic impact measuring.

Multiple parallel initiatives are contributing to these objectives ranging from some aimed at optimizing the Bank's balance sheet, mobilizing private capital, and increasing operational efficiency, to others testing a more holistic approach to achieving the Bank's twin goals (i.e. eradicating extreme poverty and boosting shared prosperity) on a liveable planet. For example, the Country Climate Development Reports[7] are already proving to be powerful tools to explore new options to create jobs, reduce emissions, and boost climate resilience with integrated development strategies.

## 13.4 The Evolving Role of Procurement

Public procurement is fundamentally important to public investment management, providing value for money from government revenues and enabling capable, efficient, inclusive, and accountable institutions. It is a key component of the 'machinery of government', helping to transform social and economic policies, financial resources, and agency-level objectives into services for the community.

Procurement also plays a central role in helping to achieve most of the objectives of governments' public investment strategies. This is particularly true for large capital investment projects intended to deliver the modern infrastructure that is critical to strengthening economic growth and improving public services. For this reason, procurement strategy needs to be part of the business case for public investments.

Complex and multidimensional concepts such as value for money and fit for purpose, which emerged as key drivers of modern public procurement, require higher professional and management skills as well as new accountability mechanisms supported by strategic technology. In this context, procurement professionals' capacity development cannot be based exclusively on rules and procedures and must necessarily be driven by a principles and performance model, especially for policymakers and where higher value-adding responsibilities relevant to complex procurement are needed. The latter responsibilities require significant professional judgement, market knowledge, and the application of alternative contracting methodologies, including complex service solutions, outsourcing, in-sourcing, contract, and risk management.

Similarly, in Bank projects, the full value of procurement can only be achieved when it is deployed strategically to support the implementation of pivotal policy initiatives and manage a diverse set of country- and project-specific risks.

Both the current authorizing environment and the significant progress made during the past several years in building borrowers' capacity support a major thrust forward to deepen the application of the Procurement Framework and take value-for-money decision-making to the next level. This next step in procurement modernization will directly support the Bank's increased ambition to meet converging global crises and help borrowers strengthen their procurement capacity and systems maximizing efficiency and effectiveness in a constrained fiscal space which demands increasingly difficult trade-offs.

These trade-offs require a balanced approach to the use of procurement as a smart governance tool to achieve economy and efficiency while also pursuing secondary policy objectives which are important to deliver both on taxpayers' expectation and global commitments made by the countries as, for example, on climate.

Climate change threatens the achievement of all key development objectives, including the Sustainable Development Goals (SDGs), the Sendai Framework for Action objectives and, especially, the sustainable eradication of poverty which is at the core of the Multilateral Development Banks' (MDB) mission. The world will simply not be able to achieve its development goals without stronger action on climate change adaptation.

The Bank is making adaptation and resilience a key priority of its 2025 Climate Change Targets[8] that elevate adaptation to an equal footing with climate mitigation actions. Multiple initiatives are designed to address this emergency. They include, for example, the Bank's commitment to align all its financing operations with the goals of the Paris Agreement in its Climate Change Action Plan 2021–2025.[9] This is the most comprehensive institutional undertaking ever done by the Bank Group to reconcile development and climate and is part of a broader multilateral development bank vision to align financing flows with the objectives of the Paris Agreement.

Green public procurement is a key contribution to drive market innovation in a direction that helps to combat climate change, promote sustainable agriculture and forestry, energy efficiency, the move to a circular economy, smart cities development, and much more. The Bank and other MDBs are engaging with their client countries to help mainstream green procurement into countries' public procurement reforms.

In an increasingly interconnected and complex world, the welfare of communities at all scales is impacted more and more by 'global public goods' from reduction of carbon emissions to food security and global initiatives to support crisis preparedness (e.g. access to vaccines and capacity to deploy them efficiently, and pandemic prevention).

Tools at governments' disposal to enhance procurement's role in supporting the achievement of both domestic and global public goods include rated criteria used in combination with lifecycle costing in the evaluation of bids/proposals. Rated criteria help to make award decisions based on the optimal balance of quality and cost, rather than the lowest price responsive bid/proposal.

Rated criteria are non-price factors taken into account when evaluating quality aspects of proposals. They are designed to address the specific risks, opportunities, issues, and quality factors in each procurement, within the country and sometimes regional context.

In high-value, complex procurements a variety of non-price factors are often critical to the delivery of successful development outcomes. Professional, evidence-based, transparent evaluation of non-price attributes incentivizes competition, promotes quality and sustainability, encourages innovation, and reduces the incidence of cost and time overruns as well as fraud and corruption during implementation. They also help to create new opportunities such as improving risk management, securing supply chains, and factoring climate impacts in award decisions.

From 1 September 2023, the Bank requires the use of rated criteria as the default approach for most international procurements. However, rated criteria in public procurement are not a new concept as they have been considered good practice in many countries for over 30 years. They have also been used for years by Bank borrowers for procurement of consultants, plants (e.g. water treatment plants, power plants, etc.), information technology, and design and build contracts. In all cases, evaluation criteria need to be proportionate and appropriate to the type, nature, market conditions, complexity, risk, value, and objective of what is being procured and must be described in the bidding documents together with the specific manner in which they will be applied.

The relative weight of price and non-monetary criteria depends on anticipated risks and opportunities in a particular operating environment, as assessed in the procurement strategy. Generally, the overall number of rated criteria should be kept to the essential minimum. Too many rated criteria may dilute important characteristics of the bid/proposal and make identification of the optimal bidder/proposer more difficult. Factors that may be considered in determining which criteria to use and the technical–financial weighting may include:

- Extent of risks associated with the procurement (i.e. the greater the risk, the higher the technical weighting)
- Degree of opportunity for procurement to contribute to broader social, economic, and environmental objectives (i.e. the greater the opportunity, the higher the technical weight)
- Potential for market-led innovation (i.e. the greater the potential for innovation, the higher the technical weight)
- Complexity of the supply chain (i.e. the greater the supply chain complexity, the higher the technical weight)

Building on the success of the Procurement Framework, the Bank will continue to use a fit-for-purpose approach to further enhance processes, improve operational efficiency, and achieve better performance in additional areas which emerge as critical to sustainable results and risk management (e.g. contract management, predictive analytics, supply chain resilience, and cybersecurity).

Oversight, reporting, and hands-on support to borrowers' contract management are critical to maintain and even enhance value for money and integrity during implementation. Target support includes:

- tracking KPIs
- undertaking deep dives on high-risk contracts
- reviewing borrowers' practice through the new contract management IT system
- tailoring hands-on support to meet the specific needs
- liaising with industry bodies to drive innovations in tracking and managing supply chain risks

A resilient supply chain is defined by its capacity for resistance and recovery. That means having the capability to resist or avoid all kinds of disruptions and their impact on the supply chain and the strength to quickly recover from critical disruptions. The COVID-19 pandemic has placed a spotlight on the risks of the continuity of, and disruption to supplies caused by supply chain vulnerabilities and surges in demand. Supply chain risks include ultimate poor product quality, human rights abuse, a large carbon footprint (supply chains generate 80% of greenhouse gas emissions), and even fraud.

Measures that procurement bodies may take to increase supply chains' resilience include:

- early identification of higher risk supply chains, bottlenecks, and vulnerable suppliers that need targeted action
- maximizing opportunities to engage with the market to build flexible capacity of both existing and new supply chains
- engaging with key partners, including other public bodies, local economic development and enterprise organizations, to prioritize and target efforts
- considering additional actions to achieve a positive social impact, protect labour rights, and generate employment and transfer of skills, where possible.

Embracing technological transformation has also increased cybersecurity risks and threats to digital infrastructure, services, and data, which rely on increasingly connected systems. As digital transformation becomes essential to the functioning of states, economies, societies, and cybersecurity solutions must keep up.

Improving identification and management of cybersecurity risks in project procurement will rely on a range of measures, such as:

- identifying and addressing project-specific cybersecurity risks during the procurement planning stage and addressing them in the Project Procurement Strategy for Development[10];
- utilizing new tools currently being developed to assess, mitigate, and manage cybersecurity risks in critical infrastructure and other projects;
- strengthening Standard Procurement Documents by including specific requirements where cybersecurity risk has been assessed as high;
- evaluating relevant experience in the identification and management of cybersecurity risks on similar projects (using rated criteria);
- requiring cybersecurity credentials such as cybersecurity accreditation (e.g. ISO 27001), where appropriate, and require a Cyber Security Risk Management Plan specific to the contract as part of the bid/proposal documents.

## 13.5 Conclusion

The Procurement Framework has already helped the Bank to respond successfully to multiple crises and continues to evolve in parallel with the Bank's broader evolution and fast-changing market and country conditions driven by a fit-for-purpose and value-for-money approach.

This evolution is centred around value-based decision-making and supports priorities such as climate, managing supply chains, and the need to mitigate a broad range of risks including environmental, social, and cybersecurity to achieve greater impact at both the local and global levels.

This agile adaptation effort will fully utilize the flexibilities provided in the Procurement Framework to: (i) drive continuous improvement and modernization of the Bank's procurement toolkit (documents, guidance, and approaches); and (ii) exercise consistent foresight to anticipate future needs/challenges with fit-for-purpose procurement functionality and approaches.

The Bank continues to closely monitor the Framework's performance and make needed enhancements, as many more projects using the Framework are added every year to the Bank's portfolio, creating a richer data set to analyse, compare, and inform this ongoing evolution.

Agile adaptation to deepen implementation of the Procurement Framework and take value-driven procurement to the next level will also require ongoing change management to ensure that all stakeholders move in step while responding with tailored solutions to countries' development and global agendas to enhance impact, integrity, and transparency. It will also require scaling up market engagement and close partnerships with a complete range of stakeholders including IFIs, donors, borrowers, industry organizations, and civil society.

## Notes

1 These data are reported by multiple sources with slight variations as, for example, by the Office of the U.S. Trade Representative, Executive Office of the President. Available at https://ustr.gov/issue-areas/government-procurement

2 The World Bank Procurement Framework includes the Bank's procurement policy, internal Directives and Procedure, and a complete set of standard procurement documents and guidance. Available at https://projects.worldbank.org/en/projects-operations/products-and-services/brief/procurement-new-framework

3 A still evolving document which outlines the Bank's commitment and implementation steps to respond to the G20's request for greater ambition in addressing increasingly complex development challenges, multiple global crisis, and the need to further mainstream Global Public Goods into country strategies. Available at www.worldbank.org/en/news/statement/2023/01/13/world-bank-group-statement-on-evolution-roadmap

4 Available at https://thedocs.worldbank.org/en/doc/9385bfef1c330ed6ed972dd9e70d0fb7-0200022021/original/DC2021-0004-Green-Resilient-final.pdf; and https://unfccc.int/process-and-meetings/the-paris-agreement; https://unfccc.int/files/meetings/paris_nov_2015/application/pdf/paris_agreement_english_.pdf

5 Procurement policy and detailed rules for borrowers prior to effectiveness of the Procurement Framework which applies to all project with a concept note date on or after 1 July 2016. Available at https://thedocs.worldbank.org/en/doc/492221459454433323-0290022014/original/ProcurementGuidelinesEnglishJuly12014.pdf

6 'Public Goods are goods that benefit everyone within a jurisdiction' and 'Global Public Goods benefit every country, irrespective of which one provides them, examples are the eradication of smallpox, nonuse of nuclear weapons, and protection of the ozone layer'. Available at http://elibrary.worldbank.org/doi/10.1596/978-1-4648-0307-9_ch2

7 Core diagnostics that integrate climate change and development issues and strategy to help prioritize actions and achieve broader development goals. Available at www.worldbank.org/en/publication/country-climate-development-reports

8 The Climate Change Action Plan 2021–2025 aims to advance the climate change aspects of the World Bank Group's Green, Resilient, and Inclusive Development (GRID) approach, which pursues poverty eradication and shared prosperity with a sustainability lens. Climate Change Action Plan 2021-2025 is available at https://openknowledge.worldbank.org/server/api/core/bitstreams/19f8b285-7c5b-5312-8acd-d9628bac9e8e/content

9 Refers to the Bank's commitment to align all its operations with the goals of the Paris Agreement. Available at www.worldbank.org/en/publication/paris-alignment/joint-mdb-paris-alignment-approach

10 A comprehensive assessment of the risks and opportunities in a particular operating environment which should be taken into account in developing an optimal procurement strategy. It includes a market assessment using modern techniques for supplier positioning and a review of environmental, social, and stakeholders' risks, among other aspects. Available at https://thedocs.worldbank.org/en/doc/847531467334322069-0290022017/original/PPSDLongForm.pdf

# 14 How public performances can be enhanced by linking innovation policies to ordinary procurement

## The Sardinian case

*Stefano Casu, Giovanni Gaspa, Susanna Maxia, and Vincenzo Francesco Perra*

### 14.1 Introduction

Potentially, public procurement can be an extraordinary tool of economic and industrial policy (Geroski, 1990; Kattel & Lember, 2010) to be used not only to maximize spending efficiency but also to stimulate the market and steer economic operators towards the production of innovative solutions, services, and products.

Every year in the European Union, over 250,000 public authorities spend around €2 trillion (13.6 % of Gross Domestic Product) on the purchase of services, works, and supplies (EU, 2023).

These very significant dimensions give the measure of how effectively using the leverage of public procurement can affect the economy of a state as well as a region.

Starting from this premise, the action of Sardegna Ricerche – and its Procurement Desk – is inspired by a first-level goal consisting of the use of the public procurement market as a tool of economic and industrial policy through the involvement of the stakeholder.

This action is aimed at strengthening the competitiveness of the public procurement market in Sardinia through the improvement of the quality of the process (administrative quality) and the purchasing and procurement tools adopted:

- by all public buyers (market demand side) and
- by the acquisition or updating of techniques, methods, and approaches of positioning on the public procurement market (supply side, i.e. economic operators).

In particular, the action has two significant macro goals, distinguishable by the side of the procurement market on which Sardegna Ricerche is positioned.

- Public demand side for goods, works, and services: aim at adapting the knowledge and approaches of Sardinian contracting authorities to increase the level

DOI: 10.4324/9781032631721-20

of correctness of procurement procedures financed by EU and national funds, and in particular those coming from the Next Generation EU Plan and National Recovery and Resilience Plan (NRRP, 2021) in full compliance with the evolution of the sector dictated by European, national, and regional regulations.

- Supply side of goods, works, and services: aim to recover the gap highlighted by the European Commission's 2015 Report (SME Performance Review, 2023) on the results achieved in implementation of the Small Business Act (2008) and to accompany SMEs in the study of the markets that are functional to the expansion of its target market as well as to the increase of its degree of competitiveness.

## 14.2 Public administration, public procurement, and innovation

Its a common belief that the concepts of public sector and innovation are antithetical because public organizations are conceived as bureaucratic, as if the power of public offices were adverse to innovation.

Innovation, on the other hand, conceived as a tool for economic development, to overcome crises, has for decades been universally accepted as a driver for the economies' growth (Schumpeter, 1934).

The public procurement market is at the core of Sardegna Ricerche's agenda since the agency considers it as an opportunity where the public administration can combine the concept of public sector and innovation. As already mentioned, it is a huge market where companies offer all kinds of goods and services to the public organizations.

Therefore, the cues for a renewed evaluation on roles, responsibilities, and competences of the Italian public administration in relation to procurement have been examined in a particular light: the one which concerns innovation.

It is true, in the face of an undoubted growing demand for innovation, that a significant part of the purchases of the public administration – probably the one that makes immense numbers of the public accounts of 'intermediate consumption expenditure' – consists of standardized, basic goods and services, which cannot be conceived as a demand for innovative products and services. Innovation is positioned on a frontier that sometimes resides at a sidereal distance from the ordinary needs of the administration. However, innovation offers a key to interpretation that can lay the foundations for imagining a systemic evolution of public administration in all areas.

According to the Directive 2014/24/EU on public procurement,

> research and innovation [...] are among the main drivers of future growth and have been put at the centre of the Europe 2020 strategy for smart, sustainable and inclusive growth. Public authorities should make the best strategic use of public procurement to spur innovation. Buying innovative products, works and services plays a key role in improving the efficiency and quality of public services while addressing major societal challenges.
>
> (Art. 47, Dir. 2014/24/EU).

In the Public Procurement Directives (2014), the European Commission has placed great emphasis on this concept. The Commission makes it clear that public procurement is of strategic importance for public organisations in order to increase the volume of research and development carried out by the public sector. EU members must also be able to use public procurement to address the societal challenges that are constantly emerging.

In this perspective Sardegna Ricerche and the Region of Sardinia have tried to combine the concept of innovation as a cornerstone and a turning point in order to reshape the organizational models of purchases: in fact, the strategic content of innovation purchases has led the European and Italian legislators to loosen, precisely for the specific needs of the subject, the links of the regulation, thus enhancing the areas of discretion that guide the public administration in the purchasing process.

Due to these peculiarities, the possible organizational models of the procurement cycle can be articulated in a diverse manner, with an emphasis on discretion, skill enhancement, and dynamic management of the procurement process.

The models illustrated express the relevance of the alternatives conceived by Green Paper on the modernization of EU public procurement policy:

> There are two possible ways to use public procurement in order to achieve the Europe 2020 policy objectives: – provide contracting authorities with the wherewithal to take into account those objectives under procedural public procurement rules ('how to buy'); – impose mandatory requirements on contracting authorities or provide for incentives to steer their decisions as to which goods and services should be procured ('what to buy').
>
> (Green Paper, 2011, point 4)

The coexistence of the two ways proposes, also in the strategic conception of procurement, the ordinary tension between rule and freedom present in all human events. It is clear that the constant interaction between economy and law, which in the field of public procurement is indissoluble and articulated, cannot be resolved with an *'aut aut'*.

In the combination of public procurement and innovation, Sardegna Ricerche has tried to move on two guidelines.

(A) First of all, Sardegna Ricerche has implemented numerous activities aimed at satisfying specific needs and requirements of public administrations and enterprises through the acquisition, development, and/or dissemination of solutions that are not necessarily new to the market or that exceed the frontier of technology, but that represent organizational or process or service innovations for the contracting authorities and businesses, such as e-procurement, digitalization, skills strengthening, and green public procurement.

(B) Second, Sardegna Ricerche has planned and implemented an integrated action plan that pursues the crucial goal of stimulating and disseminating skills and tools on innovation public procurement (or public procurement for innovation), supporting regional public administrations in purchasing research and development services.

## 14.3 Innovation procurement

Usually, citizens are more aware of ordinary services, those that are needed precisely to meet the requests submitted to the public organizations on a daily basis.

We are referring to products and services that the public sector organizations offer and that usually don't have a great innovatory value, but if we instead assume that we buy research and innovation for the services that are routinely requested by citizens, the public sector can increase research and innovation and therefore being able to act as a lever for the overall development.

This is an indirect effect, but as a primary impact it will certainly increase the quality and sustainability of public services received by citizens and at the same time providing concrete answers to significant issues – such as the environment, education, health, soil preservation, and so on.

Thanks to public procurement, public administration can establish a very profitable and fruitful combination between the public sector and innovation.

Consequently, as mentioned earlier and accurately described in the EU Guidance (2021), public procurement rules aim at not only 'how to buy' but as well at 'what to buy', in order to satisfy the primary needs of public entities bringing 'the best added value in terms of quality, cost-efficiency, environmental and social impact' offering numerous opportunities for the suppliers' market.

Furthermore, in this context, in recognizing a key role for innovation as an engine for competitiveness, at the European level the focus has gradually shifted from supply side support policies in the technology market, such as financial incentives or investment in infrastructure, to policies acting on the demand side, including public procurement.

Public procurement policy can be conceived as a genuine investment capable of raising the technological content of domestic supply, changing the structure of supply through the introduction of new products and services to the market.

The dimension of public demand is undoubtedly a central factor in guiding the supply of products and services.

The ability of public demand to fuel technological innovation lies substantially in the guarantee, offered by the public entity, to purchase new technological products, especially in the early stages of commercialization.

The crucial element is the size of the demand which offers a large market with the advantage of reducing the risks of introducing innovative products for economic operators, consequently incentivizing innovation activities. It occurs especially because it is a coordinated expression of numerous entities and public administrations (aggregate demand dictated by needs).

In addition, the public administration assuming the role of first, sole or lead buyer and user of new products or services that require a large investment in research (first buyer or lead user) can be more exacting than the private sector, although the latter also contributes to demand.

It is quite evident that the public entity is able to produce a strong stimulus to the demand for innovation in sectors such as environment, health, energy, ICT, and transport while it even assumes a decisive role when it constitutes the sole buyer, as in the emblematic case of defence.

Indeed, research and innovation have always been among the priorities of the European Union's agenda for growth and jobs (Kok Report, 2004).

This trend is confirmed by the Innovation Agenda (2022), enabling deep tech innovation through experimentation spaces and public procurement.

In particular, the issue of public demand has emerged powerfully in the context of the revision of the Lisbon Strategy (EU, 2007), which, from the outset, has been characterized by the setting of quantitative targets relating to a quantity – public and private spending on research and development as a percentage of GDP – according to analysts definable as 'input-oriented' (Bonaccorsi & Panariello, 2012). The consequence is that the resources used as inputs in research and innovation processes are measured, thus neglecting 'output-oriented' indicators, i.e. those that measure new products, processes, services, and, above all, the improvements they produce on quality of life, health, the environment (Bonaccorsi & Panariello, 2012).

## 14.4 An attempt of taxonomy for innovation procurement

Hereafter a brief description of the types of innovation procurement implemented by Sardegna Ricerche, with which public demand can be effectively answered and adequately met through public procurement rules.

### *14.4.1 Pre-commercial procurement*

Pre-commercial procurement (PCP) consists in procuring research and development services at advantageous conditions from several economic operators (EU PCP, 2007; Dimitri, 2012).

This kind of method allows enterprises to compete and to propose radically new technological solutions to the public sector in order to find solutions to unsolved problems that public administrations face in delivering services to citizens. Thus, one more time, the focus is on the quality and sustainability of public services.

The providers are the companies that compete in the different phases of this procurement, which consists of a multiphase process, and since the public organizations don't acquire the exclusive rights of the research results, at the end of the contract the companies involved can keep the results ownership.

In this way the companies are able to patent these innovative solutions and then offering them to the market (meaning both other public organizations and other enterprises) and accordingly serving as a powerful driver for the economy and for the innovative technology sector.

The use of PCP is related to a need of the public administration that cannot be met by acquiring a product or service already on the market.

The conditions for the non-applicability of state aid rules are as follows:

- the selection procedure is open, transparent, and non-discriminatory, and is based on objective and pre-defined selection and award criteria;
- research and development services are purchased at market prices;
- the award is multiple (contract awarded to several economic operators);
- the results of research and development services do not produce a benefit exclusively for the public administration that uses them in the exercise of its activity, but a sharing of benefits and risks between public administration and economic operators occurs.

### *14.4.2 Innovation partnership*

The innovation partnership was introduced in Directive 2014/24/EU (Art. 31). Recital 49 makes it clear that this specific procurement procedure responds to needs that cannot be met by resorting to solutions already available on the market, and is specifically aimed at 'developing innovative products, services and works' and 'subsequently purchasing the resulting supplies, services or works'.

As mentioned in the following, the distinction is clear between this kind of procedure and PCP.

While the innovation partnership has a more defined scope and is inspired by an idea of innovation that is more anchored in goods and services that have a more solid prospect in terms of future commercialization, in the case of PCP, research and knowledge activity is organized to identify possible solutions with respect to complex problems through the possible development, on an experimental basis, of prototypes.

In addition, the innovation partnership covers both the development and the subsequent purchase of innovative products, services, and works by the public administration.

As described in the EU Guidance (2021), the innovation partnership process takes place in three phases:

1. The selection phase occurs at the very beginning of the procedure. After a call for competition, one or more of the most suitable partners are selected on the basis of their skills and abilities. The contract(s) establishing the innovation partnership is (are) subsequently awarded based on the best price-quality ratio proposed. This phase is similar to a restricted procedure with a prior call for competition.
2. In the next phase, the partner(s) develop(s) the new solution in collaboration with the public buyer. This research and development phase can be further divided into several stages designated for evaluating concepts, developing prototypes and/or testing performance. During each stage, the number of partners may be reduced on the basis of predetermined criteria.
3. In the commercial phase, the partner(s) provides the final results, but only if they correspond to the performance levels and maximum costs agreed between the public buyer and the partner(s).

#### *14.4.3 Research and development tenders: a specific case*

Article 14 – Research and development services – of the 2014/24/EU Directive applies to public service contracts for research and development services which are covered by specific CPVs.[1] In this case, public purchasers are allowed to purchase research and development services in order to retain ownership and intellectual property rights on the research results. This type of research-related purchases is the least customized to obtain innovation and development.

### 14.5 Sardinian innovation procurement policy

The mission of the regional agency Sardegna Ricerche is to support research and innovation in the region. Sardegna Ricerche has planned and implemented an integrated action plan that pursues two main goals:

- Stimulating and disseminating innovation in the public procurement sector;
- Stimulating and disseminating skills and tools on innovation public procurement.

The set of activities implemented in the past and still ongoing include a sequence of actions which are intended to motivate and facilitate the public and private actors of the territory to make an active use of the opportunities offered by the market of public procurement and public supplies. These opportunities have the extraordinary potential to generate impact in economic, social, innovation, and cultural fields also in relation to international procurements. Sardegna Ricerche currently represents in Sardinia a reference point for procurement in general and particularly for innovation procurement.

The implementation of the set of activities stimulate the exchange of skills and expertise between the actors involved and will ensure a permanent growth for Sardegna Ricerche's team committed for the project.

#### *14.5.1 Background*

Sardegna Ricerche has been in charge of building Sardinia's Technology Park since its initial establishment. Originating from the commitment of the Autonomous Regional Government of Sardinia and the European Union, the Science and Technology Park of Sardinia, is a system of advanced facilities and services fostering innovation, development, and the industrialization of research. This has meant paying great attention to the presence in the team of human resources with excellent skills in the field of legal affairs and public procurement.

The peculiarity, however, was that these human resources summed up economic skills with expertise in the management of structural funds, especially regarding financing programmes aimed primarily at local innovative enterprises and research centres.

It was the combination of strong skills in public procurement owned by the staff and the focus on the local innovation ecosystem that created the conditions for the development of the innovation procurement project.

The initiative was based on the insights of the legal affairs team of Sardegna Ricerche, who, reflecting on the consideration and indication shared by the EU Commission, came to the same conclusion in the regional context by retracing the path of critical analysis of the local economic context.

The strategy for deepening the topic of innovative procurement necessarily had to start from the analysis of the procurement context in general.

The procurement system reform has placed at the centre of the system the public administrations identifying them first of all as 'smart buyers'. A buyer that must operate by using its acquisitions as a leverage for the rational and well-balanced growth of the economy and society. The first step taken was to convert into objective and measurable data the informal perception that Sardegna Ricerche operators perceived concerning the local context.

The result of a survey carried out by Sardegna Ricerche was that in the regional territory Sardinian companies were not competitive in procurement procedures. Therefore, in order to address the issue of innovative procurement, it was necessary to deal with the ability of Sardinian companies to compete in the public administration market.

A deeper analysis showed that only in part this was related to the size of enterprises in the area (SMEs) and consequently their reduced economic and financial capacity, as a further reason was the absence or reduced competence concerning the public procurement procedures in general. On the other hand, public administrations and public officers as well had to develop and implement long-term professionalization strategies for public procurement, tailored to their needs, resources, and administrative structures. It was understood that there was not only a lack of competitiveness among local SMEs but also a difficulty for contracting authorities to manage in an effective and efficient way public resources mainly due to organizational difficulties and the lack of human resources able to devote adequate energy to purchasing planning activities, adequate choice of the most appropriate procedures, and clear and exhaustive drafting of tender documents.

It then became clear that the best way to solve problems was to develop not only legal skills but also technical, economic and management skills and knowledge, for both public administrations and companies.

Strengthening the skills of public administrations and businesses was the necessary starting point for building and strengthening the skills and knowledge of innovative procurement.

Not all procurement can be centralized; the challenge was to bring R&D purchases at the centre of the attention of small local entities (public and private).

### *14.5.2 Action plan*

With the implementation of the programmes in favour of innovation procurement, Sardegna Ricerche tried to identify the concept of innovation as a cornerstone and turning point notion in order to reshape the organizational procurement model.

The structure of the programmes has been intended to generate an original process, totally different compared to the one oriented to centralization executed by, for example, central administrations at national level. What the Sardinian government and its agency Sardegna Ricerche together with the Sardinian contracting authorities strive to accomplish is a collective and a non-centralized cooperative pathway for innovation procurement provided on a tailor-made basis. A non-centralized path which ensures an exchange and a transfer of knowledge and skills (capacity building, capacity development, and capacity strengthening).

The main innovative aspect of this action concerns bringing complex procedures such as R&D innovation procurement to entities and public administrations that are small in size and lacking significant resources to conceive and to realize complex calls for tenders. By accompanying these administrations to launch their own calls for tenders for innovation procurement without intermediaries, this project pursues the goal of disseminating the skills needed to approach R&D even in local realities.

Due to the strategic relevance of the innovation procurement, Sardegna Ricerche has established a 'Group of Innovation Procurement (hereinafter: GPI)' (2017) to coordinate all the activities concerning the public procurement of innovation in which our agency is involved. The total budget was €1,174,000,000.

The objective of the professionalization of public procurement was understood broadly to reflect the overall improvement of the whole range of professional skills, knowledge, and experience of the people conducting or participating in tasks related to procurement. The first course of capacity-building activities was launched with the aim of starting promotional activities among entrepreneurs and public bodies starting to spread the awareness that public procurement should be seen not only as an unavoidable purchasing method for public administrations, but as a potential driver for the local economy, both for the number of public resources available and for the indirect benefits obtainable by the territory also thanks to the chance offered by the new innovative procurement tools provided for and introduced by EU legislation.

Moreover, as Sardegna Ricerche is a regional agency, it supports the governing bodies of the Region of Sardinia in the definition of policies and instruments related to research and innovation.

Subsequently, Region of Sardinia usually delegates to Sardegna Ricerche the implementation of the actions relating to the Scientific Research Technological Development and Innovation axis and in the context approved the Activity Plan and the related implementation schemes.

### *14.5.3 Implementation*

#### *14.5.3.1 The team*

The first action concerned the creation of a dedicated team, the GPI (2017), with legal, economic, and managerial skills, composed of seven total people all related to the internal staff of Sardegna Ricerche (employees and collaborators already in charge of the agency Sardegna Ricerche). To empower possessed skills and ensure maximum efficiency and timing of the all-action plan, the core staff has been the first beneficiary of all empowerment activities carried out during the project and has also been supported by external experts who joined the activities covering different roles:

- ongoing market and context analysis and strategy updating;
- consultant in the implementation phase: instruments, sub-actions as tenders and grants related to the project, application of project management approaches, methods, and tools;
- teachers' workshops and seminars.

Phase 1 and Phase 2 were designed as preparatory tools to facilitate the approach for public administrations and enterprises to innovation procurement.

#### *14.5.3.2 Phase 1. Sardegna Ricerche procurement desk*

The procurement desk addressed first some critical issues by offering an overall capacity building which includes contents such as contracts, tendering processes, and strategic public programming. The intention of Sardegna Ricerche procurement desk is to be like a coach for enterprises and public administration. It provides direct consultancy online and on-site to support our users in facing electronic marketplaces and platforms, in dealing with central purchasing bodies (both nationally and regionally). Moreover, in addition to the staff from Sardegna Ricerche the procurement desk can count on external experts highly knowledgeable in operational procedures. The Sardegna Ricerche procurement desk is also intended to be a 'meeting place', an online community creator, where enterprises, contracting authorities, and all operators in the sector in Sardinia can interact. The desk website offers to registered users a dashboard of tools that enable them to exchange useful information and identify partners. The users can also enter 'reputational' details about the tendering behaviour of enterprises and contracting authorities. Participation in the events, seminars, webinars, and workshops is open and totally free of charge. In order to foster the access to the European market of innovation procurement (including the research for funding for new projects), Sardegna Ricerche has besides implemented a modular programme named 'Innovation Project'. The project is specifically focused on the priority areas of the Sardinian Smart Specialization Strategy (S3 Strategy) and it is oriented to raise awareness and to create a professional base (consisting of public and private regional operators). Innovation project has structured in a sequence of thematic days and operational workshops for public administrations, enterprises, and start-ups. The meetings have been for sure organized to illustrate the three innovative procurement tools introduced or improved by the 2014/24/EU Directive that may promote new investments in S3 Strategy: PCP, innovation partnership, and the research and development tenders.

An additional component that enhances Sardegna Ricerche's proposal is the Master in Procurement Management organized by Sardegna Ricerche procurement desk and integrated with the University of Rome Tor Vergata (Department of Economics and Finance). The Master course (six editions in total), was the first in Sardinia that drove into all strategic issues concerning public procurement management specifically including in the schedule-specific sessions dedicated to the innovation procurement.

To conclude, it is certainly worth mentioning the nourished contents uploaded in Sardegna Ricerche procurement desk website such as videos, legal documents, webinar, infographics, and even a very useful glossary where the user will find all words and expressions connected with public procurement.

A specifically wiki guideline web page dedicated to innovative procurement has been created by Sardegna Ricerche and it works as crosswise tool to inform and support the reader.

#### *14.5.3.3 Phase 2. Technology foresight*

The foresight project identifies a systematic process involving the gathering of information in order to establish the thematic areas of interest on which to structure public procurement. It is meant to be a preparatory work, a collection of data to be realized with the collaboration of public administrations and main stakeholders, and it aims at detecting the innovation needs that are still not satisfied related to services of general interest. The idea is to promote technological solution and therefore to support R&D innovation and exploitation by stimulating the public demand through PCP. In this sense it can be understood as a 'tank of needs' that are converted into ideas and projects with different degrees of feasibility. Some of them are quickly brought to the stage of procurement; others as to be 'stored' and gradually realized into application. The final purpose of this action is to study the research areas identified by S3 Strategy in order to select the most promising ones in relation to the technology needs of Sardinian administration. The activity envisaged by Sardegna Ricerche, with the support of external professionals, has entailed: 459 administrations identified to develop the first mapping, involvement of 11 experts, 15 meetings organized with specific administrations in order to detect innovations needs, 8 workshops, 1 event, 3 breakout session days with selected administrations, 11 advisory coaching meeting, and 1 final conference.

The project is directed to satisfy the regional public sector innovation needs by promoting:

- the development of new technologies and the integration of existing ones into complex innovative systems which lead to the creation of an industrial value prototype that is able to qualify an innovative product.
- research activities aimed at the development of innovative services or products capable of satisfying the demand express by public administration.
- R&D services for new solutions not available on the market to meet public demand.

Moreover, to help the Region's businesses build specialist knowledge and step up their global competitiveness, Sardegna Ricerche has put in place an extensive range of services and programmes for product and process innovation, and a set of thematic info desk – all free of charge – extremely fruitful to foster the public procurement of innovation, delivering advanced consultancy in the following areas:

- Intellectual Property Desk which provides support for public authorities and small and medium companies as concerns patents, trademarks, design, copyright, and Intellectual Property Rights (IPR) in general.
- EU Research Desk which provides support for the Framework Programmes for research and Horizon 2020.[2]
- Start-Up Desk which aims at providing new enterprises a specific support and a general tutorship.

#### *14.5.3.4 Phase 3*

While providing through the foresight project a comprehensive overview of needs assessment in Sardinia and identifying the thematic areas of interest on which to structure public procurements, according to the S3 Strategy, Sardegna Ricerche decided to support public authorities in implementing the innovative procedures. Sardegna Ricerche published a call for proposals addressed to public administrations. In 2017, it has published the 'Call for proposals in order to foster new markets of innovation in the public administration'.

The principal goal was to enhance and define the demand of innovation of public administration, by supporting initiatives of public procurement of innovation, namely through: R&D tenders; PCP; innovation partnership.

Sardegna Ricerche by pursuing a partnering approach to the conduction of R&D programmes (experienced so far with private companies) decided to pay attention to the development of 'supporting instruments' associated to the public procurement enablement.

Some of these practical supports provided were: production tender documentation frameworks, decision-making templates to determine tender strategies, and guidelines for innovation procurements. Moving along the path, Sardegna Ricerche considered and still does, according to the individual procurement stages, to support the public administrations selected in the two calls for proposals later on explained, with the processing of the tender documentation and with the implementation of the procurement, always allowing the funded administrations, even the smallest ones, to better tailor autonomously the innovation internally. To exemplify, concerning the tender documentation production support we can mention: tender disciplinary template, draft framework agreement, IPR contract, and technical terms of contract.

#### *14.5.3.5 Phase 4*

Sardegna Ricerche published the second call for proposals addressed to public administrations. In 2018, it has been published as the

> Call for proposals for the analysis of existing public needs for technological innovation in the following public policy areas: health, environment, energy,

sustainable construction, schools, protection, enhancement and security of land, environment and heritage for the purpose of pre-commercial procurement'.[3]

The principal goal is to enhance and define the demand of innovation of the public administration, by supporting only actions of PCP.

Referring to the first call for the promotion of new markets, Sardegna Ricerche resolved to funding not only the PCPs but also other types of procedures like the R&D traditional tenders and innovation partnerships. In this first call a small grant has been fixed (not higher than €500,000) was earmarked for public administrations and public companies, making it easier for small municipalities to apply. On the contrary, for the second call for proposals dedicated to the analysis of public needs Sardegna Ricerche decided to choose the PCP model with the ambition to realize more challenging projects. Indeed, in the second call the amount foreseen was higher (up to €2.5 million) considering that for PCP a competitive multi-level competition between the economic operators is expected.

## 14.6 Conclusions

This chapter aims to illustrate the Sardinian case through a description of the rationale behind it and a governance model tested for strengthening the link between innovation and public procurement.

From the beginning, the crucial goal was as follows: how to render innovation procurement more attractive for public buyers and for SMEs?

The response of the Sardegna Ricerche working group has been to propose models utilized in general procurement with capacity-building activities adapted in innovation procurement. That is, adapting and improving the traditional methods and tools in the field of innovation procurement, following a non-centralized cooperative pathway for innovation procurement provided on a tailor-made basis.

Therefore, Sardegna Ricerche decided to avoid a centralized model supporting (even small) public administration in order to become more confident in dealing with innovation purchases.

According to the EU Guidance (2021), procurement has been organized as a step-by-step process, with evaluations after each R&D phase in order to gradually select the best technological solutions.

This allows public purchasers to steer development throughout the process to satisfy public sector needs as much as possible. The European Commission's assumed path suggests maintaining at least two participating companies until the final stage to ensure competitive conditions in the future market. By maintaining positive competitive pressure on suppliers, public buyers can boost the best solutions the market can offer.

While respecting the mandatory separation between R&D phase and the commercialization phase of final products, the action may also concern procedures (as envisaged, autonomous from PCP) of innovation partnership.

Sardegna Ricerche decided to choose the European Commission's initiative for innovation procurement programme 'Start small, scale up fast' Guidance on Innovation Procurement' (2021/C 267/01).

As this experience can be tough and challenging, the right approach should be to introduce it as a step-by-step learning process. In other words, the most difficult changes – from cultural to procedural – required for innovation procurement need not be made all at once. Designing a successful project involving innovation could even be organized from the bottom up – with the public authorities supported – by starting to focus on simple, practical problems.

The starting point has been the identification of a number of themes (e.g. ICT, smart grids, agrifood, health, aerospace, biomedicine, tourism, and cultural assets) on which to focus that would benefit from an innovative approach. Also suggested by the European Commission, it is crucial starting small in order to build credibility and confidence and, afterwards, planning bigger projects.

This step-by-step approach can lead even small public administrations towards innovation in a market and competitive environment.

Consequently, it can increase competitiveness of the SMEs, impacting political economy.

Therefore, the strategy of Sardegna Ricerche and Procurement Desk shows that public performances can be enhanced by linking innovation policies to ordinary procurement.

To sum up, the guidelines followed by Sardegna Ricerche can be summarized as follows:

- 'Fill the gap': Sardegna Ricerche aimed at overcoming the distance between public buyers and economic operators.
- 'Problem-solving': Sardegna Ricerche used innovation procurement to solve real problems.
- 'Think small': Sardegna Ricerche fostered innovation procurement even in small public administrations.
- 'Everything should be made as simple as possible, but not simpler': Sardegna Ricerche kept on facing the challenge of simplifying to innovation procurement.

## Notes

1 Codes 73000000-2 to 73120000-9, 73300000-5, 73420000-2, and 73430000-5 provided that both of the following conditions are fulfilled: (a) the benefits accrue exclusively to the contracting authority for its use in the conduct of its own affairs, and (b) the service provided is wholly remunerated by the contracting authority.

2 Horizon2020 – Details of the EU funding programme. https://research-and-innovation.ec.europa.eu/funding/funding-opportunities/funding-programmes-and-open-calls/horizon-2020_en

3 Sardegna Ricerche official website. www.sardegnaricerche.it/index.php?xsl=558&tipodoc=3&s=13&v=9&c=4200&c1=4200&id=75566&va=

## References

Bonaccorsi, A. and Panariello, T. (2012), 'Domanda pubblica e politiche per l'innovazione. Fondamenti economici e profili giuridici'. *Rivista di Politica Economica*, 1, 61–96.

Dimitri, N. (2012), 'Some law & economics considerations on the EU pre-commercial procurement of innovation, Working Papers 2012/10, Maastricht School of Management in: Piga, Treumer (ed.), *The Applied Law and Economics of Public Procurement*, Routledge, London and New York.

EU (2021), Commission Notice "Guidance on Innovation Procurement" (2021/C 267/01) Available at https://eur-lex.europa.eu/legal-okcontent/EN/TXT/PDF/?uri=CELEX:52021XC0706(03)&rid=6

EU (2023), 'Communication from the Commission: Public procurement: A data space to improve public spending', 2023/C 98 I/01.

EU Guidance (2021), C(2021) 4320 final 'Guidance on public procurement of innovation'. Available at https://commission.europa.eu/funding-tenders/tools-public-buyers/innovation-procurement_en

EU PCP (2007), Communication from the Commission to the European Parliament, the Council, the European Economic and Social Committee and the Committee of the Regions - Pre-commercial Procurement: driving innovation to ensure sustainable high quality public services in Europe COM/2007/0799 final https://eur-lex.europa.eu/legal-content/EN/TXT/?uri=CELEX%3A52007DC0799#:~:text=Communication%20from%20the%20Commission%20to%20the%20European

EU (2007), Communication from the Commission to the European Parliament, the Council, the European Economic and Social Committee and the Committee of the Regions - Member States and Regions delivering the Lisbon strategy for growth and jobs through EU cohesion policy, 2007-2013 COM/2007/0798 final Available at https://eur-lex.europa.eu/legal-content/EN/TXT/?uri=celex%3A52007DC0798

Geroski, P.A. (1990), 'Procurement policy as a tool of industrial policy', *International Review of Applied Economics*, 4(2), pp. 182–198. Available at www.tandfonline.com/doi/abs/10.1080/758523673.

Green Paper (2011), 'Green Paper on the modernisation of EU public procurement policy. Towards a more efficient European Procurement Market'. Available at https://op.europa.eu/en/publication-detail/-/publication/04a30c4a-e533-41ec-a039-231f1aa39645/language-en.

Innovation Agenda (2022), 'Communication from the Commission to the European Parliament, the Council, the European Economic and Social Committee and the Committee of the Regions. A New European Innovation Agenda COM(2022) 332 final'. Available at https://eur-lex.europa.eu/legal-content/EN/TXT/HTML/?uri=CELEX:52022DC0332.

Kattel, R. and Lember, V. (2010), 'Public procurement as an industrial policy tool: An option for developing countries?', *Journal of Public Procurement*, 10(3), pp. 368–404. Available at www.emerald.com/insight/content/doi/10.1108/JOPP-10-03-2010-B003/full/html.

Kok Report (2004), Facing the challenge. The Lisbon strategy for growth and employment. Report from the High Level Group chaired by Wim Kok. November 2004. Available at https://ec.europa.eu/councils/bx20041105/kok_report_en.pdf

NRRP (2021), National Recovery and Resilience Plan https://commission.europa.eu/strategy-and-policy/recovery-plan-europe_en#national-allocations.

EU (2020), Recovery plan for Europe. All official documents available at https://commission.europa.eu/strategy-and-policy/recovery-plan-europe_en.

EU Directives (2014), Directive 2014/23/EU of the European Parliament and of the Council of 26 February 2014 on the award of concession contracts; Directive 2014/24/EU of the European Parliament and of the Council of 26 February 2014 on public procurement and repealing Directive 2004/18/EC; Directive 2014/25/EU of the European Parliament and of the Council of 26 February 2014 on procurement by entities operating in the water, energy, transport and postal services sectors and repealing Directive 2004/17/EC.

Small Business Act (2008), 'Communication from the Commission to the Council, the European Parliament, the European Economic and Social Committee and the Committee of the Regions – "Think Small First" – A "Small Business Act" for Europe COM/2008/0394 final. Available at https://eur-lex.europa.eu/legal-content/EN/TXT/HTML/?uri=CELEX:52008DC0394

Schumpeter, J. (1934), *The Theory of Economic Development*, Harvard University Press, Cambridge, MA.

SME Performance Review (2023), SME Performance Review. Annual Report 2023/2024 Official documents. Available at https://single-market-economy.ec.europa.eu/smes/sme-strategy/sme-performance-review_en.

SSI (2016), 'Communication from the Commission to the European Parliament, the Council, the European Economic and Social Committee and the Committee of the Regions, Europe's next leaders: The start-up and scale-up initiative COM(2016) 733 final'. Available at https://eur-lex.europa.eu/legal-content/EN/TXT/HTML/?uri=CELEX%3A52016DC0733.

# Index

FSC
www.fsc.org
MIX
Papier | Fördert gute Waldnutzung
FSC® C083411

Kolibri 360 GmbH
Ferdinand-Jühlke-Straße 7
99095 Erfurt, Deutschland
produktsicherheit@kolibri360.de